Generic Goals and Generic Practices

GG 1: Achieve Specific Goals

GP 1.1: Perform Specific Practices

GG 2: Institutionalize a Managed Process

GP 2.1: Establish an Organizational Policy

GP 2.2: Plan the Process

GP 2.3: Provide Resources

GP 2.4: Assign Responsibility

GP 2.5: Train People

GP 2.6: Manage Configurations

GP 2.7: Identify and Involve Relevant Stakeholders

GP 2.8: Monitor and Control the Process

GP 2.9: Objectively Evaluate Adherence

GP 2.10: Review Status with Higher Level Management

GG 3: Institutionalize a Defined Process

GP 3.1: Establish a Defined Process

GP 3.2: Collect Improvement Information

GG 4: Institutionalize a Quantitatively Managed Process

GP 4.1: Establish Quantitative Objectives for the Process

GP 4.2: Stabilize Subprocess Performance

GG 5: Institutionalize an Optimizing Process

GP 5.1: Ensure Continuous Process Improvement

GP 5.2: Correct Root Causes of Problems

D1064502

CMMI® for Services

The SEI Series in Software Engineering

Software Engineering Institute | **Carnegie Mellon**

CMMI Second Edition — Guidelines for Process Integration and Product Improvement — Mary Beth Chrissis, Mike Konrad, Sandy Shrum

PSP — A Self-Improvement Process for Software Engineers — Watts S. Humphrey

Software Architecture in Practice Second Edition — Len Bass, Paul Clements, Rick Kazman

CMMI and Six Sigma — Partners in Process Improvement — Jeannine M. Siviy, M. Lynn Penn, Robert W. Stoddard

Software Security Engineering — A Guide for Project Managers — Julia H. Allen, Sean Barnum, Robert J. Ellison, Gary McGraw, Nancy R. Mead

Addison-Wesley

Visit **informit.com/sei** for a complete list of available publications.

The **SEI Series in Software Engineering** is a collaborative undertaking of the Carnegie Mellon Software Engineering Institute (SEI) and Addison-Wesley to develop and publish books on software engineering and related topics. The common goal of the SEI and Addison-Wesley is to provide the most current information on these topics in a form that is easily usable by practitioners and students.

Books in the series describe frameworks, tools, methods, and technologies designed to help organizations, teams, and individuals improve their technical or management capabilities. Some books describe processes and practices for developing higher-quality software, acquiring programs for complex systems, or delivering services more effectively. Other books focus on software and system architecture and product-line development. Still others, from the SEI's CERT Program, describe technologies and practices needed to manage software and network security risk. These and all books in the series address critical problems in software engineering for which practical solutions are available.

PEARSON

CMMI® for Services

Guidelines for Superior Service

Eileen C. Forrester
Brandon L. Buteau
Sandy Shrum

✦▾Addison-Wesley

Upper Saddle River, NJ • Boston• Indianapolis • San Francisco
New York • Toronto • Montreal • London • Munich • Paris • Madrid
Capetown • Sydney • Tokyo • Singapore • Mexico City

Carnegie Mellon
Software Engineering Institute

The SEI Series in Software Engineering

Many of the designations used by manufacturers and sellers to distinguish their products are claimed as trademarks. Where those designations appear in this book, and the publisher was aware of a trademark claim, the designations have been printed with initial capital letters or in all capitals.

CMM, CMMI, Capability Maturity Model, Capability Maturity Modeling, Carnegie Mellon, CERT, and CERT Coordination Center are registered in the U.S. Patent and Trademark Office by Carnegie Mellon University.

ATAM; Architecture Tradeoff Analysis Method; CMM Integration; COTS Usage-Risk Evaluation; CURE; EPIC; Evolutionary Process for Integrating COTS Based Systems; Framework for Software Product Line Practice; IDEAL; Interim Profile; OAR; OCTAVE; Operationally Critical Threat, Asset, and Vulnerability Evaluation; Options Analysis for Reengineering; Personal Software Process; PLTP; Product Line Technical Probe; PSP; SCAMPI; SCAMPI Lead Appraiser; SCAMPI Lead Assessor; SCE; SEI; SEPG; Team Software Process; and TSP are service marks of Carnegie Mellon University.

Special permission to reproduce in this book CMMI for Services, Version 1.2 Model (CMU/SEI-2009-TR-001, ESC-TR-2009-001), © 2009 by Carnegie Mellon University, is granted by the Software Engineering Institute.

The authors and publisher have taken care in the preparation of this book, but make no expressed or implied warranty of any kind and assume no responsibility for errors or omissions. No liability is assumed for incidental or consequential damages in connection with or arising out of the use of the information or programs contained herein.

The publisher offers excellent discounts on this book when ordered in quantity for bulk purchases or special sales, which may include electronic versions and/or custom covers and content particular to your business, training goals, marketing focus, and branding interests. For more information, please contact:

U. S. Corporate and Government Sales
(800) 382-3419
corpsales@pearsontechgroup.com

For sales outside the United States, please contact:

International Sales
international@pearsoned.com

Visit us on the Web: informit.com/aw

Library of Congress Cataloging-in-Publication Data

Forrester, Eileen C.

  CMMI for services : guidelines for superior service / Eileen C. Forrester, Brandon L. Buteau, Sandy Shrum.

    p. cm. — (The SEI series in software engineering)

  Includes bibliographical references and index.

  ISBN 978-0-321-63589-1 (hardcover : alk. paper)

  1. Capability maturity model (Computer software) 2. Software engineering. I. Buteau, Brandon L. II. Shrum, Sandy. III. Title.

  QA76.758.F6725 2009

  005.1—dc22

                                                                              2009031362

ISBN-13: 978-0-321-63589-1
ISBN-10:   0-321-63589-2

Text printed in the United States on recycled paper at RR Donnelley in Crawfordsville, Indiana.
Second Printing, January 2010

Roger Bate, the longtime architect of CMMI, passed away shortly after the release of the CMMI-SVC model. He was an accomplished and extraordinary man, and the authors of this book and developers of CMMI-SVC were fortunate to have worked with him on his last project. We humbly dedicate this book in his memory.

CONTENTS

PREFACE

Services make up 80 percent of the world economy and comprise more than half of U.S. Department of Defense acquisitions. The primary purpose of the CMMI for Services (CMMI-SVC) model, which is the basis of this book, is to guide service providers as they improve the way they do their work—their processes. Improved processes result in improved service performance, customer satisfaction, and profitability. When organizations using CMMI-SVC make improvements in their performance, they can ultimately improve the health of the world economy.

CMMI (Capability Maturity Model Integration) models are collections of effective practices that help organizations to improve their processes. The CMMI-SVC model, like all of the CMMI Product Suite,[1] is developed by a team from industry, government, and the Software Engineering Institute (SEI). Hundreds of reviewers suggest new content and changes for the model. Early adopters pilot the model and give further feedback. A network of hundreds of SEI partners and thousands of users apply the model to their work and report their experience and results, further improving model content. In this way, the CMMI-SVC model represents the ongoing consensus of thousands of practitioners about how to provide superior service.

---

1. There are CMMI models that focus on the development of products and services (CMMI for Development) and on the acquisition of products and services (CMMI for Acquisition). See the CMMI website for more information about these members of the CMMI Product Suite (www.sei.cmu.edu/cmmi/).

Purpose

This book provides guidance on how all types of service provider organizations can establish, manage, and improve services that meet the needs of their customers and end users.

This guidance includes the following:

- Delivering services that meet the terms of service agreements
- Managing the organization's capacity to provide services and ensure the availability of services
- Addressing service incidents effectively
- Establishing standard services and service levels that meet the strategic needs of the organization as well as the needs of customers and end users
- Ensuring the continuity of services in the face of disaster

By integrating these and other practices, CMMI-SVC helps service providers to establish, deliver, and manage services.

Organization of This Book

This book is organized into three main parts:

- Part One—About CMMI for Services
- Part Two—Generic Goals and Generic Practices, and the Process Areas
- Part Three—The Appendices and Glossary

Part One, "About CMMI for Services," consists of six chapters.

- Chapter 1, "Introduction," offers a broad view of CMMI and the Services constellation,[2] concepts of process improvement, the history of models used for process improvement, and key concepts of CMMI for Services.
- Chapter 2, "Process Area Components," describes all of the components of the CMMI-SVC process areas.
- Chapter 3, "How to Start Using CMMI," describes the important roles needed for implementing a CMMI-based process improvement program, explains how appraisals can be used, identifies training that can help, and provides tips for getting started using CMMI.

---

2. A "constellation" is defined as a collection of components that are used to construct models, training materials, and apraisal materials in an area of interest (e.g., services, development).

- Chapter 4, "Achieving Process Improvement That Lasts," explains how selected practices in all CMMI models enable the organization to make improvement part of how it does business, including descriptions of generic goals, generic practices, maturity levels, capability levels, and equivalent staging.
- Chapter 5, "Relationships among Process Areas," describes how process areas interrelate and provides insight into the interactions of the CMMI-SVC process areas.
- Chapter 6, "Essays about CMMI for Services," consists of invited essays from contributing authors. The essays cover early use of CMMI-SVC, unusual applications, use of CMMI-SVC in new domains, and solutions from field use to challenges such as including other frameworks in appraisals.

Part Two, "Generic Goals and Generic Practices, and the Process Areas," contains all of the CMMI-SVC required and expected components. It also contains related informative components, including subpractices, notes, examples, and typical work products.

Part Two contains 25 sections. The first section contains the generic goals and practices. The remaining 24 sections each represent one of the CMMI-SVC process areas.[3] Process areas contain effective practices covering topics ranging from configuration management to service delivery.

To make these process areas easy to find, they are organized alphabetically by process area acronym. Most CMMI users quickly learn the process area acronyms and abandon their longer names for their shorter abbreviations. Here's an example in which the order of the process areas by full process area title versus their abbreviations is different: Supplier Agreement Management (SAM) appears before Service Delivery (SD). Each section contains goals, practices, and examples in a format that enables you to locate information quickly.

Part Three, "The Appendices and Glossary," consists of four sections:

- Appendix A, "References," contains references you can use to locate documented sources of information, such as reports, process improvement models, industry standards, and books that are related to CMMI-SVC.
- Appendix B, "Acronyms," defines the acronyms used in the model.

---

3. A process area is a cluster of related best practices in an area that, when implemented collectively, satisfies a set of goals considered important for making significant improvement in that area. This concept is covered in detail in Chapter 2.

- Appendix C, "CMMI for Service Project Participants," contains lists of team members who participated in the development of CMMI-SVC, Version 1.2.
- Appendix D, "Glossary," defines many of the terms used in CMMI-SVC.

Extras in This Book

Readers who are familiar with the model and with prior CMMI books will find these changes and extras in this book on CMMI-SVC. We extensively revised Part One to add more material on service concepts, including a discussion of lifecyles in service environments, as well as invited essays on the use and application of CMMI-SVC. We also clarified and shortened the material on generic goals and practices, and updated the material on getting started and sustaining improvement. In Part Two, we added margin notes to all the process areas. These notes describe why the practices in a process area are valuable and rephrase what the process area is about in plainer language than the formal model language. We also added author notes in Part Two to amplify service concepts or to explain how to apply core model concepts in a service context.

How to Use This Book

Whether you are new to process improvement, new to CMMI, or already familiar with CMMI, Part One can help you understand why CMMI-SVC is the model to use for improving your service processes. Over time, you will use Part Two the most because it contains the practices of the model. The primary value of Part Three is the glossary.

Readers New to Process Improvement

If you are new to process improvement or new to the Capability Maturity Model (CMM) concept, we suggest that you read Chapter 1 first. Chapter 1 contains an overview of CMMI-based process improvement as well as descriptions of the concepts and conventions used in the rest of the CMMI-SVC model.

Next, skim Part Two, including generic goals and practices as well as the process areas, to get a feel for the scope of the practices contained in the model. Pay close attention to the purpose and introductory notes at the beginning of each process area. Also pay attention to how information is organized and presented in Part Two.

In Part Three, skim the references in Appendix A to see if additional sources would be beneficial to read before using CMMI-SVC. Read through the acronyms and glossary to become familiar with the language of CMMI. Then, go back and read the details of Part Two.

Readers Experienced with Process Improvement

If you are new to CMMI but have experience with other process improvement models, such as Information Technology Infrastructure Library (ITIL) or International Organization for Standardization (ISO) 9000, you will recognize similarities in their structure and content.

We recommend that you read Part One to understand how CMMI is different from other process improvement models. If you have experience with other models, you may want to select which sections to read first. Read Part Two, looking for practices you recognize from other models that you have used, and note variations. You may notice a different level of detail in CMMI than in the models you are accustomed to using.

Next, review the glossary and the "Important CMMI-SVC Concepts" section in Chapter 1 to understand how some terminology may differ from that used in the process improvement models you know. Concepts may be shared by CMMI and other standards, but they may use different terms to name them.

Readers Familiar with CMMI

If you have reviewed or used a CMMI model before, you will quickly recognize the CMMI concepts discussed and many of the practices presented.

Review the process areas specific to CMMI-SVC first:

- Capacity and Availability Management (CAM)
- Incident Resolution and Prevention (IRP)
- Service Continuity (SCON)
- Service Delivery (SD)
- Service System Development (SSD)
- Service System Transition (SST)
- Strategic Service Management (STSM)

Then go back and review the other process areas you are already familiar with and see the guidance for applying these practices to a service environment.

User Feedback and Questions

Your suggestions for improving CMMI are continually reviewed and used to make changes to models, appraisal methods, and training materials each time they are released. For information on how to provide feedback, see the CMMI website at www.sei.cmu.edu/cmmi /models/change-requests.html. If you have questions about CMMI, send e-mail to cmmi-comments@sei.cmu.edu.

ACKNOWLEDGMENTS

This book wouldn't have been possible without the work of multiple people from multiple organizations dedicated to CMMI-based process improvement. The CMMI-SVC model is contained in the book, which was created by the CMMI Product Team. Other helpful information was added by Eileen Forrester, Brandon Buteau, and Sandy Shrum.

The CMMI-SVC Model Development Team included members from different organizations and backgrounds. Ultimately, without the work of those involved in the CMMI project since it began in 1998, this book would not exist.

The CMMI-SVC Model Development Team developed what is now CMMI-SVC, V1.2, from the input of lots of users and reviewers. That team consisted of the following members: Drew Allison, Roger Bate, Rhonda Brown, Brandon Buteau, Eileen Clark, Eileen Forrester, Craig Hollenbach, Mike Konrad, Frank Niessink, Mary Lynn Penn, Roy Porter, Rich Raphael, Pamela Schoppert, Sandy Shrum, Jerry Simpson, and Jeff Zeidler.

We would also like to acknowledge those who directly contributed to this book.

We want to thank Bill Peterson for his support and for his leadership of the Software Engineering Process Management Program (which includes CMMI) at the SEI.

We have special thanks for the contributors to Chapter 6. All of these authors were willing to share their insights and experiences and met aggressive deadlines to do so. These contributors were Kevin

Behr, Betsey Cox-Buteau, Sally Cunningham, Kieran Doyle, Suzanne Garcia-Miller, Hillel Glazer, Robert K. Green, Gene Kim, Angela Marks, Barbara Neeb-Bruckner, Brad Nelson, Mike Phillips, and Hal Wilson. We are delighted that they agreed to contribute their experiences to our book.

We are grateful to the reviewers of this book, Agapi Svolou, Hillel Glazer, and Pat O'Toole. Their useful comments helped us to improve the book and to better convey our ideas.

Special thanks go to Addison-Wesley Publishing Partner, Peter Gordon, for his assistance, experience, and advice. We'd also like to thank Kim Boedigheimer, Anna Popick, John Fuller, Audrey Doyle, Evelyn Pyle, and Dmitri Korzh for their help with the design, editing, and final production of this book.

From Eileen Forrester

I thank my two coauthors, Sandy and Brandon. I can't imagine doing this work without you. In addition, Craig Hollenbach, who led the volunteer industry team for the first two years of the project, is an accomplished and generous collaborator. We wouldn't have this model or the book without his fine work. I also acknowledge Mike Konrad and Mike Phillips for asking me to lead the CMMI-SVC work. It's been an amazing experience, possible only because of your trust. I thank my dear friends and collaborators, Julia Allen, David Carney, Audrey Dorofee, Suzanne Garcia-Miller, and Ray Obenza, for their constant encouragement and discussion. I especially want to thank two of my many supportive family members. My nephew Alex was the biggest fan of my prior book, and at age ten asked good questions until he understood the work I do—no mean feat. My brother Joe's unflagging pride and interest in what I am working on has been an unexpected treasure at this point in my career.

From Brandon Buteau

First, I am deeply grateful to my two coauthors, Eileen and Sandy. Besides granting me the honor of joining them in working on this book, they are both exceptional collaborators and have made the experience easier than I could have possibly imagined at the beginning. I'm also thankful to Craig Hollenbach, who invited me to work on the CMMI-SVC model team at its beginning, and who trusted me with a significant leadership role in its development.

I would not have the skills today that made it possible for me to contribute to the CMMI-SVC model or this book without the early guidance of my parents. My father taught me the value of disciplined reasoning, and my mother taught me the value of subtleties in the meanings of words. The result has been my lifelong appreciation of good arguments and good definitions.

Finally, my wife, Betsey, has been a complete jewel throughout all my work on the model and the book, and has gradually progressed from being a cheerful supporter and patient sounding board to an enthusiastic advocate of CMMI-SVC practices in her own professional field. I cannot thank her enough.

From Sandy Shrum

I would like to thank my coauthors, Eileen and Brandon. My work with them, both when developing the CMMI-SVC model and assembling this book, has been a terrific and very rewarding learning experience. I'd also like to thank those on the CMMI Product Development Teams that I've worked with over the years to develop and support CMMI models. There are so many, it would be difficult to name them all.

My work with CMMI has given me opportunities I otherwise would not have had. Finally, I'd like to thank my boyfriend, Jimmy Orsag, for his loving support and advice. Through all of the hard work on both the model and the book, he encouraged me in countless ways.

PART ONE

About CMMI for Services

CHAPTER 1

INTRODUCTION

The service industry is a significant driver for worldwide economic growth. Guidance on developing and improving service processes is a critical contributor to improved performance, customer satisfaction, and profitability. The CMMI for Services (CMMI-SVC) model was designed to begin meeting that need for guidance within the CMMI Product Suite.

All CMMI-SVC model practices focus on the activities of the service provider organization. Seven process areas focus on practices specific to services, addressing capacity and availability management, service continuity, service delivery, incident resolution and prevention, service transition, service system development, and strategic service management processes. The remaining 17 process areas focus on practices that any organization should master to meet its business objectives.

Do You Need CMMI?

CMMI is being adopted by organizations all over the world. These organizations are large and small, government and private industry, and represent industries ranging from financial to health care, manufacturing to software, education to business services. What do all of these organizations have in common?

Do You Have These Common Problems?

Many organizations accept common problems as "normal," and they don't try to address them or eliminate them. What about your organization? Are you settling for less? Take a look through the following list and see if you have accepted problems that you can solve by adopting CMMI.

- Plans are made but not necessarily followed.
- Work is not tracked against the plan; plans are not adjusted.
- Expectations and service levels are not consistent; changes to them are not managed.
- Estimates are way off; over-commitment is common.
- When overruns become apparent, a crisis atmosphere develops.
- Most problems are discovered in operations or, worse yet, by the customer.
- Success depends on heroic efforts by competent staff members.
- Repeatability of effective behaviors is questionable.

Even if you've accepted that your organization could use something to reduce or eliminate these problems, some service providers reject the idea of using process improvement to address or resolve them. Some mythology has grown up around the idea of using process improvement. You may have heard some of these fallacies.

- I don't need process improvement; I have good people (or advanced technology, or an experienced manager).
- Process improvement interferes with creativity and introduces bureaucracy.
- Process improvement is useful only in large organizations and costs too much.
- Process improvement hinders agility in fast-moving markets.[1]

These common misconceptions serve only as excuses for organizations not willing to make the changes needed to move ahead, address their problems, and improve their bottom line.

Another way to look at whether your organization could benefit from CMMI is to think about whether it is often operating in crisis mode. Crisis mode is characterized by the following:

- Staff members working harder and longer
- Staff members moving from team to team
- Service teams lowering expectations to meet delivery deadlines
- Service teams adding more people to meet expectations or deadlines
- Everyone cutting corners
- A hero saving the day

---

1. See the report "CMMI or Agile: Why Not Embrace Both!" for a discussion of how CMMI and Agile can work together effectively [Anderson 2008].

How Does CMMI Help You Solve These Problems?

In its research to help organizations to develop and maintain quality products and services, the Software Engineering Institute (SEI) has found several dimensions that an organization can focus on to improve its business. Figure 1.1 illustrates the three critical dimensions that organizations typically focus on: people, procedures and methods, and tools and equipment.

What ties everything together? Processes allow you to align people, procedures and methods, and tools and equipment with the way you do business. They allow you to address scalability and provide a way to incorporate knowledge of how to do things better. Processes allow you to get leverage from your resources and to examine business trends.

People and technology are important. However, we are living in a world in which technology is changing by an order of magnitude every few years, and people typically work for many companies throughout their careers. We live in a dynamic world. A focus on process provides the infrastructure and stability necessary to be competitive when faced with these ever-present changes.

CMMs (including CMMI) focus on improving processes in an organization. They contain the essential elements of effective processes for one or more disciplines and describe an evolutionary

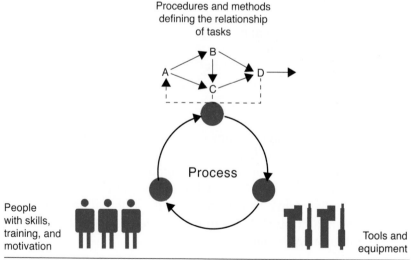

FIGURE 1.1
The Three Critical Dimensions

improvement path from ad hoc, immature processes to disciplined, mature processes with improved quality and effectiveness.

The advantage of a process focus is that it complements the emphasis the organization places on both its people and its technology.

- A well-defined process can provide the means to work smarter, not harder. That means using the experience and training of your workforce effectively. It also means shifting the "blame" for problems from people to processes, making the problems easier to address and solve.
- An appropriate process roadmap can help your organization use technology to its best advantage. Technology alone does not guarantee its effective use.
- A disciplined process enables an organization to discover which procedures and methods are most effective and to improve them as results are measured.

CMMI is a suite of products used for process improvement. These products include models, appraisal methods, and training courses.

- The models are descriptions of best practices that can help you achieve your business goals related to cost, schedule, service levels, quality, and so forth. CMMI best practices describe what to do, but not how to do it or who should do it.
- The appraisal methods evaluate an organization's processes using a CMMI model as a yardstick. SCAMPI (Standard CMMI Appraisal Method for Process Improvement) is the group of SEI appraisal methods used with CMMI models. SCAMPI uses a formalized appraisal process, involves senior management as a sponsor, focuses the appraisal on the sponsor's business objectives, and observes strict confidentiality and nonattribution of data.
- Training courses support knowledge about the use of CMMI models and appraisal methods.

The SEI has taken the process management premise that *the quality of a product (including service) is highly influenced by the quality of the process used to develop and maintain it* and defined CMMs that embody this premise. The belief in this premise is seen worldwide in quality movements, as evidenced by the International Organization for Standardization/International Electrotechnical Commission (ISO/IEC) body of standards.

How Can CMMI Benefit You?

Today, CMMI is an application of the principles introduced almost a century ago to achieve an enduring cycle of process improvement. The value of this process improvement approach has been confirmed over time. Organizations have experienced increased productivity and quality, improved cycle time, and more accurate and predictable schedules and budgets [Gibson 2006].

The benefits of CMMI have been published for years and will continue to be published in the future. See the SEI website for more information about performance results.

Although the cost of CMMI adoption is highly variable depending on many factors (organization size, culture, structure, current processes), regardless of the investment, history demonstrates a respectable return on investment.

Example returns on investment at various organizations using CMMI for Development (CMMI-DEV) include those shown in Table 1.1.

Since the CMMI-SVC model has been recently released, data on the results of its use are not yet available. The SEI will be collecting ROI data as organizations adopt the CMMI-SVC model.

See the CMMI website (www.sei.cmu.edu/cmmi/) for the latest information about CMMI adoption, including presentations by those who have adopted CMMI and want to share how they did it.

The History of CMMI

In the 1930s, Walter Shewhart began work in process improvement with his principles of statistical quality control [Shewhart 1931]. These principles were refined by W. Edwards Deming [Deming 1986], Phillip Crosby [Crosby 1979], and Joseph Juran [Juran 1988].

TABLE 1.1 Benefits Resulting from the Use of CMMI-DEV

ROI	Focus of Process Improvement Program	Organization
5:1	Quality activities	Accenture
13:1	Defects avoided per hour spent in training and defect prevention	Northrop Grumman
2:1	Overall process improvement over three years	Siemens Information Systems Ltd., India

Watts Humphrey, Ron Radice, and others extended these principles even further and began applying them to software in their work at IBM and the SEI [Humphrey 1989]. Humphrey's book, *Managing the Software Process*, provides a description of the basic principles and concepts on which many of the Capability Maturity Models (CMMs) are based.

The SEI created the first CMM designed for software organizations and published it in a book, *The Capability Maturity Model: Guidelines for Improving the Software Process* [SEI 1995].

Figure 1.2 illustrates the models that were integrated into CMMI, Version 1.2. Developing the CMMI Product Suite involved more than simply combining some existing model materials. Using processes that promote consensus, the CMMI Product Team built a framework that accommodates multiple constellations and benefits multiple industries and areas of interest.

Some service providers attempted to use the CMMI-DEV model to address their process improvement needs, but the fit required some difficult interpretations.

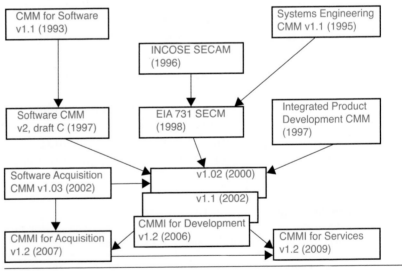

FIGURE 1.2
The History of CMMs[2]

---

2. EIA 731 SECM is the Electronic Industries Alliance standard 731, or the Systems Engineering Capability Model. INCOSE SECAM is the International Council on Systems Engineering Systems Engineering Capability Assessment Model [EIA 2002].

Then, in 2006, Northrop Grumman approached the CMMI Steering Group with the idea of a distinct CMMI for Services model. The Steering Group approved the idea, and as a result, Northrop Grumman sponsored and led a volunteer industry team. This team eventually joined with the SEI to finish developing a pilot draft of a CMMI for Services model.

After collecting piloting results and feedback from the draft's use, the CMMI-SVC development team updated and improved the draft to be what it is today, CMMI-SVC, V1.2, the model contained in this book.

CMMI Framework

The *CMMI Framework* provides the structure needed to produce CMMI models, training materials, and appraisal-related materials. The CMMI Framework is a structure that allows the use of multiple models that serve different constituencies while maintaining a strong CMMI identity. Within the CMMI Framework, model components are classified as either common to all CMMI models or applicable to a specific area of interest or constellation. The common material that is present in all CMMI models is called the "CMMI Model Foundation," or "CMF."

CMF components are combined with material applicable to a constellation (e.g., Services, Development) to produce a model. Some of this material is shared across constellations, and other material is unique to only one.

A "constellation" is defined as a collection of components that are used to construct models, training materials, and appraisal-related materials in an area of interest. CMMI-SVC belongs to the Services constellation.

CMMI for Services

CMMI-SVC draws on concepts and practices from CMMI and other service-focused standards and models, including the following:

* Information Technology Infrastructure Library (ITIL)
* ISO/IEC 20000: Information Technology—Service Management
* Control Objectives for Information and Related Technology (CobiT)
* Information Technology Services Capability Maturity Model (ITSCMM)

Familiarity with these and other service-oriented standards and models is not required to understand and use CMMI-SVC, and the Services constellation is not structured in a way that is intended to conform to any of them (except CMMI, of course). However, knowledge of other standards and models may provide a richer understanding of CMMI-SVC models and content.

The Services constellation covers services of many different types. Although the standards and models used to develop CMMI-SVC predominately cover IT services, this model was purposely written more broadly to be useful by a wide variety of different service types. These service types include information services, engineering services, maintenance, operations, logistics, and research services.

As defined in the CMMI context, a service is an intangible, nonstorable product. The CMMI-SVC model has been developed to be compatible with this broad definition. CMMI-SVC goals and practices are therefore potentially relevant to any organization concerned with the delivery of services, including enterprises in sectors such as defense, information technology (IT), health care, finance, and transportation.

Early users of CMMI-SVC, who used the model during its development and piloting, deliver services as varied as training, logistics, maintenance, refugee services, lawn care, book shelving, research, consulting, auditing, independent verification and validation, human resources, financial management, health care, and IT services.

The Services constellation contains practices that cover project management, process management, service establishment, service delivery, and supporting processes. The CMMI-SVC model shares a great deal of material with CMMI models in other constellations. Therefore, those familiar with another CMMI constellations will find much of the CMMI-SVC content familiar.

In the context of CMMI-SVC, the term *project* is interpreted to encompass all of the resources required to satisfy a service agreement with a customer. Thus, the concept of *project management* in this context is intended to be similar to the concept of *service management* in other standards and models, although the correspondence may not be exact. See more about the meaning of "project" in the Important CMMI-SVC Concepts section of this chapter.

Organizations interested in evaluating and improving their processes to *develop* systems for delivering services may use a CMMI-DEV model. This approach is especially recommended for organizations that are already using CMMI-DEV or that must develop and maintain complex systems for delivering services. However, some organizations instead may choose to use the Service System Development (SSD) process area. This process area consolidates some of the practices in the CMMI-DEV model and interprets them for service systems. In fact, we recommend that even if you use CMMI-DEV to develop your service system, you review SSD for some of its service-specific guidance.

Important CMMI-SVC Concepts

The following concepts are particularly significant in the CMMI-SVC model. Although all are defined in the glossary, they each employ words that can cover a range of possible meanings to those from different backgrounds, and so they merit additional discussion to ensure that model material that includes these concepts is not misinterpreted.

Service

The most important of these terms is the word *service* itself, which the glossary defines as a product that is intangible and nonstorable. While this definition accurately captures the intended scope of meaning for the word *service*, it does not highlight some of the possible subtleties or misunderstandings of this concept in the CMMI context.

The first point to highlight is that a service is a kind of *product*, given this definition. Many people routinely think of products and services as two mutually exclusive categories. In CMMI models, however, products and services are not disjoint categories: A *service* is considered to be a special variety of *product*. Any reference to *products* can be assumed to refer to *services* as well. If you find a need to refer to a category of products that are not services in a CMMI context, you may find it helpful to use the term *goods*, as in the commonly used and understood phrase "goods and services." (For historical reasons, portions of CMMI models still use the phrase "products and services" on occasion. However, this usage is always intended to explicitly remind the reader that services are *included* in the discussion.)

A second possible point of confusion is between *services* and *processes*, especially because both terms refer to entities that are by nature intangible and nonstorable, and because both concepts are intrinsically linked. However, in CMMI models, processes are *activities*, while services are a useful *result* of performing those activities. For example, an organization that provides training services performs training processes (activities) that are intended to leave the recipients of the training in a more knowledgeable state. This useful state of affairs (i.e., being more knowledgeable) is the *service* that the training provider delivers or attempts to deliver. If the training processes are performed but the recipients fail to become more knowledgeable (perhaps because the training is poorly designed, or the recipients don't have some necessary preliminary knowledge), then the service—the useful result—has not actually been delivered. Services are the results of processes (performed as part of a collection of resources), not the processes themselves.

A final possible point of confusion over the meaning of the word *service* will be apparent to those with a background in information technology, especially those familiar with disciplines such as service-oriented architecture (SOA) or software as a service (SaaS). In a software context, services are typically thought of as methods, components, or building blocks of a larger automated system, rather than as the results produced by that system. In CMMI models, services are useful intangible and nonstorable results delivered through the operation of a service system, which may or may not have any automated components. To completely resolve this possible confusion, an understanding of the *service system* concept is necessary.

Service System

A *service* is delivered through the operation of a *service system*, which the glossary defines as an integrated and interdependent combination of component resources that satisfies service requirements. The use of the word *system* in *service system* may suggest to some that service systems are a variety of information technology, and that they must have hardware, software, and other conventional IT components. This interpretation is too restrictive. While it is possible for some components of a service system to be implemented with information technology, it is also possible to have a service system that uses little or no information technology at all.

In this context, the word *system* should be interpreted in the broader sense of "a regularly interacting or interdependent group of items forming a unified whole," a typical dictionary definition. Also, systems created by people usually have an intended unifying purpose, as well as a capability to operate or behave in intended ways. Consider a package delivery system, a health care system, or an education system as examples of service systems with a wide variety of integrated and interdependent component resources.

Some may still have trouble with this interpretation because they may feel that the way they deliver services is not systematic, does not involve identifiable "components," or is too small or difficult to view through the lens of a systems perspective. While this difficulty may in some cases be true for service provider organizations with relatively immature practices, part of the difficulty may also be traced to an overly narrow interpretation of the word *resources* in the definition of service system.

The full extent of a service system encompasses *everything* required for service delivery, including work products, processes, tools, facilities, consumable items, and human resources. Some of these resources may belong to customers or suppliers, and some may be transient (in the sense that they are only part of the service system for a limited time). But all of these resources become part of a service system if they are needed in some way to enable service delivery.

Because of this broad range of included resource types and the relationships among them, a service system can be something large and complex, with extensive facilities and tangible components (e.g., a service system for health care or for transportation). Alternatively, a service system could be something consisting primarily of people and processes (e.g., for an independent verification and validation service). Since every service provider organization using the CMMI-SVC model must have at a minimum both people and process resources, they should be able to apply the service system concept successfully.

Service providers who are not used to thinking of their methods, tools, and personnel for service delivery from a broad systems perspective may need to expend some effort to reframe their concept of service delivery to accommodate this perspective. The benefits of doing so are great, however, because critical and otherwise unnoticed resources and dependencies among resources will become visible for the first time. This insight will enable the service provider organization to effectively improve its operations over time without being caught by surprises or wasting resources on incompletely addressing a problem.

Services and Service Systems in CMMI for Services versus SOA and SaaS

If you know something about SOA or SaaS, you might be a bit nonplussed by the preceding briefly stated distinction between the various meanings of the term *service,* followed by a forward reference to a discussion of the term *service system,* where neither SOA nor SaaS is mentioned at all. Here's some additional clarification. (If you're not interested in SOA or SaaS, you can skip over this discussion.)

Although there are a variety of interpretations of SOA and SaaS, they all tend to focus on information systems of one form or another and how they are designed to deliver value. SOA emphasizes certain characteristics of the architecture of these systems (e.g., the alignment of components with business functions), whereas SaaS considers different aspects of system architecture while emphasizing the flexibility of how software capabilities are delivered to end users. Because CMMI for Services, SOA, and SaaS practitioners all use the terms *service* and *system* somewhat differently, and because it's quite possible for CMMI for Services, SOA, and SaaS to all be employed in a single context, some confusion is likely if you are not sensitive to those differences.

In the CMMI for Services perspective, a service is the result of a process, and *system* (i.e., a service system) refers to all the resources required to deliver services. When done properly, the operation of a service system causes service delivery. Service systems may incorporate subsystems that are themselves information technology systems, but these IT systems might represent only a small fraction of a total service system infrastructure.

In the SOA perspective, a service is an IT system component that provides a distinct and loosely coupled function accessible through a standard, contractually governed interface. At the top level, the structure of these services is expected to correlate well with the structure of business functions that an organization performs, and SOA designs often involve analyses of one or more enterprise architectures to establish needed commonalities. No matter what level of abstraction, the term *service* in SOA is most likely to be applied to actions, methods, functions, and "things that are done" rather than to their results; and the term *system* typically refers to something that at its core is an IT system of some kind.

In the SaaS perspective, software is delivered as a service (e.g., a subscription service) without the need for the customer to pay for the full cost up front. The term *service* in SaaS therefore seems closer to the CMMI for Services usage than the SOA usage, but it's important to be clear. A SaaS service is not a software component that is made available (as in SOA), but rather is the on-demand availability of that component (and others) along with capabilities such as dynamic updates, tailorability, and load balancing. SaaS services are delivered via an IT system, but this may be only a portion of a larger service system that supplies other services, such as help desk support or network management.

Service Agreement

A *service agreement* is the foundation of the joint understanding between a service provider and a customer of what to expect from their mutual relationship. The glossary defines a service agreement as a binding, written record of a promised exchange of value between a service provider and a customer. Service agreements can appear in a wide variety of forms, ranging from simple posted menus of services and their prices, to tickets or signs with fine print that refers to terms and conditions described elsewhere, to complex multipart documents that are included as part of legal contracts. Whatever they may contain, it is essential that service agreements be recorded in a form that both the service provider and the customer can access and understand so that misunderstandings are minimized.

The "promised exchange of value" implies that each party to the agreement commits to providing the other party or parties with something they need or want. A common situation is for the service provider to deliver needed services and for the customer to pay money in return, but many other types of arrangements are possible. For example, an operating level agreement (OLA) between organizations in the same enterprise may require only that the customer organization notify the service provider organization when certain services are needed. Service agreements for public services provided by governments, municipal agencies, and nonprofit organizations may simply document what services are available, and identify what steps end users must follow to get those services. In some cases, the only thing the service provider needs or wants from the customer or end user is specific information required to enable service delivery.

See the glossary for additional discussion of the terms *service agreement*, *service level agreement*, *customer*, and *end user*.

Service Request

Even given a service agreement, customers and end users must be able to notify the service provider of their needs for specific instances of service delivery. In the CMMI-SVC model, these notifications are called "service requests," and they can be communicated in every conceivable way, including face-to-face encounters, phone calls, all varieties of written media, and even nonverbal signals (e.g., pressing a button to call a bus to a bus stop).

However it is communicated, a service request identifies one or more desired services that the request originator expects to fall within the scope of an existing service agreement. These requests are often generated over time by customers and end users as their needs develop. In this sense, service requests are *expected* intentional actions that are an essential part of service delivery; they are the primary triggering events that cause service delivery to occur. (Of course, it is possible for the originator of a request to be mistaken about whether the request is actually within the scope of agreed services.)

Sometimes specific service requests may be incorporated directly into the service agreements themselves. This incorporation of service requests in the service agreement is often the case for services that are to be performed repeatedly or continuously over time (e.g., a cleaning service with a specific expected cleaning schedule or a network management service that must provide 99.9 percent network availability for the life of the service agreement). Even in these situations, ad hoc service requests may also be generated when needed, and the service provider should be prepared to deliver services in response to both types of requests.

Service Incident

Even with the best planning, monitoring, and delivery of services, unintended events may occur that are unwanted. Some instances of service delivery may have lower than expected or lower than acceptable degrees of performance or quality, or may be completely unsuccessful. The CMMI-SVC model refers to these difficulties as "service incidents." The glossary defines a service incident as an indication of an actual or potential interference with a service. The single word *incident* is used in place of *service incident* when the context makes the meaning clear.

Like requests, incidents require some recognition and response by the service provider; but unlike requests, incidents are *unintended* events, although some types of incidents may be anticipated. Whether or not they are anticipated, incidents must be resolved in some way by the service provider. In some service types and service provider organizations, service requests and incidents are both managed and resolved through common processes, personnel, and tools. The CMMI-SVC model is compatible with this kind of approach but does not require it, as it is not appropriate for all types of services.

The use of the word *potential* in the definition of service incident is deliberate and significant; it means that incidents do not always have to involve actual interference with or failure of service delivery. Indications that a service *may* have been insufficient or unsuccessful are also incidents, as are indications that it may be insufficient or unsuccessful in the future. (Customer complaints are an almost universal example of this type of incident because they are always indications that service delivery may have been inadequate.) This aspect of incidents is often overlooked, but it is important: Failure to address and resolve potential interference with services is likely to lead eventually to actual interference, and possibly to a failure to satisfy service agreements.

Project

While it refers to a concept that is used across all CMMI models, the term *project* deserves some special clarification in the context of the CMMI-SVC model. It is likely that no other single word in the model has the same potential to raise misunderstandings, questions, and even objections.

Those with prior experience using other CMMI models, or who routinely think of their work as part of a project-style work arrangement, may wonder where the difficulty lies. The CMMI glossary defines a project as a managed set of interrelated resources that delivers one or more products or services to a customer or end user, and continues by declaring that a project has a definite beginning (i.e., project startup) and typically operates according to a plan. These characteristics are conventional of a project according to many definitions, so why is there an issue? Why might there be a difficulty with applying terms such as *project planning* or *project management* in some service provider organizations?

One simple reason is that many people work on or know of projects that have a definite end as well as a definite beginning; such projects are focused on accomplishing an objective by a certain time. In fact, the glossary in prior versions of CMMI models (i.e., prior to V1.2) specifically included a definite end as part of the definition of *project*. This more restrictive definition reflected the original focus of CMMI (and the other maturity models that preceded it), which was principally on development efforts that normally come to some expected end once an overall objective has been reached. While some services follow this same pattern, many are delivered over time without an expected definite end (e.g., services from businesses that intend to offer them indefinitely, or typical municipal services). Service providers in these contexts would naturally be reluctant to describe their service delivery work as a project under this definition.

However, for the latest (V1.2) CMMI models, the definition of *project* was deliberately changed to eliminate this limitation, in part to allow the term to be applied easily to the full range of service types. Projects must be planned, but they do not *need* to have a planned end, and this broader definition can therefore make sense in the context of all service delivery (provided that CMMI model users are willing to suppress an expectation that all projects must come to an end).

Even given this adjustment, some people may still have difficulty thinking of the delivery of services as being a *project*, which often carries the connotation of trying to accomplish an overall objective by following some preset plan. Many services are delivered in response to what are effectively small independent objectives established over time—individual service requests—in ways that are not planned in advance according to predetermined milestones. In these circumstances, service providers are often not used to thinking of a single objective to be accomplished. Therefore, characterizing their work arrangements as projects may seem awkward at best.

For this reason, the CMMI-SVC model explicitly interprets the term *project* to encompass all of the resources required to satisfy a service agreement with a customer. Satisfaction of the terms of the service agreement becomes the overall objective under which individual service requests are handled. Planning the effort to satisfy the service agreement is required in the form of work structures, resource allocations, schedules, and other typical project planning work products and processes. If you think of a service agreement as outlining the scope of a project in this way, the use of *project* in a service context becomes less of a problem.

Even better, the glossary includes notes explaining that a project can be composed of projects. These additional notes mean that interrelated sets of service agreements or service agreements covering multiple customers can be treated as projects, as can distinct subsets of work within the scope of a single service agreement. For example, the development of a new version of a service system or the transition of a new service delivery capability into operational use can be treated as a project as well.

In the end, of course, organizations will use whatever terminology is comfortable, familiar, and useful to them, and the CMMI-SVC model does not require this approach to change. However, all CMMI models need a convenient way to refer consistently and clearly to the fundamental groupings of resources that organize work to achieve significant objectives. Given the glossary definition and the preceding discussion, the term *project* is still adequate and effective for this purpose, although its meaning has had to grow in scope over time. This adaptation is not a surprise, because CMMI models themselves have grown in scope over time, and are likely to continue to do so in the future. CMMI-SVC users are strongly encouraged to consider how they too may adapt their way of thinking to reflect greater flexibility, and thereby gain the benefits of different ways of improving services.

Stakeholder, Customer, and End User

In the model glossary, a *stakeholder* is defined as a group or individual who is affected by or is in some way accountable for the outcome of an undertaking. Stakeholders include any and all parties with a legitimate interest in the results of service delivery, such as service provider executives, staff members, customers, end users, suppliers, partners, and oversight groups. Remember that any given reference to stakeholders in the model covers all types of stakeholders, and not just the ones that might be most obvious in the particular context.

The model defines a *customer* as the party (individual, project, or organization) responsible for accepting the product or for authorizing payment. A customer must also be external to the project that develops (delivers) a product (service), although both the customer and the project may be part of the same larger organization. While this concept seems clear enough, the glossary includes some ambiguous language about how the term *customer* can include "other relevant stakeholders" in some contexts, such as *customer requirements*. Although this caveat reflects an accepted legacy usage of the term from earlier versions of CMMI models, it could be potentially confusing in a service context, where the distinction between customers and other stakeholders (especially end users) can be especially significant.

The CMMI for Services model addresses this concern in two ways. First, it avoids the term *customer requirements* except in those contexts where it refers to the requirements of *customers* in the narrow sense (those who accept a product or authorize payment). Second, the model includes added material in the glossary to distinguish between customers and end users, and to define the term *end user* itself.

The model defines an *end user* as the party (individual, project, or organization) that ultimately receives the benefit of a delivered service. While end users and customers therefore cover distinct roles in service establishment and delivery, both can often be represented by a single party. For example, a private individual who receives financial services from a bank is probably both the customer and the end user of those services. However, in health care services, the customers often include organizations such as employers and government agencies that negotiate (or dictate) health care plan coverage for the ultimate health care beneficiaries, who are the end users of those services. (Many of these end users may be customers as well, if they have a responsibility to pay for all or part of some services.)

To summarize: It's important to keep in mind the actual scope of the terms *stakeholder*, *customer*, and *end user* as you review and apply the CMMI for Services model in your unique service context so that you don't overlook or confuse crucial interactions and interfaces in your service system.

CHAPTER 2

PROCESS AREA COMPONENTS

This chapter describes the components found in each process area and in the generic goals and generic practices. Understanding the meaning of these components is critical to using the information in Part Two effectively. If you are unfamiliar with Part Two, you may want to skim the Generic Goals and Generic Practices section and a couple of process area sections to get a general feel for the content and layout before reading this chapter.

Required, Expected, and Informative Components

Model components are grouped into three categories—required, expected, and informative—that reflect how to interpret them.

Required Components

Required components describe what an organization must achieve to satisfy a process area. This achievement must be visibly implemented in an organization's processes. The required components in CMMI are the specific and generic goals. Goal satisfaction is used in appraisals as the basis for deciding whether a process area has been satisfied.

Expected Components

Expected components describe what an organization may implement to achieve a required component. Expected components guide those who implement improvements or perform appraisals. The expected components in CMMI are the specific and generic practices.

Before goals can be considered to be satisfied, either their practices as described or acceptable alternatives to them must be present in the planned and implemented processes of the organization.

Informative Components

Informative components provide details that help organizations understand the required and expected components. Subpractices, typical work products, goal and practice titles, goal and practice notes, examples, and references are some varieties of informative model components.

The CMMI glossary of terms is not a required, expected, or informative component of CMMI models. You should interpret the terms in the glossary in the context of the model component in which they appear.

Using Required, Expected, and Informative Components

Some users have grouped the required and expected components into what they call "normative" components, thereby minimizing the importance of (and even sometimes ignoring) the informative components. Distinguishing normative and informative material can be useful in selecting model components that align with your business needs. It can also reduce fears about the size of the model and what material is actually implemented. However, all three kinds of components contribute to your understanding of CMMI best practices and are meant to be used together.

Ignoring the informative material will provide you with an extremely limited view of CMMI. The informative material includes many examples, interpretations, and explanations that are useful to you when interpreting and applying the goals and practices. Using only the required and expected material is akin to reading only an outline of a book, and not the full text. When you overlook the informative material, you miss the connections, details, and value that transcends whether the material is required or expected in an appraisal.

Model Components on the Page

The typographical conventions used in this model were designed to enable you to select what you need and use it effectively. We present model components in formats that allow you to find them quickly on the page.

Figures 2.1 and 2.2 are sample pages from process areas in Part Two; they show the different process area components, labeled so that you can identify them. Notice that components differ typographically so that you can easily identify each one.

Process Area
Name

Process Area
Category

Maturity Level

Purpose

Introductory
Notes

DECISION ANALYSIS AND RESOLUTION
A Support Process Area at Maturity Level 3

Purpose

The purpose of Decision Analysis and Resolution (DAR) is to analyze possible decisions using a formal evaluation process that evaluates identified alternatives against established criteria.

IN OTHER WORDS

DAR is about using a formal decision-making process on the decisions that matter most in your business.

Introductory Notes

The Decision Analysis and Resolution process area involves establishing guidelines to determine which issues should be subject to a formal evaluation process and applying formal evaluation processes to these issues.

A formal evaluation process is a structured approach to evaluating alternative solutions against established criteria to determine a recommended solution.

A formal evaluation process involves the following actions:

WHY DO THE PRACTICES IN DAR?

You will make better decisions. Because the rationale for important decisions is clear, support for these decisions is higher. Over time, everyone is more inclined to trust the decision-making process because it is sensible and visible.

- Establishing the criteria for evaluating alternatives
- Identifying alternative solutions
- Selecting methods for evaluating alternatives
- Evaluating alternative solutions using established criteria and methods
- Selecting recommended solutions from alternatives based on evaluation criteria

Rather than using the phrase "alternative solutions to address issues" each time, in this process area, one of two shorter phrases is used: "alternative solutions" or "alternatives."

A formal evaluation process reduces the subjective nature of a decision and provides a higher probability of selecting a solution that meets multiple demands of relevant stakeholders.

DAR

267

FIGURE 2.1
Sample Page from Decision Analysis and Resolution

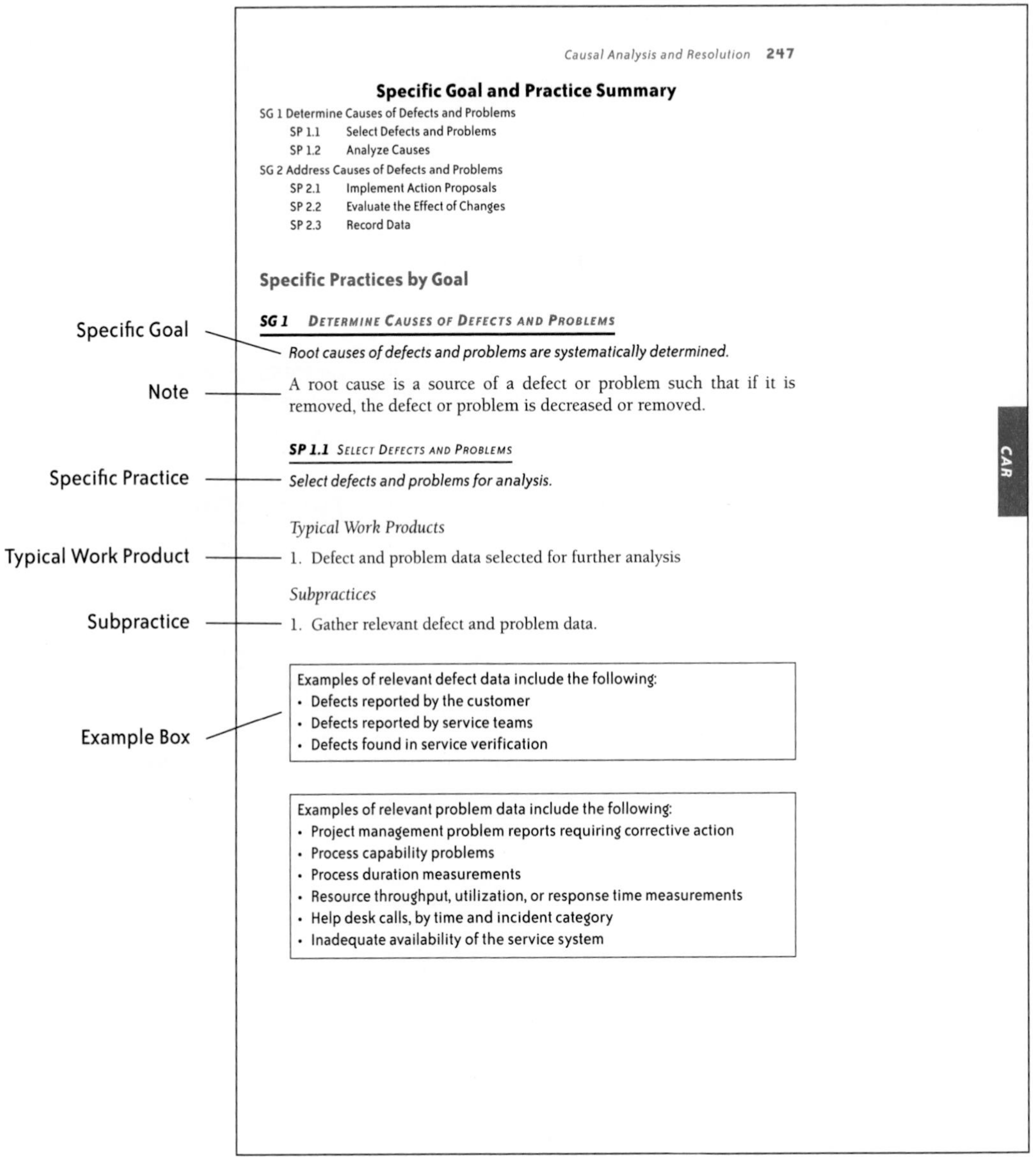

Specific Goal and Practice Summary

SG 1 Determine Causes of Defects and Problems
    SP 1.1   Select Defects and Problems
    SP 1.2   Analyze Causes
SG 2 Address Causes of Defects and Problems
    SP 2.1   Implement Action Proposals
    SP 2.2   Evaluate the Effect of Changes
    SP 2.3   Record Data

Specific Practices by Goal

SG 1   **DETERMINE CAUSES OF DEFECTS AND PROBLEMS**

Root causes of defects and problems are systematically determined.

A root cause is a source of a defect or problem such that if it is removed, the defect or problem is decreased or removed.

SP 1.1 SELECT DEFECTS AND PROBLEMS

Select defects and problems for analysis.

Typical Work Products

1. Defect and problem data selected for further analysis

Subpractices

1. Gather relevant defect and problem data.

> Examples of relevant defect data include the following:
> - Defects reported by the customer
> - Defects reported by service teams
> - Defects found in service verification

> Examples of relevant problem data include the following:
> - Project management problem reports requiring corrective action
> - Process capability problems
> - Process duration measurements
> - Resource throughput, utilization, or response time measurements
> - Help desk calls, by time and incident category
> - Inadequate availability of the service system

CAR

Labels (left margin callouts):
- Specific Goal
- Note
- Specific Practice
- Typical Work Product
- Subpractice
- Example Box

FIGURE 2.2
Sample Page from Causal Analysis and Resolution

Model Component Relationships

The model components associated with Part Two are summarized in Figure 2.3 to illustrate their conceptual relationships and to identify which components are required, expected, and informative.

Components Descriptions

The following sections provide detailed descriptions of CMMI model components.

Process Areas

A process area is a cluster of related practices in an area that, when implemented collectively, satisfies a set of goals considered important for making improvement in that area.

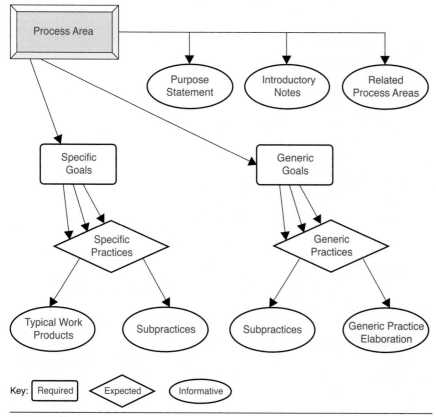

FIGURE 2.3
CMMI Model Components

The 24 process areas are presented in alphabetical order by acronym:

- Capacity and Availability Management (CAM)
- Causal Analysis and Resolution (CAR)
- Configuration Management (CM)
- Decision Analysis and Resolution (DAR)
- Integrated Project Management (IPM)
- Incident Resolution and Prevention (IRP)
- Measurement and Analysis (MA)
- Organizational Innovation and Deployment (OID)
- Organizational Process Definition (OPD)
- Organizational Process Focus (OPF)
- Organizational Process Performance (OPP)
- Organizational Training (OT)
- Project Monitoring and Control (PMC)
- Project Planning (PP)
- Process and Product Quality Assurance (PPQA)
- Quantitative Project Management (QPM)
- Requirements Management (REQM)
- Risk Management (RSKM)
- Supplier Agreement Management (SAM)
- Service Continuity (SCON)
- Service Delivery (SD)
- Service System Development (SSD)[1]
- Service System Transition (SST)
- Strategic Service Management (STSM)

Purpose Statements

A purpose statement describes the purpose of the process area and is an informative component.

For example, the purpose statement of the Organizational Process Definition process area is "The purpose of Organizational Process Definition (OPD) is to establish and maintain a usable set of organizational process assets and work environment standards."

---

1. The SSD process area is an "addition."

Introductory Notes

The introductory notes section of the process area describes the major concepts covered in the process area and is an informative component.

An example from the introductory notes of the Project Planning process area is "Planning begins with requirements that define the product and project."

Related Process Areas

The Related Process Areas section lists references to related process areas and reflects the high-level relationships among the process areas. The Related Process Areas section is an informative component.

An example of a reference found in the Related Process Areas section of the Project Planning process area is "Refer to the Risk Management process area for more information about identifying and analyzing risks."

Specific Goals

A specific goal describes the unique characteristics that must be present to satisfy the process area. A specific goal is a required model component and is used in appraisals to help determine whether a process area is satisfied.

For example, a specific goal from the Configuration Management process area is "Integrity of baselines is established and maintained."

Only the *statement* of the specific goal is a required model component. The *title* of a specific goal (preceded by the goal number) and notes associated with the goal are considered informative model components.

Generic Goals

Generic goals are called "generic" because the same goal statement applies to multiple process areas. A generic goal describes the characteristics that must be present to institutionalize the processes that implement a process area. A generic goal is a required model component and is used in appraisals to determine whether a process area is satisfied. (See the Generic Goals and Generic Practices section in Part Two for a more detailed description of generic goals.)

An example of a generic goal is "The process is institutionalized as a defined process."

Only the *statement* of the generic goal is a required model component. The *title* of a generic goal (preceded by the goal number) and notes associated with the goal are considered informative model components.

Specific Goal and Practice Summaries

The specific goal and practice summary provides a high-level summary of the specific goals, which are required components, and the specific practices, which are expected components. The specific goal and practice summary is an informative component.

Specific Practices

A specific practice is the description of an activity that is considered important in achieving the associated specific goal. The specific practices describe the activities that are expected to result in achievement of the specific goals of a process area. A specific practice is an expected model component.

For example, a specific practice from the Project Monitoring and Control process area is "Monitor commitments against those identified in the project plan."

Only the *statement* of the specific practice is an expected model component. The *title* of a specific practice (preceded by the practice number) and notes associated with the specific practice are considered informative model components.

Typical Work Products

The typical work products section lists sample output from a specific practice. These examples are called "typical work products" because there are often other work products that are just as effective but are not listed. A typical work product is an informative model component.

For example, a typical work product for the specific practice "Monitor Project Planning Parameters" in the Project Monitoring and Control process area is "Records of significant deviations."

Subpractices

A subpractice is a detailed description that provides guidance for interpreting and implementing a specific or generic practice. Subpractices may be worded as if prescriptive, but they are actually an informative component meant only to provide ideas that may be useful for process improvement.

For example, a subpractice for the specific practice "Take Corrective Action" in the Project Monitoring and Control process area is "Determine and document the appropriate actions needed to address identified issues."

Generic Practices

Generic practices are called "generic" because the same practice applies to multiple process areas. A generic practice is the description of an activity that is considered important in achieving the associated generic goal. A generic practice is an expected model component.

For example, a generic practice for the generic goal "The process is institutionalized as a managed process" is "Provide adequate resources for performing the process, developing the work products, and providing the services of the process."

Only the *statement* of the generic practice is an expected model component. The *title* of a generic practice (preceded by the practice number) and notes associated with the practice are considered informative model components.

Generic Practice Elaborations

Generic practice elaborations appear after a generic practice to provide guidance on how the generic practice should be applied uniquely to process areas. A generic practice elaboration is an informative model component.

For example, a generic practice elaboration after the generic practice "Establish and maintain an organizational policy for planning and performing the process" for the Project Planning process area is "This policy establishes organizational expectations for estimating planning parameters, making internal and external commitments, and developing the plan for managing the project."

Additions

An addition can be informative material, a specific practice, a specific goal, or a process area that extends the scope of a model or emphasizes a particular aspect of its use. In this document, all additions are related to the Service System Development process area.

The Service System Development process area is an addition. Another example of an addition is the reference in the Integrated Project Management process area that appears after specific practice 1.1, subpractice 6, "Conduct peer reviews of the project's defined process." The addition states "Refer to the Service System Development process area for more information about performing peer reviews."

Supporting Informative Components

There are many places in the model where further information is needed to describe a concept. This informative material is provided in the form of the following components:

- Notes
- Examples
- References

Notes

A note is text that can accompany nearly any other model component. It may provide detail, background, or rationale. A note is an informative model component.

For example, a note that accompanies the specific practice "Implement Action Proposals" in the Causal Analysis and Resolution process area is "Only changes that prove to be of value should be considered for broad implementation."

Examples

An example is a component comprising text and often a list of items, usually in a box, that can accompany nearly any other component and provides one or more instances to clarify a concept or described activity. An example is an informative model component.

The following is an example that accompanies the subpractice "Document noncompliance issues when they cannot be resolved in the project" under the specific practice "Communicate and Ensure the Resolution of Noncompliance Issues" in the Process and Product Quality Assurance process area.

Examples of ways to resolve noncompliance in the project include the following:
- Fixing the noncompliance
- Changing the process descriptions, standards, or procedures that were violated
- Obtaining a waiver to cover the noncompliance

References

A reference is a pointer to additional or more detailed information in related process areas and can accompany nearly any other model component. A reference is an informative model component.

For example, a reference that accompanies the specific practice "Compose the Defined Process" in the Quantitative Project Management process area is "Refer to the Organizational Process Definition process area for more information about the organization's process asset library, which might include a process element of known and needed capability."

Numbering Scheme

Specific and generic goals are numbered sequentially. Each specific goal begins with the prefix "SG" (e.g., SG 1). Each generic goal begins with the prefix "GG" (e.g., GG 2).

Specific and generic practices also are numbered sequentially. Each specific practice begins with the prefix "SP," followed by a number in the form "x.y" (e.g., SP 1.1). The x is the same number as the goal to which the specific practice maps. The y is the sequence number of the specific practice under the specific goal.

An example of specific practice numbering is in the Project Planning process area. The first specific practice is numbered SP 1.1 and the second is SP 1.2.

Each generic practice begins with the prefix "GP," followed by a number in the form "x.y" (e.g., GP 1.1).

The x corresponds to the number of the generic goal. The y is the sequence number of the generic practice under the generic goal. For example, the first generic practice associated with GG 2 is numbered GP 2.1 and the second is GP 2.2.

CHAPTER 3

HOW TO START USING CMMI

If you are new to CMMI, you may not know how to establish a process improvement program that will benefit your organization. This chapter is designed to help you learn how to get started using CMMI models, appraisal methods, and training to get you on your way to improving your organization's processes.

Important Roles in Process Improvement

Before discussing some of the actions that must be taken to establish a CMMI-based process improvement program, it is important to explain the roles involved in such a program.

The roles involved in a process improvement program are critical to the success of any changes your organization wishes to make to its processes. These roles include the executive sponsor, management steering group, process group, and working groups. In some organizations, one person may perform more than one role.

The Executive Sponsor

For major change to happen, you must have executive sponsorship for the change. An executive sponsor must be a top-level executive in the organization and must be committed to the process improvement program from beginning to end.

The executive sponsor helps to ensure success through the following actions:

• Uses influence and provides resources to help the organization adopt CMMI
• Chooses the best people to manage the process improvement program

- Monitors the process improvement program to ensure that it is getting the resources it needs to be successful
- Is an advocate and spokesperson for the process improvement program

As an advocate for CMMI-based process improvement, the executive sponsor must ensure that other executives fully support the process improvement program and understand these three reasons to adopt CMMI.

1. CMMI improves performance, cost, and schedule.
2. CMMI enables collaboration with external stakeholders to integrate their expectations into day-to-day activities.
3. CMMI improves the organization's ability to compete.

Executives who have successful process improvement programs typically take the following actions:

- They ask someone they trust to learn more about CMMI and report back to them.
- They speak with executives who have adopted CMMI in other organizations, participate in discussion groups and blogs, or attend a conference to learn from others who have adopted CMMI.

Management Steering Group

The organization's top managers form the management steering group. They are a team that oversees the improvement program and meets regularly. Their work includes reviewing progress and making decisions about what improvements should be made. This group typically is responsible for the following:

- Creating the strategic plan for the program
- Allocating resources to complete work for the program
- Providing guidance to the process group
- Removing barriers to success

The Process Group

The quality of the process group is another critical key to the success of a process improvement program. The process group is the center of all process work in the organization. It is responsible for the following:

- Being a role model for others in the organization
- Monitoring process improvement activities
- Supporting teams by providing help with chartering, training, planning, and so on
- Reporting progress and issues to the management steering group
- Being a champion for process improvement
- Teaching and encouraging others in the organization about process improvement

The Process Group Leader

The process group leader is the person who leads the process group and works with the executive sponsor to bring about change. This leader must understand quality management methods and be able to work with senior management effectively. The leader's main function is to manage the process improvement program to get results.

An effective process group leader has formally defined responsibilities, has a full-time job as the process group leader, and is a member of the management team. The process group leader should be given at least two years to get the process improvement program up and running and should be given an adequate budget.

Working Groups

Working groups are subgroups or extensions of the process group that are assigned to implement changes assigned by the process group. Working groups typically address a particular area for improvement. Working groups are often responsible for the following:

- Describing the organization's processes
- Comparing those processes to CMMI model goals and practices and the organization's business objectives
- Defining new processes
- Finding ways to help the new processes be adopted by the organization

The SCAMPI Lead Appraiser or Team Leader

When it is time to do an appraisal, the lead appraiser (for SCAMPI A appraisals) or team leader (for SCAMPI B or C appraisals) works closely with the executive sponsor to set the objectives for an appraisal. (See the section The Purpose and Function of Appraisals later in this chapter for more information about when an appraisal is appropriate.)

The lead appraiser or team leader manages, coordinates, and makes decisions during an appraisal. Another responsibility is to communicate progress and issues with the executive sponsor. The person in this role can be an employee of the organization or a hired consultant.

The Appraisal Team

The appraisal team is the group of individuals who perform the work of an appraisal. They gather information about the organization's processes and judge whether the processes satisfy the goals of the CMMI model the organization is using. The experience of the appraisal team affects the quality and credibility of the appraisal. Team members should have in-depth knowledge of the organization and its processes as well as a good understanding of CMMI. (All appraisal team members must receive training before they can be members of an appraisal team.)

The experience of the appraisal team can supplement the knowledge of the lead appraiser or team leader to ensure the right level of knowledge and skills for the appraisal.

SCAMPI Appraisals

In general, an appraisal measures an organization's processes against descriptions of effective practices. These descriptions of practices are in the reference model being used—a CMMI model. The appraisal method used with CMMI is the SCAMPI method. This method has three different classes of appraisal.

SCAMPI class A is the most rigorous method and is the only method that can result in a rating.

SCAMPI class B is a flexible, less rigorous method that uses a standard scale for evaluating processes.

SCAMPI class C is the most flexible and least rigorous method that uses a scale defined by the organization for evaluating processes.

For more information about SCAMPI, see the SEI website at www.sei.cmu.edu/appraisal-program/appraisal-classes.html.

The Purpose and Function of Appraisals

An appraisal can be used at various points in an organization's process improvement program to (1) identify weaknesses that should be addressed, (2) monitor the success of the program, and (3) prove that the program has achieved a level of success. Typically, SCAMPI B or C appraisals are used for (1) and (2), and a SCAMPI A appraisal is used for (3).

Appraisal Ratings

Many organizations conduct a SCAMPI A appraisal to achieve a maturity level rating or capability level rating. These ratings can be used to formally acknowledge the organization's successful process improvement to date.

Appraisal ratings can be published on the SEI website with the organization's permission. Many choose to publish their ratings so that they can refer customers and others to the site as evidence of their achievement. See the SEI website for published appraisal results at http://sas.sei.cmu.edu/pars/.

Finding the Right SCAMPI Lead Appraiser or Team Leader

See the Get the Right Help section in this chapter for more information about how to find and hire the right lead appraiser or team leader for your process improvement program.

Appraisal Quality Assurance

The SEI has a quality assurance policy and processes to ensure the high quality of appraisal results. Besides ensuring that all lead appraisers and team leaders meet stringent requirements before they can become lead appraisers or team leaders, the quality assurance team reviews data from appraisals.

These reviews ensure that the appropriate processes were followed during appraisals and that the lead appraiser or team leader took appropriate action during the appraisal. These reviews ensure that when you hire a lead appraiser or team leader, you are getting what you are paying for.

CMMI Training

Training plays an important role throughout a process improvement program. Those who are involved in the various roles necessary to improve the organization's processes must have the knowledge and skills to make it happen.

All of those involved in the process group and working groups must be trained in CMMI concepts. The executive sponsor must understand the concepts and methods of CMMI-based process improvement. Lead appraisers, team leaders, and instructors must have the appropriate training and credentials to be effective.

The SEI has many different training courses available. (Some training is available only from the SEI.) SEI Partners also have different training courses available. Your organization may also want to supplement purchased training with organization-specific training.

Here are some of the SEI training courses that may be useful to your organization:

- CMMI-Based Process Improvement Overview
- Mastering Process Improvement
- Introduction to CMMI for Services, Version 1.2
- Introduction to CMMI, Version 1.2 (based on CMMI-DEV)
- Acquisition Supplement for CMMI, Version 1.2
- Services Supplement for CMMI, Version 1.2
- Defining Software Processes
- Intermediate Concepts of CMMI, Version 1.2
- Understanding CMMI High Maturity Practices
- CMMI and Six Sigma: Strategies for Joint Implementation
- SCAMPI Lead Appraiser Training
- SCAMPI B and C Team Leader Training
- CMMI Instructor Training

For descriptions of these training courses and more information about SEI training courses, see the SEI website at www.sei.cmu.edu/products/courses/#CMMI.

An Approach to Getting Started

Process improvement is about evaluating and possibly changing the way your organization operates. At first you don't know where this change will focus, how much will have to change, or who should be involved in making this change happen. All of this uncertainty can make process improvement seem overwhelming at first.

Collect Information

Before you begin, you must collect information from the many available sources of information about CMMI.

The SEI website contains information about CMMI that is maintained to report on new CMMI-related reports, events, tools, and courses. See www.sei.cmu.edu/cmmi/, the CMMI home page, for the latest CMMI news and links to more information related to CMMI. See www.sei.cmu.edu/cmmi/tools/svc for all the latest information on CMMI-SVC.

The latest available CMMI models are available on the SEI website, as are appraisal method descriptions, presentations, and answers to frequently asked questions. The website contains CMMI-related reports, articles, and links to books about CMMI. You'll also find links to early adopters of new models who can provide advice and information they have found helpful.

Information about CMMI-related courses is provided in the SEI Education and Training listing at www.sei.cmu.edu/products/courses/. This listing contains descriptions of SEI courses and when they are offered. A three-day introductory course is available for the CMMI for Services model. If you would like to know when this course is scheduled, check the Education and Training listing or contact cmmi-comments@sei.cmu.edu.

The SEI has a large number of partner organizations serving a worldwide clientele. Many of these partners are licensed to provide CMMI training and appraisal services. Many of these partners also provide help for planning process improvement programs, implementing model best practices, and other related services. Some of these partner organizations have websites, publications, and tools that can help you to use CMMI for process improvement. To see a list of SEI Partners that offer CMMI-related services, visit www.sei.cmu.edu/partners/directory/organization/.

Annual conferences are sources of information about CMMI. Conferences are great places to talk to those who have process improvement programs in their organization. Many of the presentations at these conferences recount the results of CMMI-based process improvement and the different variations of how they used the model, appraisals, and training to meet their process improvement and business objectives.

The SEPG conference series consists of four conferences: SEPG North America, SEPG Europe, SEPG Latin America, and SEPG Asia Pacific. See www.sei.cmu.edu/sepg/ for more information on these conferences.

Another annual conference is the CMMI Technology Conference and User Group. This conference is held every November in Denver and is cosponsored by NDIA and the SEI. Check the NDIA website (www.ndia.org) and the SEI website (www.sei.cmu.edu/events/) in the summer to see more information about the upcoming conference.

A number of online groups, clubs, forums, and communities of CMMI users exchange information on a wide variety of CMMI-related topics. If you belong to an online social network, find out if it already has a CMMI-related group. We know of CMMI groups on Yahoo! and LinkedIn. A number of bloggers also write about CMMI.

Know Where You Are

Next, you want to collect information about your organization. If you already know what part of the organization should be the focus of process improvement (at least at first), then you are ahead of the game.

Collect information about your organization in order to help you build a picture of the status quo. Compare current processes to the practices in the CMMI model you plan to use. You can do this informally, or you can use an established method, such as a SCAMPI appraisal, to create your picture of the status quo.

The picture that you create can take any form that you find useful. If senior management is accustomed to seeing a particular kind of representation, consider using it or something akin to it. You will have to present your analysis of the status quo to management, so it must be something that they can understand quickly and easily.

Figure 3.1 illustrates a picture of the status quo done using estimates of the percentage of process area goals already in place in the organization. Light green cells represent opportunities for improvement, dark green cells represent strengths, black cells represent areas not applicable to the organization's process improvement objectives (or not present in the model), and gray cells identify the process areas targeted for early improvement.

Figure 3.2 illustrates a picture of the status quo done using capability levels to rate the degree to which process areas are already in place in the organization. This picture is commonly called a "capability profile" and can be the output of a SCAMPI appraisal.

Gather information about your organization's culture. You may need to conduct a survey of managers, project leaders, and staff members to gauge their resistance to change. High resistance to change will require more investment of time, money, and effort than low resistance to change. If you find one area of the organization that embraces change easily, it might be a place to start with process improvement. Success in that area will provide momentum and evidence to build support for change in other areas of the organization.

A large number of books are devoted to organizational change. If your organization is highly resistant to change, investigate ways to overcome this shortcoming to accommodate process improvement as

	Process Management			Project Management						Service Establishment and Delivery					Support			
	OT	OPF	OPD	IPM	PP	PMC	SAM	RSKM	REQM	SD	IRP	STSM	SSD	SST	PPQA	CM	DAR	MA
GG3	0%	0%	0%	0%	0%	10%	14%	0%	0%	0%	0%	0%	0%	0%	0%	0%	0%	0%
GG2	0%	0%	9%	0%	13%	33%	22%	14%	31%	25%	50%	27%	53%	36%	36%	36%	0%	0%
GG1	45%	18%	18%	0%	22%	44%	90%	24%	39%	50%	57%	81%	53%	50%	44%	44%	0%	0%
SG3	■	■	■	■	56%	■	■	41%	■	56%	100%	88%	88%	■	63%	56%	■	■
SG2	45%	27%	18%	100%	0%	61%	90%	65%	53%	86%	94%	53%	69%	63%	63%	63%	7%	31%
SG1	45%	27%	18%	0%	0%	50%	100%	24%	39%	72%	64%	94%	88%	59%	44%	63%	7%	0%

Legend:
- Achieved goal satisfaction
- Did not achieve goal satisfaction
- Not applicable (■)
- Focus of concern

FIGURE 3.1
Picture of Status Quo Using Percentage of Goal Satisfaction

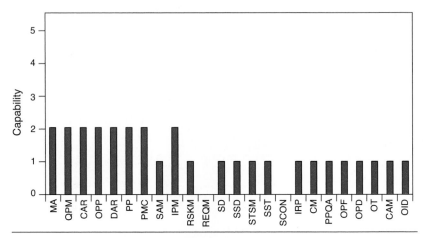

FIGURE 3.2
Picture of Status Quo Using Capability Level Ratings

well as other improvements (e.g., technology) that can benefit your organization.

Know Where You Are Going

Now that you have a picture of the status quo, you can create a corresponding picture of where you want to be. If the difference between where you want to be and where you are is very great, it makes sense to define incremental steps in getting from the status quo to your objective. Characterizing your objective using the same style of picture as your status quo picture will provide a clear and concrete path to success.

To build your picture of where you are going, gather the views of management, project leaders, and staff members to understand their objectives for improvement. Your aim is to create a picture of success that reflects the objective of each set of stakeholders, provides a clear path to integrated improvement, and ensures the support of all stakeholders required for the process improvement program to succeed. If you cannot build a picture of success that all can support, you are not ready to begin.

Figure 3.3 illustrates a picture of the organization's process improvement objective using estimates of the percentage of process area goals desired. Light green cells represent goals that do not need to be completely satisfied, dark green cells represent goals that must be satisfied, and black cells represent areas not currently applicable to the organization's process improvement objectives (or not present in the model).

	Process Management				Project Management					Service Establishment and Delivery					Support			
	OT	OPF	OPD	IPM	PP	PMC	SAM	RSKM	REQM	SD	IRP	STSM	SSD	SST	PPQA	CM	DAR	MA
GG3	0%	0%	0%	0%	100%	100%	14%	100%	100%	100%	100%	100%	100%	100%	100%	100%	100%	100%
GG2	0%	0%	9%	0%	100%	100%	22%	100%	100%	100%	100%	100%	100%	100%	100%	100%	100%	100%
GG1	45%	18%	18%	0%	100%	100%	90%	100%	100%	100%	100%	100%	100%	100%	100%	100%	100%	100%
SG3					100%		100%			100%	100%		100%		100%	100%		
SG2	45%	27%		100%	100%	100%	90%	100%		100%	100%	100%	100%	100%	100%	100%	100%	100%
SG1	45%	27%	18%	0%	100%	100%	100%	100%	100%	100%	100%	100%	100%	100%	100%	100%	100%	100%

Achieved goal satisfaction

Did not achieve goal satisfaction

Not applicable

FIGURE 3.3
Process Improvement Objective Using Percentage of Goal Satisfaction

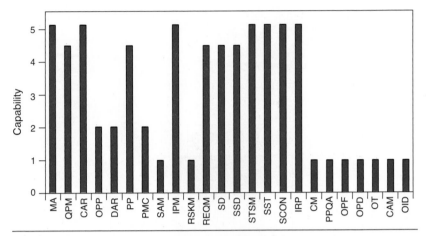

FIGURE 3.4
Process Improvement Objectives Using Capability Level Ratings

Figure 3.4 illustrates a picture of the organization's process improvement objectives using capability levels to rate the degree to which process areas will be achieved to reach process improvement objectives. This picture is commonly called a "target profile" and can be the output of a SCAMPI A appraisal.

Compare the picture of the status quo with the picture of where you are going. The difference between the two is the focus of your process improvement program. Develop a periodic (e.g., monthly, weekly) report that demonstrates your process improvement program's progress as it reaches its objectives.

Commit Resources

Remember that a process improvement program is a project. It must have the resources it needs to survive and succeed, including a plan, budget, and staff.

Choose the best staff members to manage the process improvement program. Ensure that they have the appropriate skills, experience, responsibility, and authority to be successful. Monitor the process improvement program over time to ensure that it is vital and strong.

Get the Right Help

If you want to hire experts to help you to achieve process improvement in your organization, consider hiring an SEI Partner organization. These organizations offer training, appraisal services, and process improvement advice.

Take these basic steps to ensure that you are selecting the right CMMI Partner for your organization.

1. Check the SEI website to confirm that a CMMI Partner is currently active. Only currently active partners are listed on the website. These SEI Partners receive the latest materials and information from the SEI pertaining to the services the SEI Partner is authorized to provide.
2. Interview at least three SEI Partner organizations so that you can compare their knowledge, services, and prices.
3. Ask the SEI Partner organization for a list of the services it provides, how they recommend that your organization adopt CMMI, and how they charge for their services. If you know you need help with a particular part of CMMI, be sure to ask the partner about their experience with that specific aspect of CMMI.
4. If you plan to have a SCAMPI appraisal as part of your relationship with the SEI Partner, ask if you will be able to interview and select your SCAMPI lead appraiser or team leader.
5. If you plan to purchase training as part of your relationship with the SEI Partner, ask if you will be able to interview and select your instructor.
6. Ask the SEI Partner organization what types of customers it has served before and how these customers differ from and resemble your organization. Ask for references. There is no better recommendation than from a satisfied customer.

Selecting a SCAMPI Lead Appraiser or Team Leader

Take these basic measures to ensure that you are selecting the right SCAMPI lead appraiser or team leader for your organization.

1. Check the SEI website to see if the SCAMPI lead appraiser or team leader is currently certified or authorized, respectively. Only currently certified SCAMPI lead appraisers and authorized SCAMPI team leaders are listed on the SEI website.
2. Ask the lead appraiser or team leader about his or her experience, including how many appraisals he or she has led and how many he or she has participated in. See if the lead appraiser or team leader has worked with organizations similar to yours. Find out if he or she is both a lead appraiser and a team leader.
3. Ask the lead appraiser or team leader what his or her approach is to collecting evidence, analyzing data, and presenting information that the organization can use to plan its future process improvement.

4. Ask the lead appraiser or team leader what types of customers he or she has served before and how these customers differ from and resemble your organization.

5. Ask the lead appraiser or team leader about his or her availability for answering questions before and after the appraisal.

Selecting a CMMI Instructor

Take these basic measures to ensure that you are selecting the right training instructor for your organization.

1. Check the SEI website to see if the instructor is authorized for the course you want. Only currently authorized or certified instructors are listed on the SEI website.

2. Ask the instructor about his or her experience, including how many courses he or she has taught and when he or she taught last.

3. Ask the instructor what his or her approach is to teaching and how he or she interprets the materials the SEI provides.

4. Ask the instructor what types of students he or she has taught before and how these students differ from and resemble the students you have in your organization.

5. Ask the instructor about his or her availability for answering questions before and after the class is held.

How to Get There

Each organization should develop an improvement strategy that meets its needs. Consequently, before you can determine the best improvement strategy, you must know the organization's business objectives. The improvement strategy, to be effective, must support and be designed to meet the organization's business objectives.

Scope of Improvement

Your process improvement strategy must target a portion of your organization, called an "organizational unit." If you have a very small organization, it may make sense to target the entire organization. However, for most organizations, a work unit, department, site, or set of projects is an appropriate beginning.

Choose the organizational unit carefully. Your first organizational unit is ideally one for which the process group can demonstrate the value of process improvement as quickly as possible. Such an approach will help to get others involved and eager to expand the process improvement into other areas.

If you hire an SEI Partner organization, its consultant may provide advice in the selection of an organizational unit for process improvement.

Reference Model Selection

Not only must you select the organizational unit you wish to improve, but you also must select the objectives for your process improvement program. Part of this selection is deciding which CMMI model to use and which process areas or capability levels (or maturity levels) to target.

Since you've selected the CMMI for Services model, you have already decided which model you want to use. If you want to achieve a particular maturity level, you have already selected the minimum set of process areas you wish to target for improvement.

However, there are other considerations. Which process areas are most critical to support the core of your business? For example, if you differentiate yourself from your competitors by your ability to make your services available under any circumstances, then the Service Continuity process area would immediately be identified as a critical process area for you.

If you are not interested in a maturity level or capability profile as part of your improvement, you are free simply to select the process areas most important to your organization.

If you hire an SEI Partner organization, its consultant may provide advice in the selection of the appropriate model scope for process improvement in your organization.

CMMI adoption is not a one-size-fits-all approach. CMMI can be used with other improvement approaches effectively. Some organizations have adopted CMMI with or in addition to other approaches such as the following:

- Agile methods
- Balanced Scorecard
- CobiT
- IEEE standards
- ISO 9000/20000
- ITIL
- People CMM
- RUP

- Six Sigma
- TSP/PSP

An Appraisal Approach

Since an appraisal measures the organization's processes against descriptions of effective practices, selecting which parts of the organization to appraise and which processes to appraise is critical. Such a selection is made based on the organization's business objectives and the process weaknesses identified by an informal mapping of CMMI goals and practices to the organization's processes.

In general, your appraisal strategy will closely follow the organizational unit and model scope selected for your process improvement program. However, that isn't required. You could select a representative subset of your process improvement program for appraisal.

As mentioned before, an appraisal can serve many purposes, including the following: (1) Identify weaknesses that should be addressed, (2) monitor the success of the program, and (3) prove that the program has achieved a level of success. Your appraisal strategy will cover when and which kind of appraisal you will use for which purpose as part of your overall process improvement program.

For example, you may begin with a SCAMPI C appraisal to identify strengths and weaknesses. Based on the information gained from this appraisal you plan to determine the model scope and organizational units to pursue. A SCAMPI B appraisal might be scheduled a year from then to determine if the improvement project is on track. Finally, you might project a date when you think the process improvement program will have achieved its objectives and schedule a SCAMPI A appraisal to confirm it.

That is just one example. Your plan may be different based on your organization's needs and resources. If you hire an SEI Partner organization, its consultant may provide advice about creating an appraisal strategy.

A Training Program

If your organization is small, the best value is to purchase training from the SEI or an SEI Partner organization. If your organization is *very* large, you may want to consider becoming an SEI Partner and sending employees through training to become authorized instructors. Contact the SEI for more information and advice on the best approach for you.

A Strategy for Change

You need to make a number of decisions to establish a process improvement program. Without the right information, the risk of suboptimal decisions for your unique organizational context increases. That is why research and networking with others who have tried and succeeded with process improvement are invaluable in determining what is best for your organization.

Do You Want an Appraisal Rating or Not?

Appraisal ratings can be invaluable for organizations whose customers expect to see a maturity level or capability profile that will help them distinguish between providers. Sometimes an appraisal rating can be a factor that can help you differentiate yourself from the competition.

However, not all organizations need a rating. They can benefit from the process improvement benefits of CMMI, but the appraisal ratings are of little value to them. If this situation describes your organization, then you are lucky. Your CMMI-based process improvement program can be very flexible, and you can select the process areas most critical to your business objectives.

Do You Want to Hire an SEI Partner or Not?

You might assume that if you don't want an appraisal rating, you don't need help from an SEI Partner, but that isn't necessarily true. If you have employees with extensive experience with CMMI and SCAMPI appraisals, you may not need to hire an SEI Partner. However, if you plan to select process areas solely on the basis of their benefit to your organization, you may need more help in selecting process areas that best answer your business needs.

Is Your Organization Ready for Change?

There are a variety of ways to determine whether your organization is ready for change. The culture of the organization must be receptive to change, and management must be willing to be consistent and support the change.

Before initiating a process improvement program, it is important to know the risks involved in undertaking such a program. Determine if your organization is ready for change by doing the following:

• Examining the history of the organization to evaluate how it has handled change in the past

- Determining how committed each level of management is to making change happen
- Identifying areas of resistance to change from those in the organization who would be affected by the change
- Identifying areas of the organization that should not change because they are working well

After collecting this information and analyzing it, you should be able to determine if the organization is ready for change and what the risks are for beginning a process improvement program.

These elements must be present in the organization for effective change to take place.

- A reason for change must exist. Members of the organization must be aware of organizational issues that are having an impact on the business.
- Executive management is leading the change.
- The top management team is committed to the change.
- A process group has valued resources assigned to it, including a process change leader who has a mandate to initiate change.
- A system of performance measures is in place that can be used to drive and track change.

If you hire an SEI Partner organization, its consultant may provide advice in determining the readiness of your organization for change and identifying the risks to making changes in your organization.

CHAPTER 4

ACHIEVING PROCESS IMPROVEMENT THAT LASTS

Overview

This chapter explains how CMMI models ensure lasting process improvement. Making improvements to achieve business objectives is only half the job. The other half is ensuring that these improvements persist.

Lasting Improvement

Lasting improvement requires establishing processes that are *institutionalized*, which means they are absorbed into the organization's standard way of doing business. Institutionalized processes are more likely to persist during times of stress.

So, how do processes become institutionalized? Research has shown that to become institutionalized, processes must be supported by the organization. In CMMI models, this support is embodied in the generic goals and practices. When the organization implements these practices, it increases the permanence of its processes. That is why implementing only the specific practices of a process area is not enough; you must also implement the generic goals and practices.

The degrees of process institutionalization that CMMI models support are expressed in the types of processes the generic goals and practices enable.

As generic goals and practices are implemented for a process area, the practices of the process are more likely to last. Processes can be expressed as process types, which include incomplete, managed, defined, quantitatively managed, and optimizing processes.

These process types are described in the following subsections. Each succeeding process type reflects its increasing permanence in the organization.

Incomplete Process

An *incomplete process* is a process that either is not performed or is partially performed. One or more of the specific goals of the process area are not satisfied and none of the generic goals are satisfied.

Performed Process

A *performed process* is a process that accomplishes the work necessary to produce work products and enables the work needed to establish, deliver, and manage services. The specific goals and specific practices of the process area are implemented.

Managed Process

A *managed process* is a *performed process* that establishes discipline and control to ensure continued performance in times of stress.

The organization establishes the requirements and objectives for the process. The status of the work products and delivery of the services are visible to management at defined points (e.g., at major milestones and at the completion of major tasks). Commitments are established among those performing the work and the relevant stakeholders and are revised as necessary. Work products are reviewed with relevant stakeholders and are controlled. The work products and services satisfy their specified requirements.

A critical distinction between a *performed process* and a *managed process* is the extent to which the process is managed. A managed process is planned (the plan may be part of a more encompassing plan) and the execution of the process is managed against the plan. Corrective actions are taken when the actual results and performance deviate significantly from the plan. A *managed process* achieves the objectives of the plan and is institutionalized for consistent performance.

Defined Process

A *defined process* is a *managed process* that the organization tailors from its set of standard processes according to its tailoring guidelines; has a maintained process description; and contributes work products, measures, and other process improvement information to organizational process assets.

See the glossary for the definitions of organization's set of standard processes, organizational process assets, and standard process.

The organization's set of standard processes is the basis of a defined process. The infrastructure to support current and future use of the organization's set of standard processes is established and improved over time.

There are two critical distinctions between a managed process and a defined process.

The first is the scope of standards, process descriptions, and procedures. A managed process can apply to only one project, whereas a defined process is tailored from the organization's set of standard processes.

The second distinction is the rigor used to describe processes. A defined process is managed more proactively using an understanding of the interrelationships of the process activities and detailed measures of the process and its work products.

A defined process clearly states the following:

- Purpose
- Inputs
- Entry criteria
- Activities
- Roles
- Measures
- Verification steps
- Outputs
- Exit criteria

Quantitatively Managed Process

A *quantitatively managed process* is a *defined process* that is controlled using statistical and other quantitative techniques. Quality and process-performance attributes are measurable and controlled throughout the project.

Performance models are used to set performance objectives for service provider performance and to help achieve business objectives. Quantitative objectives for quality and process performance are established and used as criteria in managing the process. Quality and process performance are understood in statistical terms and are managed throughout the life of the process. Quantitative objectives are established based on the capability of the organization's set of standard processes; the organization's business objectives; and the needs of the customer, end users, organization, and process implementers, subject to the availability of resources. The people performing the process are directly involved in quantitatively managing the process.

The subprocesses that are significant contributors to overall process performance are statistically managed. For these subprocesses, special causes of process variation are identified and, where appropriate, the source of the special cause is addressed to prevent its recurrence.

For selected subprocesses, specific measures of process performance are collected and statistically analyzed. When selecting them for analyses, it is critical to understand the relationships between processes and subprocesses and their impact on performance. Such an approach helps to ensure that quantitative and statistical management is applied where it has the most overall value to the business.

Quality and process-performance measures are incorporated into the organization's measurement repository to support future decision making.

Quantitatively managing the performance of a process includes the following activities:

- Identifying the subprocesses to be statistically managed
- Identifying and measuring work product and process attributes that are important to quality and process performance
- Identifying and addressing special causes of subprocess variations
- Managing the selected subprocesses, to bring their performance within natural bounds (i.e., making the subprocess performance statistically stable and predictable based on the selected work product and process attributes)
- Predicting the ability of the process to satisfy quantitative quality and process-performance objectives
- Taking appropriate corrective action when quality and process-performance objectives will not be satisfied

The difference between a quantitatively managed process and a defined process is the predictability of process performance. A quantitatively managed process controls its performance using statistical and other quantitative techniques and is quantitatively predictable. A defined process is typically only qualitatively predictable.

Optimizing Process

An *optimizing process* is a *quantitatively managed process* that has a continually improving range of process performance through both incremental and innovative improvements. An optimizing process continually improves process performance through incremental and innovative technological improvements.

Quantitative process improvement objectives are established, continually revised to reflect changing business objectives, and used as criteria in managing process improvement. Both the defined processes and the organization's set of standard processes are two common targets of measurable improvement activities.

Selected incremental and innovative technological process improvements are systematically managed and deployed. The effects of the improvements are measured and evaluated against quantitative process improvement objectives.

In a process that is optimized, common causes of process variation are addressed by improving the process to shift the mean or decrease variation when the process is restabilized. (See the definition of *common cause of process variation* in the glossary.)

The difference between a *quantitatively managed process* and an *optimizing process* is that a quantitatively managed process addresses special causes of process variation and provides statistical predictability of results. An optimizing process continuously improves by addressing common causes of process variation. Although a quantitatively managed process may produce predictable results, the results may not be sufficient in an increasingly competitive business environment.

Understanding Generic Practices

Generic practices ensure a degree of permanence in a variety of ways that include but are not limited to the following:

- Creating policies and securing sponsorship
- Ensuring that the work unit and/or organization has the resources it needs
- Managing the performance of the process, managing the integrity of its work products, and involving relevant stakeholders
- Reviewing with higher level management and objectively evaluating conformance to process descriptions, procedures, and standards

The generic goals and practices are listed in the first section of Part Two, including notes and subpractices that further explain them.

Applied sequentially and in order, the generic goals describe characteristics of processes that are increasingly institutionalized from *performed processes* to *optimizing processes*.

Generic goals and their practices are designed to be applied to processes associated with each process area.

Achieving GG 1 for a process area is the same as achieving the specific goals of a selected process area.

Achieving GG 2 for a process area is managing the performance of processes associated with the process area. This management includes a policy that indicates you will perform the process, a plan for performing the process, resources, assigned responsibilities, training, controlled work products, and so on.

Achieving GG 3 for a process area assumes that an organizational standard process exists that can be tailored to result in the process you will use.

Achieving GG 4 or GG 5 for a process area is conceptually feasible but may not be economical except, perhaps, in situations where the domain has become stable for an extended period or in situations in which the process area or domain is a critical business driver.

The generic goals and generic practices are used as part of achieving capability and maturity level ratings. Table 4.1 illustrates the relationships between the generic goals and practices and the maturity and capability levels.

TABLE 4.1 Model Elements Affecting Process Institutionalization

Generic Goals and Generic Practices	*Capability Levels*	*Maturity Levels*
GG 1	CL 1: Performed	(not applicable)
GG 2	CL 2: Managed	ML 2: Managed
GG 3	CL 3: Defined	ML 3: Defined
GG 4	CL 4: Quantitatively Managed	ML 4: Quantitatively Managed
GG 5	CL 5: Optimizing	ML 5: Optimizing

Understanding Capability Levels

The capability level of a process area indicates how lasting the associated processes are likely to be. A process area is given a capability level rating based on the highest generic goal satisfied.

Implementing only the specific practices of a process area will achieve capability level 1, which means that the process is performed, but it may not last.

As the organization implements the generic practices for a process, it increases the chances that the process will become part of the way the organization does business. Capability levels measure this increase in permanence for each process area by generic goal (or group of generic practices) as described in Table 4.2.

TABLE 4.2 Capability Levels and Generic Goals

Capability Levels	Generic Goals
CL 1: Performed	GG 1 All SPs in the process area
CL 2: Managed	GG 1 All SPs in the process area GG 2 GP 2.1, 2.2, 2.3, 2.4, 2.5, 2.6, 2.7, 2.8, 2.9, and 2.10
CL 3: Defined	GG 1 All SPs in the process area GG 2 GP 2.1, 2.2, 2.3, 2.4, 2.5, 2.6, 2.7, 2.8, 2.9, and 2.10 GG 3 GP 3.1, 3.2
CL 4: Quantitatively Managed	GG 1 All SPs in the process area GG 2 GP 2.1, 2.2, 2.3, 2.4, 2.5, 2.6, 2.7, 2.8, 2.9, and 2.10 GG 4 GP 4.1, 4.2
CL 5: Optimizing	GG 1 All SPs in the process area GG 2 GP 2.1, 2.2, 2.3, 2.4, 2.5, 2.6, 2.7, 2.8, 2.9, and 2.10 GG 3 GP 3.1, 3.2

Continues

TABLE 4.2 Capability Levels and Generic Goals *(Continued)*

Capability Levels	Generic Goals
	GG 4
	GP 4.1, 4.2
	GG 5
	GP 5.1, 5.2

Implementation of all generic practices for every process area is not realistic. Each process area can benefit from the GPs at capability levels 2 and 3 to make the associated improvement more permanent. However, once you get to generic goals 4 and 5, the emphasis changes to quantitative control. These generic practices should focus only on subprocesses that are indicators for the critical aspects of your business. Therefore, these generic practices should be limited to a subset of process areas.

Measuring subprocesses, statistically managing them, and subsequently optimizing their selection and performance is a way to control a process to ensure that it continues to meet the needs of the organization and its customers. That is the purpose and function of generic goals 4 and 5.

However, most processes need generic goals 2 and 3 and the level of control and permanence that they ensure.

Understanding Maturity Levels

Maturity levels indicate how advanced an organization's processes are as a whole. Each process area has a maturity level assigned to it; for example, "CM is a maturity level 2 process area." To achieve a maturity level, all of the goals of the process areas belonging to that maturity level must be satisfied.

In other words, maturity level 2 (the lowest available maturity level) means that more than just the generic goals and practices are implemented; it also means that a whole set of process areas was implemented.

An organization achieves a maturity level rating based on the highest generic goal implemented and the highest maturity level process areas satisfied. (Maturity levels are less directly related to generic practices than capability levels, but they do relate.) Maturity levels are implemented in order from 2 through 5.

As the organization achieves increasing maturity levels, it reinforces the process that will become part of the way the organization does business. Maturity levels measure this increase in permanence as described in Table 4.3.

Implementation of all generic practices for every process area is not realistic. Once you reach maturity levels 4 and 5, the maturity levels no longer rely on the generic practices to increase control and permanence: These characteristics are achieved by the maturity level 4 and 5 process areas.

The maturity level 4 and 5 process areas should focus only on subprocesses that are indicators for the critical aspects of your business.

TABLE 4.3 Maturity Levels, Process Areas, and Generic Goals

Maturity Levels	*Process Areas and Generic Goals*
ML 2: Managed	CM, MA, PMC, PP, PPQA, REQM, SAM, SD
	GG 2
	GP 2.1, 2.2, 2.3, 2.4, 2.5, 2.6, 2.7, 2.8, 2.9, and 2.10
ML 3: Defined	CM, MA, PMC, PP, PPQA, REQM, SAM, SD
	CAM, DAR, IPM, IRP, OPD, OPF, OT, RSKM, SCON, SSD, SST, STSM
	GG 2
	GP 2.1, 2.2, 2.3, 2.4, 2.5, 2.6, 2.7, 2.8, 2.9, and 2.10
	GG 3
	GP 3.1, 3.2
ML 4: Quantitatively Managed	CM, MA, PMC, PP, PPQA, REQM, SAM, SD
	CAM, DAR, IPM, IRP, OPD, OPF, OT, RSKM, SCON, SSD, SST, STSM
	OPP, QPM
	GG 2
	GP 2.1, 2.2, 2.3, 2.4, 2.5, 2.6, 2.7, 2.8, 2.9, and 2.10
	GG 3
	GP 3.1, 3.2
ML 5: Optimizing	CM, MA, PMC, PP, PPQA, REQM, SAM, SD
	CAM, DAR, IPM, IRP, OPD, OPF, OT, RSKM, SCON, SSD, SST, STSM
	OPP, QPM
	CAR, OID
	GG 2
	GP 2.1, 2.2, 2.3, 2.4, 2.5, 2.6, 2.7, 2.8, 2.9, and 2.10
	GG 3
	GP 3.1, 3.2

Measuring subprocesses, statistically managing them, and subsequently optimizing their selection and performance is a way to control a process to ensure that it continues. That is the purpose and function of the process areas staged at maturity levels 4 and 5.

Comparing Capability Levels and Maturity Levels

Capability levels support the continuous representation of the model. Maturity levels support the staged representation of the model.

Process areas are viewed differently in the two representations. Figure 4.1 compares how process areas are used in the continuous and staged representations.

The continuous representation enables the organization to focus its process improvement efforts by choosing those process areas, or sets of interrelated process areas, that best benefit the organization and its business objectives. Although there are some limits on what an organization can choose because of the dependencies among process areas, the organization has considerable freedom in its selection.

To assist those using the continuous representation, process areas are organized into four categories: Process Management, Project Management, Service Establishment and Delivery, and Support. These categories emphasize some of the key relationships that exist among the process areas.

Once you select process areas, you must also select how much you would like to improve the processes associated with those process areas (i.e., select the appropriate capability level). Capability levels and generic goals and practices support the improvement of processes associated with individual process areas. For example, an organization may wish to reach capability level 2 in one process area and capability level 4 in another. As the organization achieves a capability level, it sets its sights on the next capability level for one of these same process areas or decides to widen its view and address additional process areas relevant to its business goals.

This selection of a combination of process areas and capability levels is typically described in a "target profile." A target profile defines all of the process areas to be addressed and the targeted capability level for each. This profile governs which goals and practices the organization will address in its process improvement efforts.

Most organizations, at a minimum, target capability level 1, which requires that all specific goals of the process area be achieved. However, organizations that target capability levels higher than 1 concentrate on

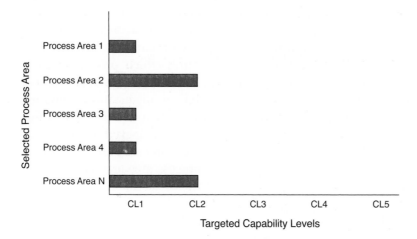

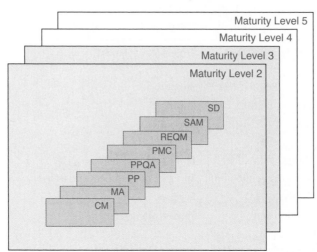

= Groups of process areas chosen for process improvement to achieve maturity level 3

FIGURE 4.1
Process Areas in Continuous and Staged Representations

the institutionalization of selected processes in the organization by implementing the associated generic goals and practices.

In contrast, the staged representation provides a predetermined path of improvement from maturity level 1 to maturity level 5 that involves achieving the goals of the process areas at each maturity level. To assist those using the staged representation, process areas are grouped by maturity level, indicating which process areas to implement to achieve each maturity level. For example, at maturity level 2, there is a set of process areas that an organization would use to guide its process improvement until it satisfies all the goals of all these process areas. Once maturity level 2 is achieved, the organization focuses its efforts on maturity level 3 process areas, and so on. The generic goals that apply to each process area are also predetermined. Generic goal 2 applies to maturity level 2 and generic goal 3 applies to maturity levels 3 through 5.

Table 4.4 provides a list of CMMI-SVC process areas and their associated categories and maturity levels.

TABLE 4.4 Process Areas and Their Associated Categories and Maturity Levels

Process Area	Category	Maturity Level
Capacity and Availability Management (CAM)	Project Management	3
Causal Analysis and Resolution (CAR)	Support	5
Configuration Management (CM)	Support	2
Decision Analysis and Resolution (DAR)	Support	3
Integrated Project Management (IPM)	Project Management	3
Incident Resolution and Prevention (IRP)	Service Establishment and Delivery	3
Measurement and Analysis (MA)	Support	2
Organizational Innovation and Deployment (OID)	Process Management	5
Organizational Process Definition (OPD)	Process Management	3
Organizational Process Focus (OPF)	Process Management	3
Organizational Process Performance (OPP)	Process Management	4
Organizational Training (OT)	Process Management	3
Project Monitoring and Control (PMC)	Project Management	2
Project Planning (PP)	Project Management	2

TABLE 4.4 Process Areas and Their Associated Categories and Maturity Levels *(Continued)*

Process Area	Category	Maturity Level
Process and Product Quality Assurance (PPQA)	Support	2
Quantitative Project Management (QPM)	Project Management	4
Requirements Management (REQM)	Project Management	2
Risk Management (RSKM)	Project Management	3
Supplier Agreement Management (SAM)	Project Management	2
Service Continuity (SCON)	Project Management	3
Service Delivery (SD)	Service Establishment and Delivery	2
Service System Development (SSD)*	Service Establishment and Delivery	3
Service System Transition (SST)	Service Establishment and Delivery	3
Strategic Service Management (STSM)	Service Establishment and Delivery	3

* The SSD process area is an "addition," which means that it is optional when selecting process areas to implement.

Equivalent Staging

Up to this point, we have not discussed process appraisals in much detail. The SCAMPI method[1] is used to appraise organizations using CMMI, and one result of an appraisal is a rating [SEI 2006b, Ahern 2005]. If the continuous representation is used for an appraisal, the rating is called a "capability level." If the staged representation is used for an appraisal, the rating is called a "maturity level" (e.g., maturity level 3).

Either type of rating can tell you a great deal about your organization's process capability and maturity. However, capability level ratings are more difficult to use than maturity level ratings for the purpose of objectively comparing your organization with other organizations. How can you compare capability levels and maturity levels? Is such a comparison even possible?

Such a comparison is accomplished using a method called "equivalent staging," which depends on an understanding of capability level profiles. A capability level profile is a list of process areas and the corresponding capability level achieved for each. This profile

1. The Standard CMMI Appraisal Method for Process Improvement (SCAMPI) method is described in Chapter 5.

enables an organization to track its capability level by process area. The profile is called an "achievement profile" when it represents the organization's actual progress for each process area. Alternatively, the profile is called a "target profile" when it represents the organization's planned process improvement objectives.

Figure 4.2 illustrates a combined target and achievement profile. The green portion of each bar represents what has been achieved. The unshaded portion represents what remains to be accomplished to meet the target profile.

An achievement profile, when compared with a target profile, enables an organization to plan and track its progress for each selected process area. Maintaining capability level profiles is advisable when using the continuous representation.

Target staging is a sequence of target profiles that describes the path of process improvement for the organization to follow. When building target profiles, the organization should pay attention to the dependencies between generic practices and process areas. If a

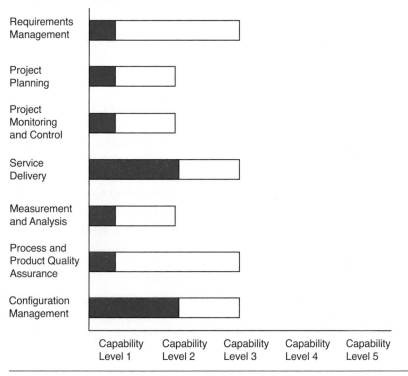

FIGURE 4.2

An Example of a Target and Achievement Profile

generic practice depends on a process area, either to enable the generic practice or to provide a prerequisite product, the generic practice may be much less effective when the process area is not implemented.[2]

Although there are many reasons to use the continuous representation, ratings consisting of capability level profiles are limited in their ability to provide organizations with a way to generally compare themselves with other organizations. Capability level profiles could be used if each organization selected the same process areas; however, maturity levels have been used to compare organizations for years and already provide predefined sets of process areas.

Because of this situation, the CMMI Product Team created equivalent staging. Equivalent staging enables an organization using the continuous representation for an appraisal to convert a capability level profile to the associated maturity level rating.

The most effective way to depict equivalent staging is to provide a sequence of target profiles, each of which is equivalent to a maturity level rating of the staged representation. The result is a target staging that is equivalent to the maturity levels of the staged representation.

Figure 4.3 shows a summary of the target profiles that must be achieved when using the continuous representation to be equivalent to maturity levels 2 through 5. Each shaded area in the capability level columns represents a target profile that is equivalent to a maturity level.

The following rules summarize equivalent staging.

- To achieve maturity level 2, all process areas assigned to maturity level 2 must achieve capability level 2 or higher.
- To achieve maturity level 3, all process areas assigned to maturity levels 2 and 3 must achieve capability level 3 or higher.
- To achieve maturity level 4, all process areas assigned to maturity levels 2, 3, and 4 must achieve capability level 3 or higher.
- To achieve maturity level 5, all process areas must achieve capability level 3 or higher.

These rules and the table for equivalent staging are complete; however, you may ask why target profiles 4 and 5 do not extend into the CL4 and CL5 columns. The reason is that maturity level 4 process areas describe a selection of the subprocesses to be stabilized

---

2. See Table 7.1 (p. 220) in the Generic Goals and Generic Practices section of Part Two for more information about the dependencies between generic practices and process areas.

Name	Abbr	ML	CL1	CL2	CL3	CL4	CL5
Configuration Management	CM	2					
Measurement and Analysis	MA	2					
Project Monitoring and Control	PMC	2					
Project Planning	PP	2		Target Profile 2			
Process and Product Quality Assurance	PPQA	2					
Requirements Management	REQM	2					
Service Delivery	SD	2					
Supplier Agreement Management	SAM	2					
Capacity and Availability Management	CAM	3					
Decision Analysis and Resolution	DAR	3					
Integrated Project Management	IPM	3					
Incident Resolution and Prevention	IRP	3			Target Profile 3		
Organizational Process Definition	OPD	3					
Organizational Process Focus	OPF	3					
Organizational Training	OT	3					
Risk Management	RSKM	3					
Service Continuity	SCON	3					
Service System Develpment[3]	SSD	3					
Service System Transition	SST	3					
Strategic Service Management	STSM	3					
Organizational Process Performance	OPP	4					
Quantitative Project Management	QPM	4		Target Profile 4			
Causal Analysis and Resolution	CAR	5					
Organizational Innovation and Deployment	OID	5		Target Profile 5			

FIGURE 4.3
Target Profiles and Equivalent Staging

3. This process area is an "SSD Addition."

based, in part, on the quality and process-performance objectives of the organization and projects. Not every process area will be addressed in the selection, and CMMI does not presume in advance which process areas might be addressed in the selection.

So, the achievement of capability level 4 for process areas cannot be predetermined, because the choices depend on the selections made by the organization in its implementation of the maturity level 4 process areas. Thus, Figure 4.3 does not show *target profile 4* extending into the *CL4* column, although some process areas will have achieved capability level 4. The situation for *maturity level 5* and *target profile 5* is similar.

The existence of equivalent staging should not discourage users of the continuous representation from establishing target profiles that extend above capability level 3. Such a target profile would be determined in part by the selections the organization made to meet its business objectives.

CHAPTER 5

RELATIONSHIPS AMONG PROCESS AREAS

In this chapter, we describe the key relationships among process areas. These relationships among multiple process areas, including the information and artifacts that flow from one process area to another—illustrated by the figures and descriptions in this chapter—help you to see a larger view of process implementation and improvement.

Successful process improvement initiatives must be driven by the business objectives of the organization. For example, a common business objective is to reduce the time it takes to respond to customers. The process improvement objective derived from that might be to improve incident management processes. Those improvements rely on best practices in the Service Delivery and Incident Resolution and Prevention process areas.

Although we group process areas in this chapter to simplify the discussion of their relationships, process areas often interact and have an effect on one another regardless of their group, category, or level. For example, the Decision Analysis and Resolution process area (a Support process area at maturity level 3) contains specific practices that address the formal evaluation process used in the Service Continuity process area (a Service Establishment and Delivery process area at maturity level 3) to select functions that are essential to the organization and must be covered in the service continuity plan.

Being aware of the key relationships that exist among CMMI process areas will help you to apply CMMI in a useful and productive way. Relationships among process areas are described in more detail in the references in each process area and specifically in the Related Process Areas section of each process area in Part Two. Refer to Chapter 2 for more information about references.

The process areas of the CMMI-SVC model have numerous inter-relationships that are based on a transfer or sharing of information, work products, and other resources by their associated practices. This section focuses on identifying only the relationships encompassing the service-specific process areas. These relationships are best understood by functionally associating them into two distinct groups that span both maturity levels and process area categories:

- Establishing and delivering services
- Managing services

Process area relationships are illustrated in flow diagrams that focus on key dependencies for the sake of clarity; not all possible interactions between process areas are shown, and not all process areas are shown. The process areas that have been omitted from these diagrams (primarily the Process Management and Support process areas) have potential relationships with all of the process areas that *are* shown, and their inclusion would make it difficult to focus on the key CMMI-SVC relationships.

Relationships That Drive Service Establishment and Delivery

Figure 5.1 shows process areas associated with the establishment of service delivery capabilities as driven by requirements from service agreements with customers, as well as with service delivery.

All of the process areas shown in this diagram are in the Service Establishment and Delivery process area category. Note that the Service Delivery process area occupies a central role in these relationships.

Service establishment and delivery process areas represent the "core" of the CMMI for Services model in a longitudinal sense: All of the relationships here can be laid out over time, in the form of interchanges that span a service lifecycle. Working through these relationships for each process area is one way to lay the groundwork for a discussion of service lifecycles, which is at the end of this chapter.

The Strategic Service Management (STSM) process area stands at the beginning of the metaphorical timeline. STSM practices cover collecting and analyzing information about customers' and end users' strategic service needs, and using this (and other) information to identify and define the requirements for standard services. These requirements, their derived requirements, and requirements for non-standard services are all handled by the Requirements Management

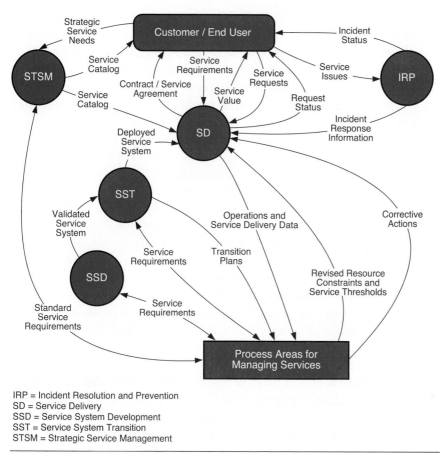

IRP = Incident Resolution and Prevention
SD = Service Delivery
SSD = Service System Development
SST = Service System Transition
STSM = Strategic Service Management

FIGURE 5.1
Key Process Area Relationships for Establishing and Delivering Services

(REQM) process area (which appears and is discussed in Relationships That Drive Service Management). STSM practices also cover producing a service catalog that is used by customers and end users to select and request services, and is used by the organization to help regulate what services actually are delivered (covered by the Service Delivery process area).

Next in line is the Service System Development (SSD) process area. SSD practices start with service requirements and transform them via requirements development, design, implementation, integration, verification, and validation into a new service system (or into significant changes to an existing service system). This transformation often yields derived requirements that should be managed as well (by REQM).

The Service System Transition (SST) process area covers the deployment of the validated service system produced by SSD. SST practices move the service system into operational use while minimizing impacts on concurrent service delivery. During the preparations for this deployment as well as during the deployment itself, SST practices are guided by previously established requirements, and may generate additional derived requirements of their own.

Everything comes together in the Service Delivery (SD) process area. SD practices include working with customers to identify their specific service requirements and establish service agreements. Service catalogs established by STSM may make this easier. The deployed service system is then operated (also covered by SD) to produce service value (i.e., delivered services) in response to specific service requests that are covered by the established agreements. SD practices include providing status information on these requests back to the originating customers, as well as providing overall operations and service delivery measures to other service management process areas. Feedback from the service management practices then regulates ongoing service delivery. Finally, information about how to respond to specific incidents enables an effective operational integration of incident and service request responses.

To handle actual or possible interference with the delivery of services, the Incident Resolution and Prevention (IRP) process area practices include receiving information about such incidents from customers and end users (as well as from internal sources). IRP practices cover determining how best to respond to each incident, sending that information on to service delivery activities to enable incident closure, and keeping the customers and end users updated with incident status.

The appearance of these process areas and relationships in Figure 5.1 should be interpreted with caution: They are not the only important ones for effective service establishment and delivery. A few other significant process areas and relationships include the following.

- The Configuration Management (CM) process area covers keeping configurations and configuration items of service system components produced by SSD under control.
- The Organizational Process Definition (OPD) process area covers creating the standard processes needed to deliver the standard services defined in STSM processes. OPD also covers providing these processes and related service lifecycles to SSD processes to guide the design of service system development.

- The Organizational Training (OT) process area covers implementing the training strategy created by SST processes to prepare staff members for the rollout of a new or changed service system.
- The Causal Analysis and Resolution (CAR) process area covers identifying and addressing the root causes of problems identified during Incident Resolution and Prevention processes.

Relationships That Drive Service Management

Figure 5.2 shows process areas associated with the management of services at the project level. Most of the process areas shown in this diagram are in the Project Management process area category, with the exception of Service Delivery. The reason this diagram refers to "service management" rather than "project management" is that the Service Delivery process area contributes both to Project Management

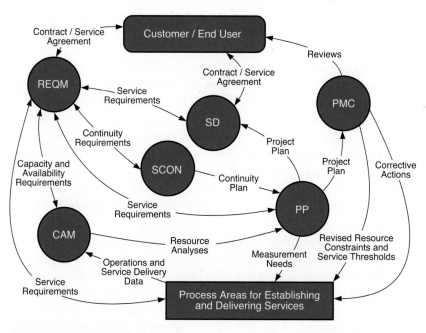

CAM = Capacity and Availability Management
PMC = Project Monitoring and Control
PP = Project Planning
REQM = Requirements Management
SCON = Service Continuity
SD = Service Delivery

FIGURE 5.2
Key Process Area Relationships for Service Management

and to Service Establishment and Delivery but can be part of only a single process area category in a CMMI model. Since Service Delivery is formally categorized in the Service Establishment and Delivery process area category, its inclusion in this figure means that *project management* is not a sufficiently broad description for what is shown.

The process areas that are most central to the management of services have their own critical relationships, many of which are illustrated in Figure 5.2. Because they cover activities that are performed more or less throughout the entire service lifecycle, there's no particularly obvious order for considering them, so an alphabetical sorting is sufficient.

The Capacity and Availability Management (CAM) process area receives information about capacity and availability requirements, service system operations, and other service delivery data. CAM practices are used to analyze this information to produce estimates of the types and quantities of resources needed over time to deliver services, based upon the use of service system representations. These analyses may also yield modifications to previously established requirements.

The Project Monitoring and Control (PMC) process area is driven by project-level plans, as well as by operational-level plans (not shown in Figure 5.2) created on the fly during service delivery and by service system operations and service delivery data (also not shown in Figure 5.2). PMC practices determine whether current and anticipated service system operations are consistent with overall project plans and establish corrective actions or needed revisions to resource constraints or service thresholds. In addition, customers and end users are kept informed with information about overall operations.

The Project Planning (PP) process area represents the logical foundation of project management in a services context. PP practices develop and maintain a project plan that builds upon resource analyses performed by CAM and covers all the service system resources. PP also establishes commitments to the plan from necessary stakeholders. This plan is constrained by the overall service requirements established for the project, from one or more service agreements with actual or anticipated customers. As other project-related plans are developed (e.g., a service continuity plan), PP practices ensure that they are harmonized and consistent with the overall project plan. Finally, PP establishes the project-level data measurement needs that determine what data should be collected during service system operations.

The Requirements Management (REQM) process area is the focal point for tracking requirements for any aspect of the project. REQM practices both collect and distribute requirements from many other process areas, including those originating in service agreements with customers. This coordination facilitates requirements change management, bidirectional traceability, and the detection of inconsistencies between requirements and the full range of work products of the project.

To provide assurance that critical services can be delivered no matter what happens, the Service Continuity (SCON) process area implements a specialized form of risk management. This work is often performed across an organization rather than in any single project, because the risks created by major disasters frequently have an organization-wide scope. SCON practices are used to identify essential service resources and functions based on priority service requirements, and then to prepare, verify, and validate plans to ensure that catastrophic events will not completely wipe out a service provider's capability to deliver all services.

The Service Delivery (SD) process area appears in the discussions of both types of process areas and relationships (service delivery and service management), because SD includes both types of activities. From a service management perspective, SD practices include the creation of service agreements with customers. The service requirements from those agreements, plus the resource constraints and schedules identified in the project plan, allow SD to establish a targeted service delivery approach that will satisfy all stakeholders. This approach guides the operational-level responses to service requests during ongoing service delivery.

As with the process areas and relationships that drive service establishment and delivery, the service management process areas and relationships that appear in Figure 5.2 are not the only ones relevant to effective service management. The CMMI for Services model contains cross-references between these and many other process areas that identify these types of relationships. As you learn and understand the distribution of goals and practices across the entire model, you will probably realize the existence of other relationships that are not explicitly identified.

Lifecycles

Anyone who has managed or worked in a service business knows that work activities change over time in a way that reflects the dependencies among those activities as well as their dependence on the activities of other relevant stakeholders. For example, from a high-level perspective, you need a service agreement in place before you begin delivering services; you have to create a service system of some kind before you roll it out into operational use; and so on. These types of time-phased relationships can be organized and abstracted into groups of activities called "phases," and the phases can be structured and ordered into patterns called "lifecycles."

Although the concept of a lifecycle is fairly commonly used and understood in the context of domains such as manufacturing and product development, it is less often considered in the context of service delivery. Because the CMMI for Services model makes a variety of references to lifecycles, and because a proper understanding of them is helpful for achieving higher levels of process maturity, service lifecycles and ways of modeling them are worth an extended discussion.

The Importance of Lifecycles

Lifecycles are valuable because they provide a consistent and improvable basis of planning for any repeatable pattern of work activities over time. They provide a common framework within which business processes can be ordered. Organizations that don't use lifecycles may have to create from scratch the plans needed to accomplish new work each time, without the benefit of prior experience and the knowledge of a normal order of events. This type of approach to work planning over time can lead to wasted effort, lower-quality plans, and higher risks.

Rather than describing every last detail of a set of related work activities and events over time, lifecycles usually abstract the most significant information into a manageable number of chunks or phases. For different types of lifecycles, these phases can cover different degrees of scope ranging from single tasks to entire lines of business. Lifecycle phases can also have a varying granularity ranging from minutes to years in length, depending on the scope of the phase and nature of the service domain. For example, contrast the likely phases of a service request lifecycle in a service domain that emphasizes speedy response (e.g., fast food restaurants) with those in a service domain that emphasizes extreme caution (e.g., historical artifact conservation).

Effective and balanced abstraction of information is what determines the value of lifecycles. Too much detail and a lifecycle will likely require too much modification to be used repeatedly. Too little detail and a lifecycle may be missing important guidance. To be valuable, a lifecycle must have the necessary reusable information for *your* organization. With the right balance of information, good lifecycles allow you to more effectively plan for needed changes, smoothly transition from one phase of activity to another, and consistently control the pace of your work over time.

Lifecycles in CMMI for Services

The CMMI for Services model mentions a number of different types of lifecycles, including those for products, projects, services, incidents, and service systems. (Sometimes these are referred to as "lifecycle models," which indicate the existence of a relatively small set of standardized lifecycles created, selected, or adapted by an organization.) However, little guidance is provided on how these and other lifecycles might be defined in a service context, or how they may interrelate, so it may be difficult to know where to begin.

This discussion outlines some examples to help you get started with your lifecycle definitions, but caution is warranted: These are only *examples* of what is possible. Some of these examples may be more broadly useful than others, but it is important for you to tailor them to meet the needs of your organization, or create other lifecycles that may be specifically relevant to your situation. The Organizational Process Definition process area contains a practice that specifically focuses on the creation of effective lifecycle models by your organization.

Service Lifecycles

Because the primary focus of CMMI for Services is on services rather than on products in general, we can use the concept of a *service* as the entry point into the discussion of lifecycles. The lifecycle of a service might best be interpreted as lasting the entire period of time that a particular service is actually available plus the additional time needed to make that service available and remove it from availability. A service lifecycle covers the fullest possible extent of events and activities related over time in any way to the actual delivery of service, and might therefore include the following phases:

1. Conceptualization: determining what services must be provided for different types of customers
2. Development: determining how services will be provided and establishing the resources needed to do so

3. Actualization: establishing agreements to deliver services and actually delivering services to satisfy those agreements

4. Retirement: removing a service that is no longer needed

Since a service lifecycle encompasses the complete scope of all activities related to service delivery, it's quite reasonable to expect that all the different process areas of the CMMI for Services model are potentially applicable in one or more of these phases. However, one process area stands out as being of interest *primarily* in service lifecycles and less so in other lifecycles: Strategic Service Management. This process area focuses on the conceptualization of services in ways that are independent of service agreements with individual customers. Strategic Service Management practices help you to define a standard foundation of services for all of your customers.

Project Lifecycles

The CMMI for Services model handles the concept of a project in a flexible way. Some organizations have a single ongoing project that operates a service system for different customers through different service agreements over time. Other organizations might have a separate project for each major service agreement with a different customer. And some might treat the creation of a new service system as an independent project.

Service provider organizations follow so many different business models that it's impossible to establish a meaningful single project lifecycle to cover them all. The project lifecycles you define should reflect your own project management needs. For example, if your organization treats each service agreement as a separate project, your project lifecycle might include the following phases:

1. Agreement: negotiating with your customer and establishing your service agreement

2. Preparation: planning, organizing, and allocating your resources, as well as establishing your service delivery approach and your service system (if needed)

3. Delivery: providing services to your customers in response to service requests, handling incidents, and managing and maintaining your service system

4. Termination: completing your service agreements, disposing of service system resources, and archiving project data

These same phases might occur in a different order if your organization has projects that cover multiple service agreements; preparation might precede agreement, and you might have multiple agreement phases.

Like a service lifecycle, a project lifecycle is broad in scope, and most process areas of the CMMI for Services model have practices that are applicable to project lifecycles. However, several service-specific process areas stand out as being particularly relevant to most project lifecycles:

- Service Delivery, which covers responding to service requests and maintaining your service system, as well as the establishment of service agreements and your service delivery approach
- Capacity and Availability Management, which monitors, analyzes, and reports on the capacity and availability of your service system
- Incident Resolution and Prevention, which resolves service incidents and helps to keep your service operation running smoothly

Service System Lifecycles

The lifecycle of a service system may fall completely within a single project lifecycle, or it may span several project lifecycles. Alternatively, a long-running project might span several service system lifecycles. However your service system lifecycles are aligned, you should define their phases to comprehensively cover all the necessary processes. For example, a "waterfall" type of service system lifecycle might have the following phases:

1. Analysis: determining what your service system will do by developing and refining the requirements for services to a sufficient level of detail
2. Design: identifying the types of service system components, functions, and interfaces needed to address identified requirements, and allocating those requirements to appropriate components
3. Implementation: assembling, building, and integrating components into a working service system
4. Transition: placing a new or changed service system into operational use
5. Operation: delivering services, handling incidents, and maintaining the service system
6. Retirement: removing service system components or the entire service system from active use

Other service system lifecycles can be similarly adapted from other product development lifecycle models such as incremental or evolutionary models. You should also consider that different service and project contexts may require very different emphases and time scales for the various phases. For example, an organization providing professional services with a simple service system might have the operations phase occupying the bulk of the service system lifecycle. Another organization might build custom complex service systems under contract for each customer, in which case the analysis, design, and implementation phases might be more significant.

Two service-specific process areas stand out as being particularly relevant to most service system lifecycles:

- Service System Development: analyzing, designing, developing, integrating, verifying, and validating your service system
- Service System Transition: preparing to deploy your service system into operational use, and actually deploying it

In addition, the Service Delivery, Capacity and Availability Management, and Incident Resolution and Prevention process areas all contribute useful practices to the operational phase of a service system's lifecycle.

Service Request Lifecycles

Depending on the length and complexity of the service requests your organization handles, the lifecycle of a single service request may be so simple that you might choose to describe it as a single process rather than as a lifecycle with multiple phases and processes. Either way, your service requests are likely to include at least the following steps or phases:

1. Initiation: receiving and recording a communication from a customer of a particular need for a service
2. Analysis: determining an initial appropriate method for responding to the request, and identifying and assigning resources sufficient to execute the response
3. Response: providing the requested service
4. Closure: confirming that the customer received the anticipated service, and recording appropriate service information, including customer satisfaction data

Some service requests may involve lifecycles with the possibility of iterations of analysis and response, or the response phase may itself be divisible into further phases. In any case, the Service Delivery process area is the one process area of the CMMI for Services model that is most relevant to service requests and their lifecycles.

Incident Lifecycles

For some organizations, the lifecycle of an incident may often be similar in outline to a service request lifecycle, with the exception that incidents are not usually "initiated" intentionally. And some incident lifecycles may also be so short as to be best addressed through a single process. The necessary activities will probably include the following steps or phases:

1. Detection: identifying and recording the existence of a possible interference with service delivery
2. Analysis: determining an initial appropriate method for responding to the incident, and identifying and assigning resources sufficient to execute the response
3. Response: performing the identified method for correcting or mitigating the incident
4. Closure: confirming that the incident has been resolved and recording appropriate incident information

In many incident management contexts, the initial response may be inadequate to bring the incident to closure, and cycles of analysis and response may be necessary (including escalation that identifies and assigns additional resources). The Incident Resolution and Prevention process area is the one process area of the CMMI for Services model that is most relevant to service incidents and their lifecycles.

Putting Lifecycles Together

With so many different types of lifecycles to consider, you may have some difficulty imagining how they are interrelated. A lifecycle diagram is useful for this purpose, and it can serve as the starting point for defining your own lifecycles. Figure 5.3 provides an example of one way that these service-related lifecycles can be integrated and aligned.

In this hypothetical example, the service provider organization provides a separate set of services independently to each major customer based on a separately negotiated service agreement. Each

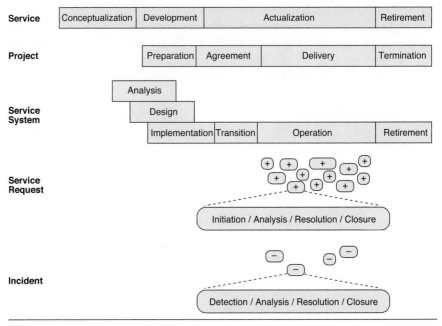

FIGURE 5.3
An Example of Service-Related Lifecycle Alignment

service agreement defines the scope of a separate project. A separate service system is developed for each project, and that system is ready for use by the time the service agreement is finalized. Service delivery then occurs whenever the provider organization handles customer-generated service requests; different requests take different amounts of time and resources to handle (see the "+" bars in the diagram). Sometimes service delivery is incomplete or inadequate, and there are incidents that need to be handled as well (see the "−" bars in the diagram); these also can require different amounts of time and resources to achieve closure.

Of course, your own organization may have one or more ways of integrating these and other lifecycles that are quite different from this example. A service system lifecycle might span multiple projects with the same customer or with different customers. A single long-running project might span multiple service system lifecycles, or might need to include a product development lifecycle for tangible items that are delivered to customers along with services. Some types of service requests might be resolved across the entire duration of a service agreement, and some might be resolved through automated processes. An additional separate lifecycle for pursuing major business opportunities may be appropriate. In the end, your own business structure and work patterns are the primary drivers that determine what lifecycles are needed, how they should be defined, and how they should be tied together.

CHAPTER 6

ESSAYS ABOUT CMMI FOR SERVICES

This chapter consists of essays written by invited contributing authors. All of these essays are related to CMMI for Services. Some of them are straightforward applications of CMMI-SVC to a particular field; for example, reporting a pilot use of the model in an IT organization. We also have an essay describing how CMMI-SVC could have been used and would have helped in a service environment that the author experienced in a prior job. Other essays are prospective applications to disciplines or domains that haven't traditionally applied CMMI, such as education and legal services.

In addition, we sought some unusual treatments of CMMI-SVC: Could it be used to bolster corporate social responsibility? Can CMMI-SVC be used in development contexts? Can CMMI-SVC be used with Agile methods—or are services already agile? Finally, several essayists describe how to approach known challenges using CMMI-SVC: adding security concerns to an appraisal, using the practices of CMMI-SVC to capitalize on what existing research tells us about superior IT service, and reminding those who buy services to be responsible consumers, even when buying from users of CMMI-SVC.

In this way, we have sought to introduce ideas about using CMMI-SVC both for those who are new to CMMI and for those who are very experienced with prior CMMI models. These essays demonstrate the promise, applicability, and versatility of CMMI for Services.

Using CMMI-SVC in a DoD Organization

By Mike Phillips

Author Comments: Mike Phillips is the program manager for the entire CMMI Product Suite and an authorized CMMI instructor. Before his retirement from the

U.S. Air Force, he managed large programs, including a large operation that could have benefited from CMMI-SVC, had it existed at the time. He looks back at this experience and describes how some of the practices in the Air Force unit he led would have met the goals in the CMMI-SVC model, and how other model content would have helped them if the model were available to them at that time.

In this essay, I highlight some of the ways in which CMMI for Services practices could have been used in a DoD organization and where their use might have solved challenges that we failed to handle successfully. After all, process improvement does not simply document what we do (although that does have a value for improving the capability of new employees who must learn tasks quickly). It also illuminates ways to satisfy our customers and end users.

The organization that I describe in this essay is a U.S. Air Force unit based in Ohio that, at the time, provided a rich mix of services to its customers in a broad research and development domain. It was called a "Test Wing," and it employed 1,800 military and civilian employees who supported customers across the entire Department of Defense. The goal of the Test Wing's customers was to investigate the performance and usability of various potential military systems and subsystems. These systems and subsystems were typically avionic units such as radios and radar systems. They were being tested for potential use in aircraft in the Air Force's operational fleet. However, other military services and agencies were also customers of this Test Wing.

While a wide range of examples could be included, this essay focuses on a segment of the Test Wing. This segment's activities demonstrate the interaction between CMMI's service-specific process areas and some of the process areas that are common to all three of the current CMMI constellations.

Organizational Elements and CMMI Terminology

A "Wing" in the Air Force describes a large organization that often occupies an entire "mini city"—often employing thousands of people. The primary work conducted at the Test Wing that I'm describing focused on delivering test services. It, in turn, contained groups dedicated to the following:

- *Operating* the Test Wing's collection of aircraft
- *Maintaining* those aircraft

- *Planning and executing modifications* to the aircraft to allow new systems to be installed and tested
- *Planning the test missions and analyzing and reporting the resulting data* to the customers who had requested the service

Each of these work units had a variety of organizational descriptors, but the term *project* was not used with any frequency. (As a test pilot in the Test Wing, I recall being told at times that I would be given a "special project," which normally meant additional work to be conducted outside the normal flight rhythm. So, reactions of potential team members to "projects" were often cautious and somewhat negative.)

The CMMI-SVC model defines projects in relation to individual service agreements. For small organizations focused on delivering a single service successfully, that focus is vitally important to their success. However, as organizations grow larger in size and complexity, the term *project* often must be reinterpreted to ensure the best use of the idea of a "project." For example, in the Test Wing, each service agreement tended to be of relatively short duration. We called the activities associated with these agreements "missions." These missions might involve a single aircraft and crew or a collection of aircraft and crews.

To support one memorable service agreement, we had to deploy three aircraft to three different countries to capture telemetry data. These data were captured from a launch vehicle with three successive boosting stages placing a satellite into orbit. To monitor the first stage of the launch from California, the aircraft had to take off in Mexico and fly out over the Pacific. The second stage boost required data collection in Polynesia. The final stage required that an aircraft take off from South Africa and fly toward the South Pole. This mission (or "project" using CMMI-SVC terminology) lasted only three months from the earliest plans to the completion of data gathering. Virtually every work unit of the Test Wing committed members to the successful fulfillment of the service agreement.

These missions had a familiar business rhythm. We had existing agreements to work from, but each new mission called for a specific approach to meet the customer's needs (Service Delivery SP 2.1) and adequate preparation for the operation (Service Delivery SP 2.2). It was not uncommon for the "critical path" to include securing visas for the passports of a dozen crew members deploying to a distant country.

In this environment, a team spanning many work units needed to satisfy a particular service agreement. The value of fully understanding and executing the practices of Service Delivery cannot be overstated. These practices include the following:

- Analyzing existing agreements and service data
- Establishing the service agreement
- Establishing the service delivery approach
- Preparing for service system operations
- Establishing a request management system
- Receiving and processing service requests
- Operating the service system
- Maintaining the service system

Composing these service-agreement-specific teams for missions also involved the practices in CMMI-SVC that are found in Integrated Project Management (using the project's defined process and coordinating and collaborating with relevant stakeholders). Each mission required careful analysis of the elements needed to satisfy the customer requiring our services, and then delivering that service—in this case, around the world.

To make missions such as this happen required planning and managing the various work units involved. Organizational units—in our case, "squadrons"—needed an annual plan for how to successfully execute multiple service agreements with team members who needed to gain and maintain proficiency in unusual aircraft. So, at the squadron level, Project Planning, Project Monitoring and Control, and Capacity and Availability Management practices were used. This approach is similar to the approach used by other service provider organizations that need to describe services around a particular aspect of the service: sometimes a resource and sometimes a competence that helps to scope the types of services provided.

This approach leads to the definition of "project" in the CMMI-SVC glossary. The glossary entry states, "A project can be composed of projects." The discussion of "project" in Chapter 3 illustrates this aspect of projects as well.

Although the CMMI-SVC model was not available to us at the time, every crew was expected to be adept at Incident Resolution and Prevention. The dynamic nature of test-related activities made for many opportunities to adjust mission plans to meet a changing situation. Aircraft would develop problems that required workarounds.

Customer sites would find that support they expected to provide had encountered difficulties that drove changes in the execution of the service agreement. An anomaly on the test vehicle would require rapid change to the support structure as the test was under way. Because many of the test support types were similar, "lessons learned" led to changes in the configuration of our test data gathering and to the actual platforms used as part of the testing infrastructure for the collection of types of equipment being tested. Incident prevention was a strongly supported goal, much like we see in SG 3 of Incident Resolution and Prevention.

Two other process areas merit a brief discussion as well: Service Continuity and Service System Transition. You may not be surprised if you have worked for the military that Service Continuity activities were regularly addressed. Various exercises tested our ability to quickly generate and practice the activities needed to recover from disasters, whether these were acts of war or acts of nature, such as hurricanes. We also had continuity plans and rehearsed how we would maintain critical operations with varying loss of equipment functionality.

Service System Transition, on the other hand, provided the Test Wing staff with a reflection of how technology influenced our service systems. We frequently found ourselves needing to add newer aircraft with differing capabilities and to retire older aircraft and other resources—all while supporting customer needs.

So, CMMI-SVC represents the kind of flexible model that maps well into a military research and test environment, as well as many of the other environments described. The practices often remind us of ways to further improve our methods to achieve the goal of effective, disciplined use of our critical processes.

What We Can Learn from High-Performing IT Organizations to Stop the Madness in IT Outsourcing

By Gene Kim and Kevin Behr

Author Comments: These two authors—who lead the IT Process Institute and work as C level executives in commercial practice—have spent a decade researching the processes in IT that lead to high performance. Based on research in more than 1,500 IT organizations, they describe what processes make the difference between high performance and low or even medium performance. Their observations about the distinguishing characteristics of high performers are consistent with the goals and practices in CMMI for Services. They further note the potential downside of the pervasive trend of outsourcing IT services. Without adept and informed management of these outsourced IT contracts, harm is suffered by both provider and client. In response to this trend, they call on CMMI practitioners to use their experience and techniques to bring sanity to the world of IT outsourcing.

Introduction

Since 1999, a common area of passion for the coauthors has been studying high-performing IT operations and information security organizations. To facilitate our studies, in 2001 we cofounded the IT Process Institute, which was chartered to facilitate research, benchmarking, and development of prescriptive guidance.

In our journey, we studied high-performing IT organizations both qualitatively and quantitatively. We initially captured and codified the observed qualitative behaviors they had in common in the book *The Visible Ops Handbook: Starting ITIL in Four Practical Steps.*[1]

Seeking a better understanding of the mechanics, practice, and measurements of the high performers, we used operations research techniques to understand what specific behaviors resulted in their remarkable performance. This work led to the largest empirical research project of how IT organizations work; we have benchmarked more than 1,500 IT organizations in six successive studies.

What we learned in that journey will likely be no surprise to CMMI-SVC practitioners. High-performing IT organizations invest in the right processes and controls, combine that investment with a management commitment to enforcing appropriate rigor in daily operations, and are rewarded with a four- to five-times advantage in productivity over their non-high-performing IT cohorts.

In the first section of this essay, we will briefly outline the key findings of our ten years of research, describing the differences between high- and low-performing IT organizations, both in their performance and in their controls.

In the second section, we will describe a disturbing problem that we have observed for nearly a decade around how outsourced IT services are acquired and managed, both by the client and by the outsourcer. We have observed a recurring cycle of problems that occur in many (if not most) IT outsourcing contracts, suggesting that an inherent flaw exists in how these agreements are solicited, bid upon,

---

1. Behr, Kevin; Kim, Gene; and Spafford, George. *The Visible Ops Handbook: Starting ITIL in Four Practical Steps.* IT Process Institute, 2004. Introductory and ordering information is available at www.itpi.org. Since its publication, more than 120,000 copies have been sold.

and then managed. We believe these problems are a root cause of why many IT outsourcing relationships fail and, when left unaddressed, will cause the next provider to fail as well.

We will conclude with a call to action to the IT process improvement, management, and vendor communities, which we believe can be both a vanguard and a vanquisher of many of these dysfunctions. Our hope is that you will act and take decisive action, either because you will benefit from fixing these problems or because it is already your job to fix them.

Our Ten-Year Study of High-Performing IT Organizations

From the outset, high-performing IT organizations were easy to spot. By 2001, we had identified 11 organizations that had similar outstanding performance characteristics. All of these organizations had the following attributes:

- High service levels, measured by high mean time between failures (MTBFs) and low mean time to repair (MTTR)
- The earliest and most consistent integration of security controls into IT operational processes, measured by control location and security staff participation in the IT operations lifecycle
- The best posture of compliance, measured by the fewest number of repeat audit findings and lowest staff count required to stay compliant
- High efficiencies, measured by high server-to-system-administrator ratios and low amounts of unplanned work (reactive work that is unexpectedly introduced during incidents, security breaches, audit preparation, etc.)

Common Culture among High Performers

As we studied these high performers, we found three common cultural characteristics.

A culture of change management: In each of the high-performing IT organizations, the first step when the IT staff implements changes is *not* to first log into the infrastructure. Instead, it is to go to some change advisory board and get authorization that the change should be made. Surprisingly, this process is not viewed as bureaucratic, needlessly slowing things down, lowering productivity, and decreasing the quality of life. Instead, these organizations view change management as absolutely critical to the organization for maintaining its high performance.

A culture of causality: Each of the high-performing IT organizations has a common way to resolve service outages and impairments. They realize that 80 percent of their outages are due to changes and that 80 percent of their MTTR is spent trying to find what changed. Consequently, when working on problems, they look at changes first in the repair cycle. Evidence of this can be seen in the incident management systems of the high performers: Inside the incident record for an outage are all the scheduled and authorized changes for the affected assets, as well as the actual detected changes on the asset. By looking at this information, problem managers can recommend a fix to the problem more than 80 percent of the time, with a first fix rate exceeding 90 percent (i.e., 90 percent of the recommended fixes work the first time).

A culture of planned work and continuous improvement: In each of the high-performing IT organizations, there is a continual desire to find production variance early before it causes a production outage or an episode of unplanned work. The difference is analogous to paying attention to the low-fuel warning light on an automobile to avoid running out of gas on the highway. In the first case, the organization can fix the problem in a planned manner, without much urgency or disruption to other scheduled work. In the second case, the organization must fix the problem in a highly urgent way, often requiring an all-hands-on-deck situation (e.g., six staff members must drop everything they are doing and run down the highway with gas cans to refuel the stranded truck).

For longtime CMMI practitioners, these characteristics will sound familiar, and the supports for them available in the model will be obvious. For those IT practitioners new to CMMI, CMMI-SVC has not only the practices to support these cultural characteristics, but also the organizational supports and institutionalization practices that make it possible to embrace these characteristics and then make them stick.

The Performance Differences between High and Low Performers

In 2003, our goal was to confirm more systematically that there was an empirically observable link between certain IT procedures and controls to improvements in performance. In other words, one doesn't need to implement all the processes and controls described in the various practice frameworks (ITIL for IT operations, CobiT or ISO 27001 for information security practitioners, etc.).

The 2006 and 2007 ITPI IT Controls Performance Study was conducted to establish the link between controls and operational performance. The 2007 Change Configuration and Release Perform- ance Study was conducted to determine which best practices in these areas drive performance improvement. The studies revealed that, in comparison with low-performing organizations, high-per- forming organizations enjoy the following effectiveness and effi- ciency advantages:

- Higher throughput of work
- Fourteen times more production changes
- One-half the change failure rate
- One-quarter the first fix failure rate
- Severity 1 (representing the highest level of urgency and impact) out- ages requiring one-tenth the time to fix
- One-half the amount of unplanned work and firefighting
- One-quarter of the frequency of emergency change requests
- Server-to-system-administrator ratios that are two to five times higher
- More projects completed with better performance to project due date
- Eight times more projects completed
- Six times more applications and IT services managed

These differences validate the Visible Ops hypothesis that IT con- trols and basic change and configuration practices improve IT oper- ations effectiveness and efficiency. But the studies also determined that the same high performers have superior information security effectiveness as well. The 2007 IT controls study found that when high performers had security breaches, the following conditions were true.

The security breaches are far less likely to result in loss events (e.g., financial, reputational, and customer). High performers are half as likely as medium performers and one-fifth as likely as low per- formers to experience security breaches that result in loss.

The security breaches are far more likely to be detected using automated controls (as opposed to an external source, such as the newspaper headlines or a customer). High performers automatically detect security breaches 15 percent more often than medium per- formers and twice as often as low performers.

Security access breaches are detected far more quickly. High per- formers have a mean time to detect measured in minutes, compared with hours for medium performers and days for low performers.

These organizations also had one-quarter the frequency of repeat audit findings.

Which Controls Really Matter

By 2006, we had established by analyzing the link between controls and performance that not all controls are created equal. By that time, we had benchmarked about one thousand IT organizations, and had concluded that of all the practices outlined in the ITIL process and CobiT control frameworks, we could predict 60 percent of their performance by asking three questions: To what extent does the IT organization define, monitor, and enforce the following three types of behaviors?

- A standardized configuration strategy
- A culture of process discipline
- A systematic way of restricting privileged access to production systems

In ITIL, these three behaviors correspond to the release, controls, and resolution process areas, as we had posited early in our journey. In CMMI-SVC, these correspond to the Service System Transition, Service System Development, and Incident Resolution and Prevention process areas.

Throughout our journey, culminating in having benchmarked more than 1,500 IT organizations, we find that culture matters, and that certain processes and controls are required to ensure that those cultural values exist in daily operations.

Furthermore, ensuring that these controls are defined, monitored, and enforced can predict with astonishing accuracy IT operational, information security, and compliance performance.

Although behaviors prescribed by this guidance may be common sense, they are far from common practice.

What Goes Wrong in Too Many IT Outsourcing Programs

When organizations decide to outsource the management and ongoing operations of IT services, they should expect not only that the IT outsourcers will "manage their mess for less," but also that those IT outsourcers are very effective and efficient. After all, as the logical argument goes, managing IT is their competitive core competency.

However, what we have found in our journey spanning more than ten years is that the opposite is often true. Often the organizations that have the greatest pressure to outsource services are also the organizations with the weakest management capabilities and the lowest amount of process and control maturity.

We postulate two distinct predictors of chronic low performance in IT.

IT operational failures: Technology in general provides business value only when it removes some sort of business obstacle. When business processes are automated, IT failures and outages cause business operations to halt, slowing or stopping the extraction of value from assets (e.g., revenue generation, sales order entry, bill of materials generation, etc.).

When these failures are unpredictable both in occurrence and in duration (as they often are), the business not only is significantly affected, but also loses trust in IT. This is evidenced by many business executives using IT as a two-letter word with four-letter connotations.

IT capital project failures: When IT staff members are consumed with unpredictable outages and firefighting, by definition this is often at the expense of planned activity (i.e., projects). Unplanned work and technical escalations due to outages often cause top management to "take the best and brightest staff members and put them on the problem, regardless of what they're working on." So, critical project resources are pulled into firefighting, instead of working on high-value projects and process improvement initiatives.

Managers will recognize that these critical resources are often unavailable, with little visibility into the many sources of urgent work. Dates are often missed for critical path tasks with devastating effects on project due dates.

From the business perspective, these two factors lead to the conclusion that IT can neither keep the existing lights on nor install the new lighting that the business needs (i.e., operate or maintain IT and complete IT projects). This conclusion is often the driver to outsource IT management.

However, there is an unstated risk: An IT management organization that cannot manage IT operations in-house may not be able to manage the outsourcing arrangement and governance when the moving parts are outsourced.

A Hypothetical Case Study

This case study reflects a commonly experienced syndrome while protecting the identities of the innocent. The cycle starts as the IT management function is sourced for bids. These are often long-term and expensive contracts, often in the billions of dollars, extending over many years. And as the IT outsourcing providers exist in a competitive and concentrated industry segment, cost is a significant factor.

Unfortunately, the structure of the cost model for many of the outsourcing bids is often fundamentally flawed. For instance, in a hypothetical five-year contract bid, positive cash flow for the outsourcer is jeopardized by year 2. Year 1 cost reduction goals are often accomplished by pay reductions and consolidating software licenses. After that, the outsourcer becomes very reliant on change fees and offering new services to cover up a growing gap between projected and actual expenditures.

By year 3, the outsourcer often has to reduce their head count, often letting their most expensive and experienced people go. We know this because service levels start to decline: There are an ever-increasing number of unplanned outages, and more Severity 1 outages become protracted multiday outages, and often the provider never successfully resolves the underlying or root cause.

This leads to more and more service level agreement (SLA) penalties, with money now being paid from the outsourcer to the client (a disturbing enough trend), but then something far more disturbing occurs. The service request backlog of client requests continues to grow. If these projects could be completed by the outsourcer, some of the cash flow problems could be solved, but instead, the outsourcer is mired with reactive and unplanned work.

So, client projects never get completed, project dollars are never billed, and client satisfaction continues to drop. Furthermore, sufficient cycles for internal process improvement projects cannot be allocated, and service levels also keep dropping. Thus continues the downward spiral for the outsourcer. By year 4 and year 5, customer satisfaction is so low that it becomes almost inevitable that the client puts the contract out for rebid by other providers.

And so the cycle begins again. The cumulative cost to the client and outsourcer, as measured by human cost, harm to stakeholders, damage to competitive ability, and loss to shareholders, is immense.

An Effective System of IT Operations

We believe that it doesn't really matter who is doing the work if an appropriate system for "doing IT operations" is not in place. The system starts with how IT contributes to the company's strategy (What must we do to have success?). A clear understanding of what is necessary, the definition of the work to be done, and a detailed specification of quantity, quality, and time are critical to creating accountability and defect prevention. Only then can a system of controls be designed to protect the goals of the company and the output of those controls used to illuminate success or failure.

This situation is betrayed by the focus on SLAs by IT management—which is classic after-the-fact management—versus a broader systemic approach that prevents issues with leading indicator measurements. The cost of defects in this scenario is akin to manufacturing, where orders of magnitude in expense reduction are realized by doing quality early versus picking up wreckage and finding flight recorders and reassembling a crashed airplane to figure out what happened and who is at fault.

Call to Action

In our research, we find a four- to five-times productivity difference between high and low performers.

IT operations

- Are Severity 1 outages measured in minutes or hours versus days or weeks?
- What percentage of the organization's fixes work the first time? Because they have a culture of causality, high performers average around 90 percent versus 50 percent for low performers.
- What percentage of changes fail, causing some sort of episode of unplanned work? High performers have a culture of change management and average around 95 percent to 99 percent, versus around 80 percent for low performers.

Compliance

- What percentage of audit findings are repeat findings? In high performers, typically fewer than 5 percent of audit findings are not fixed within one year.

Security

- What percentage of security breaches are detected by an automated internal control? In high performers, security breaches are so quickly detected and corrected that they rarely impact customers.

Many of these can be collected by observation, as opposed to substantive audits, and are very accurate predictors of daily operations. Formulating the profile of an outsourcer's daily operations can help to guide the selection of an effective outsourcer, as well as ensuring that the selected outsourcer remains effective.

We can verify that an effective system of operations exists by finding evidence of the following.

- The company has stated its goals.
- IT has defined what it must do to help the company reach its goals.
- IT understands and has documented the work that needs to be done (e.g., projects and IT operations).
- IT has created detailed specifications with respect to the quantity of work, the quality required to meet the company's goals, and the time needed to do this work.
- IT understands the capabilities needed to deliver the aforementioned work in terms of time horizons, and other key management skills and organization must be constructed to do the work.
- IT has created a process infrastructure to accomplish the work consistently in tandem with the organizational design.
- IT has created an appropriate system of controls to instrument the effectiveness of the execution of the system and its key components.

CMMI for Services includes practices for all of these and, with its associated appraisal method, the means to gather the evidence of these practices. Without an understanding of the preceding profile (and there is much more to consider), outsourcing success would be more akin to winning the lottery than to picking up a telephone in your office and getting a dial tone.

Plans Are Worthless

By Brad Nelson

Author Comments: From early in the development of the CMMI-SVC model, we began to hear concerns from users about the guidance or policy that might be imposed by government acquirers on providers bidding on service contracts. We sought the participation of experts such as Brad Nelson on our Advisory Group to ensure that we were considering these issues. In this essay, the author, who works on industrial policy for the Office of the Secretary of Defense, makes clear that it is appropriate capability that is sought, not the single digits of a maturity level rating. Further, he describes the ongoing responsibility of the government acquirer, rather than just the responsibility of the provider.

The Limits of the Maturity Level Number

The CMMI model developed by the CMMI Product Development Team (involving representatives from industry, government, and the Software Engineering Institute [SEI] of Carnegie Mellon) can be thought of as an advanced process planning tool. CMMI defines maturity levels ranging from level 1—ad hoc performance—through level 5—process and subprocess optimization.

Stated colloquially, a level 1 organization accomplishes goals without a well-developed organizational memory to ensure that good decisions leading to work accomplishment will be repeated. It's sometimes said that a level 1 organization is dependent on individual heroes who react well to events and other people. On the other end of the spectrum, a level 5 organization has measureable processes that repeatedly guide good decisions, and those processes are continuously improved.

A level 5 organization has a breadth and depth of institutional capability and culture to reliably optimize workflows and isn't dependent on any one person. It's certainly reasonable to expect a much higher probability of project success from a level 5 organization than from a level 1 organization. The SEI certifies individuals to provide CMMI maturity level appraisals using a Standard CMMI Appraisal Method for Process Improvement (SCAMPI). Given this well-organized CMMI infrastructure, wouldn't it make sense for a buyer to require minimum maturity level ratings for potential suppliers?

What's wrong with Department of Defense (DoD) staff members who provide opinions that "DoD does not place significant emphasis on capability level or maturity level ratings…?"[2] Don't they get it?

Some understanding of this opinion might be gained through the examination of a quote from General Dwight D. Eisenhower, who said that "plans are worthless but planning is everything." It's quite a pithy saying, and a couple of things can be quickly inferred. The first is that given complex endeavors with a large number of variables, plans are at high risk of obsolescence. The second is that the familiarization and insights gained from the planning process are invaluable to making informed adaptations to changing conditions.

Perhaps oversimplifying a bit, a plan is a static artifact, and those who rely on static artifacts do so at their own peril. The real value of a plan is that its completion facilitates the detailed situational awareness of the planner and his or her ability to perform well in a changing environment. But don't continuously improving level 5 organizations avoid the trap of static process planning?

While it may appear like "hairsplitting" to some, it's critical to observe that the preceding discussion of the value of a plan applies to

2. CMMI Guidebook for Acquirers Team. *Understanding and Leveraging a Supplier's CMMI Efforts: A Guidebook for Acquirers (CMU/SEI-2007-TR-004)*. Pittsburgh: Software Engineering Institute, Carnegie Mellon University, March 2007; www.sei.cmu.edu/publications/documents /07.reports/07tr004.html.

the CMMI *rating*, not process plans. In fact, it's actually the CMMI rating that's the static artifact.

Viewed from a different angle, even though a high-maturity organization may have process plans that are adapted and optimized over time, the appraiser's observation of that organization is static. Organizations and the people in them change over time. Furthermore, careful consideration must be given to the relationship between a SCAMPI appraiser's observations of prior work by one group of people to the new work with possibly different people. What was relevant yesterday may not be relevant today.

Considerations for the Responsible Buyer

When committing hard-earned money to a purchase, a buyer hopes for the best results. Going beyond hope, a smart buyer looks for indicators that a seller actually has the capability to achieve expected results. An experienced smart buyer establishes requirements to accomplish the desired results by a capable supplier. Understanding what a CMMI rating is and isn't helps the smart and experienced buyer evaluate CMMI ratings appropriately.

To estimate a supplier's probability of success, a good buyer must first understand what is being purchased. A buyer expecting that a supplier's mature processes will enhance their probabilities of success must do more than hope that a past CMMI rating is applicable to the current project. Due diligence requires the buyer to analyze the relevance of a potential supplier's processes to their particular project.

When this analysis is done, it should carry substantially more weight than a CMMI rating. When it's not done and significant weight is given to a rating, the buyer is effectively placing their due diligence in the hands of the appraiser. This is an obvious misuse of the rating. A CMMI rating can be one of many indicators of past performance, but a rating is a "rating" and not a "qualification." CMMI appraisers do not qualify suppliers.

Remaining Engaged after Buying

Once a savvy buyer chooses a qualified supplier, the buyer's real work begins. In the words of ADM Hyman Rickover, father of the nuclear navy, "You get what you inspect, not what you expect." This principle is applied every day by smart, experienced buyers when they plan and perform contract monitoring. It's an axiom that performance monitoring should focus on results rather than process.

Nevertheless, intermediate results of many endeavors are ambiguous, and forward-looking process monitoring can reduce the ambiguity and point to future results. CMMI can provide valuable goals and benchmarks that help a supplier to develop mature processes leading to successful results, and SCAMPI ratings can provide constructive independent feedback to the process owner.

A rating, though, carries with it no binding obligation to apply processes at appraised levels to particular projects or endeavors. A rating is not a qualification, and it's also not a license. Qualifications and licenses imply mutual responsibilities and oversight by the granting authority. Once a CMMI rating is granted, neither responsibilities nor oversight is associated with it.

A failure or inability to maintain process performance at a rated level carries no penalty. There is no mechanism for the SEI or a SCAMPI appraiser to reduce or revoke a rating for inadequate performance. The appraiser has no monitoring function he or she uses after providing an appraisal rating at a point in time, and certainly has no responsibility to a buyer.

The obligation to perform to any particular standard is between the buyer and the supplier. Essentially, if a buyer depends on a supplier's CMMI rating for project performance and uses it as justification for reducing project oversight, it would be a misunderstanding and misuse of the CMMI rating as well as an abdication of their own responsibility.

Seeking Accomplishment as Well as Capability

It is intuitive that mature processes enable high-quality completion of complex tasks. CMMI provides an advanced framework for the self-examination necessary to develop those processes. The satisfaction of reaching a high level of capability represented by a CMMI rating is well justified. It is possible, though, to lose perspective and confuse capability with accomplishments.

It's been said that astute hiring officials can detect job applicants' resumes that are overweighted with documented capabilities and underweighted with documented accomplishments. This may be a good analogy for proposal evaluation teams. The familiar phrase "ticket punching" cynically captures some of this imbalance. Herein lies another reason why CMMI can be quite valuable, yet entirely inappropriate, as a contract requirement.

In the cold, hard, literal world of contracts and acquisition, buyers must be careful what they ask for. Buyers want suppliers that embrace minimum levels of process maturity, but "embrace" just doesn't make for good contract language. While it might at first seem to be a good substitute to require CMMI ratings instead, it can inadvertently encourage a cynical "ticket punching" approach to the qualification of potential suppliers. Because ratings themselves engender no accountability, there should be no expectation that ratings will improve project outcomes.

Pulling this thread a bit more, it's not uncommon to hear requests for templates to develop the CMMI artifacts necessary for an appraisal. While templates could be useful to an organization embracing process maturity, they could also be misused by a more cynical organization to shortcut process maturation and get to the artifact necessary for a "ticket punching" rating. Appraisers are aware of this trap and do more than merely examine the standard artifacts. But as a practical matter, it can be difficult to distinguish between the minimum necessary to get the "ticket punch" and a more sincere effort to develop mature processes.

If an influential buyer such as the Department of Defense were to require CMMI ratings, it would likely lead to more CMMI ticket punching rather than CMMI embracing. The best that the DoD can do to accomplish the positive and avoid the negative has already been stated as "not placing significant emphasis on capability level or maturity level ratings, but rather promot[ing] CMMI as a tool for internal process improvement."[3]

Summary

To summarize, it certainly appears reasonable to expect more mature organizations to have a higher probability of consistently achieving positive results than less mature organizations. CMMI ratings are external indicators that provide information, but they are only indicators. A savvy buyer must know what the indicators mean and what they don't mean. Ultimately, accountability for project success is between the buyer and the seller. CMMI and SCAMPI ratings are well structured to provide important guidance and feedback to an organization on its process maturity, but responsible buyers must perform their own due diligence, appraisal of supplier capabilities, and monitoring of work in progress.

---

3. Ibid.

How to Appraise Security Using CMMI for Services

By Kieran Doyle

Author Comments: CMMI teams have regularly considered how to include security (and how much of it to include) in the various CMMI models. For the most part, coverage of security is modest and is treated as a class of requirement or risk. However, service organizations using CMMI-SVC, especially IT service organizations, would like to handle security concerns more fully. In this essay, Kieran Doyle, an instructor and certified high-maturity appraiser with Lamri, explains how security content from ISO 27001 can be included in a CMMI-SVC appraisal. His advice, based on a real case, is also useful for anyone using CMMI-SVC alongside another framework, such as ITIL or ISO standards.

"We would like to include security in the scope of our CMMI for Services appraisal." With these words, the client lays down the gauntlet. The subtext is, "We are already using something that includes security. I like CMMI, but I want to continue covering everything that I am currently doing." These were the instructions received from a recent change sponsor within a Scandinavian government organization. So, from where does the challenge emerge to include security in the appraisal scope? More importantly, is there a way to use the power of CMMI and SCAMPI to address *all* of the client's needs?

Information security is already an intrinsic part of both the Information Technology Infrastructure Library (ITIL) and the international standard for IT service management, ISO 20000. Both are in common use in the IT industry. The ISO 20000 standard provides good guidance on *what* is needed to implement an appropriate IT service management system. ITIL provides guidance on *how* IT service management may be implemented.

So, there is at least an implied requirement with many organizations that CMMI-SVC should be able to deal with most if not all of the topics that ISO 20000 and ITIL already address; and by and large it does! Indeed, there are probably advantages to using all three frameworks as useful tools in your process and business improvement toolbox.

As I've mentioned, ISO 20000 provides guidance on the requirements for an IT service management system. But it does not have the *evolutionary* structure that CMMI contains. In other words, CMMI-SVC can provide a roadmap along which the process capability of the organization can evolve.

Similarly, ITIL is a useful library of *how* to go about implementing IT service processes. In ITIL Version 3, this sense of it being a *library* of good ideas has come even more to the fore. But it needs something like CMMI-SVC to structure why we are doing it, and to help select the most important elements in the library for the individual implementation.

Thus, ISO 20000, ITIL, and CMMI-SVC work extremely well together. But CMMI-SVC doesn't cover IT security, and it is not unreasonable for organizations already using ISO 20000 or ITIL to ask a lead appraiser if they can include their security practices in the appraisal scope, particularly when conducting baseline and diagnostic appraisals. So, how can we realistically answer this question?

One answer is just to say, sorry, CMMI-SVC is not designed to cover this area, at least not yet. But there is a different tack we can use.

The SCAMPI approach is probably one of the most rigorous appraisal methods available. Although it is closely linked with CMMI, it can potentially be used with any reference framework to evaluate the processes of an organization. So, if we had a suitable reference framework, SCAMPI could readily cope with IT security.

What might such a reference framework look like? Well, we could look to ISO 27001 for ideas. This standard provides the *requirements* for setting up, then running and maintaining, the *system* that an organization needs for effective IT information security. How could we use this standard with the principles of both CMMI and SCAMPI?

One thing that CMMI, in all its shapes, is very good at helping organizations do is to institutionalize their processes. As longtime CMMI users know, the generic goals and practices are extremely effective at getting the right kind of management attention for setting up and keeping an infrastructure that supports the continued, effective operation of an organization's processes. No matter what discipline we need to institutionalize, CMMI's generic goals and practices would need to be in the mix somewhere.

So, in our appraisal of an IT security system, we would need to look for evidence of its institutionalization. The generic practices as they currently stand in CMMI-SVC can be used to look for evidence of planning the IT security processes, providing adequate resources and training for the support of the IT security system, and so on. But it turns out that ISO 27001 has some useful content in this respect as well.

Certain clauses in the ISO 27001 standard map very neatly to the CMMI generic practices. For example, consider the following:

- Clause 4.3, Documentation Requirement: contains aspects of policy (GP 2.1) and configuration control (GP 2.6).
- Clause 5, Management Responsibility: details further aspects of policy (GP 2.1) plus the provision of resources (GP 2.3), training (GP 2.5), and assigning responsibility (GP 2.4).
- Clause 6, Internal ISMS Audits: requires that the control activities, processes, and procedures of the IT security management system are checked for conformance to the standard and that they perform as expected (GP 2.9).
- Clause 7, Management Review of the IT Security Management System: necessitates that managers make sure that the system continues to operate suitably (GP 2.10). But additionally, this management check may take input from measurement and monitoring type activities (GP 2.8).
- Clause 8, IT Security Management System Improvement: looks to ensure continuous improvement of the system. Some of this section looks similar to GP 2.9, but there is also a flavor of GP 3.1 and GP 3.2.

So, collecting evidence in a Practice Implementation Indicator (PII) for IT security as we do in SCAMPI, we could use these sections of the ISO 27001 like GPs to guide our examination. But what is it about the material that is more unique to setting up and running an IT security management system? In CMMI, this material would be contained in the specific goals and practices.

Looking once more to ISO 27001, we find material that is a suitable template for this type of content. The following clauses of the standard appear appropriate.

- Clause 4.2.1, Establish the Information Security Management System: This deals with scoping the security system; defining policies for it; defining an approach to identifying and evaluating security threats and how to deal with them; and obtaining management approval for the plans and mechanisms defined.
- Clause 4.2.2, Implement and Operate the Information Security Management System: This deals with formulating a plan to operate the security system to manage the level of threat and then implementing that plan.
- Clause 4.2.3, Monitor and Review the Information Security Management System: This uses the mechanisms of the system to monitor threats to information security. Where action is required to address a threat (e.g., a security breach), it is implemented and tracked to a satisfactory conclusion.

- Clause 4.2.4, Maintain and Improve the Information Security Management System: This uses the data from measuring and monitoring the system to implement corrections or improvements of the system.

Incorporating this content into the typical structure of a CMMI process area could provide a suitable framework for organizing the evidence in a SCAMPI type appraisal of IT security management. Often, CMMI process areas are structured with one or more specific goals concerned with "Preparing for operating a process or system" and one or more specific goals dealing with "Implementing or providing the resultant system." The match of this structure to the relevant ISO 27001 clauses is very appropriate.

We could structure our specific component of the PII to look for evidence in two main blocks.

1. Establishing and Maintaining an Information Security Management System: This involves activities guided by the principles in section 4.2.1 of the standard and would look something like this.
   - Identify the scope and objectives for the information security management system.
   - Identify the approach to identifying and assessing information security threats.
   - Identify, analyze, and evaluate information security threats.
   - Select options for treating information security threats relevant to the threat control objectives.
   - Obtain commitment to the information security management system from all relevant stakeholders.

2. Providing Information Security Using the Agreed Information Security Management System: This would then involve implementing the system devised in part (a) and would look something like this.
   - Implement and operate the agreed information security management system.
   - Monitor and review the information security management system.
   - Maintain and improve the information security management system.

Such an approach allows us to more easily include this discipline in the scope of a SCAMPI appraisal and enables the prior data collection and subsequent verification that is a signature of SCAMPI appraisals. *It means that a non-CMMI area can be included alongside CMMI process areas with ease.*

The intention has been to give organizations a tool that they can use to address IT security within their CMMI-SVC improvement initiatives. Such a pragmatic inclusion will make it easier for organizations to take advantage of the evolutionary and *inclusive* approach to service management improvement offered by CMMI-SVC. This makes CMMI-SVC adoption a case of building on the good work done to date.

Public Education in an Age of Accountability

By Betsey Cox-Buteau

Author Comments: The field of education is among the service types in which we frequently hear people say that they hope to see application of CMMI for Services. (The other two areas most commonly mentioned are health care and finance.) Because good results in education are important to society, process champions are eager to see the benefits of process improvement that have been realized in other fields. Betsey Cox-Buteau is a school administrator and consultant, who works with struggling schools to improve test scores and professional development. Here she makes the case for how CMMI-SVC could make a difference in U.S. schools.

Orienting Education to Delivering Services

For generations, schools have been more about "teaching" than about "student learning." It has often been said that the job of the teacher is to teach and the job of the student is to learn. Over time, some teachers have adopted this as an excuse to shrug off the need to change their pedagogy to produce higher levels of learning among all students. "I teach the curriculum—if the students don't learn it, then it's their fault." This attitude can no longer be tolerated. The school's professional community is responsible for seeing that *all* students learn and that they make adequate progress toward specific curriculum goals. It has now become the teacher's responsibility not just to deliver curriculum instruction, but also to *ensure* that each student actually learns the curriculum and is able to apply it. Teachers must adjust their pedagogy to meet the needs of all of their students so that all can learn.

In other words, the staffs of our schools have been adjusting to the notion that their profession is becoming defined as a service industry. Hence, the CMMI for Services model comes to us at an opportune moment in the history of public education.

Along with curriculum accountability, schools are always experiencing pressure to hold down the cost of educating their students. Public schools are expected to provide the best education at the lowest cost per student. Even school districts in wealthier communities face this pressure, especially during difficult economic times. This dual expectation is a call for the most efficient education system possible, a system that provides society with well-prepared young workers and invested members of a democratic society, and a system that streamlines processes and delivers the greatest level of student learning for the investment. Where do these expectations leave school administration?

School administrators have very little formal training in business practices or process improvement methods, and they tend to inherit a predetermined system of service delivery practices when they walk into a new position. These inherited practices are often unclear; in most cases they are documented poorly or not at all. Incoming administrators rarely have the opportunity to learn from their predecessors before they leave the job. Often, new administrators find that they must learn the old system from the office secretary, if the secretary stayed when the old boss left. This practice leads to a fair amount of "reinventing the wheel" each time a new person comes into a school system to lead it. For school superintendents nationwide, that is an average of every five to six years.[4] The figures for school principals are similar.

Federal Legislation Drives Change

On January 8, 2002, then-President George W. Bush signed into law the No Child Left Behind (NCLB) Act of 2001. This legislation was unprecedented in its federal reach into every public school in the nation. That reach shook the foundation of a very old system that has remained largely an ad hoc operation in the majority of America's school districts for more than 100 years. For the first time, if public schools wished to continue to receive federal funds, they had to demonstrate progress toward a goal of 100 percent of children reading and performing math at their grade level by the year 2014.

---

4. Glass, Thomas E.; Bjork, Lars; and Brunner, C. Cryss. "The Study of the American School Superintendency, 2000. A Look at the Superintendent of Education in the New Millennium." American Association of School Administrators (Arlington, VA: 2000); www.eric.ed.gov:80 /ERICWebPortal/custom/portlets/recordDetails/detailmini.jsp?_nfpb=true&_&ERICExtSearch _SearchValue_0=ED440475&ERICExtSearch_SearchType_0=no&accno=ED440475.

To measure progress toward that goal, each state was required to formulate an annual assessment process. Under these new requirements, if schools did not show adequate yearly progress (AYP), they would fall subject to varying levels of consequences to be imposed by their state. The consequences included allowing students to attend other schools in their district, creating written school improvement plans, and replacing teachers and administrators. School boards and administrations had to reconsider the frequently used excuse that public schools were different from businesses because their products were human beings; therefore, business standards and processes did not apply to them. The NCLB Act forced all stakeholders to revisit the real product of a public school because of this new accountability. The product of the public school is now being defined as "student learning," and it is measurable.

As the curriculum accountability required by the NCLB Act has become institutionalized over time through state testing, and the focus tightens on data analysis regarding levels of student learning, the concept that schools provide a service to students, parents, and society has become clearer to those who work in our schools and those who create educational policy.

A Service Agreement for Education

So, how can public education begin to take advantage of the CMMI for Services model? The education service system is already in place, and students have been graduating for a long, long time, so the system must be working, *right*? It may be "working" in some sense, but the same questions present themselves to each new administrator when he or she comes into a building or a central office. Is the present system working *well*? Is it efficient? Are the processes institutionalized, or will they fade away over time? It is time for school administrators, from the central office to the individual buildings, to examine the processes involved in their service system and determine their efficacy against their "service agreement" with taxpayers. The CMMI for Services model provides many process areas within which to accomplish these tasks.

For example, look at any school's mission statement. It often begins something like this: "Our school is dedicated to serving the individual academic, social-emotional, and physical needs of each student, to create lifelong learners...." Are these goals real? Are they measurable? If so, do our public schools have in place a reliable method to measure the achievement of these goals? If schools begin to look at themselves as service providers, then their services must be defined in a measurable manner. When the goals are measurable the processes to deliver those services can be measured and analyzed. Using the resulting data, the services can be redesigned, refined, and institutionalized.

Although the nomenclature is different, the "mission statement" is in essence a school's "service agreement" with its customers. The CMMI for Services model offers guidance in the Service Delivery process area (SP 1.1 and 1.2) to address the process for developing a measurable service agreement. Once a measurable service agreement is in place, all the stakeholders will have a firm foundation on which to build the processes necessary to successfully meet the requirements of that agreement.

A Process for Consistent Curriculum Delivery

One of those requirements critical to the measurable service agreement is the delivery of curriculum. This area is another in which the CMMI for Services model could move a school system toward a streamlined, dynamic curriculum delivery system. Public schools are ripe for a well-documented structuring of the delivery of their services in curriculum delivery, due to the accountability requirements of the NCLB Act. Curriculum delivery is tied directly to student learning and ultimately to test scores. The challenge here is to be consistent in how we assess student learning so that progress (or the lack of it) can be recognized and understood.

Standardized processes should be in place for the review of learning assessment data, which in turn refocuses and improves the delivery of the curriculum. Ideally, curriculum review against assessment data should remain in place no matter who is in the front or central office. All too often, the superintendent or building principal leaves, and the curriculum review and improvement process breaks down. There are many reasons for this breakdown, not the least of which is personnel turnover. One of the many possible applications of the Process and Product Quality Assurance process area of the CMMI for Services model is curriculum development. This would benefit much of the curriculum development and delivery by enabling a curriculum delivery review system and measuring employee compliance with that delivery.

A Process for Efficient Decision Making

Beyond the more obvious areas of application, such as curriculum delivery, other education practices can benefit from the discipline of the CMMI for Services model. For example, the decision making in school buildings can be as simple as a librarian choosing a book or as involved as a large committee choosing a curriculum program. Decisions can be made by a harried teacher attempting to avoid internal conflict or by a principal who wants to defuse the anger of a parent. Many decisions are made. Some decisions affect few, and some affect many. Some decisions may have long-lasting implications for a child's life or for a parent's or taxpayer's trust in the system; and that trust (or lack of it) shows up in the voting booth each year. If the processes of each service delivery subsystem are mature and transparent, the provider and the customers will be satisfied and will trust each other. When applied to refine the decision-making process in a school district, the Decision Analysis and Resolution process area of the model can be instrumental in ensuring that personnel make the best decisions possible using a standard, approved, and institutionalized process; the result is the establishment of greater trust with the customer.

Providing for Sustained Improvement

In this era of rapid turnover in school administration, the institutionalization of effective processes is paramount to the continuity of providing high-quality service to all stakeholders. As superintendents and school principals move to other administrative positions and school districts, the use of the model's generic goals and practices can provide a means of ensuring that these effective system processes will have lasting continuity. Each time a process area is established and refined, the generic goals and practices provide a framework in place behind it that helps to keep the improvements "locked in" even after later personnel changes. Policies documenting the adopted processes, positions of responsibility named for the implementation and follow-through of these new procedures, and other generic practices will remain intact and in effect long after any one person moves through the organization.

Other Applications for the Model

These process areas are just a few of the many process areas of the CMMI for Services model that would be beneficial when applied to the public education system. Others would include

- Integrated Project Management, for the inclusion of stakeholders, (i.e., parents and the community) in the education of their children
- Measurement and Analysis, to ensure the correct and continuous use of data to inform all aspects of the educational process

- Organizational Innovation and Deployment, to ensure an orderly and organized process for the piloting and adoption of new curricula, educational programs, delivery methods, and technologies
- Organizational Process Definition, to organize the standard processes in a school district ranging from purchasing supplies to curriculum review cycles
- Organizational Process Performance, to establish the use of data to provide measures of improvement of the processes used in the district in an effort to continually improve them
- Organizational Training, to establish the ongoing training of teachers and other staff members so that as they transition into and out of a building or position, continuity of the delivery of curriculum and other services is maintained
- Service System Transition, to establish a smooth transition from one way of doing things to another, while minimizing disruption to student learning

A Better Future for American Education

With no expectation of a lifting or significant easing of the present assessment and accountability measures placed on public schools by society's expectations and drivers such as the No Child Left Behind Act, these institutions of student learning can benefit from the application of this model. If our schools are to deliver the highest rate of student learning using the least amount of taxpayer dollars, the CMMI for Services model is a natural and essential tool for accomplishing this goal.

National Government Services Uses CMMI-SVC and Builds on a History with CMMI-DEV

By Angela Marks and Bob Green

Author Comments: National Government Services works in the health care domain and is among the earliest adopters of CMMI-SVC. The organization has a long history of successful use of CMMI-DEV. Like many users of CMMI, the organization does some development and some service. In its case, the predominant mission is service, and the CMMI-SVC model is a good fit for its work. However, the service system it relies on is large and complex enough that the Service System Development (SSD) process area in CMMI-SVC is not sufficient for its purposes. The organization needs to use the Engineering process areas in CMMI-DEV instead. This is one of the tailorings that the builders of

CMMI-SVC envisioned to accommodate the full range of service users and the reason that SSD is an "addition" (or is optional). Working with SEI Partner Gary Norausky, National Government Services has field-tested the notion of CMMI-SVC use with added Engineering process areas from CMMI-DEV—with good results.

Introduction

How does a mid-size CMMI-DEV maturity level 3 organization leverage its experience, knowledge, extant library of processes, and existing structures in a successful implementation of CMMI-SVC? This was the question that the IT Governance Team at National Government Services, the nation's largest Medicare contractor, faced as it created and evaluated a strategic plan for its participation in the January 2009 four-day CMMI-SVC pilot evaluation.

Because of the nonprescriptive nature of the CMMI models, National Government Services used a unique approach that paid off, especially in terms of a soft return on investment, by carefully integrating CMMI-DEV and CMMI-SVC. That strategy forms the context of this case study.

Overview and Strategy

During its strategy development sessions, the IT Governance Team at National Government Services, working with Norausky Process Solutions, created a plan to leverage its strong development background in the implementation of CMMI-SVC, complementing that which was already in place and refining extant processes.

Rather than viewing CMMI-SVC as another separate and distinct model, National Government Services set out to merge CMMI-DEV and CMMI-SVC with the goal of augmenting its current library of process assets as well as using this blended approach and further institutionalizing its self-mandate to strive for continuous process improvement in the way it does business. In short, National Government Services was successful in getting the best out of both constellations. A reasonable question, then, is how National Government Services could be confident its strategic approach would work. *Tailoring* best sums up the answer.

Model Tailoring

A critical element of the IT Governance Team's strategy included incorporating the best of both constellations; namely, the best of CMMI-DEV and CMMI-SVC. National Government Services posits that tailoring serves as the best strategic approach for accomplishing a nonbinary approach to augmenting IT service delivery. For example, the IT Governance Team, using a tailoring matrix approach, easily established Incident Resolution and Prevention (IRP) and Service Continuity (SCON) practices by using extant practices that were already deeply embedded in the company's disaster recovery processes and culture.

National Government Services' study of the CMMI-SVC model made evident the fact that *tailoring* is a critical aspect, or component, of Strategic Service Management (STSM), where the purpose is *to establish and maintain standard services in concert with strategic needs and plans.* Because National Government Services is a CMMI-DEV maturity level 3 organization, the focus was on tailoring as a way to put several pieces of the CMMI-DEV and CMMI-SVC models together.

Pieces of Two Puzzles

By way of an analogy, National Government Services initially viewed CMMI-DEV and CMMI-SVC as two boxes of a multiplicity of puzzle pieces that, in the end, assemble to create a single picture. National Government Services had already assembled the majority of the pieces from the CMMI-DEV box and was reaching deep into the CMMI-SVC box to find the pieces that would complete the picture.

As National Government Services explored CMMI-SVC, it began to recognize that CMMI-SVC adds dimension to and completes the delivery manner, and methods, of its suite of processes and products. By tailoring existing processes, National Government Services was able to achieve a full-spectrum means of doing business and meeting customer needs.

Results of the Strategy

Critical to National Government Services' strategic approach was the IT Governance Team, which serves as the Engineering Process Group. The IT Governance Team realized that CMMI-DEV covers only certain areas of IT, but the augmentation of CMMI-DEV with CMMI-SVC enabled the IT Governance Team to introduce standardized process improvement opportunities into such nondevelopment areas of IT as Systems Security, Networking/Infrastructure, and Systems Service Desks. Additionally, National Government Services has been implementing ITIL and has found that CMMI-SVC complements ITIL.

A key aspect of National Government Services' *model-blending strategy* was our discovery of the CMMI-DEV practices that were used to form the Service System Development (SSD) process area. SSD, the purpose of which is *to analyze, design, develop, integrate, verify, and validate service systems, including service system components, to satisfy existing or anticipated service agreements*, is satisfied by strongly developed practices in CMMI-DEV process areas such as Requirements Development (RD), Technical Solution (TS), Product Integration (PI), Verification (VER), and Validation (VAL).

Since SSD provides an alternative means of achieving the practices of the "Engineering" process areas of the CMMI-DEV constellation, National Government Services determined that SSD was not necessary, because its robust development processes provided full coverage of this area. By invoking Decision Analysis and Resolution (DAR), a process area in both models, National Government Services determined that, due to the scope of its projects, which tend to be large, it was easier to establish the necessary behaviors under the CMMI-DEV process areas. For its portfolio of projects, National Government Services uses the SSD process area to provide guidance for tailoring its CMMI-DEV process areas to augment service delivery of its large-scale, complex service systems.

In this way, National Government Services builds on its success with CMMI-DEV while applying CMMI-SVC to the service delivery work that is its core mission. Such an approach illustrates why CMMI was created and how it is designed to work. The models are part of an integrated framework that enables organizations such as National Government Services to gain an advantage from what it has learned using one CMMI model when beginning implementation with another.

Treating Systems Engineering as a Service

By Suzanne Garcia-Miller

Author Comments: Somewhat to the surprise of the authors of CMMI for Services, we have seen keen interest from developers in applying the model to their work. In this essay, Suzanne Garcia-Miller, a noted CMMI author and an applied researcher working on systems of systems and other dynamic system types, writes about the value to be gained by treating development, and systems engineering in particular, as a service.

Many of us who have worked in and around CMMs for a long time are accustomed to applying them to a system development lifecycle. Sometimes, when applying the practices to settings that provide valuable services to others (e.g., independent verification and validation agents for U.S. government contracts, or providers of data-mining services for market research firms in the commercial sector), we provided an ad hoc service to help an organization in that setting to tailor its implementation of the CMM in use (usually CMMI-DEV in recent years). We did this tailoring by

- Interpreting definitions in different ways (e.g., looking at a *project* as the time span associated with a service level agreement)
- Providing ideas for different classes of work products not typically discussed in development-focused models (e.g., the service level agreement as a key element of a project plan)
- Interpreting the scope of one or more process areas differently than originally described (e.g., the scope of the Requirements Management process area being interpreted as the requirements associated with a service agreement [usually a contract])

With the publication of CMMI for Services, V1.2, organizations whose primary business focus is service delivery now have an opportunity to use good practices from their business context to improve the capability of their delivery and support processes. And an emerging discipline called "service systems engineering" explicitly focuses on applying the tools, techniques, and thinking style of systems engineering to services of many types. (A Google search in May 2009 on "service systems engineering" as a phrase yielded more than 7,000 hits.)

In preparing to teach this new CMMI-SVC constellation, especially in the early days of its adoption, many of the students attending pilot course offerings were people much more experienced with a product development context using CMMI-DEV. Several of us were struck by the difficulty more than a few experienced people were having when trying to "shift gears" into a service mindset. To help them (and myself, who sometimes inadvertently slipped into "tangible product mode"), I started thinking about the service aspects of pretty much everything I came into contact with: service aspects of research, service aspects of teaching CMMI courses, service aspects of systems-of-systems governance, and, inevitably, service aspects of systems engineering.

In thinking about conversations going back as far as the development of the initial Systems Engineering CMM (1993–1995), I remember struggles to capture what was different about systems engineering as a discipline. In trying to capture important practices, we kept coming across the problem of trying to express "practices" associated with

- The holistic viewpoint that a good systems engineer brings to a project
- The conflict resolution activities (among both technical and organizational elements) that are a constant element of a systems engineer's role
- The myriad coordination aspects of a systems engineer's daily existence
- Being the ongoing keeper of the connection between the technical and the business or mission vision that was the source of the system being developed
- Switching advocacy roles depending on who the systems engineer is talking to—being the user's advocate when the user isn't in the room; being the project manager's advocate when his or her viewpoint is under-represented in a tradeoff study

Looking back with the benefit of hindsight, I can easily conceive of these as difficulties in trying to fit the *service* of systems engineering into a model focused on the *product development* to which systems engineering is applied. I also remember a paper that Sarah Sheard wrote about the 12 roles of systems engineering [Sheard 1996]. Out of those 12 roles, at least three of them, Customer Interface, Glue among Subsystems, and Coordinator, were heavily focused on services: intangible and nonstorable products (CMMI-SVC 1.2). When looking for references for this viewpoint of systems engineering as a service on the Web, I found little that addressed the service aspect of systems engineering within the typical context of complex system development.

To satisfy myself that I wasn't taking my services obsession too far, I pulled out some key definitions related to service delivery from CMMI-SVC, V1.2, and thought about how systems engineering being performed in the context of complex system development could be viewed as a service. Table 6.1 reflects my initial thoughts on this subject, and I hope they will engender a dialogue that will be productive to the systems engineering community.

TABLE 6.1 Nominal Mapping of Systems Engineering Aspects to CMMI-SVC Service Terms

CMMI-SVC Term and Definition	How Systems Engineering Reflects (or Could Reflect) This Service Element
Service: in the CMMI Product Suite, a product that is intangible and nonstorable. (Services are delivered through the use of service systems that have been designed to satisfy service requirements. Many service providers deliver combinations of services and goods. A single service system can deliver both types of products.)	Systems engineering has many "intangible, nonstorable" aspects, particularly when you consider the customer interface, "keeper of the vision," and coordinator roles that are typical of systems engineering [Sheard 1996]. A service is often something without a definable end. This aspect of a service reflects one of the roles that systems engineers fill in many enterprises—the keeper of lessons learned that should be transferred from one instance of a product to the next. Although the end of the systems engineer's role might be defined as the point when the system is retired, in practical terms that system could be sustained for 20 to 40 years (the lifespan of many physical and software-based systems). Such a lifespan implies that the ongoing services of systems engineering will be required for an indefinite period. Different systems engineering authors take more of either a "lifecycle" viewpoint or a "program management" viewpoint for categorizing systems engineering activities. It may be tempting to say that the service aspect of systems engineering is confined to the program management viewpoint. Taking this perspective would miss the services that are provided by systems engineers in terms of conflict resolution among different technical and organizational interfaces for the system, as well as the hours of technical communication that are provided to improve the system development team's understanding of overall system aspects that they affect or are affected by.

TABLE 6.1 Nominal Mapping of Systems Engineering Aspects to CMMI-SVC Service Terms *(Continued)*

CMMI-SVC Term and Definition	How Systems Engineering Reflects (or Could Reflect) This Service Element
Service system: an integrated and interdependent combination of component resources that satisfies service requirements. (A service system encompasses *everything* required for service delivery, including work products, processes, facilities, tools, consumables, and human resources. Note that a service system includes the people necessary to perform the service system's processes.)	What is the *service system* for systems engineering? Such things as systems engineering processes, simulation and analysis tools, prototyping facilities, customer requirements, and mission concepts may not be things we are accustomed to thinking about in terms of service delivery, but they are all service components of the coordination, conflict resolution, communication, and integration services that systems engineers provide over the life of a system.
Service system component: a resource required for a service system to successfully deliver services. (Components may include processes and people.)	In addition to the service components mentioned in the discussion of the service system, other service system components that might relate directly to the communication aspect of systems engineering, for example, could include the telecommunication facilities (e.g., videoconference, Web-based collaboration tools, physical team rooms) needed to support a geographically distributed engineering team.
Service requirements: the complete set of requirements that affect service delivery and service system development. (Service requirements include both technical and nontechnical requirements.)	The service requirements for systems engineering are often stated in terms of a systems engineering organization's charter, or roles and responsibilities, as well as in terms of the competencies that are required to staff the function.
Service request: a communication from a customer or end user that one or more specific instances of service delivery are desired. These requests are made within the context of a service agreement.	The service requests that a systems engineer receives are formal (a charter for performing a tradeoff study on some aspect of the system under development) and informal ("Joe, will you please come talk to me and Anita about how to interpret the interface requirements for subsystems X and Y?").

Continues

TABLE 6.1 Nominal Mapping of Systems Engineering Aspects to CMMI-SVC Service Terms *(Continued)*

CMMI-SVC Term and Definition	How Systems Engineering Reflects (or Could Reflect) This Service Element
Service agreement: a binding, written record of a promised exchange of value between a service provider and a customer. (A "promised exchange of value" means a joint recognition and acceptance of what each party will provide to the other to satisfy the agreement.)	One expression of a service agreement for systems engineering, especially in complex system development projects, is likely to be the Systems Engineering Management Plan, which can be seen as essentially defining the agreed services (in terms of activities) that the systems engineering function will provide to the system development project.
Service level agreement: a service agreement that specifies delivered services; service measures; levels of acceptable and unacceptable services; and expected responsibilities, liabilities, and actions of both the provider and the customer in anticipated situations.	The service level agreement is one element of a service mindset that I have not explicitly expressed for a systems engineering function. However, it is interesting to think about the "implied" service levels that are taken for granted in many organizations in relation to systems engineering.
Service incident: an indication of an actual or potential interference with a service.	It is easy to think of things that interfere with the delivery of systems engineering services—everything from people who don't show up at a meeting they have committed to attend, to political machinations to avoid abiding by an interface agreement.
Service catalog: a list or repository of standardized service definitions. Service catalogs may include varying degrees of detail about available service levels, quality, prices, negotiable/tailorable items, and terms and conditions.	The definition of standard systems engineering services may well be embodied in a set of systems engineering policies, processes, or procedures. However, outside of a systems engineering consulting house context, I haven't seen details about service levels, quality, prices, and so on, normally expressed in these types of documents.

Having completed the mapping, and, with some exception, finding it easy to interpret systems engineering from a services mindset, the next question for me is this: What value could systems engineering practitioners derive from looking at their roles and activities in this way? I'll close this essay with a few of my ideas framed as questions, with the hope that the systems engineering community will go beyond my initial answers.

- How does viewing systems engineering as a service change the emphasis of systems engineering competencies (knowledge, skills, and process abilities)?

  By making the service aspect of systems engineering explicit, the need for competencies related to the service aspects (coordination, conflict resolution, etc.) can also be made explicit, perhaps resulting in more value being placed on systems engineers who go beyond performing the translation of one development work product into another.

- What would a service level agreement for systems engineering look like?

  I can think of several systems engineers of my current acquaintance who would love to have an explicit service level agreement for expected turnaround times on different types of requests, availability for different types of activities, and stipulations related to defective work product inputs (with willingness to commit to mutually agreed on defect rates for their work product outputs). My instinct is that working on producing such an agreement would actually embody many of the project management and support practices of CMMI-DEV (an interesting research topic for a systems engineering master's thesis, perhaps?).

- How do you separate the "product" and "service" aspects of a systems engineer's role?

  A trivial approach to separating the systems engineer's product and service aspects would be to say that the activities related to transforming work products from one state to another (e.g., requirements into designs and test plans) would be product-focused, and all the other "ongoing" activities (coordination, conflict resolution, interface management, customer communications) would be service-focused. However, the CMMI-SVC service system concept includes the work products that are produced as part of the service system. I'm inclined to think that the systems engineering function as a whole on a development project could productively be perceived as a service, with the work product transformations being part of that service.

- Systems engineers, and the other participants they work closely with, coproduce value as they transform an idea into a working, validated product. In many types of services, it is that simultaneous coproduction of value that is the essence of service and service quality. I know many systems engineers who think that their contribution revolves around their ability to see beyond the piece parts to the entire system. I think the next evolution of systems engineering is to see beyond the system to its entire socio-technical context, which drives the whole of systems engineering into a service mindset. What is the benefit of thinking about systems engineering as a service?

The answer to this question will ultimately determine which perspective practicing systems engineers will apply to their work. To me, the benefit will be in looking at systems engineering in the same holistic fashion that systems engineers try to use when looking at the system they are building. In particular, a service viewpoint focuses on stakeholders in a richer, more nuanced way than is typical with a product viewpoint. With a service viewpoint, we are constantly looking for measures of customer and stakeholder satisfaction, not just product delivery.

If the systems we were building 20 years ago were the most complex we would ever be faced with, then a product-centric view might continue to be productive. But the complexity we face today isn't just bigger; it is also dynamic, with the pace of user and operational needs being conceived clearly outstripping traditional suppliers' ability to respond to them from a traditional, product-centric view. Service concepts bring some of the fluidity to the relationship needed between users and suppliers to support dynamic complexity. And who better than systems engineers to be at the forefront of defining new ways to support those needs, through service systems that include not just the traditional tangible products but also the situationally required knowledge, skills, and abilities to compose and reconfigure system elements into an ongoing evolution of solutions?

Are Services Agile?

By Hillel Glazer

Author Comments: Practitioners who are champions of Agile principles and practitioners using CMMI have been realizing recently just how much they have in common rather than what separates them. This isn't a recent insight for Hillel Glazer from Entinex, however, who has been a thought leader in both communities for some time. In this essay, Hillel considers the ways in which services may already be agile and what CMMI for Services might bring to the conversation about using Agile and CMMI together. He is a certified instructor and high maturity lead appraiser for CMMI.

Some argue that "agile" in the context of software development came about in response to an unhealthy trend. That trend distracted the attention of development projects from customer service and product excellence to demonstrable proof of process fidelity. That love affair with tools and an obsession with plans, contracts, and rigidity usurped relationships with customers and calcified responsiveness.

Look at the Agile Manifesto:

We are uncovering better ways of developing
software by doing it and helping others do it.
Through this work we have come to value:

Individuals and interactions *over processes and tools*
Working software *over comprehensive documentation*
Customer collaboration *over contract negotiation*

Responding to change *over following a plan*
That is, while there is value in the items on
the right, we value the items on the left more.

The values in the Agile Manifesto are clearly in favor of individuals, interactions, results, customers, and responsiveness: all attributes classically characteristic of the business and the operation of a service.

Services are not performed in the vacuum of a cubicle where the people doing the work can throw their results "over the wall." Under most circumstances, services require a human touch somewhere in the delivery of the service. Further, services generally require people to work together—whether in sync with policy and management or in coordination with coworkers.

The impact, output, and outcome of services are often detectable by the customer immediately. This characteristic of services makes meeting expectations through demonstrable results imperative to the service provider. People who can recall a great service experience will note that the experience was not with a machine or with a document, but with a person in the business who was working with them to meet their needs.

Truly, if a single attribute of services can be found among the many service situations, it's that services generally account for a wide variety of inputs. These inputs are often unpredictable and as often unknowable until some aspect of the service is provided. Overall, it is very much a dynamic situation in which a broad spectrum of inputs must be normalized to fit the pattern the organization created to provide the consistent "level of service" customers come to expect.

One might argue that whether intentionally, surreptitiously, or serendipitously, the progenitors, proponents, and practitioners of agile principles and methods were creating a systematic approach to serving software clients better. In other words, in many ways, agile puts the "services" back into software development.

Providing services for a living involves processes that are among the least likely to work well in "cookie-cutter" fashion. It's true that at a macro level, many instantiations of a service will have common elements or fit a pattern for that class of service. For example, in a hospital there are the check-in and registration steps, the evaluation and analysis steps, diagnosis, prognosis, treatment or prescription, follow-up and discharge, and so forth. But at the specific, case-by-case point of delivery ("project" or "patient" in our example), the services have the potential to be as unique as the customer (patient) receiving the service.

To enhance the provision of services amid the delivery of those services is akin to the classic metaphor of "changing the tires on a moving car." To achieve this state, the processes involved in providing and improving services must themselves be responsive, adaptive, nonobstructive, and unobtrusive.

CMMI for Services was created with a keen eye toward this reality; in other words, the modelers did not want improvement processes that hinder service delivery processes. With this in mind, service-oriented process areas in CMMI-SVC (as well as the CMMI Model Foundation process areas) are written (and additional informative material is included) to discourage processes that overtake the service to be provided and to accommodate the dynamic environment in which services are provided.

While agility and responsiveness are critical to services and to agile software development, a simple concept cannot be overemphasized and must not be dismissed: Think through what will be done before it's time to do it.

The creators of CMMI for Services do not expect that each time a customer walks into a bank or a patient is rushed into the emergency room, a project plan will be created. However, they do expect that when the banking customer steps into the branch or the patient emerges through the doors, the respective organizations have a pretty good idea of what they will be doing with the incoming service request or "project."

When someone calls the help desk, the person who takes the call should not have to invent how to proceed, what information to collect, and where or how to record the information he or she gathers. A restaurant does not invent its menu with each customer and invent recipes with each order, even though some tailoring is usually allowed.

CMMI for Services operates at this level. It also has provisions for situations in which the customer does, in fact, have an unusual request, or the organization has to stretch its operations to meet a new need or has to create a "project" to meet a particular need. We want the print, copy, and ship locations to make our custom order to our specifications, but we don't want them having to learn on the job whether what we've requested is a custom order or to learn on the job how to operate the copier machine.

In CMMI for Services, the seven constellation-specific process areas are designed to facilitate the continuous delivery of services while also providing the infrastructure for the continuous collection of experience and data to help to improve those services. In each process area case, the notion of standardization prevails. Knowing which services a customer expects, which services a customer can expect, and which services a customer should not expect may seem like an obvious consideration, but reconciling expectations is likely an experience most readers can relate to when it comes to a bad service experience. Knowing which services are routine and which aren't seems like a commonsense, basic notion. Despite its simplicity, these are necessary early steps in the ability to improve services.

These ideas fit well with the development ideas of "agility." A relentless focus on the customer and on value enhances the relationship between provider and customer. Innovation and creativity used to meet the needs of a customer may trump established processes in most well-run service organizations. Established processes can provide the basis for reliable service, but these processes must not be allowed to hinder the meeting of customer expectations. Ideally, the established processes themselves are set up to encourage innovation and improvement and may even help the provider anticipate additional needs and tailoring.

It is important for users of this constellation to never abandon their customer orientation and their ability to respond to the dynamics of their service operations in pursuit of demonstrating a faithful implementation of a process improvement model.

- Service agreements need be no more formal than a list of services provided, costs, and other means of establishing expectations. A published, visible service menu or an order form may suffice.

- The means by which incidents are resolved and prevented should be no more complicated than the nature of the incidents, but having no means to resolve or prevent incidents would be as unforgivable to a service operation as not testing the product would be to a product operation.

- Managing the service operation's capacity and availability seems basic enough, though anyone on hold waiting on the phone has clearly experienced the implementation (or lack thereof) of this idea. To an agile organization, knowing where and why bottlenecks occur facilitates workarounds and preferably the avoidance of bottlenecks. What can be more disruptive to a service or its ability to be agile than the total and complete loss of use of the primary operation? This situation is accounted for in disaster-recovery and continuity of operations concepts found in any well-run service organization and also in the CMMI-SVC constellation. In agile organizations, this would be the ultimate expression of responding to change where the organization can continue to provide value-added services despite the absence of its usual facility, let alone its processes. But deciding which services must be forgone, which services can still be provided, and how they will be provided under unusual circumstances should be known ahead of needing to implement the backup plan.

- Ever experience the bumps and hiccups associated with a service provider trying out a new service or switching from one way of delivering its service to another? Such spikes in the usual operational scenario can be avoided with some consideration of the impact of the change on the customers, on the operations, and on the people who provide the services. This consideration of impact is as much a courtesy as it is a necessity, agile or otherwise.

- While developing products relies on resources just as much as services do, in the context of services, and in a strong parallel to the values of agility, a strategic view of services to be provided relies heavily on the individuals and their interactions. In particular, service businesses must plan the availability of the right kind of people and forecast the types of services to be provided. In some ways, anticipating the direction of markets and resources and deciding which services to standardize and which to keep on the periphery until the market demonstrates the demand and validity of a service are somewhat forward-thinking concepts. But in any business, these are not far-fetched concepts, merely ones that prudent companies pursue. When providing services is your business, these activities are how you ensure that you are relevant now to your customers' needs and remain relevant in the future. Finally, there's a remaining aspect of the CMMI-SVC that bears a clear resemblance to concepts that promote an agile organization: The notion of having to develop a service system in CMMI for Services was derived from taking the absolute minimum practices from the Engineering process areas of CMMI for Development and incorporating them into a single process area in CMMI-SVC. What in CMMI-DEV were five unique process areas, comprising 13 goals and 40 practices, were whittled down to one process area comprising 3 goals and 12 practices. For organizations whose primary efforts are in services and not developing systems (at least not developing very complicated ones), CMMI-SVC provides an abridged version of improvement practices in the engineering space. And those organizations that need simple service systems, perhaps consisting of just people and procedures, can opt out of this process area.

Where agile development parts ways with CMMI-SVC is that most services themselves tend to not work well when delivered in increments or provided iteratively. People don't want part of their shirts laundered and pressed, they don't want some of their stock purchased at the target price, they don't want a portion of their house saved from fire, and they don't want to be taken 30 percent of the way to the airport. Customers also don't want the services rendered for them to be experiments in early or frequent failures. They don't want their change miscounted, they don't want their meals undercooked, and they'd prefer to avoid someone getting lost on the way to the airport.

Nonetheless, despite this departure from agile in the "development" sense, other concepts of agility, such as eliminating wasteful effort, promoting self-organization, and facilitating trust and high morale among the team, are all hallmarks of well-run service organizations.

Should organizations seek to adopt agile approaches to services and an improvement schema that allows agile approaches to flourish, the lessons learned from CMMI-DEV apply equally well to CMMI-SVC.

- CMMI (regardless of constellation) is a model; how to actually create an improvement system using this model will be unique to each organization.
- The artifacts of an improvement system come from the operation of the improvement system.
- Appraisals for CMMI determine whether (not how well) its improvement system shows signs that it was created using CMMI as the improvement model.

- It's critical that the context of an improvement system—the service itself—be the arbiter of how to evaluate the artifacts created by that system.

Each service system requires a custom-fit improvement system, or customers will leave. To do otherwise would not be agile and would not be good service. And that would be entirely unforgiveable.

Legal Services in a Changing World

By Sally Cunningham

Author Comments: In this essay, Sally Cunningham, a licensed attorney in the Commonwealth of Pennsylvania with extensive experience in all aspects of technology transition, licensing, contracts, and negotiation, considers a couple of the drivers facing legal organizations and argues the case for what model-based process discipline has to offer to this well-established profession. One might assume that, like education, the law already has an extremely codified approach to their work practices. But the author notes that the recent disruptive forces may call for management practices in the CMMI for Services model.

Two trends are affecting law firms in the twenty-first century. The first is globalization. The second is consolidation. Much like other similar service industries, law firms are consolidating. Bigger firms provide more and different types of services. For a law firm to survive in today's global economy, the management of legal services must change from the old view, where knowing the law comes first and managing the firm's business comes second, to possessing business expertise and disciplined management. One of the major concerns of any law firm, in addition to providing effective counsel or winning cases for its clients, is running an efficient and fiscally responsible business. How can CMMI-SVC help a law firm to manage this major concern?

The use of electronic billing by law firms has been gaining such momentum over the past few decades that any firm not taking advantage of electronic billing will be outperformed by competitors. This transition began in the 1990s and continues to this day. In addition, many law firms use electronic billing for much more than billing and collections. They also use electronic billing for budgeting, tracking spending against budgets or reserves, and spending in categories such as types of cases (civil versus criminal), companies, or outside counsel. Reports can also be run to fulfill Sarbanes-Oxley financial reporting requirements.

Imagine that you are a law firm senior administrator and have just been told that it is your firm's time to move from tracking cases by having weekly meetings using an old-fashioned spreadsheet as a way of managing to an electronic billing system. How will you manage the transition?

Here is one way to proceed using the process areas of CMMI-SVC. Using the Supplier Agreement Management (SAM) process area, a project management process area at maturity level 2, will assist you in acquiring a system that is best suited for your firm's particular needs.

To make a selection, you must know what kind of reporting you desire and whether a given supplier can facilitate these reports. The Service System Development process area will assist you in developing and analyzing requirements. Also, it is important to decide whether you want to purchase a COTS product and conform your billing system to that COTS product or whether your requirements are so unique that you need a customized COTS system. The supplier agreement management process can assist in defining and deciding supplier agreement details, such as delivery of the product, training, and level of ongoing technical support.

SAM SP 1.1, Determine Acquisition Type, will help you decide whether you want installation of software on your law firm servers or whether you are interested in a Web-based application service provider (ASP). Although an ASP seems convenient, you must determine how to assess vendor vulnerabilities, such as security and commingling of your firm's data with that of other firms.

SAM SP 1.2, Select Suppliers, will assist you in establishing and documenting criteria for evaluating potential suppliers, identifying potential suppliers, evaluating proposals and risks, and evaluating suppliers' ability to perform the work. This specific practice will also help you determine what type of work products you desire in order to select suppliers. Examples are market studies, lists of suppliers, preferred vendor lists, trade studies, letters of interest, and proposals.

You have effectively used the SAM process area to help you make a change to your service system. Now, using the Service System Transition (SST) process area will assist you in planning, communicating, managing, deploying, and confirming that your service system components effectively make the transition to the delivery environment.

Any adoption of a new process or technology requires that an organization be fully committed from the highest level of the organization, including administrative and financial resources. Being fully committed, however, is only half the battle. In addition to being fully committed, an organization must know how to define the comprehensive process of preparing for, executing, and confirming deployment of a system.

SST SP 1.1, Analyze Service System Transition Needs, will enable you to identify and mitigate issues associated with the transition. You will have to baseline the current system. For example, your firm may have a bookkeeper who collects detailed data from billing spreadsheets and uses that data to create paper invoices, which are mailed to clients. Then you must determine if the data created by the new electronic billing system is adequate to accurately bill clients. In addition, management oversight must be analyzed. In old-fashioned law firms, the partners would physically sign off on matters of litigation, billing, and so forth. It was presumed that by the time a person made partner, he or she was experienced enough to understand correct filings and billings. Using this specific practice will help you analyze, identify, and mitigate potential issues as you transition from a paper-based billing system to an electronic billing system.

SST SP 1.3, Prepare Stakeholders for Changes, ensures that the transition is not impaired because of failure to prepare relevant stakeholders for all of the changes caused by introducing the new electronic billing system. It will be important to establish and maintain a transition notification or communication strategy for both external and internal stakeholders. To ensure continuity in cash flow, external stakeholder clients must be aware of the new electronic billing system, must know when the transition will occur, and must understand any changes that will affect the way they pay bills. Internal stakeholders must be aware of changes and must be trained to use the new system. It is also important for both external and internal stakeholders to understand procedures and tools for customer and user feedback.

SST SP 2.1, Deploy Service System Components, will help you to develop a tactical plan for the transition to electronic billing that you can use for deployment. You will need to set a "go live" date for the transition. In addition, you need to have a plan for validating that the deployed electronic billing system is operating as expected. Once you have validated that the electronic billing system is operating as expected, you may start the process of retiring and archiving those old spreadsheets and paper invoices and appropriately removing them from the billing delivery environment.

SST SP 2.2, Assess and Control the Impacts of the Transition, ensures that transition activities extending past installation of the new electronic billing system are addressed. This assessment period often extends for months because it takes time to gather data and ensure that the new system is positively affecting relevant stakeholders. In addition, this practice ensures that the electronic billing system does not degrade other parts of the system, such as accounts receivable.

Many communication methods can be used during all phases of a service system transition. It is important to proactively communicate information about deployment of the electronic billing system. Examples are e-mail notification, embedded system notifications, and Frequently Asked Questions (FAQs).

This example highlights a few of the CMMI-SVC process areas that may assist a law firm in managing critical service provider processes. In a climate of globalization, increasing law firm size, economic uncertainty, and increasing competition, law firms need to be able to focus on being the best service provider possible. CMMI-SVC provides the tools required for a law firm to focus on process improvement with a goal of increased productivity and quality.

In addition to converting to an electronic billing system, suppose that the senior partners of the law firm have told you they want to expand internationally to remain competitive in the business of law. The partners of the firm want you to explore international expansion as part of their strategic business planning process and then implement and manage this expansion. Where do you begin?

Using the Strategic Service Management (STSM) process area is a great start. The purpose of STSM is to establish and maintain standard services in concert with strategic needs and plans. STSM will assist you in analyzing capabilities and needs for services that span multiple customers and agreements and establishing and maintaining standard services, service levels, and descriptions that reflect these capabilities and needs.

STSM SP 1.1, Gather and Analyze Relevant Data, will help you gather and analyze data that can help with planning the location and types of global services to be provided. Data that need to be examined are both internal and external. You must gather data on the organization's capabilities and strategic needs as well as the needs of its market. For example, it is well known that the United States and the United Kingdom dominate capital market, corporate, and mergers and acquisitions legal work around the world. You must determine whether your firm is capable of considering this market, whether it is a good strategic direction, and whether and where the market is already saturated with U.S. and U.K. firms.

Once you decide that the firm has the capacity and capability to go global, you can proceed by using STSM SP 1.2, Establish Plans for Standard Services, to confirm the strategic business objective of international expansion. In addition, you will have a framework to recommend requirements for standard services based on strategic business objectives, the firm's capabilities, and strategic needs. Internationalization of a law firm is complex and comes with great costs as well as benefits. It is important to move forward carefully, as most law firms do not have outside investors. The seed funding for expansion comes from the partners and is limited. A typical work product in this SP is a description of the planned standard services. Therefore, if your description of planned standard services is the offering of corporate legal services, you may then start to explore certain markets and make decisions such as location and whether to start the firm with organic growth or acquire an existing law firm in the chosen location.

Once standard services are defined, you may use STSM SP 2.1, Establish Properties of Standard Services and Service Levels, to establish and maintain standard services. Depending on how many countries your firm chooses in which to expand, you may have multiple standard services and service levels to address the different needs of customers. This is especially true since the law varies from country to country. Considering the difference in cultures and laws of various countries, it is especially important when engaging in international expansion to define critical attributes of standard services and then to divide common and variable parts of standard services based on the needs of your clients in the particular countries you choose for expansion.

The last practice in the STSM process area is STSM SP 2.2, Establish Descriptions of Standard Services. This practice will assist you in establishing and maintaining descriptions of the law firm's defined standard services. This practice area is especially critical for international expansion. When the firm expands to the point where many remote employees will never meet each other, it is extremely important to document knowledge and processes in a manner that is effective and appropriate for all intended providers and users of the firm's standard services. Typical products include a description of the services to be provided and adjunct materials, such as ethics and compliance instructions for the legal staff, business development instructions, retainer templates, and other forms of legal documents. These instructions must be available to all in a location that encourages use by the full range of intended users. The perfect place for this material in a firm that is expanding globally is a well-done intranet with an organized document library and process asset library.

Using only two of the process areas in CMMI-SVC, you can see how the model provides practices essential to dealing with two important drivers in legal services. Of course, the rest of the model has practices drawn from many types of services that can improve other operations for legal services as well. Every CMMI model allows the organization to select which practices are most relevant for their business goals. With this example, I've shown how CMMI-SVC can be used proactively to meet two of the specific challenges to survival that law firms face today.

CMMI and Corporate Social Responsibility

By Barbara Neeb-Bruckner

Author Comments: In this essay, Barbara Neeb-Bruckner notes the possible leverage to be gained in using CMMI by corporations that are interested in their performance on social requirements. Barbara is currently a student of sustainable tourism management at Eberswalde University of Applied Sciences and was formerly a senior executive consultant at Wibas IT maturity services GmbH and CM consultant at Motorola A/S. She paints a promising case of "win-win" for those organizations that care about issues such as environmental sustainability by pointing out the foundation CMMI offers for considering social issues and governance. While Barbara considers the scenario for corporations, what she writes could also apply to nonprofit organizations, which are frequently committed to being responsible citizens in their communities as well. Barbara is writing her master's thesis on CMMI for Services and corporate responsibility in the tourism industry.

There are fundamental similarities between CMMI and Corporate Social Responsibility (CSR). These similarities light the way for these two approaches to work together and enhance the results experienced by organizations adopting them together.

What Is Corporate Social Responsibility?

While the term *Corporate Social Responsibility* (CSR) may seem to be relatively new to the corporate world, the concept itself has evolved over several decades. The various definitions of CSR range from the simplistic to the complex, and a collection of terms and ideas (some used interchangeably) are associated with it, including corporate sustainability, corporate citizenship, corporate social investment, the triple bottom line, socially responsible investment, business sustainability, and corporate governance.

The European Union defines CSR as a "concept whereby companies integrate social and environmental concerns in their business operations and in their interaction with their stakeholders on a voluntary basis."

This definition emphasizes that CSR is a voluntary concept that covers social and environmental issues; should not be separate from business strategy and operations; and influences how enterprises interact with their internal and external stakeholders (e.g., employees, customers, neighbors, nongovernmental organizations, and public authorities).

CSR is based on the ideas of sustainable development, which according to the Brundtland Report, also known as "Our Common Future" and published in 1987 by the United Nations World Commission on Environment and Development, comprise the environment, the economy, and the society. These three factors are often called the "three pillars of sustainability." In view of increasing global challenges, companies and their employees must find new, sustainable ways of operating their businesses in which ecological, social, and economic factors play equally important roles.

Similarities between CSR and CMMI

CSR and CMMI are both voluntary ventures that demand stakeholder involvement. CSR and CMMI must also be implemented "hand in hand" with business strategies and operations to be successful.

In 2007, Kori Udovicki of the United Nations Development Programme said of CSR, "Strategically and systematically integrated into their business, CSR helps companies to better address reputation risks, attract investors, improve relations with stakeholders, and become more competitive in mature markets." Replace "CSR" with "CMMI" and the statement is still true.

CSR and CMMI both target improvement, though each is driven by different motivations. CMMI, as a process improvement model, helps organizations to optimize their underlying processes to achieve more efficient results and a competitive advantage. Most businesses compete on either price, level of quality, or service as their competitive advantage. Can additional economic, environmental, or social advantages be used for competitive purposes as well, such as community support, better brand identity, reduced waste disposal costs, or better employee working conditions?

Today consumers, investors, governments, and employees have become more sophisticated and more aware of whether corporate behavior is "good" or not. In this new business environment, a company's reputation has become one of its most valuable assets. CSR has become one of the key components of corporate reputation. Further, CSR is increasingly being seen as an important and integral part of normal business operations.

How do you know where you're going if you don't know where you are? Before improving, organizations using both CMMI and CSR approaches require a detailed analysis of their current strengths and weaknesses before any improvement planning and implementation is done.

Depending on the organization's culture and the willingness of people to adopt changes, it may take time until the changes are adopted and institutionalized. For example, when project or service managers are adopting CMMI, it may be new to them to get commitment to the project or service plan from the team members or to explicitly plan stakeholder involvement. Likewise, when adopting CSR, it may be a new concept for an organization to buy and use environmentally friendly paper company-wide or for employees to replace business trips with videoconferencing.

The implementation of CMMI or CSR is not a one-time activity; it is a collection of ongoing activities to remedy existing process deficiencies and to respond to new legal, organizational, societal, or customer requirements.

The SEI recommends that those adopting CMMI "interpret the process areas using an in-depth knowledge of CMMI, their organization, the business environment, and the specific circumstances involved." The same recommendation applies to CSR. To be successful, CSR requirements must be mapped to the organization's needs.

These similarities are not surprising. Both CMMI and CSR are based on common sense and describe best practices that contribute to the economic, ecological, and social "well-being" of an entity, its members, and its surroundings. Of course, organizations have started improvement activities without having a specific model or concept to guide them; these activities were just based on experience and morals. Only later, once the CMMI model or CSR concept became known, did organizations discover that these improvement activities were consistent with these approaches.

Similar but Different

Despite the similarities described, some differences do exist between CMMI and CSR. CMMI is a well-defined quality model maintained by an organization (the SEI). CSR is a concept that is missing a standard definition. CMMI is applied to organizations only, whereas CSR applies also to nations or even the world.

You can attend a CMMI training course and earn a certificate that is recognized worldwide. CSR training is provided by multiple sources (e.g., the World Bank Institute, universities, business schools), but the courses are as heterogeneous as the CSR definitions.

Unlike CMMI, interpretations of CSR exist for particular industry sectors. The majority of these focus on CSR reporting, not on the implementation of CSR practices. The Global Reporting Initiative (GRI) has developed a reporting framework with supplements for certain sectors, such as automotive, telecommunications, and tour operations. (These are documented at www.globalreporting.org.) The Center for Ecology and Development (KATE) has developed material for CSR reporting in tourism and also suggests a "CSR Certification of Tourism Enterprises." (These are documented at www.kate-stuttgart.org.)

CMMI has well-described appraisal methods and qualification opportunities for independent appraisers. These sorts of opportunities have just started to develop with CSR. However, a generally accepted holistic CSR certification system does not yet exist. Some approaches already certify management systems that include elements of CSR. For example, the Eco Management and Audit Scheme (EMAS) enables European companies to validate their corporate environmental management. And the ISO 14001 standard has an environmental management system similar to EMAS that does not include environmental reporting. With the planned development of ISO 26000, a globally applicable framework for CSR is emerging, but it does not yet include certification.

Combining CMMI and CSR

Having identified similarities between CMMI and CSR, it seems obvious to consider bringing these approaches together. Would it be possible to implement CMMI and at the same time satisfy CSR requirements? Would sustainable behavior be promoted by having CMMI practices in place? The answer is "yes" to both questions.

CSR can profit from the structured and well-defined methods promoted by CMMI best practices. Clear communication structures, defined responsibilities, regular process monitoring, resolving noncompliances, and so on should be in place to ensure a successful implementation of CSR. The call for ecological, social, and economic development by CSR adds requirements to the organization's process asset library, such as the following:

* Additional stakeholders (e.g., public authorities, the organization's environmental manager)
* Measures (called "indicators" in CSR) to satisfy additional information needs (e.g., percentage of women in management positions, rate of fluctuation of employees, total environmental protection expenditures and investments by type, total weight of waste by type and disposal method)
* Additional risks (e.g., the risk of additional cost for meeting environmental demands)

Conversely, CMMI can benefit from CSR ideas by understanding that not all improvement programs provide direct shareholder value and increase the return on investment (ROI) in its traditional definition of looking at benefits compared to costs. For those who advocate for CSR, all businesses (public and private) have a fundamental responsibility to give back to their communities and our world. This is a moral value that cannot easily be measured, and the returns may not come in dollars and cents.

Business in the Community, a Prince's Charity in the United Kingdom, states it well: "Corporate responsibility has never been more important to ensure that the short-term pressures on business decisions are balanced against longer-term business value in the current recession. Responsible businesses must do the following:

* Have confidence in the products and services they are buying or selling
* Have internal controls in place to reduce risk and maximize opportunity
* Focus on long-term success (e.g., economic, social, environmental) rather than just short-term returns
* Apply key principles to ensure boards provide effective oversight of these responsibilities."

These statements of responsibility could be added to a CMMI brochure explaining the benefits of applying this model.

Critical Success Factors

The implementation of CMMI or CSR in an organization can be described as organizational development tasks with similar success factors, which include the following.

Senior Management Sponsorship

Research has shown that the most powerful initial step of process improvement is to build organizational support through strong senior management sponsorship. To gain senior management's sponsorship, it is often beneficial to expose them to the performance results experienced by others who have used CMMI to improve their processes or have performed CSR reporting.

Clear Direction

For all of those implementing either of these approaches or being affected by them, it must be clear why changes are being made, how they are planned to be implemented, and what the ultimate goal is.

Training and Coaching

Those implementing changes or being affected by them must have the required training and coaching.

Measurable Goals

Goals must be formulated in a way that ensures they are measurable so that everybody knows when the goals are achieved.

Analysis of Existing Processes

Existing processes must be analyzed, and improvement actions must be derived from identified weaknesses.

Iterative Process

Organizational development will fail if the organization implements too many changes at the same time. The organization needs sufficient time to adopt new structures, responsibilities, procedures, work products, and so forth.

A Practical Example: CMMI-SVC in Tourism

In the context of CMMI-SVC, sustainability includes considering environmental, socio-cultural, and economic issues when establishing, delivering, and managing services. The goal of responsible tourism is to change tourism for the long-term benefit of local people, tourists, the environment, and the tourism industry.

KATE supports the application of CSR principles to tourism. It has stated that CSR management in tourism has great potential if taken seriously. Only committed employees and local hosts who are convinced of the effects of their work, coupled with a healthy environment, will result in successful service providers and satisfied customers. Tourism is not an easy service to develop, manage, and deliver. Many jobs in tourism are characterized by seasonal employment, low wages, and long working hours. With regard to CSR, questions to be addressed include the following: How many jobs are created and under what conditions? Does tourism contribute to capacity building and does it increase the level of employment?

How can CMMI-SVC support or even promote CSR concepts for the tourism industry? The following examples in Table 6.2 demonstrate how using Global Sustainable Tourism Criteria (GSTC) and CMMI-SVC can support each other. GSTC are part of the response of the tourism community to the United Nations' Millennium Development Goals and are available at www.sustainabletourismcriteria.org/. Similar to CMMI-SVC, GSTC indicate what should be done, not how to do it.

TABLE 6.2 Examples of How GSTC and CMMI-SVC Support Each Other

GSTC	CMMI-SVC
Sustainability Management System	
The first step toward embracing sustainable business practices entails creating a sustainability management system (SMS) that includes transparent, documented policies and procedures, implementation, and communication plans. A well-written sustainability policy will define and clearly communicate organizational goals (A.1).	After implementing this model, a management system will be in place. CMMI-SVC demands organizational policies (GP 2.1), which is an ideal place to include management's expectations on sustainable behavior; expectations on electrical energy saving or waste treatment could be formulated as a policy. Project Planning (PP) should define all aspects of the effort, including stakeholder interaction, which is a common practice to describe in such a communication plan.
Employee Training	
All personnel receive periodic training regarding their role in the management of environmental, socio-cultural, health, and safety practices. A defined training program on the SMS aspects will enable employees to understand the company's goals and objectives (A.3).	The purpose of the generic practice "Train people" (GP 2.5) is to ensure that people have the necessary skills and expertise to perform or support the processes. The Organizational Training (OT) process area elaborates on the training program to support the organization's strategic business objectives in the most efficient way. Training on CSR theory and on environmental, socio-cultural, health, and safety practices could be included.

Continues

TABLE 6.2 Examples of How GSTC and CMMI-SVC Support Each Other *(Continued)*

GSTC	CMMI-SVC
Customer Satisfaction	
Customer satisfaction is measured and corrective action is taken where appropriate. Monitoring of customers' satisfaction with internal operations, relations with the community and other stakeholders, and the effectiveness of sustainable programs enables the company to make improvements on a regular basis (A.4).	Customer and end-user complaints are types of service incidents that are dealt with in the Incident Resolution and Prevention (IRP) process area. For example, an incident could be the bad foreign language skills of a guide, which may be reported by customers in an end-of-trip feedback form. The measurement of customer satisfaction will be covered by the Measurement and Analysis (MA) process area with the information derived and evaluated from the same end-of-trip feedback forms.
Fair Trade	
Local and fair-trade services and goods are purchased by the business, where available (B.3).	Criteria for selecting suppliers (SAM SP 1.2)—for example, hotels or restaurants—could involve fair-trade goods.
Code of Behavior	
The company follows established guidelines or a code of behavior for visits to culturally or historically sensitive sites, to minimize visitor impact and maximize enjoyment (C.1).	Education about local and indigenous people's cultural customs, values, and beliefs as well as appropriate verbal and nonverbal behavior can be included in the training (GP 2.5, OT) of guides. Guidelines for Responsible Travel—for example, regarding dress code or photography at the destination—could be included in the service agreements (SD SP 1.2) between a tour operator and customers.
Purchasing Policy	
Environmentally friendly products for building materials, capital goods, food, and consumables are favored (D.1.1).	This can be included in a management policy and dealt with in more detail in the Supplier Agreement Management (SAM) process area.

What's Next?

With an increasing focus on CSR and related concepts, such as "greening" the supply chain and running "cleaner" operations, companies are examining every phase of their product or service lifecycle. Further research is required to understand where and to what extent CSR can benefit from CMMI and vice versa.

It would be appropriate to consider the structured approach of CMMI for process improvement, training, and appraisals when planning a CSR initiative. The implementation of CSR in an organization could profit from CMMI's generic practices, which support the institutionalization of new or changed processes. CMMI's Requirements Management (REQM) process area can help to bring new CSR requirements into an organization in a controlled way, and the Measurement and Analysis (MA) process area can help to find, collect, and analyze measurement data required for CSR. In general, existing services could be replaced by more sustainable services using the Service System Transition (SST) process area. Benchmarking CSR would be easier if organizations were also CMMI-compliant.

Expanding the Universe of CMMI with the CMMI for Services Constellation

By Hal Wilson

Author Comments: Hal Wilson was the sponsor of the volunteer industry team that created the CMMI for Services model. In this essay, he gives some of the history that led to the concept of CMMI constellations, describes the motivations that caused Northrop Grumman to invite competitors to collaborate on this model, delineates the surprising range of possible applications for CMMI-SVC, and indicates how CMMI-SVC will be used at his company.

Why Did We Ever Attempt to Create CMMI-SVC?

When the CMMI-SE/SW model was created, the initial emphasis naturally was on creating a more complete and valuable development model to replace separate software and systems engineering models. But with an eye to the future, the process areas were kept generic to embrace all kinds of organizations that might want to use CMMI, and the CMMI Steering Group created a concept of operations that included a mechanism to propose additions to CMMI. However, at that time, no one really understood the complications that would be created when additions of new areas of interest were attempted.

When the addition of security and safety to the CMMI Framework was first attempted, it became clear that some portions of CMMI-SE/SW contained embedded presumptions that the model would be used only for development, primarily because of the development legacy from which CMMI-SE/SW was created. The Steering Group asked the late Roger Bate, the architect of CMMI, to address the problem. I was fortunate to be asked to participate with Roger on the effort. After some debate, we came up with the current *constellation* architecture, which recognized that some process areas contained in the CMMI Framework were the base upon which all models could be built. We designated those as part of the CMMI Model Framework (CMF). Then we realized that some process areas would really be better focused on their specific domains. We chose to use the term *constellation* because it wasn't already being used by modelers and would avoid confusion and presumption that comes when a more commonly used term is applied to a new concept. While we were thinking on the subject, Roger naturally began to consider how the new architecture could be applied. We immediately began to think of applications such as maintenance and support, network management, and service delivery in general. The Constellation Architecture was fleshed out by an architecture team led by Roger Bate and approved by the CMMI Steering Group, and adding new constellations went onto the back burner.

Soon afterward, several events occurred that influenced my role in the eventual creation of CMMI for Services (CMMI-SVC). Within Northrop Grumman, we were receiving pressure from some of our DoD customers who managed service delivery contracts to perform CMMI appraisal on their contracts. Unfortunately, the only model available, CMMI-DEV, required appraising against the engineering process areas, which were development-centric. After much experimentation, we concluded that the organization would have to use some "fast and loose" process definitions to make service delivery look enough like development processes. Therefore, we were unable to provide a maturity level appraisal against the full CMMI-DEV model. In exploring this situation with other DoD contractors, we found that many of our competitors among the larger companies had experienced the same situation and opted not to stretch the definitions of development to qualify a service-delivery-oriented set of processes to qualify for a development appraisal. We got feedback that two companies had completed appraisals for services using the development model and had achieved appraisal ratings for CMMI-DEV. However, that led to what could be considered an undesirable situation, because the service organizations now had credentials that identified them as mature developers with software and systems engineering capabilities even though they didn't actually do development. To me, having been involved on the CMMI Steering Group from its inception and having a strong personal commitment to protecting the CMMI benchmark, such a result placed the CMMI-DEV benchmark in jeopardy, especially when an organization that does not perform development receives a credential that asserts that it is mature and qualified against a development model. At that point, I was strongly committed to pursuing and resolving this problem and made a proposal to the CMMI Steering Group to get approval to begin development of a Services constellation.

The Path to Success Isn't Always Straightforward

After we received approval to proceed with Services constellation development, the development team found very strong and broad-based support among the service practitioners who represented multiple service disciplines in an international setting. While not many of the smaller companies could afford to participate in the generation of the new model content, the team got numerous offers to comment and review as development of the model went forward. The development team was relatively small and active, but they represented a wide-ranging set of specialties and interests in the service delivery arena. In addition, they were supported by a large cadre of interested reviewers who brought an even wider spectrum of perspectives.

I was particularly encouraged when we did a review of the service domains that the development team represented. The initial perception by some within the sponsor community was that the team was primarily IT-services-oriented. In fact, the 13-member development team was very diverse in its experience, with certain individuals representing more than one domain because of their extensive experience. In addition, the team had a review group of more than 50 organizations that regularly provided input to multiple drafts. The performed pilots also addressed multiple domains and provided solid feedback on the ability of the new model to be applied and appraised. As we were proceeding through the review cycle, we were asked to provide the background of the team with respect to the types of service disciplines they supported. I was amazed when a poll of the developers showed that members had experience in 76 service areas within 20 major markets.

Protecting the CMMI Legacy and Maintaining Commonality and Consistency

One of the immediate areas of interest for the larger companies that had an active base in CMMI-DEV within their development organizations was the ability to apply their organizational and general management and support practices as much as possible in the Services constellation. The Services team adopted that philosophy from the outset and needed little urging from Roger Bate to consider the CMMI Model Framework as the base from which to proceed. They managed to keep that commitment through the entire development so that organizations with a CMMI-DEV heritage have a great legacy that they can apply to the Organizational, Management, and Support process areas.

The team realized from the outset that there were models related to the IT environment that were effective but very IT-focused. The team decided to maintain the generic structure and focus of CMMI and use the informative material only to cite detailed examples that might include specific areas of interest. Because the team did not want to create "yet another model" for the early adopters of good IT processes, they incorporated references to existing models into the informative material so that practitioners could continue to use those practices and still get the benefit of the broader perspective of good management, organizational, and support processes included in the CMF.

Along the way to completion of CMMI-SVC, there were questions about how well the constellation addressed small service companies, particularly since smaller companies weren't involved in the development team. Encouraged by the DoD sponsor organization, the development team gained the support of the Professional Services Council on the expert reviewing team. Other champions of additional industries and organization sizes were added as participants in the CMMI-SVC Advisory Group. They brought an additional level of service diversity to the review process and added value to CMMI-SVC.

In addition, the team took their responsibility seriously and made a point of keeping impacts to the CMMI Model Framework and the number of service-specific process areas to a minimum. They realized early in their work that a cost was associated with being too prolific in creating process areas that are unique to a constellation. As a result, they actually reduced the final number of process areas as they went from their first draft to the final version. They deserve a lot of credit for keeping the value to the service delivery practitioners in the forefront of their deliberations.

One of the challenges faced by the service development team during the creation of CMMI-SVC was to gather and then maintain the appropriate support base as issues were raised and tough decisions had to be made. Particularly encouraging to me as the initial sponsor of the CMMI-SVC effort was the long-term dedication and commitment that the development team and their reviewer community demonstrated during the several years of activity, particularly when the Steering Group delayed CMMI-SVC while CMMI-ACQ was being completed and moved through the SEI production process. The team was able to keep their focus and, by communicating with the services community across the globe, maintained the involvement of their support group. As an indication of their effectiveness, there were more than 18,000 downloads of the CMMI-SVC review drafts by individuals interested in the services model before its release. I am particularly grateful to the development team for maintaining their incredible commitment even when faced with the challenges and delays they had to experience, even though they didn't create most of them.

Northrop Grumman's Plans for Using CMMI-SVC

It would be natural to ask whether Northrop Grumman, which proposed and led the development of the Services constellation, will actually use it now that it is completed. The answer is easy. While leading the team that was developing CMMI-SVC, a Northrop Grumman organization participated in the piloting of CMMI-SVC and demonstrated for ourselves and hopefully for the development team that there was value in using the CMMI-SVC model. The pilot appraisal showed that the new model did indeed solve the very problems that kept us from adopting CMMI-DEV for our services projects. That being said, we are also working toward being among the first CMMI-SVC appraisal activities when the formal appraisal window opens at the end of August 2009. We have several areas in our services business base that are anxious to proceed with an appraisal. Even with the economic problems that all companies are experiencing, we still plan to get started with one or more appraisals before the end of 2009.

Northrop Grumman has more CMMI maturity level 5 appraisals than any other company in the world (15 as of June 2009), but we don't anticipate that we'll achieve high maturity status in services for some time. Our primary goal in moving forward with CMMI-SVC is to improve our service delivery performance. In the process of improving, we will consider the business case for moving toward higher maturity. We obviously are convinced that high maturity pays off for development organizations, but we're not sure where the payoff sweet spot will be for services. The programs are often smaller and of shorter duration, making the benefits after achievement of higher maturity less obvious.

Regardless, we're convinced that the discipline that comes with using CMMI across our organizations and the value of getting new programs started right will make the adoption of CMMI-SVC a positive step in improving service to our customers and financial performance to our shareholders.

PART TWO

Generic Goals and Generic Practices, and the Process Areas

GENERIC GOALS AND GENERIC PRACTICES

This section describes in detail all the generic goals and generic practices of CMMI—model components that directly address process institutionalization. Also included are their associated subpractices, notes, examples, references, and generic practice elaborations.

Generic practice elaborations appear after generic practices to show how these practices should uniquely be applied to various process areas. Not all process areas are represented, since application of generic practices to process areas sometimes needs no explanation and other times requires explanation or examples.

Applying Generic Practices

Generic practices are components that are common to all process areas. Think of generic practices as reminders. They serve the purpose of reminding you to do things right and are expected model components.

For example, when you are achieving the specific goals of the Configuration Management process area, you are establishing and maintaining the integrity of work products using configuration identification, configuration control, configuration status accounting, and configuration audits. One of the generic practices that applies to the Configuration Management process area is "Establish and maintain an organizational policy for the planning and performing the process." (GP 2.2). When applied to this process area, this generic practice reminds you to establish a policy for conducting configuration management activities in the organization.

When you are satisfying the specific goals of the Organizational Training process area, you are developing the skills and knowledge of people in your organization so that they can perform their roles effectively and efficiently. When applying the generic practice "Establish and maintain the plan for performing the process." (GP 2.2) to the Organizational Training process area, this generic practice reminds you to plan the activities involved in developing the skills and knowledge of people in the organization.

Generic Goals and Generic Practices

Below are all of the generic goals and generic practices contained in the CMMI-SVC model. The generic goals are organized in numerical order, GG 1 through GG 5. The generic practices are also organized in numerical order under the generic goal they support.

GG 1 ACHIEVE SPECIFIC GOALS

The process supports and enables achievement of the specific goals of the process area by transforming identifiable input work products to produce identifiable output work products.

GP 1.1 PERFORM SPECIFIC PRACTICES

Perform the specific practices of the process area to develop work products and provide services to achieve the specific goals of the process area.

The purpose of this generic practice is to produce the work products and deliver the services that are expected by performing the process. These practices may be done informally without following a documented process description or plan. The rigor with which these practices are performed depends on the individuals managing and performing the work and may vary considerably.

GG 2 INSTITUTIONALIZE A MANAGED PROCESS

The process is institutionalized as a managed process.

GP 2.1 ESTABLISH AN ORGANIZATIONAL POLICY

Establish and maintain an organizational policy for planning and performing the process.

The purpose of this generic practice is to define the organizational expectations for the process and make these expectations visible to those in the organization who are affected. In general, senior management is responsible for establishing and communicating guiding principles, direction, and expectations for the organization.

Not all direction from senior management will bear the label "policy." The existence of appropriate organizational direction is the expectation of this generic practice, regardless of what it is called or how it is imparted.

CAR Elaboration

This policy establishes organizational expectations for identifying and systematically addressing root causes of defects and other problems.

CM Elaboration

This policy establishes organizational expectations for establishing and maintaining baselines, tracking and controlling changes to work products (under configuration management), and establishing and maintaining integrity of the baselines. This policy must address authorizing and implementing emergency changes.

DAR Elaboration

This policy establishes organizational expectations for selectively analyzing possible decisions using a formal evaluation process that evaluates identified alternatives against established criteria. The policy should also provide guidance on which decisions require a formal evaluation process.

IPM Elaboration

This policy establishes organizational expectations for establishing and maintaining the project's defined process from project startup through the life of the project, using the project's defined process in managing the project, and coordinating and collaborating with relevant stakeholders.

IRP Elaboration

This policy establishes organizational expectations for establishing an approach to incident resolution and prevention; identifying, controlling, and addressing incidents; and for selected incidents, determining workarounds or addressing underlying causes.

MA Elaboration

This policy establishes organizational expectations for providing measurement results and for aligning measurement objectives and activities with identified information needs and objectives.

OID Elaboration

This policy establishes organizational expectations for identifying and deploying process and technology improvements that contribute to meeting quality and process-performance objectives.

OPD Elaboration

This policy establishes organizational expectations for establishing and maintaining a set of standard processes for use by the organization, making organizational process assets available across the organization, and establishing rules and guidelines for integrated teams.

OPF Elaboration

This policy establishes organizational expectations for determining process improvement opportunities for the processes being used and for planning, implementing, and deploying process improvements across the organization.

OPP Elaboration

This policy establishes organizational expectations for establishing and maintaining process-performance baselines for the organization's set of standard processes.

OT Elaboration

This policy establishes organizational expectations for identifying the strategic training needs of the organization and providing that training.

PMC Elaboration

This policy establishes organizational expectations for monitoring performance against the project plan and managing corrective action to closure when actual performance or results deviate significantly from the plan.

PP Elaboration

This policy establishes organizational expectations for estimating planning parameters, making internal and external commitments, and developing the plan for managing the project.

PPQA Elaboration

This policy establishes organizational expectations for objectively evaluating whether processes and associated work products adhere to applicable process descriptions, standards, and procedures and ensuring that noncompliance is addressed.

This policy also establishes organizational expectations for process and product quality assurance being in place for all projects. Process and product quality assurance must possess sufficient independence from project management to provide objectivity in identifying and reporting noncompliance issues.

QPM Elaboration

This policy establishes organizational expectations for quantitatively managing the project using quality and process-performance objectives and statistically managing selected subprocesses within the project's defined process.

REQM Elaboration

This policy establishes organizational expectations for managing requirements and identifying inconsistencies between the requirements and project plans and work products.

RSKM Elaboration

This policy establishes organizational expectations for defining a risk management strategy and identifying, analyzing, and mitigating risks.

SAM Elaboration

This policy establishes organizational expectations for establishing, maintaining, and satisfying supplier agreements.

SCON Elaboration

This policy establishes organizational expectations for establishing a service continuity plan that enables resumption of key services following a significant disruption in service delivery, providing training in the execution of the plan, and verifying and validating the plan.

SD Elaboration

This policy establishes organizational expectations for defining a service delivery approach, establishing service agreements, processing service requests, and delivering services.

SSD Elaboration

This policy establishes organizational expectations for the following:

- Collecting stakeholder needs, formulating service and service system component requirements, and analyzing and validating those requirements
- Performing the iterative cycle in which service system solutions are selected, service system and service system component designs are developed, interface compatibility is managed, service system designs are implemented, and service system components are integrated
- Establishing and maintaining verification and validation methods, procedures, criteria, and environments; performing peer reviews; and verifying selected work products.

SSD Addition

SST Elaboration

This policy establishes organizational expectations for planning, implementing, and managing the transition of service system components into the delivery environment.

STSM Elaboration

This policy establishes organizational expectations for establishing and maintaining a set of standard services for use by the organization and making standard service descriptions available across the organization.

GP 2.2 PLAN THE PROCESS

Establish and maintain the plan for performing the process.

The purpose of this generic practice is to determine what is needed to perform the process and to achieve the established objectives, to prepare a plan for performing the process, to prepare a process description, and to get agreement on the plan from relevant stakeholders.

The practical implications of applying a generic practice vary for each process area. For example, the planning described by this generic practice as applied to the Project Monitoring and Control process area may be carried out in full by the processes associated with the Project Planning process area. However, this generic practice, when applied to the Project Planning process area, sets an expectation that the project planning process itself be planned. Therefore, this generic practice may either reinforce expectations set elsewhere in CMMI or set new expectations that should be addressed.

Refer to the Project Planning process area for more information about developing a project plan.

Establishing a plan includes documenting the plan and a process description. Maintaining the plan includes updating it to reflect corrective actions or changes in requirements or objectives.

The plan for performing the process typically includes the following:

- Process description
- Standards and requirements for the work products and services of the process
- Specific objectives for the performance of the process (e.g., quality, time scale, cycle time, use of resources)

- Dependencies among the activities, work products, and services of the process
- Resources (e.g., funding, people, tools) needed to perform the process
- Assignment of responsibility and authority
- Training needed for performing and supporting the process
- Work products to be controlled and the level of control to be applied
- Measurement requirements to provide insight into the performance of the process, its work products, and its services
- Involvement of identified stakeholders
- Activities for monitoring and controlling the process
- Objective evaluation activities of the process
- Management review activities for the process and the work products

Subpractices

1. Define and document the plan for performing the process.
   This plan may be a stand-alone document, embedded in a more comprehensive document, or distributed across multiple documents. In the case of the plan being distributed across multiple documents, ensure that a coherent picture of who does what is preserved. Documents may be hardcopy or softcopy.

2. Define and document the process description.
   The process description, which includes relevant standards and procedures, may be included as part of the plan for performing the process or may be included in the plan by reference.

3. Review the plan with relevant stakeholders and get their agreement.
   This review of the plan includes reviewing that the planned process satisfies the applicable policies, plans, requirements, and standards to provide assurance to relevant stakeholders.

4. Revise the plan as necessary.

CAM Elaboration

This plan for performing the capacity and availability management process can be included in (or referenced by) the project plan, which is described in the Project Planning process area.

CAR Elaboration

This plan for performing the causal analysis and resolution process can be included in (or referenced by) the project plan, which is described in the Project Planning process area. This plan differs from the action proposals and associated action items described in several specific practices in this process area. The plan called for in this generic practice addresses the project's overall causal analysis and resolution process (perhaps tailored from a standard process maintained by the organization). In contrast, the process action proposals and associated action items address the activities needed to remove a specific root cause under study.

CM Elaboration

This plan for performing the configuration management process can be included in (or referenced by) the project plan, which is described in the Project Planning process area.

DAR Elaboration

This plan for performing the decision analysis and resolution process can be included in (or referenced by) the project plan, which is described in the Project Planning process area.

IPM Elaboration

This plan for performing the integrated project management process unites the planning for the project planning and monitor and control processes. The planning for performing the planning-related practices in Integrated Project Management is addressed as part of planning the project planning process. This plan for performing the monitor-and-control-related practices in Integrated Project Management can be included in (or referenced by) the project plan, which is described in the Project Planning process area.

Refer to Table 7.1 (p. 220) in Generic Goals and Generic Practices for more information about the relationship between generic practice 2.2 and project planning processes.

IRP Elaboration

This plan for performing the incident resolution and prevention process can be included in (or referenced by) the project plan, which is described in the Project Planning process area. This plan typically is based on an estimation of the volume and type of service incidents.

MA Elaboration

This plan for performing the measurement and analysis process can be included in (or referenced by) the project plan, which is described in the Project Planning process area.

OID Elaboration

This plan for performing the organizational innovation and deployment process differs from the deployment plans described in a specific practice in this process area. The plan called for in this generic practice addresses the comprehensive planning for all of the specific practices in this process area, from collecting and analyzing improvement proposals through measuring improvement effects. In contrast, the deployment plans called for in the specific practices of this process area address the planning needed for the deployment of individual process and technology improvements.

OPD Elaboration

This plan for performing the organizational process definition process can be part of (or referenced by) the organization's process improvement plan.

OPF Elaboration

This plan for performing the organizational process focus process, which is often called "the process improvement plan," differs from the process action plans described in specific practices in this process area. The plan called for in this generic practice addresses the comprehensive planning for all of the specific practices in this process area, from establishing organizational process needs through incorporating process-related experiences into organizational process assets.

OPP Elaboration

This plan for performing the organizational process-performance process can be included in (or referenced by) the organization's process improvement plan, which is described in the Organizational Process Focus process area. Or it may be documented in a separate plan that describes only the plan for the organizational process-performance process.

OT Elaboration

This plan for performing the organizational training process differs from the tactical plan for organizational training described in a specific practice in this process area. The plan called for in this generic practice addresses the comprehensive planning for all of the specific practices in this process area, from establishing strategic training needs through assessing the effectiveness of organizational training.

In contrast, the organizational training tactical plan called for in the specific practice of this process area addresses the periodic planning for the delivery of individual training offerings.

PMC Elaboration

This plan for performing the project monitoring and control process can be part of (or referenced by) the project plan, as described in the Project Planning process area.

PP Elaboration

Refer to Table 7.1 (p. 220) in Generic Goals and Generic Practices for more information about the relationship between generic practice 2.2 and the Project Planning process area.

PPQA Elaboration

Examples of resources provided include the following tools:
- Evaluation tools
- Noncompliance tracking tools

QPM Elaboration

This plan for performing the quantitative project management process can be included in (or referenced by) the project plan, which is described in the Project Planning process area.

REQM Elaboration

This plan for performing the requirements management process can be part of (or referenced by) the project plan as described in the Project Planning process area.

RSKM Elaboration

This plan for performing the risk management process can be included in (or referenced by) the project plan, which is described in the Project Planning process area. The plan called for in this generic practice addresses the comprehensive planning for all of the specific practices in this process area. In particular, this plan provides the overall approach for risk mitigation but is distinct from mitigation plans (including contingency plans) for specific risks. In contrast, the risk mitigation plans called for in the specific practices of this process area addresses more focused items, such as the levels that trigger risk-handling activities.

SAM Elaboration

Portions of this plan for performing the supplier agreement management process can be part of (or referenced by) the project plan as described in the Project Planning process area. Often, however, some portion of the plan resides outside of the project with a group such as contract management.

SCON Elaboration

This plan for performing the service continuity process can be included in (or referenced by) the project plan, which is described in the Project Planning process area. Alternatively, this plan can be included as part of a broader business continuity plan maintained at the organizational level.

In either case, the plan for performing the service continuity process differs from the service continuity plans described in a specific practice in this process area. The plan called for in this generic practice addresses the comprehensive planning for all of the specific practices in this process area, from identifying and prioritizing essential functions through analyzing results of verification and validation. In contrast, the service continuity plans called for in one of the specific practices of this process area address how to restore key services following a significant disruption in service delivery.

SD Elaboration

This plan for performing the service delivery process can be included in (or referenced by) the project plan, which is described in the Project Planning process area.

SSD Elaboration

This plan for performing the service system development process can be part of (or referenced by) the project plan as described in the Project Planning process area.

SST Elaboration

Overall planning for service system transition can be included in (or referenced by) the project plan, which is described in the Project Planning process area. In addition, planning associated with the transition of a particular service system is typically addressed in a service system transition plan.

This plan for performing the service system transition process differs from the plans for service system transition described in a specific practice in this process area. The plan called for in this generic practice addresses the comprehensive planning for all of the specific practices in this process area, from analyzing service system transition needs through assessing and controlling the impacts of the transition. In contrast, the service system transition plans called for in the specific practice of this process area address planning for specific transitions of the service system.

STSM Elaboration

This plan for performing the strategic service management process differs from the plans for standard services described in the specific practices of this process area. The plan called for in this generic practice addresses comprehensive planning for all the specific practices in the process area.

GP 2.3 PROVIDE RESOURCES

Provide adequate resources for performing the process, developing the work products, and providing the services of the process.

The purpose of this generic practice is to ensure that the resources necessary to perform the process as defined by the plan are available when they are needed. Resources include adequate funding, appropriate physical facilities, skilled people, and appropriate tools.

The interpretation of the term "adequate" depends on many factors and can change over time. Inadequate resources may be addressed by increasing resources or by removing requirements, constraints, and commitments.

CAM Elaboration

> Examples of resources provided include the following:
> - Remote analysis tools
> - Monitoring tools

CAR Elaboration

> Examples of resources provided include the following:
> - Database systems
> - Process modeling tools
> - Statistical analysis packages
> - Methods and analysis techniques (e.g., Ishikawa or fishbone diagrams, Pareto analysis, histograms, process capability studies, control charts)

CM Elaboration

> Examples of resources provided include the following:
> - Configuration management tools
> - Data management tools
> - Archiving and reproduction tools
> - Database programs

DAR Elaboration

> Examples of resources provided include the following:
> - Simulators and modeling tools
> - Prototyping tools
> - Tools for conducting surveys

IPM Elaboration

> Examples of resources provided include the following:
> - Problem tracking and reporting packages
> - Groupware
> - Video conferencing
> - Integrated decision databases
> - Integrated product support environments

IRP Elaboration

> Examples of resources provided include the following:
> - Help desk tools
> - Remote analysis tools
> - Automated monitoring tools
> - Incident management systems

MA Elaboration

Measurement personnel may be employed full time or part time. A measurement group may or may not exist to support measurement activities across multiple projects.

> Examples of resources provided include the following:
> - Statistical packages
> - Packages that support data collection over networks

OID Elaboration

Examples of resources provided include the following:
- Simulation packages
- Prototyping tools
- Statistical packages
- Dynamic systems modeling
- Subscriptions to online technology databases and publications
- Process modeling tools

OPD Elaboration

A process group typically manages organizational process definition activities. This group typically is staffed by a core of professionals whose primary responsibility is coordinating organizational process improvement. This group is supported by process owners and people with expertise in various disciplines such as the following:

- Project management
- The appropriate engineering disciplines
- Configuration management
- Quality assurance

Examples of resources provided include the following:
- Database management systems
- Process modeling tools
- Web page builders and browsers

OPF Elaboration

Examples of resources provided include the following:
- Database management systems
- Process improvement tools
- Web page builders and browsers
- Groupware
- Quality-improvement tools (e.g., cause-and-effect diagrams, affinity diagrams, Pareto charts)

OPP Elaboration

Special expertise in statistics and statistical process control may be needed to establish process-performance baselines for the organization's set of standard processes.

> Examples of resources provided include the following:
> - Database management systems
> - System dynamics models
> - Process modeling tools
> - Statistical analysis packages
> - Problem-tracking packages

OT Elaboration

> Examples of resources provided include the following:
> - Subject matter experts
> - Curriculum designers
> - Instructional designers
> - Instructors
> - Training administrators

Special facilities may be required for training. When necessary, the facilities required for the activities in the Organizational Training process area are developed or purchased.

> Examples of resources provided include the following:
> - Instruments for analyzing training needs
> - Workstations to be used for training
> - Instructional design tools
> - Packages for developing presentation materials

PMC Elaboration

> Examples of resources provided include the following:
> - Cost tracking systems
> - Effort reporting systems
> - Action item tracking systems
> - Project management and scheduling programs

PP Elaboration

Special expertise, equipment, and facilities in project planning may be required. Special expertise in project planning may include the following:

- Experienced estimators
- Schedulers
- Technical experts in applicable areas (e.g., product domain, technology)

Examples of resources provided include the following:
- Spreadsheet programs
- Estimating models
- Project planning and scheduling packages

PPQA Elaboration

Examples of resources provided include the following:
- Evaluation tools
- Noncompliance tracking tools

OPP Elaboration

Special expertise in statistics and statistical process control may be needed to define the techniques for statistical management of selected subprocesses, but staff will use the tools and techniques to perform statistical management. Special expertise in statistics may also be needed for analyzing and interpreting the measures resulting from statistical management.

Examples of resources provided include the following:
- System dynamics models
- Automated test-coverage analyzers
- Statistical process and quality control packages
- Statistical analysis packages

REQM Elaboration

Examples of resources provided include the following:
- Requirements tracking tools
- Traceability tools

RSKM Elaboration

Examples of resources provided include the following:
- Risk management databases
- Risk mitigation tools
- Prototyping tools
- Modeling and simulation tools

SAM Elaboration

Examples of resources provided include the following:
- Preferred supplier lists
- Requirements tracking programs
- Project management and scheduling programs

SCON Elaboration

Service continuity relies on obtaining special as well as adequate resources. Remote locations, secure networks, facilities, and equipment should be identified, procured, and prepared in advance to ensure continued service system operations in the event of a significant disruption. Special training facilities and related resources may be needed to prepare those responsible for implementing the service continuity plan. Finally, special testing facilities, equipment, and tools may need to be developed or purchased for use in verifying and validating service continuity preparations.

Examples of resources provided include the following:
- Backup communication mechanisms and networks
- File backup and restore utilities
- Workstations to be used for training
- Modeling and simulation tools
- Test-management tools

SD Elaboration

Service delivery requires the operation of an appropriate service system that includes a trained staff, infrastructure, tools, processes, consumables, and other resources. In addition, the operation of the service system imposes a continuing need for adequate resources.

For example, over time components of the service system may need to be upgraded, replaced, or retired; service delivery staff may need to be retrained, augmented, rotated, or reduced; and consumables may need to be replenished to ensure that the service is delivered in accordance with service agreements.

Some of the components of the service system may need to be developed or purchased, and this constraint may require obtaining resources as described in the Service System Development and Supplier Agreement Management process areas.

Examples of resources provided include the following:
- Request management systems
- Automated monitoring tools

SSD Elaboration

Examples of resources provided include the following:
- Requirements specification tools
- Simulation and modeling tools
- Prototyping tools
- Scenario definition and tracking tools
- Design specification tools
- Fabrication and assembly tools
- Test management tools
- Test case generation tools
- Monitoring tools
- Test facilities and environments

SSD ADDITION

SST Elaboration

Examples of resources provided include the following:
- Transition support staff
- Installation and deployment tools
- Mechanisms for back out and restore

STSM Elaboration

Senior managers, strategic planners, product managers, product line managers, or portfolio managers typically manage strategic service management practices.

Examples of resources provided include the following:
• Sources of data on strategic needs and capabilities
• Document management or configuration management tools
• Product management techniques

GP 2.4 ASSIGN RESPONSIBILITY

Assign responsibility and authority for performing the process, developing the work products, and providing the services of the process.

The purpose of this generic practice is to ensure that there is accountability for performing the process and achieving the specified results throughout the life of the process. The people assigned must have the appropriate authority to perform the assigned responsibilities.

Responsibility can be assigned using detailed job descriptions or in living documents, such as the plan for performing the process. Dynamic assignment of responsibility is another legitimate way to perform this generic practice, as long as the assignment and acceptance of responsibility are ensured throughout the life of the process.

Subpractices

1. Assign overall responsibility and authority for performing the process.
2. Assign responsibility and authority for performing the specific tasks of the process.
3. Confirm that the people assigned to the responsibilities and authorities understand and accept them.

IRP Elaboration

Responsibility is assigned both for first-tier service incident handling (e.g., by a help desk) and for second-tier handling (e.g., by support groups organized by service, platform, function, or technology).

PPQA Elaboration

Responsibility is assigned to those who can perform process and product quality assurance evaluations with sufficient independence and objectivity to guard against subjectivity or bias.

SCON Elaboration

Responsibility is assigned to a backup management team for the organization (or project) to take over management responsibilities in the event of a significant disruption.

SD Elaboration

Responsibility is assigned for establishing service agreements, accepting service requests, communicating status information (e.g., by a help desk), operating and maintaining the service system, processing service requests, and resolving service incidents (e.g., by support groups organized by service, platform, function, or technology).

SST Elaboration

Responsibility is assigned for planning, implementing, and managing the transition. In addition, stakeholder notification activities are explicitly assigned to ensure open communication and buy-in. Rollback and back-out assignments are made in the event that the transition is not successful.

GP 2.5 TRAIN PEOPLE

Train the people performing or supporting the process as needed.

The purpose of this generic practice is to ensure that people have the necessary skills and expertise to perform or support the process.

Appropriate training is provided to those who will be performing the work. Overview training is provided to orient people who interact with those performing the work.

> Examples of methods for providing training include self study; self-directed training; self-paced, programmed instruction; formalized on-the-job training; mentoring; and formal and classroom training.

Training supports the successful performance of the process by establishing a common understanding of the process and by imparting the skills and knowledge needed to perform the process.

Refer to the Organizational Training process area for more information about developing skills and knowledge of people so they can perform their roles effectively and efficiently.

CAM Elaboration

> Examples of training topics include the following:
> - Roles, responsibilities, and authority of the capacity and availability management staff
> - Capacity and availability management standards, procedures, and methods

CAR Elaboration

> Examples of training topics include the following:
> - Quality management methods (e.g., root cause analysis)

CM Elaboration

> Examples of training topics include the following:
> - Roles, responsibilities, and authority of the configuration management staff
> - Configuration management standards, procedures, and methods
> - Configuration library system

DAR Elaboration

> Examples of training topics include the following:
> - Formal decision analysis
> - Methods for evaluating alternative solutions against criteria

IPM Elaboration

> Examples of training topics include the following:
> - Tailoring the organization's set of standard processes to meet the needs of the project
> - Procedures for managing the project based on the project's defined process
> - Using the organization's measurement repository
> - Using organizational process assets
> - Integration management
> - Intergroup coordination
> - Group problem solving

IRP Elaboration

Examples of training topics include the following:
- Service incident criteria
- Interacting with those who report service incidents and those who are affected by them
- Incident management system
- Analysis techniques (e.g., Ishikawa or fishbone diagrams, Pareto analysis, histograms)

MA Elaboration

Examples of training topics include the following:
- Statistical techniques
- Data collection, analysis, and reporting processes
- Development of goal-related measurements (e.g., Goal Question Metric)

OID Elaboration

Examples of training topics include the following:
- Planning, designing, and conducting pilots
- Cost/benefit analysis
- Technology transition
- Change management

OPD Elaboration

Examples of training topics include the following:
- CMMI and other process and process improvement reference models
- Planning, managing, and monitoring processes
- Process modeling and definition
- Developing a tailorable standard process
- Developing work environment standards
- Ergonomics

OPF Elaboration

> Examples of training topics include the following:
> - CMMI and other process improvement reference models
> - Planning and managing process improvement
> - Tools, methods, and analysis techniques
> - Process modeling
> - Facilitation techniques
> - Change management

OPP Elaboration

> Examples of training topics include the following:
> - Process and process improvement modeling
> - Quantitative and statistical methods (e.g., estimating models, Pareto analysis, control charts)

OT Elaboration

Refer to Table 7.1 (p. 220) in Generic Goals and Generic Practices for more information about the relationship between generic practice 2.5 and the Organizational Training process area.

> Examples of training topics include the following:
> - Knowledge and skills needs analysis
> - Instructional design
> - Instruction techniques (e.g., train the trainer)
> - Refresher training on subject matter

PMC Elaboration

> Examples of training topics include the following:
> - Project monitoring and control
> - Risk management
> - Data management

PP Elaboration

Examples of training topics include the following:
- Estimating
- Budgeting
- Negotiating
- Risk identification and analysis
- Data management
- Planning
- Scheduling

PPQA Elaboration

Examples of training topics include the following:
- Application domain
- Customer relations
- Process descriptions, standards, procedures, and methods for the project
- Quality assurance objectives, process descriptions, standards, procedures, methods, and tools

QPM Elaboration

Examples of training topics include the following:
- Process modeling and analysis
- Process measurement data selection, definition, and collection

REQM Elaboration

Examples of training topics include the following:
- Application domain
- Requirements definition, analysis, review, and management
- Requirements management tools
- Configuration management
- Negotiation and conflict resolution

RSKM Elaboration

Examples of training topics include the following:
- Risk management concepts and activities (e.g., risk identification, evaluation, monitoring, mitigation)
- Measure selection for risk mitigation

SAM Elaboration

Examples of training topics include the following:
- Regulations and business practices related to negotiating and working with suppliers
- Acquisition planning and preparation
- Commercial off-the-shelf product acquisition
- Supplier evaluation and selection
- Negotiation and conflict resolution
- Supplier management
- Testing and transition of acquired products
- Receiving, storing, using, and maintaining acquired products

SCON Elaboration

Examples of training topics include the following:
- Service system and its components
- Business functions and resources used to support the operation of the service system (and thus service delivery)
- Contents of the service continuity plan
- Relevant local, state, and federal disaster-preparedness activities

SD Elaboration

Examples of training topics include the following:
- Roles, responsibilities, and authority of the service delivery staff
- Service agreement, service requests, and service delivery standards, procedures, and methods
- Request management system
- Other service system components

SSD Elaboration

SSD ADDITION

Examples of training topics include the following:
- Specialized knowledge in a particular service domain
- Requirements definition, analysis, elicitation, specification, modeling, and tracking
- Design methods
- Common service system component and interface design patterns
- Standards (e.g., product, safety, human factors, security, delivery, environmental)
- Integration methods, tools, and facilities
- Verification and validation principles, standards, methods, tools, and facilities
- Peer review preparation and procedures
- Meeting facilitation

SST Elaboration

Examples of training topics include the following:
- Transition planning and monitoring
- Transition notification strategies
- Rollback and back-out approaches
- Post-deployment review process

STSM Elaboration

Examples of training topics include the following:
- Strategic planning techniques, such as scenario planning, SWOT, and needs analysis
- Market research techniques
- Product planning and management
- Portfolio management
- Marketing communication

GP 2.6 *MANAGE CONFIGURATIONS*

Place designated work products of the process under appropriate levels of control.

The purpose of this generic practice is to establish and maintain the integrity of the designated work products of the process (or their descriptions) throughout their useful life.

The designated work products are specifically identified in the plan for performing the process, along with a specification of the appropriate level of control.

Different levels of control are appropriate for different work products and for different points in time. For some work products, it may be sufficient to maintain version control (i.e., the version of the work product in use at a given time, past or present, is known, and changes are incorporated in a controlled manner). Version control is usually under the sole control of the work product owner (which may be an individual, group, or team).

Sometimes, it may be critical that work products be placed under formal or baseline configuration management. This type of control includes defining and establishing baselines at predetermined points. These baselines are formally reviewed and approved, and serve as the basis for further development of the designated work products.

Refer to the Configuration Management process area for more information about establishing and maintaining a configuration management and a change management system for controlling work products.

Additional levels of control between version control and formal configuration management are possible. An identified work product may be under various levels of control at different points in time.

CAM Elaboration

Examples of work products placed under control include the following:
- Capacity and availability management records
- Capacity and availability management reports

CAR Elaboration

Examples of work products placed under control include the following:
- Action proposals
- Action proposals selected for implementation
- Causal analysis and resolution records

CM Elaboration

Refer to Table 7.1 (p. 220) in Generic Goals and Generic Practices for more information about the relationship between generic practice 2.6 and the Configuration Management process area.

Levels of control must be sufficient to meet business needs, mitigate the risk of failure, and address service criticality.

Examples of work products placed under control include the following:
- Access lists
- Change status reports
- Change request database copies
- Configuration control board meeting minutes
- Archived baselines

DAR Elaboration

Examples of work products placed under control include the following:
- Guidelines for when to apply a formal evaluation process
- Evaluation reports containing recommended solutions

IPM Elaboration

Examples of work products placed under control include the following:
- The project's defined process
- Project plans
- Other plans that affect the project
- Integrated plans
- Actual process and product measurements collected from the project

---

IRP Elaboration

Examples of work products placed under control include the following:
- Incident management records
- Incident resolution and prevention reports
- Action proposals
- Workaround description and instructions
- Incident database copies

MA Elaboration

> Examples of work products placed under control include the following:
> - Specifications of base and derived measures
> - Data collection and storage procedures
> - Base and derived measurement data sets
> - Analysis results and draft reports
> - Data analysis tools

OID Elaboration

> Examples of work products placed under control include the following:
> - Documented lessons learned from pilots
> - Revised process- and technology-improvement measures, objectives, priorities, and deployment plans
> - Updated training material

OPD Elaboration

> Examples of work products placed under control include the following:
> - Organization's set of standard processes
> - Descriptions of lifecycle models
> - Tailoring guidelines for the organization's set of standard processes
> - Definitions of the common set of product and process measures
> - Organization's measurement data

OPF Elaboration

> Examples of work products placed under control include the following:
> - Process improvement proposals
> - Organization's approved process action plans
> - Training materials used for deploying organizational process assets
> - Guidelines for deploying the organization's set of standard processes on new projects
> - Plans for the organization's process appraisals

OPP Elaboration

Examples of work products placed under control include the following:
- Organization's quality and process-performance objectives
- Definitions of the selected measures of process performance
- Baseline data on the organization's process performance

OT Elaboration

Examples of work products placed under control include the following:
- Organizational training tactical plan
- Training records
- Training materials and supporting artifacts
- Instructor evaluation forms

PMC Elaboration

Examples of work products placed under control include the following:
- Project schedules with status
- Project measurement data and analysis
- Earned value reports

PP Elaboration

Examples of work products placed under control include the following:
- Work breakdown structure
- Project plan
- Data management plan
- Stakeholder involvement plan

PPQA Elaboration

Examples of work products placed under control include the following:
- Noncompliance reports
- Evaluation logs and reports

QPM Elaboration

> Examples of work products placed under control include the following:
> - Subprocesses to be included in the project's defined process
> - Operational definitions of the measures, their collection points in the subprocesses, and how the integrity of the measures will be determined
> - Collected measures

REQM Elaboration

> Examples of work products placed under control include the following:
> - Requirements
> - Requirements traceability matrix

RSKM Elaboration

> Examples of work products placed under control include the following:
> - Risk management strategy
> - Identified risk items
> - Risk mitigation plans

SAM Elaboration

> Examples of work products placed under control include the following:
> - Statements of work
> - Supplier agreements
> - Memoranda of agreement
> - Subcontracts
> - Preferred supplier lists

SCON Elaboration

> Examples of work products placed under control include the following:
> - Service continuity plan
> - Material used for training staff in the service continuity plan
> - Training records
> - Verification and validation procedures and criteria
> - Verification and validation reports

SD Elaboration

Examples of work products placed under control include the following:
- Service agreements
- Service delivery and request management reports
- Request management database

SSD Elaboration

Examples of work products placed under control include the following:
- Stakeholder requirements
- Service system architecture
- Service, service system, service system component, and interface requirements
- Service system, service system component, and interface designs
- Criteria for design and service system component reuse
- Skill specifications and staffing solutions
- Implemented designs (e.g., operating procedures, fabricated consumable components)
- Integrated service system component evaluations
- Service system component integration sequences
- Integration procedures and criteria
- Verification and validation procedures and criteria
- Verification and validation reports
- Peer review training material
- Peer review data
- User, installation, delivery, incident management, and maintenance documentation

---

SSD ADDITION

SST Elaboration

Examples of work products placed under control include the following:
- Transition plan
- Service system analysis reports
- Deployment reports and records
- Transition assessments and post-deployment review reports

STSM Elaboration

> Examples of work products placed under control include the following:
> • Organization's set of standard service descriptions
> • Descriptions of service levels
> • Tailoring guidelines for the organization's set of standard services

GP 2.7 IDENTIFY AND INVOLVE RELEVANT STAKEHOLDERS

Identify and involve the relevant stakeholders of the process as planned.

The purpose of this generic practice is to establish and maintain the expected involvement of stakeholders during the execution of the process.

Involve relevant stakeholders as described in an appropriate plan for stakeholder involvement. Involve stakeholders appropriately in activities such as the following:

• Planning
• Decisions
• Commitments
• Communications
• Coordination
• Reviews
• Appraisals
• Requirements definitions
• Resolution of problems/issues

Refer to the Project Planning process area for more information about planning stakeholder involvement.

The objective of planning stakeholder involvement is to ensure that interactions necessary to the process are accomplished, while not allowing excessive numbers of affected groups and individuals to impede process execution.

Subpractices

1. Identify stakeholders relevant to this process and their appropriate involvement.

    Relevant stakeholders are identified among the suppliers of inputs to, the users of outputs from, and the performers of the activities within the process. Once the relevant stakeholders are identified, the appropriate level of their involvement in process activities is planned.

2. Share these identifications with project planners or other planners as appropriate.

3. Involve relevant stakeholders as planned.

CAM Elaboration

Examples of activities for stakeholder involvement include the following:
- Reviewing capacity and availability management reports and resolving issues
- Working closely with stakeholders when it is not possible to directly influence the demand for the use of resources

CAR Elaboration

Examples of activities for stakeholder involvement include the following:
- Conducting causal analysis
- Assessing action proposals

CM Elaboration

Examples of activities for stakeholder involvement include the following:
- Establishing baselines
- Reviewing configuration management system reports and resolving issues
- Assessing the impact of changes for configuration items
- Performing configuration audits
- Reviewing results of configuration management audits

DAR Elaboration

Examples of activities for stakeholder involvement include the following:
- Establishing guidelines for which issues are subject to a formal evaluation process
- Establishing evaluation criteria
- Identifying and evaluating alternatives
- Selecting evaluation methods
- Selecting solutions

IPM Elaboration

Refer to Table 7.1 (p. 220) in Generic Goals and Generic Practices for more information about the relationship between generic practice 2.7 and the Manage Stakeholder Involvement specific practice in this process area.

Examples of activities for stakeholder involvement include the following:
- Resolving issues about the tailoring of organizational process assets
- Resolving issues among the project plan and other plans that affect the project
- Reviewing project performance to align with current and projected needs, objectives, and requirements

---

IRP Elaboration

Examples of activities for stakeholder involvement include the following:
- Establishing an approach to incident resolution and prevention
- Identifying service incidents and recording information about them
- Analyzing service incidents to determine the best course of action
- Reviewing the result of actions for resolving service incidents

---

MA Elaboration

Examples of activities for stakeholder involvement include the following:
- Establishing measurement objectives and procedures
- Assessing measurement data
- Providing meaningful feedback to those responsible for providing the raw data on which the analysis and results depend

---

OID Elaboration

Examples of activities for stakeholder involvement include the following:
- Reviewing process- and technology-improvement proposals that may have major impacts on process performance or on customer and end-user satisfaction
- Providing feedback to the organization on the status and results of the process- and technology-improvement deployment activities

---

Feedback typically involves the following:
- Informing those who submit process- and technology-improvement proposals about the disposition of their proposals
- Regularly informing relevant stakeholders about the plans and status for selecting and deploying process and technology improvements
- Preparing and distributing a summary of process- and technology-improvement selection and deployment activities

OPD Elaboration

Examples of activities for stakeholder involvement include the following:
- Reviewing the organization's set of standard processes
- Reviewing the organization's lifecycle models
- Resolving issues on tailoring guidelines
- Assessing definitions of the common set of process and product measures
- Reviewing work environment standards

OPF Elaboration

Examples of activities for stakeholder involvement include the following:
- Coordinating and collaborating on process improvement activities with process owners, those who are or will be performing the process, and support organizations (e.g., training staff, quality assurance representatives)
- Establishing the organizational process needs and objectives
- Appraising the organization's processes
- Implementing process action plans
- Coordinating and collaborating on the execution of pilots to test selected improvements
- Deploying organizational process assets and changes to organizational process assets
- Communicating the plans, status, activities, and results related to planning, implementing, and deploying process improvements

OPP Elaboration

> Examples of activities for stakeholder involvement include the following:
> - Establishing the organization's quality and process-performance objectives and their priorities
> - Reviewing and resolving issues on the organization's process-performance baselines
> - Reviewing and resolving issues on the organization's process-performance models

OT Elaboration

> Examples of activities for stakeholder involvement include the following:
> - Establishing a collaborative environment for discussion of training needs and training effectiveness to ensure that the organization's training needs are met
> - Identifying training needs
> - Reviewing the organizational training tactical plan
> - Assessing training effectiveness

PMC Elaboration

Refer to Table 7.1 (p. 220) in Generic Goals and Generic Practices for more information about the relationship between generic practice 2.7 and the Monitor Stakeholder Involvement specific practice in the Project Monitoring and Control process area.

> Examples of activities for stakeholder involvement include the following:
> - Assessing the project against the plan
> - Reviewing commitments and resolving issues
> - Reviewing project risks
> - Reviewing data management activities
> - Reviewing project progress
> - Managing corrective actions to closure

PP Elaboration

Refer to Table 7.1 (p. 220) in Generic Goals and Generic Practices for more information about the relationship between generic practice 2.7 and the Plan Stakeholder Involvement specific practice in the Project Planning process area.

> Examples of activities for stakeholder involvement include the following:
> - Establishing estimates
> - Reviewing and resolving issues on the completeness and correctness of project risks
> - Reviewing data management plans
> - Establishing project plans
> - Reviewing project plans and resolving issues on work and resource issues

PPQA Elaboration

> Examples of activities for stakeholder involvement include the following:
> - Establishing criteria for the objective evaluations of processes and work products
> - Evaluating processes and work products
> - Resolving noncompliance issues
> - Tracking noncompliance issues to closure

QPM Elaboration

> Examples of activities for stakeholder involvement include the following:
> - Establishing project objectives
> - Resolving issues among the project's quality and process-performance objectives
> - Appraising performance of the selected subprocesses
> - Identifying and managing the risks in achieving the project's quality and process-performance objectives
> - Identifying what corrective action should be taken

REQM Elaboration

Select relevant stakeholders from customers, end users, developers, producers, testers, suppliers, marketers, maintainers, disposal personnel, and others who may be affected by, or may affect, the product as well as the process.

Examples of activities for stakeholder involvement include the following:
* Resolving issues on the understanding of requirements
* Assessing the impact of requirements changes
* Communicating bidirectional traceability
* Identifying inconsistencies among project plans, work products, and requirements

RSKM Elaboration

Examples of activities for stakeholder involvement include the following:
* Establishing a collaborative environment for free and open discussion of risk
* Reviewing the risk management strategy and risk mitigation plans
* Participating in risk identification, analysis, and mitigation activities
* Communicating and reporting risk management status

SAM Elaboration

Examples of activities for stakeholder involvement include the following:
* Establishing criteria for evaluation of potential suppliers
* Reviewing potential suppliers
* Establishing supplier agreements
* Resolving issues with suppliers
* Reviewing supplier performance

SCON Elaboration

Examples of activities for stakeholder involvement include the following:
* Identifying essential functions and resources that support service delivery
* Reviewing the service continuity plan
* Reviewing training materials
* Verification and validation activities

SD Elaboration

Examples of activities for stakeholder involvement include the following:
- Establishing service agreements
- Submitting service requests
- Reviewing service request management reports and resolving issues
- Reviewing the result of actions for resolving service requests

SSD Elaboration

Examples of activities for stakeholder involvement include the following:
- Reviewing and assessing the adequacy of requirements in meeting needs, expectations, constraints, and interfaces
- Establishing operational concepts and scenarios
- Establishing service and service system requirements
- Assessing cost, schedule, intended resource needs, and risk
- Developing alternative solutions and selection criteria
- Obtaining approval on external interface specifications and design descriptions
- Developing the service system architecture
- Assessing the make, buy, or reuse alternatives for service system components
- Implementing the design
- Reviewing interface descriptions for completeness
- Establishing the service system integration procedures, criteria, and sequences
- Integrating and assembling service system components
- Selecting the service system components to be verified and validated
- Establishing the verification and validation methods, procedures, and criteria
- Reviewing results of service system component verification and validation
- Resolving issues with customers or end users identified during verification and validation

SSD ADDITION

SST Elaboration

Examples of activities for stakeholder involvement include the following:
- Planning and monitoring service system transition
- Notifying stakeholders about transition status and issues
- Post-deployment review

STSM Elaboration

> Examples of activities for stakeholder involvement include the following:
> - Confirming business objectives
> - Reviewing the organization's set of standard services
> - Reviewing the descriptions of standard services
> - Reviewing the organization's service levels
> - Resolving issues on tailoring guidelines

GP 2.8 MONITOR AND CONTROL THE PROCESS

Monitor and control the process against the plan for performing the process and take appropriate corrective action.

The purpose of this generic practice is to perform the direct day-to-day monitoring and controlling of the process. Appropriate visibility into the process is maintained so that appropriate corrective action can be taken when necessary. Monitoring and controlling the process involves measuring appropriate attributes of the process or work products produced by the process.

Refer to the Measurement and Analysis process area for more information about developing and sustaining a measurement capability used to support management information needs.

Refer to the Project Monitoring and Control process area for more information about providing an understanding of the project's progress so that appropriate corrective actions can be taken when the project's performance deviates significantly from the plan.

Subpractices

1. Measure actual performance against the plan for performing the process.

    The measures are of the process, its work products, and its services.

2. Review accomplishments and results of the process against the plan for performing the process.

3. Review activities, status, and results of the process with the immediate level of management responsible for the process and identify issues.

    The reviews are intended to provide the immediate level of management with appropriate visibility into the process. The reviews can be both periodic and event driven.

4. Identify and evaluate the effects of significant deviations from the plan for performing the process.

5. Identify problems in the plan for performing the process and in the execution of the process.

6. Take corrective action when requirements and objectives are not being satisfied, when issues are identified, or when progress differs significantly from the plan for performing the process.

There are inherent risks that should be considered before any corrective action is taken.

Corrective action may include the following:

- Taking remedial action to repair defective work products or services
- Changing the plan for performing the process
- Adjusting resources, including people, tools, and other resources
- Negotiating changes to the established commitments
- Securing change to the requirements and objectives that must be satisfied
- Terminating the effort

7. Track corrective action to closure.

CAM Elaboration

> Examples of measures and work products used in monitoring and controlling include the following:
> - Total number of customer hours lost per month to interruptions of normal service from causes associated with capacity and availability management
> - Number of hours lost per customer per month to interruptions of normal service from causes associated with capacity and availability management
> - Percent of service response time requirements not met due to causes associated with capacity and availability management
> - Accuracy of forecasts of trends in resource use

CAR Elaboration

> Examples of measures and work products used in monitoring and controlling include the following:
> - Number of root causes removed
> - Change in quality or process performance per instance of the causal analysis and resolution process
> - Schedule of activities for implementing a selected action proposal

CM Elaboration

> Examples of measures and work products used in monitoring and controlling include the following:
> - Number of changes to configuration items
> - Number of configuration audits conducted
> - Schedule of configuration control board or audit activities

DAR Elaboration

> Examples of measures and work products used in monitoring and controlling include the following:
> - Cost-to-benefit ratio of using formal evaluation processes
> - Schedule for the execution of a trade study

IPM Elaboration

> Examples of measures and work products used in monitoring and controlling include the following:
> - Number of changes to the project's defined process
> - Schedule and effort to tailor the organization's set of standard processes
> - Interface coordination issue trends (i.e., number identified and number closed)
> - Schedule for project tailoring activities

IRP Elaboration

> Examples of measures and work products used in monitoring and controlling include the following:
> - Capacity, performance, and availability data that signal potential service incidents
> - Number of service incidents received
> - Lead time for resolving service incidents compared to the lead times defined in the service level agreement
> - Number of transfers between support groups before a service incident is resolved
> - Schedule for implementing an action proposal to prevent a class of service incidents from reoccurring

MA Elaboration

Examples of measures and work products used in monitoring and controlling include the following:
- Percentage of projects using progress and performance measures
- Percentage of measurement objectives addressed
- Schedule for collection and review of measurement data

OPD Elaboration

Examples of measures and work products used in monitoring and controlling include the following:
- Percentage of projects using the process architectures and process elements of the organization's set of standard processes
- Defect density of each process element of the organization's set of standard processes
- Number of worker's compensation claims due to ergonomic problems
- Schedule for development of a process or process change

OPF Elaboration

Examples of measures and work products used in monitoring and controlling include the following:
- Number of process improvement proposals submitted, accepted, or implemented
- CMMI maturity level or capability level earned
- Schedule for deployment of an organizational process asset
- Percentage of projects using the current organization's set of standard processes (or tailored version of the current set)
- Issue trends associated with implementing the organization's set of standard processes (i.e., number of issues identified and number closed)

OPP Elaboration

Examples of measures and work products used in monitoring and controlling include the following:
- Trends in the organization's process performance with respect to changes in work products and task attributes (e.g., size growth, effort, schedule, quality)
- Schedule for collecting and reviewing measures to be used for establishing a process-performance baseline

---

OT Elaboration

Examples of measures and work products used in monitoring and controlling include the following:
- Number of training courses delivered (e.g., planned versus actual)
- Post-training evaluation ratings
- Training program quality survey ratings
- Schedule for delivery of training
- Schedule for development of a course

PMC Elaboration

Refer to Table 7.1 (p. 220) in Generic Goals and Generic Practices for more information about the relationship between generic practice 2.8 and the Project Monitoring and Control process area.

Examples of measures and work products used in monitoring and controlling include the following:
- Number of open and closed corrective actions
- Schedule with status for monthly financial data collection, analysis, and reporting
- Number and types of reviews performed
- Review schedule (planned versus actual and slipped target dates)
- Schedule for collection and analysis of monitoring data

PP Elaboration

Examples of measures and work products used in monitoring and controlling include the following:
- Number of revisions to the plan
- Cost, schedule, and effort variance per plan revision
- Schedule for development and maintenance of program plans

PPQA Elaboration

Examples of measures and work products used in monitoring and controlling include the following:
- Variance of objective process evaluations planned and performed
- Variance of objective work product evaluations planned and performed
- Schedule for objective evaluations

QPM Elaboration

Examples of measures and work products used in monitoring and controlling include the following:
- Profile of subprocesses under statistical management (e.g., number planned to be under statistical management, number currently being statistically managed, number that are statistically stable)
- Number of special causes of variation identified
- Schedule of data collection, analysis, and reporting activities in a measurement and analysis cycle as it relates to quantitative management activities

REQM Elaboration

Examples of measures and work products used in monitoring and controlling include the following:
- Requirements volatility (percentage of requirements changed)
- Schedule for coordination of requirements
- Schedule for analysis of a proposed requirements change

RSKM Elaboration

Examples of measures and work products used in monitoring and controlling include the following:
- Number of risks identified, managed, tracked, and controlled
- Risk exposure and changes to the risk exposure for each assessed risk, and as a summary percentage of management reserve
- Change activity for risk mitigation plans (e.g., processes, schedule, funding)
- Occurrence of unanticipated risks
- Risk categorization volatility
- Comparison of estimated versus actual risk mitigation effort and impact
- Schedule for risk analysis activities
- Schedule of actions for a specific mitigation

SAM Elaboration

Examples of measures and work products used in monitoring and controlling include the following:
- Number of changes made to the requirements for the supplier
- Cost and schedule variance per supplier agreement
- Number of supplier work product evaluations completed (planned versus actual)
- Number of supplier process evaluations completed (planned versus actual)
- Schedule for selecting a supplier and establishing an agreement

SCON Elaboration

Examples of measures and work products used in monitoring and controlling include the following:
- Number of changes made to the list of functions and resources identified as essential to service delivery
- Cost, schedule, and effort expended for ensuring service continuity
- Percentage of those trained in the service continuity plan who must be trained again
- Service continuity plan verification and validation problem report status (i.e., how long each problem report has been open)

SD Elaboration

Examples of measures and work products used in monitoring and controlling include the following:
- Time taken to prepare the service agreement
- Number of service requests received
- Time taken to resolve service requests compared to the times defined in the service level agreement
- Number of transfers between support groups before a service request is resolved

SSD Elaboration

Examples of measures and work products used in monitoring and controlling include the following:
- Cost, schedule, and effort expended for rework
- Defect density of requirements specifications
- Schedule for activities to develop a set of requirements
- Percentage of requirements addressed in the service system or service system component design
- Size and complexity of the service system, service system components, interfaces, and documentation
- Defect density of design and integration work products
- Integration evaluation problem report trends (e.g., number written, number closed)
- Integration evaluation problem report aging (i.e., how long each problem report has been open)
- Verification and validation profiles (e.g., the number of verifications and validations planned and performed, the number of defects found)
- Number of defects detected by defect category
- Verification and validation problem report trends (e.g., number written, number closed)
- Verification and validation problem report status (i.e., how long each problem report has been open)
- Schedule for conduct of specific requirements, design, integration, verification, and validation activities

SST Elaboration

Examples of measures and work products used in monitoring and controlling include the following:
- Planned versus actual transition time
- Number of transition-related service incidents received
- Number of unexpected back-out and rollback instances, including magnitude of disruption to service system delivery
- Results of post-deployment review and stakeholder surveys

SSD ADDITION

STSM Elaboration

> Examples of measures and work products used in monitoring and controlling include the following:
> - Percentage of contracts using the organization's set of standard services
> - Number of customer requests that breach defined service levels
> - Frequency of use of particular services
> - Schedule for development of a service description change

GP 2.9 OBJECTIVELY EVALUATE ADHERENCE

Objectively evaluate adherence of the process against its process description, standards, and procedures, and address noncompliance.

The purpose of this generic practice is to provide credible assurance that the process is implemented as planned and adheres to its process description, standards, and procedures. This generic practice is implemented, in part, by evaluating selected work products of the process. (See the definition of "objectively evaluate" in the glossary.)

Refer to the Process and Product Quality Assurance process area for more information about objectively evaluating processes and work products.

People not directly responsible for managing or performing the activities of the process typically evaluate adherence. In many cases, adherence is evaluated by people within the organization, but external to the process or project, or by people external to the organization. As a result, credible assurance of adherence can be provided even during times when the process is under stress (e.g., when the effort is behind schedule, when the effort is over budget).

CAR Elaboration

> Examples of activities reviewed include the following:
> - Determining causes of defects
> - Addressing causes of defects

> Examples of work products reviewed include the following:
> - Action proposals selected for implementation
> - Causal analysis and resolution records

CM Elaboration

> Examples of activities reviewed include the following:
> - Establishing baselines
> - Tracking and controlling changes
> - Establishing and maintaining the integrity of baselines

> Examples of work products reviewed include the following:
> - Archives of baselines
> - Change request database

DAR Elaboration

> Examples of activities reviewed include the following:
> - Evaluating alternatives using established criteria and methods

> Examples of work products reviewed include the following:
> - Guidelines for when to apply a formal evaluation process
> - Evaluation reports containing recommended solutions

IPM Elaboration

> Examples of activities reviewed include the following:
> - Establishing, maintaining, and using the project's defined process
> - Coordinating and collaborating with relevant stakeholders

> Examples of work products reviewed include the following:
> - The project's defined process
> - Project plans
> - Other plans that affect the project
> - Work environment standards

IRP Elaboration

> Examples of activities reviewed include the following:
> - Establishing an approach to incident resolution and prevention
> - Identifying service incidents and recording information about them
> - Communicating the status of service incidents

Examples of work products reviewed include the following:
- Service incident database
- Workarounds
- Action proposals
- Service incident records

MA Elaboration

Examples of activities reviewed include the following:
- Aligning measurement and analysis activities
- Providing measurement results

Examples of work products reviewed include the following:
- Specifications of base and derived measures
- Data collection and storage procedures
- Analysis results and draft reports

OID Elaboration

Examples of activities reviewed include the following:
- Selecting improvements
- Deploying improvements

Examples of work products reviewed include the following:
- Deployment plans
- Revised process- and technology-improvement measures, objectives, priorities, and deployment plans
- Updated training material

OPD Elaboration

Examples of activities reviewed include the following:
- Establishing organizational process assets
- Establishing rules and guidelines for structuring and forming integrated teams

Examples of work products reviewed include the following:
- Organization's set of standard processes
- Descriptions of lifecycle models
- Tailoring guidelines for the organization's set of standard processes
- Organization's measurement data

OPF Elaboration

Examples of activities reviewed include the following:
- Determining process improvement opportunities
- Planning and coordinating process improvement activities
- Deploying the organization's set of standard processes on projects at their startup

Examples of work products reviewed include the following:
- Process improvement plans
- Process action plans
- Process deployment plans
- Plans for the organization's process appraisals

OPP Elaboration

Examples of activities reviewed include the following:
- Establishing process-performance baselines and models

Examples of work products reviewed include the following:
- Process-performance plans
- Organization's quality and process-performance objectives
- Definitions of the selected measures of process performance

OT Elaboration

Examples of activities reviewed include the following:
- Identifying training needs and making training available
- Providing necessary training

Examples of work products reviewed include the following:
- Organizational training tactical plan
- Training materials and supporting artifacts
- Instructor evaluation forms

PMC Elaboration

Examples of activities reviewed include the following:
- Monitoring project performance against the project plan
- Managing corrective actions to closure

Examples of work products reviewed include the following:
- Records of project performance
- Project review results

PP Elaboration

Examples of activities reviewed include the following:
- Establishing estimates
- Developing the project plan
- Obtaining commitments to the project plan

Examples of work products reviewed include the following:
- Work breakdown structure
- Project plan
- Data management plan
- Stakeholder involvement plan

PPQA Elaboration

Refer to Table 7.1 (p. 220) in Generic Goals and Generic Practices for more information about the relationship between generic practice 2.9 and the Process and Product Quality Assurance process area.

Examples of activities reviewed include the following:
- Objectively evaluating processes and work products
- Tracking and communicating noncompliance issues

Examples of work products reviewed include the following:
- Noncompliance reports
- Evaluation logs and reports

QPM Elaboration

Examples of activities reviewed include the following:
- Quantitatively managing the project using quality and process-performance objectives
- Statistically managing selected subprocesses within the project's defined process

Examples of work products reviewed include the following:
- Subprocesses to be included in the project's defined process
- Operational definitions of the measures
- Collected measures

REQM Elaboration

Examples of activities reviewed include the following:
- Managing requirements
- Identifying inconsistencies among project plans, work products, and requirements

Examples of work products reviewed include the following:
- Requirements
- Requirements traceability matrix

RSKM Elaboration

Examples of activities reviewed include the following:
- Establishing and maintaining a risk management strategy
- Identifying and analyzing risks
- Mitigating risks

Examples of work products reviewed include the following:
- Risk management strategy
- Risk mitigation plans

SAM Elaboration

Examples of activities reviewed include the following:
- Establishing and maintaining supplier agreements
- Satisfying supplier agreements

Examples of work products reviewed include the following:
- Plan for supplier agreement management
- Supplier agreements

SCON Elaboration

Examples of activities reviewed include the following:
- Establishing the service continuity plan
- Conducting training in the service continuity plan
- Verifying and validating the service continuity plan

Examples of work products reviewed include the following:
- Service continuity plan
- Training materials
- Verification and validation methods, procedures, and criteria

SD Elaboration

Examples of activities reviewed include the following:
- Establishing service agreements
- Processing service request
- Maintaining the service system

Examples of work products reviewed include the following:
- Service agreements
- Service delivery approach

SSD Elaboration

Examples of activities reviewed include the following:
- Collecting stakeholder needs
- Formulating and analyzing service, service system, and component requirements
- Selecting service system solutions
- Developing service system and service system component designs
- Ensuring interface compatibility
- Implementing service system designs
- Integrating and assembling service system components
- Verifying and validating service systems
- Performing peer reviews

Examples of work products reviewed include the following:
- Service, service system, and component requirements
- Interface requirements
- Service system architecture
- Service system, service system component, and interface designs
- Criteria for design and service system component reuse
- Skill specifications and staffing solutions
- Implemented designs (e.g., operating procedures, fabricated consumable components)
- Integrated service system component evaluations
- Service system component integration sequences
- Integration procedures and criteria
- Verification and validation procedures and criteria
- Verification and validation reports
- Peer review training material
- Peer review data
- User, installation, delivery, incident management, and maintenance documentation

SST Elaboration

Examples of activities reviewed include the following:
- Transition planning
- Transition training
- Deployment activities, including validation and assessment

Examples of work products reviewed include the following:
- Service system transition plan
- Installation records
- Post-deployment review report

STSM Elaboration

Establishing organizational standard services is an example of an activity to be reviewed.

Examples of work products reviewed include the following:
- Organization's set of standard services
- Descriptions of standard services
- Descriptions of service levels
- Tailoring guidelines for the organization's set of standard services

GP 2.10 REVIEW STATUS WITH HIGHER LEVEL MANAGEMENT

Review the activities, status, and results of the process with higher level management and resolve issues.

The purpose of this generic practice is to provide higher level management with the appropriate visibility into the process.

Higher level management includes those levels of management in the organization above the immediate level of management responsible for the process. In particular, higher level management includes senior management. These reviews are for managers who provide the policy and overall guidance for the process, and not for those who perform the direct day-to-day monitoring and controlling of the process.

Different managers have different needs for information about the process. These reviews help ensure that informed decisions on the planning and performing of the process can be made. Therefore, these reviews are expected to be both periodic and event driven.

IRP Elaboration

Higher level management is kept informed of the status of significant service incidents, including results of workarounds and prevention activities.

OPF Elaboration

These reviews are typically in the form of a briefing presented to the management steering committee by the process group and the process action teams.

Examples of presentation topics include the following:
- Status of improvements being developed by process action teams
- Results of pilots
- Results of deployments
- Schedule status for achieving significant milestones (e.g., readiness for an appraisal, progress toward achieving a targeted organizational maturity level or capability level profile)

REQM Elaboration

Proposed changes to commitments to be made external to the organization are reviewed with higher level management to ensure that all commitments can be accomplished.

RSKM Elaboration

Reviews of project risk status are held on a periodic and event-driven basis with appropriate levels of management to provide visibility into the potential for project risk exposure and appropriate corrective action.

Typically, these reviews include a summary of the most critical risks, key risk parameters (such as likelihood and consequence of the risks), and the status of risk mitigation efforts.

SCON Elaboration

These reviews are typically in the form of a briefing presented to higher level management.

Examples of presentation topics include the following:
- Identification of significant changes in the business functions and resources essential to service delivery
- Status of preparations for service continuity including training activities
- Verification and validation issues and results

SST Elaboration

Higher level management is kept informed of the status of transitions, including successful and unsuccessful transition attempts and deployment results.

GG 3 INSTITUTIONALIZE A DEFINED PROCESS

The process is institutionalized as a defined process.

GP 3.1 ESTABLISH A DEFINED PROCESS

Establish and maintain the description of a defined process.

The purpose of this generic practice is to establish and maintain a description of the process that is tailored from the organization's set of standard processes to address the needs of a specific instantiation. The organization should have standard processes that cover the process area, as well as have guidelines for tailoring these standard processes to meet the needs of a project or organizational function. With a defined process, variability in how the processes are performed across the organization is reduced, and process assets, data, and learning can be effectively shared.

Refer to the Integrated Project Management process area for more information about establishing and maintaining the project's defined process.

Refer to the Organizational Process Definition process area for more information about standard processes and tailoring criteria and guidelines.

The descriptions of the defined processes provide the basis for planning, performing, and managing the activities, work products, and services associated with the process.

Subpractices

1. Select from the organization's set of standard processes those processes that cover the process area and best meet the needs of the project or organizational function.
2. Establish the defined process by tailoring the selected processes according to the organization's tailoring guidelines.
3. Ensure that the organization's process objectives are appropriately addressed in the defined process.
4. Document the defined process and the records of the tailoring.
5. Revise the description of the defined process as necessary.

IPM Elaboration

Refer to Table 7.1 (p. 220) in Generic Goals and Generic Practices for more information about the relationship between generic practice 3.1 and the Integrated Project Management process area.

GP 3.2 COLLECT IMPROVEMENT INFORMATION

Collect work products, measures, measurement results, and improvement information derived from planning and performing the process to support the future use and improvement of the organization's processes and process assets.

The purpose of this generic practice is to collect information and artifacts derived from planning and performing the process. This generic practice is performed so that the information and artifacts can be included in the organizational process assets and made available to those who are (or who will be) planning and performing the same or similar processes. The information and artifacts are stored in the organization's measurement repository and the organization's process asset library.

> Examples of relevant information include the effort expended for the various activities, defects injected or removed in a particular activity, and lessons learned.

Refer to the Integrated Project Management process area for more information about contributing work products, measures, and documented experiences to the organizational process assets.

Refer to the Organizational Process Definition process area for more information about establishing organizational process assets.

Subpractices

1. Store process and product measures in the organization's measurement repository.

    The process and product measures are primarily those that are defined in the common set of measures for the organization's set of standard processes.

2. Submit documentation for inclusion in the organization's process asset library.

3. Document lessons learned from the process for inclusion in the organization's process asset library.

4. Propose improvements to the organizational process assets.

CAR Elaboration

> Examples of work products, measures, measurement results, and improvement information include the following:
> - Action proposals
> - Number of action proposals that are open and for how long
> - Action proposal status reports

CM Elaboration

> Examples of work products, measures, measurement results, and improvement information include the following:
> - Trends in the status of configuration items
> - Configuration audit results
> - Change request aging reports

DAR Elaboration

> Examples of work products, measures, measurement results, and improvement information include the following:
> - Number of alternatives considered
> - Evaluation results
> - Recommended solutions to address significant issues

IPM Elaboration

Refer to Table 7.1 (p. 220) in Generic Goals and Generic Practices for more information about the relationship between generic practice 3.2 and the Integrated Project Management process area.

> Examples of work products, measures, measurement results, and improvement information include the following:
> - Project's defined process
> - Number of tailoring options exercised by the project to create its defined process
> - Interface coordination issue trends (i.e., number identified and number closed)
> - Number of times the process asset library is accessed for assets related to project planning by project personnel
> - Records of expenses related to holding face-to-face meetings versus holding meetings using collaborative equipment, such as teleconferencing and videoconferencing

IRP Elaboration

Examples of work products, measures, measurement results, and improvement information include the following: • Trends in time required to resolve service incidents • Number of times the incident management system is accessed and for what purpose (e.g., identify workaround for known incident) • Results of applying workarounds and implementing action proposals

OID Elaboration

Examples of work products, measures, measurement results, and improvement information include the following: • Lessons learned captured from relevant stakeholders that identify barriers to deployment from previous technology insertions • Documented measures of the costs and benefits resulting from deploying innovations • Report of a comparison of similar development processes to identify the potential for improving efficiency

OPD Elaboration

Examples of work products, measures, measurement results, and improvement information include the following: • Submission of lessons learned to the organization's process asset library • Submission of measurement data to the organization's measurement repository • Status of the change requests submitted to modify the organization's standard process • Record of nonstandard tailoring requests

OPF Elaboration

Examples of work products, measures, measurement results, and improvement information include the following:
- Criteria used for prioritizing candidate process improvements
- Appraisal findings that address strengths and weaknesses of the organization's processes
- Status of improvement activities against the schedule
- Records of tailoring the organization's set of standard processes and implementing them on identified projects

OPP Elaboration

Examples of work products, measures, measurement results, and improvement information include the following:
- Process-performance baselines
- Percent of measurement data that is rejected because of inconsistencies with the process-performance measurement definitions

OT Elaboration

Examples of work products, measures, measurement results, and improvement information include the following:
- Results of training effectiveness surveys
- Training program performance assessment results
- Course evaluations
- Training requirements from an advisory group

PMC Elaboration

Examples of work products, measures, measurement results, and improvement information include the following:
- Records of significant deviations
- Criteria for what constitutes a deviation
- Corrective action results

PP Elaboration

> Examples of work products, measures, measurement results, and improvement information include the following:
> - Project data library structure
> - Project attribute estimates
> - Risk impacts and probability of occurrence

PPQA Elaboration

> Examples of work products, measures, measurement results, and improvement information include the following:
> - Evaluation logs
> - Quality trends
> - Noncompliance report
> - Status reports of corrective action
> - Cost of quality reports for the project

QPM Elaboration

> Examples of work products, measures, measurement results, and improvement information include the following:
> - Records of statistical and quality management data from the project, including results from the periodic review of the actual performance of the statistically managed subprocesses against established interim objectives of the project
> - Process and product quality assurance report that identifies inconsistent but compliant implementations of subprocesses being considered for statistical management

REQM Elaboration

> Examples of work products, measures, measurement results, and improvement information include the following:
> - Requirements traceability matrix
> - Number of unfunded requirements changes after baselining
> - Lessons learned in resolving ambiguous requirements

RSKM Elaboration

Examples of work products, measures, measurement results, and improvement information include the following:
- Risk parameters
- Risk categories
- Risk status reports

SAM Elaboration

Examples of work products, measures, measurement results, and improvement information include the following:
- Results of supplier reviews
- Trade studies used to select suppliers
- Revision history of supplier agreements
- Supplier performance reports
- Results of supplier work product and process evaluations

SCON Elaboration

Examples of work products, measures, measurement results, and improvement information include the following:
- Revision history for the list of threats and vulnerabilities that could significantly disrupt the delivery of services
- Risk exposure to significant service disruption
- Changes to risk exposure
- Costs associated with service continuity activities
- Verification and validation analysis reports

SD Elaboration

Examples of work products, measures, measurement results, and improvement information include the following:
- Number of issues raised over terms in the service agreement (following its implementation)
- Measures of service system component use, availability, and performance
- Trends in lead time for responding to service requests
- Reviews of the results of service request responses

SSD Elaboration

Examples of work products, measures, measurement results, and improvement information include the following:
- List of requirements for a service or service system that are ambiguous
- Number of requirements introduced at each phase of the project life-cycle
- Lessons learned from the requirements allocation process
- Results of make, buy, or reuse analyses
- Design defect density
- Results of applying new methods and tools
- Records of the receipt of service system components, exception reports, confirmation of configuration status, and results of readiness checking
- Percent of total development effort spent in service system integration (actual to date plus estimate to complete)
- Defects found in the service system and test environment during service system integration, verification, and validation
- Peer review records that include conduct time and average preparation time

SSD ADDITION

SST Elaboration

Examples of work products, measures, measurement results, and improvement information include the following:
- Deployment assessment artifacts
- Post deployment review results and lessons learned

STSM Elaboration

Examples of work products, measures, measurement results, and improvement information include the following:
- Customer requests for new services
- Customer questions to clarify service descriptions
- Status of change requests submitted to modify the organization's standard services
- Record of nonstandard tailoring requests

GG 4 *INSTITUTIONALIZE A QUANTITATIVELY MANAGED PROCESS*

The process is institutionalized as a quantitatively managed process.

GP 4.1 *ESTABLISH QUANTITATIVE OBJECTIVES FOR THE PROCESS*

Establish and maintain quantitative objectives for the process, which address quality and process performance, based on customer needs and business objectives.

The purpose of this generic practice is to determine and obtain agreement from relevant stakeholders about specific quantitative objectives for the process. These quantitative objectives can be expressed in terms of product quality, service quality, and process performance.

Refer to the Quantitative Project Management process area for more information about selecting subprocesses to be statistically managed as well as selecting measures and analytic techniques.

The quantitative objectives may be specific to the process, or they may be defined for a broader scope (e.g., for a set of processes). In the latter case, these quantitative objectives may be allocated to some of the included processes.

These quantitative objectives are criteria used to judge whether the products, services, and process performance will satisfy the customers, end users, organization management, and process implementers. These quantitative objectives go beyond the traditional end-product objectives. They also cover intermediate objectives that are used to manage the achievement of the objectives over time. They reflect, in part, the demonstrated performance of the organization's set of standard processes. These quantitative objectives should be set to values that are likely to be achieved when the processes involved are stable and within their natural bounds.

Subpractices

1. Establish the quantitative objectives that pertain to the process.
2. Allocate the quantitative objectives to the process or its sub-processes.

GP 4.2 *STABILIZE SUBPROCESS PERFORMANCE*

Stabilize the performance of one or more subprocesses to determine the ability of the process to achieve the established quantitative quality and process-performance objectives.

The purpose of this generic practice is to stabilize the performance of one or more subprocesses of the defined process, which are critical contributors to overall performance, using appropriate statistical and other quantitative techniques. Stabilizing selected subprocesses supports predicting the ability of the process to achieve the established quantitative quality and process-performance objectives.

Refer to the Quantitative Project Management process area for more information about selecting subprocesses for statistical management and statistically managing subprocess performance.

A stable subprocess shows no significant indication of special causes of process variation. Stable subprocesses are predictable within the limits established by the natural bounds of the subprocess. Variations in the stable subprocess are due to a constant system of chance causes, and the magnitude of the variations can be small or large.

Predicting the ability of the process to achieve the established quantitative objectives requires a quantitative understanding of the contributions of the subprocesses that are critical to achieving these objectives and establishing and managing against interim quantitative objectives over time.

Selected process and product measures are incorporated into the organization's measurement repository to support process-performance analysis and future fact-based decision making.

Subpractices

1. Statistically manage the performance of one or more subprocesses that are critical contributors to the overall performance of the process.
2. Predict the ability of the process to achieve its established quantitative objectives considering the performance of the statistically managed subprocesses.
3. Incorporate selected process-performance measurements into the organization's process-performance baselines.

GG 5 INSTITUTIONALIZE AN OPTIMIZING PROCESS

The process is institutionalized as an optimizing process.

GP 5.1 ENSURE CONTINUOUS PROCESS IMPROVEMENT

Ensure continuous improvement of the process in fulfilling the relevant business objectives of the organization.

The purpose of this generic practice is to select and systematically deploy process and technology improvements that contribute to meeting established quality and process-performance objectives.

Refer to the Organizational Innovation and Deployment process area for more information about selecting and deploying incremental and innovative improvements that measurably improve the organization's processes and technologies.

Optimizing the processes that are agile and innovative depends on the participation of an empowered workforce aligned with the business values and objectives of the organization. The organization's ability to rapidly respond to changes and opportunities is enhanced by finding ways to accelerate and share learning. Improvement of the processes is inherently part of everybody's role, resulting in a cycle of continual improvement.

Subpractices

1. Establish and maintain quantitative process improvement objectives that support the organization's business objectives.

    The quantitative process improvement objectives may be specific to the individual process, or they may be defined for a broader scope (i.e., for a set of processes) with the individual processes contributing to achieving these objectives. Objectives that are specific to the individual process are typically allocated from quantitative objectives established for a broader scope.

    These process improvement objectives are derived primarily from the organization's business objectives and from a detailed understanding of process capability. These objectives are the criteria used to judge whether the process performance is quantitatively improving the organization's ability to meet its business objectives. These process improvement objectives are often set to values beyond current process performance, and both incremental and innovative technological improvements may be needed to achieve these objectives. These objectives may also be revised frequently to continue to drive the improvement of the process (i.e., when an objective is achieved, it may be set to a new value that is again beyond the new process performance).

    These process improvement objectives may be the same as, or a refinement of, the objectives established in the "Establish Quantitative Objectives for the Process" generic practice, as long as they can serve as both drivers and criteria for successful process improvement.

2. Identify process improvements that would result in measurable improvements to process performance.

    Process improvements include both incremental changes and innovative technological improvements. The innovative technological improvements are typically pursued as efforts that are separately planned, performed, and managed. Piloting is often performed. These efforts often address specific areas of the processes that are determined by analyzing process performance and identifying specific opportunities for significant measurable improvement.

3. Define strategies and manage deployment of selected process improvements based on the quantified expected benefits, the estimated costs and impacts, and the measured change to process performance.

> The costs and benefits of these improvements are estimated quantitatively and the actual costs and benefits are measured. Benefits are primarily considered relative to the organization's quantitative process improvement objectives. Improvements are made to both the organization's set of standard processes and the defined processes.

> Managing deployment of the process improvements includes piloting changes and implementing adjustments where appropriate, addressing potential and real barriers to deployment, minimizing disruption to ongoing efforts, and managing risks.

GP 5.2 CORRECT ROOT CAUSES OF PROBLEMS

Identify and correct the root causes of defects and other problems in the process.

The purpose of this generic practice is to analyze defects and other problems that were encountered in a quantitatively managed process, to correct the root causes of these types of defects and problems, and to prevent these defects and problems from occurring in the future.

Refer to the Causal Analysis and Resolution process area for more information about identifying causes of defects and problems and taking action to prevent them from occurring in the future.

Even though the Causal Analysis and Resolution process area has a project context, it can be applied to processes in other contexts as well.

Root cause analysis can be applied beneficially to processes that are not quantitatively managed. However, the focus of this generic practice is to act on a quantitatively managed process, though the final root causes may be found outside of that process.

Process Areas That Support Generic Practices

While generic goals and generic practices are the model components that directly address the institutionalization of a process across the organization, many process areas likewise address institutionalization by supporting the implementation of the generic practices. Such process areas contain one or more specific practices that when implemented may also fully implement a generic practice or generate a work product that is used in the implementation of a generic practice.

Knowing these relationships will help you effectively implement the generic practices.

An example is the Configuration Management process area and GP 2.6, "Place designated work products of the process under appropriate levels of control." To implement the generic practice for one or more process areas, you might choose to implement the Configuration Management process area, all or in part, to implement the generic practice.

Another example is the Organizational Process Definition process area and GP 3.1, "Establish and maintain the description of a defined process." To implement this generic practice for one or more process areas, you should first implement the Organizational Process Definition process area, all or in part, to establish the organizational process assets that are needed to implement the generic practice.

Table 7.1 describes (1) the process areas that support the implementation of generic practices and (2) the recursive relationships between generic practices and their closely related process areas. Both types of relationships are important to remember during process improvement to take advantage of the natural synergies that exist between the generic practices and their related process areas.

Given the dependencies that generic practices have on these process areas, and given the more *holistic* view that many of these process areas provide, many organizations implement these process areas early, in whole or in part, before or concurrent with implementing the associated generic practices.

There are also a few situations in which the result of applying a generic practice to a particular process area would seem to make a whole process area redundant, but, in fact, it does not. It may be natural to think that applying GP 3.1, "Establish a Defined Process," to the Project Planning and Project Monitoring and Control process areas gives the same effect as the first specific goal of Integrated Project Management, "Use the Project's Defined Process."

Although it is true that there is some overlap, the application of the generic practice to these two process areas provides defined processes covering project planning and project monitoring and control activities. These defined processes do not necessarily cover support activities (e.g., configuration management), other project management processes (e.g., supplier agreement management), or the engineering processes. In contrast, the project's defined process, provided by the Integrated Project Management process area, covers all appropriate project management, engineering, and support processes.

TABLE 7.1 Generic Practice and Process Area Relationships

Generic Practice	Roles of Process Areas in Implementation of the Generic Practice	How the Generic Practice Recursively Applies to Its Related Process Area(s)*
GP 2.2 Plan the Process	**Project Planning:** The project planning process can implement GP 2.2 in full for all project-related process areas (except for Project Planning itself).	GP 2.2 applied to the project planning process can be characterized as "plan the plan" and covers planning project planning activities.
GP 2.3 Provide Resources GP 2.4 Assign Responsibility	**Project Planning:** The part of the project planning process that implements Project Planning SP 2.4, "Plan the Project's Resources," supports the implementation of GP 2.3 and GP 2.4 for all project-related process areas (except perhaps initially for Project Planning itself) by identifying needed processes, roles, and responsibilities to ensure the proper staffing, facilities, equipment, and other assets needed by the project are secured.	
GP 2.5 Train People	**Organizational Training:** The organizational training process supports the implementation of GP 2.5 as applied to all process areas by making the training that addresses strategic or organization-wide training needs available to those who will perform or support the process. **Project Planning:** The part of the project planning process that implements Project Planning SP 2.5, "Plan Needed Knowledge and Skills," together with the organizational training process, supports the implementation of GP 2.5 in full for all project-related process areas.	GP 2.5 applied to the organizational training process covers training for performing the organizational training activities, which addresses the skills required to manage, create, and accomplish the training.
GP 2.6 Manage Configurations	**Configuration Management:** The configuration management process can implement GP 2.6 in full for all project-related process areas as well as some of the organizational process areas.	GP 2.6 applied to the configuration management process covers change and version control for the work products produced by configuration management activities.

* When the relationship between a generic practice and a process area is less direct, the risk of confusion is reduced; therefore, we do not describe all recursive relationships in the table (e.g., for generic practices 2.3, 2.4, and 2.10).

TABLE 7.1 Generic Practice and Process Area Relationships *(Continued)*

Generic Practice	Roles of Process Areas in Implementation of the Generic Practice	How the Generic Practice Recursively Applies to Its Related Process Area(s)
GP 2.7 Identify and Involve Relevant Stakeholders	**Project Planning:** The part of the project planning process that implements Project Planning SP 2.6, "Plan Stakeholder Involvement," can implement the stakeholder identification part (first two subpractices) of GP 2.7 in full for all project-related process areas.	GP 2.7 applied to the project planning process covers the involvement of relevant takeholders in project planning activities.
	Project Monitoring and Control: The part of the project monitoring and control process that implements Project Monitoring and Control SP 1.5, "Monitor Stakeholder Involvement," can aid in implementing the third subpractice of GP 2.7 for all project-related process areas.	GP 2.7 applied to the project monitoring and control process covers the involvement of relevant stakeholders in project monitoring and control activities.
	Integrated Project Management: The part of the integrated project management process that implements Integrated Project Management SP 2.1, "Manage Stakeholder Involvement," can aid in implementing the third subpractice of GP 2.7 for all project-related process areas.	GP 2.7 applied to the integrated project management process covers the involvement of relevant stakeholders in integrated project management activities.
GP 2.8 Monitor and Control the Process	**Project Monitoring and Control:** The project monitoring and control process can implement GP 2.8 in full for all project-related process areas.	GP 2.8 applied to the project monitoring and control process covers the monitoring and controlling of the project's monitor and control activities.
	Measurement and Analysis: For all processes, not just project-related processes, the Measurement and Analysis process area provides general guidance about measuring, analyzing, and recording information that can be used in establishing measures for monitoring actual performance of the process.	
GP 2.9 Objectively Evaluate Adherence	**Process and Product Quality Assurance:** The process and product quality assurance process can implement GP 2.9 in full for all process areas (except perhaps for Process and Product Quality Assurance itself).	GP 2.9 applied to the process and product quality assurance process covers the objective evaluation of quality assurance activities.

Continues

TABLE 7.1 Generic Practice and Process Area Relationships *(Continued)*

Generic Practice	*Roles of Process Areas in Implementation of the Generic Practice*	*How the Generic Practice Recursively Applies to Its Related Process Area(s)*
GP 2.10 Review Status with Higher Level Management	**Project Monitoring and Control:** The part of the project monitoring and control process that implements Project Monitoring and Control SP 1.6, "Conduct Progress Reviews," and SP 1.7, "Conduct Milestone Reviews," supports the implementation of GP 2.10 for all project-related process areas, perhaps in full, depending on higher level management involvement in these reviews.	
GP 3.1 Establish a Defined Process	**Integrated Project Management:** The part of the integrated project management process that implements Integrated Project Management SP 1.1, "Establish the Project's Defined Process," can implement GP 3.1 in full for all project-related process areas. **Organizational Process Definition:** For all processes, not just project-related processes, the organizational process definition process establishes the organizational process assets needed to implement GP 3.1.	GP 3.1 applied to the integrated project management process covers establishing defined processes for integrated project management activities.
GP 3.2 Collect Improvement Information	**Integrated Project Management:** The part of the integrated project management process that implements Integrated Project Management SP 1.7, "Contribute to Organizational Process Assets," can implement GP 3.2 in part or in full for all project-related process areas. **Organizational Process Focus:** The part of the organizational process focus process that implements Organizational Process Focus SP 3.4, "Incorporate Experiences into Organizational Process Assets," can implement GP 3.2 in part or in full for all process areas. **Organizational Process Definition:** For all processes, the organizational process definition process establishes the organizational process assets needed to implement GP 3.2.	GP 3.2 applied to the integrated project management process covers collecting improvement information derived from planning and performing integrated project management activities.

TABLE 7.1 Generic Practice and Process Area Relationships *(Continued)*

Generic Practice	Roles of Process Areas in Implementation of the Generic Practice	How the Generic Practice Recursively Applies to Its Related Process Area(s)
GP 4.1 Establish Quantitative Objectives for the Process	**Quantitative Project Management:** The part of the quantitative project management process that implements Quantitative Project Management SP 1.1, "Establish the Project's Objectives," supports the implementation of GP 4.1 for all project-related process areas by providing objectives from which the objectives for each particular process can be derived. If these objectives become established as part of implementing subpractices 5 and 8 of Quantitative Project Management SP 1.1, then the quantitative project management process implements GP 4.1 in full. **Organizational Process Performance:** The part of the organizational process-performance process that implements Organizational Process Performance SP 1.3, "Establish Quality and Process Performance Objectives," supports the implementation of GP 4.1 for all process areas.	GP 4.1 applied to the quantitative project management process covers establishing quantitative objectives for quantitative project management activities. GP 4.1 applied to the organizational process-performance process covers establishing quantitative objectives for organizational process-performance activities.
GP 4.2 Stabilize Subprocess Performance	**Quantitative Project Management:** The part of the quantitative project management process that implements Quantitative Project Management SG 2, "Statistically Manage Subprocess Performance," can implement GP 4.2 in full for all project-related process areas to which a statistically managed subprocess can be mapped. **Organizational Process Performance:** For all processes, not just project-related processes, the organizational process performance process establishes organizational process assets that may be needed to implement GP 4.2.	GP 4.2 applied to the quantitative project management process covers the stabilization of selected subprocesses within quantitative project management activities.
GP 5.1 Ensure Continuous Process Improvement	**Organizational Innovation and Deployment:** The organizational innovation and deployment process can implement GP 5.1 in full for all process areas providing that quality and process-performance objectives for the organization have been defined. (The latter would be the case, say, if the Organizational Process Performance process area has been implemented.)	GP 5.1 applied to the organizational innovation and deployment process covers ensuring continuous process improvement of organizational innovation and deployment activities.

Continues

TABLE 7.1 Generic Practice and Process Area Relationships *(Continued)*

Generic Practice	Roles of Process Areas in Implementation of the Generic Practice	How the Generic Practice Recursively Applies to Its Related Process Area(s)
GP 5.2 Correct Root Causes of Problems	**Causal Analysis and Resolution:** The causal analysis and resolution process can implement GP 5.2 in full for all project-related process areas.	GP 5.2 applied to the causal analysis and resolution process covers identifying root causes of defects and other problems in causal analysis and resolution activities.

CAPACITY AND AVAILABILITY MANAGEMENT
A Project Management Process Area at Maturity Level 3

Purpose

The purpose of Capacity and Availability Management (CAM) is to ensure effective service system performance and ensure that resources are provided and used effectively to support service requirements.

Introductory Notes

The Capacity and Availability Management process area involves establishing and maintaining capacity and availability at a justifiable cost and with an efficient use of resources. Capacity and availability management activities may be performed at different levels of the organization, including across different services.

The Capacity and Availability Management process area involves the following activities:

- Establishing and maintaining a capacity and availability management strategy
- Providing and allocating resources appropriately
- Monitoring, analyzing, understanding, and reporting on current and future demand for services, use of resources, capacity, service system performance, and service availability
- Determining corrective actions to ensure appropriate capacity and availability while balancing costs against resources needed and supply against demand

"Capacity" is the degree to which one thing may support, hold, process, or produce another thing. In the context of services, capacity may refer to the maximum amount of service delivery or maximum number of service requests that a service system can handle successfully within a fixed period of time. The definition and measurement of

225

capacity may differ for different types of services and service systems and may be defined in the service agreement. In addition, capacity definitions and measures may be derived from service agreements, rather than reflected there. If the service agreement has no explicit capacity requirements, it may still imply derived capacity requirements for the service or service system. For some services, capacity may be the maximum size, volume, or throughput of service system components.

Examples of capacity include the following:
- Number of vehicles requiring maintenance that can be received on the maintenance premises within a 24-hour period
- Number of loan application forms that can be processed within an 8-hour period
- Size or volume of a disk drive
- Square feet of floor space that can be cleaned per hour
- Number of pounds that a loader can hold at one time
- Total amount of fluid that can be absorbed by a service system component
- Number of calls per day that can be handled by a call center
- Number of appraisals that can be performed per year

As part of establishing the capacity and availability management strategy, the following are determined:

- Resources appropriate to manage
- Aspects of the service system that affect service availability and should be measured, monitored, analyzed, and managed

---

Examples of resources include personnel, hardware, power, and available space.

"Availability" is the degree to which something is accessible and usable when needed. In the context of services, availability may refer to the set of times, places, and other circumstances in which services are to be delivered, service requests are to be honored, or other aspects of a service agreement are to be valid. Different projects may have different definitions and measurements of availability for different types of services and service systems and for various perspectives of availability (e.g., business perspective, end-user perspective, customer perspective, service provider perspective). The definition of availability requires an understanding of how service system components support service requirements for availability, which may be defined in the service agreement. In addition, availability requirements and measures may both depend on and affect other closely related requirements, such as maintainability, reliability, sustainability, and security.

Examples of service system components for which availability may be a concern include the following:
- Anesthesia equipment
- Cafeteria staff
- Maintenance supplies
- Transportation components (e.g., cabs, buses, trucks, drivers)
- Call center staff
- Lead appraisers

Availability is one of the most visible indicators of service quality in the eyes of the end user and customer. For some services, understanding the relationships between reliability, maintainability, etc., and availability is important to managing availability.

Availability of services may depend on the following:
- Availability of service system components
- Resilience of the service system to failure
- Quality of the maintenance performed on the service system
- Quality of the support provided to the service system
- Effectiveness of service processes
- Security practices

"Capacity management" is focused on how best to provide resources to meet service requirements. "Availability management" is focused on delivering a sustained level of availability to meet service requirements. However, at a high level, many of the best practices for capacity management and availability management are similar enough to be combined, and they become closely coupled. Capacity management provides the means for achieving sustained availability to meet service requirements. (For some services, it provides spare capacity and resilience as well.)

The simultaneous production and consumption of services is one of the unique characteristics of services. This characteristic presents some challenges for managing the capacity and availability of services. If the capacity and availability to provide the service is not present when demand occurs, the customer must wait, resulting in costs of one kind or another (e.g., lower customer satisfaction, lost business as customers give up on waiting, financial penalties). Costs may also be associated with excess capacity when estimated demand does not occur (e.g., cost of employees on the payroll sitting idle, purchasing costs of excess capacity).

Examples of capacity management challenges include the following:
- Providing enough and the right kind of hotel rooms to meet demand without double booking or ending up with empty hotel rooms
- Providing enough baggage handlers for the volume of travelers at an airport without having excess or idle baggage handlers

---

Examples of availability management challenges include the following:
- Ensuring that landscaping services are delivered, landscaping equipment is maintained, and landscaping personnel are able to take days off (e.g., holidays, annual leave) as defined in relevant agreements
- Monitoring the reliability of landscaping equipment and personnel (e.g., the absentee rate among landscaping personnel)
- Determining corrective action when service availability drops below levels in the service agreement

---

Capacity and availability management includes establishing service system representations and using these representations to do the following:

- Supporting negotiation of appropriate service agreements
- Planning
- Decision making
- Considering corrective actions
- Providing and allocating resources to meet current and future service requirements

"Service system representations," such as models, simulations, diagrams, maps, and prototypes, provide insight into how a service system will behave given specific work volumes and varieties. These representations may be built using spreadsheets, commercial off-the-shelf (COTS) tools (e.g., simulation packages), or tools developed in-house. For some services, the representations may be known as historical baselines, trend analyses, analytical models, analysis of waiting times in queues, simulation models, statistical models (e.g., regression models or time series models), causal models (e.g., probabilistic networks), or application sizing.

The scope of capacity and availability management can be one service system or multiple service systems. If the service provider is operating multiple service systems, capacity and availability management processes can be performed independently on each discrete service system, but the organization may realize reduced value.

CAM

CAPACITY, AVAILABILITY, AND SERVICE SYSTEM REPRESENTATIONS

Since capacity and availability are distinct attributes of service systems and their components, a question naturally arises: Why did the CMMI for Services model team place the management of these important properties in the same process area? The introductory notes in this process area suggest two different answers to this question: "... at a high level, many of the best practices for capacity management and availability management are similar enough to be combined, and they become closely coupled. Capacity management provides the means for achieving sustained availability to meet service requirements." So, capacity and availability are handled together by the model because they share some common goals and practices, and because they are managing a common collection of entities (resources) to achieve objectives that are distinct but intrinsically intertwined.

Additional reasons for integrating capacity management with availability management are that both depend on the use of explicit service system representations, these representations may be integrated in ways yielding both capacity and availability information, and capacity and availability estimates derived from these representations may be dependent on each other. Overall capacity of a service system can often be increased by extending the availability of key resources, either by adding additional resources or by extending their in-service cycle length; and overall availability of a service can often be increased by providing enlarged capacity. There are too many contexts where it simply doesn't make sense to manage capacity and availability independently of each other.

Continues

Some CMMI for Services reviewers have also questioned why the model team chose to use the somewhat fuzzy term *service system representations* rather than the more intuitive term *service system models* in CAM. The informative material in the CAM process area discusses service system representations at length in SP 1.3 without ever addressing this question, although it is careful to explain why service system representations and process-performance models are distinct. The need for that careful explanation actually provides a hint of the real answer: The term *model* is already overloaded in the CMMI context with two distinct and specialized meanings (one related to process performance and one related to entire CMMI products). The CMMI for Services model team concluded that it would create too much confusion to establish a third distinct specialized meaning for the word *model* when referring to artifacts that describe components, relationships, and properties of service systems. The team selected the term *representation* rather than *model* as a way to prevent this potential significant confusion (at the price of occasional questions raised about service system representations).

Related Process Areas

Refer to the Incident Resolution and Prevention process area for more information about identifying, controlling, and addressing incidents.

Refer to the Service Continuity process area for more information about establishing and maintaining plans to ensure continuity of services during and following any significant disruption of normal operations.

Refer to the Service Delivery process area for more information about maintaining the service system.

Refer to the Strategic Service Management process area for more information about establishing strategic needs and plans for standard services.

Refer to the Measurement and Analysis process area for more information about specifying measures.

Refer to the Project Planning process area for more information about establishing the project strategy and developing a project plan.

Specific Goal and Practice Summary

SG 1 Prepare for Capacity and Availability Management
      SP 1.1   Establish a Capacity and Availability Management Strategy
      SP 1.2   Select Measures and Analytic Techniques
      SP 1.3   Establish Service System Representations
SG 2 Monitor and Analyze Capacity and Availability
      SP 2.1   Monitor and Analyze Capacity
      SP 2.2   Monitor and Analyze Availability
      SP 2.3   Report Capacity and Availability Management Data

Specific Practices by Goal

SG 1 PREPARE FOR CAPACITY AND AVAILABILITY MANAGEMENT

Preparation for capacity and availability management is conducted.

Preparation for capacity and availability management includes the following activities:

- Establishing and maintaining a strategy for managing capacity and availability to meet service requirements
- Selecting measures and analytic techniques to support availability and capacity management objectives
- Establishing and maintaining service system representations to understand current capacity, availability, and service system performance (i.e., describe what the normal capacity, availability, and service levels are)

Thresholds are established and maintained to define exception conditions in the service system, recognize breaches or near breaches of service requirements, and identify service incidents. In addition to understanding the capacity and availability of the current service system, capacity, availability, and service levels are estimated based on trends in service resource use, service system performance, and expected service requirements.

SP 1.1 ESTABLISH A CAPACITY AND AVAILABILITY MANAGEMENT STRATEGY

Establish and maintain a strategy for capacity and availability management.

A strategy for capacity and availability management is based on service requirements, failure and change request trend analysis, current resource use, and service system performance. Service system representations can help to develop a strategy for capacity and availability management. A strategy may address the minimum, maximum, and average use of services (i.e., service resources) over the short, medium, and long term as appropriate for the duration of the service.

It may be appropriate for some services to identify, plan for, and manage the availability of surge capacity or "reach-back" resources to respond to sudden, unexpected increases in demand. For some service types, the management of the obsolescence of certain resources and services factor into the strategy for capacity and availability management.

Service system design documentation can help to determine resources and aspects of the service system to be measured, monitored, analyzed, and managed. However, design documents may not be available or may not accurately and comprehensively reflect all aspects of the live service environment that affect capacity and availability. Therefore, it is important to monitor and analyze *actual* capacity and availability data. Service strategies, information from day-to-day service delivery and monitoring, and service requirements from current service agreements can assist with these determinations.

Refer to the Service Delivery process area for more information about establishing service agreements.

Refer to the Service System Transition process area for more information about preparing for service system transition.

Refer to the Strategic Service Management process area for more information about establishing standard services.

The strategy for capacity and availability management may reflect factors such as constraints due to limited customer funding and the customer's acceptance of certain risks related to capacity and availability.

The service provider may not be able to influence or control demand and resource adjustments but is still required to formulate a strategy that best meets service requirements. If the service provider can influence or control demand and resource adjustments, the strategy may be more sophisticated than in situations in which the service provider cannot exercise such influence or control.

Typical Work Products

1. Capacity and availability management strategy

Subpractices

1. Document resource and service use, performance, and availability.
2. Estimate future resource and service capacity and availability requirements.

3. Develop a capacity strategy that meets service requirements, meets the demand for resources and services, and addresses how resources are provided, used, and allocated.

4. Develop an availability strategy that meets service requirements and addresses delivering a sustained level of availability.

   It may be appropriate for some services to include in the strategy an availability testing schedule, a service system maintenance strategy, and planned service outages.

   Refer to the Service Continuity process area for more information about preparing for service continuity.

   Refer to the Service Delivery process area for more information about maintaining the service system.

   Refer to the Service System Transition process area for more information about preparing for service system transition.

5. Document monetized costs and benefits of the strategy and any assumptions.

6. Periodically revise the strategy.

   It may also be necessary to revise the strategy on an event-driven basis.

SP 1.2 SELECT MEASURES AND ANALYTIC TECHNIQUES

Select measures and analytic techniques to be used in managing the capacity and availability of the service system.

The measures specified for managing capacity and availability may require the collection of business data, financial data, service data, technical data, service resource use data, performance data, and other data about the capacity and availability of the service system. Measurement objectives and the selection of measures and analytic techniques for capacity and availability management are largely influenced by the service agreement and specific properties of the service system.

Considerations for selection of measures also include which activities are being supported, reporting requirements, and how the information will be used. Supplier agreements should reflect or support the selected measures and analytic techniques as appropriate.

Refer to the Service Delivery process area for more information about establishing the service agreement.

Refer to the Measurement and Analysis process area for more information about aligning measurement and analysis activities.

Refer to the Supplier Agreement Management process area for more information about establishing supplier agreements.

Examples of availability measures include the following:
- Percentage available within agreed hours (this availability can be overall service availability or service component availability)
- Percentage unavailable within agreed hours (this unavailability can be overall service unavailability or service component unavailability)
- Duration of downtime due to failure (typically minutes, hours, or hours per week)
- Failure frequency
- Scope of impact (e.g., number of users who were affected, number of minutes that users lost productivity, number of transactions or vital business functions not processed or carried out, number of application services impeded)
- Response time of the service system to service incidents, transaction response times, and service response times (this response time can be a capacity measure or availability measure)
- Reliability (e.g., number of service breaks, mean time between failures, mean time between service incidents)

Examples of capacity measures are as follows:
- Use of service resources that are limited
- Use of service components
- Unused service resources that are limited
- Unused service components
- Throughput (e.g., number of concurrent users, number of transactions to be processed)
- Queue length (maximum and average)
- Number of a particular type of resource or one or more specific resources in use a selected number of times (this use can be monitored by calendar time)

Typical Work Products

1. Operational definitions of capacity and availability measures
2. Traceability of capacity and availability measures to service requirements
3. Tools to support collection and analysis of capacity and availability data
4. Target measures or ranges to be met for selected measured attributes

Subpractices

1. Identify measures from organizational process assets that support capacity and availability management objectives.

2. Identify and specify additional measures that may be needed to support achieving capacity and availability management objectives for the service.

3. Analyze the relationship between identified measures and service requirements, and derive objectives that state specific target measures or ranges to be met for each measured attribute.

> This analysis may provide input to the descriptions of standard services and service levels.

> *Refer to the Strategic Service Management process area for more information about establishing standard services.*

SP 1.3 ESTABLISH SERVICE SYSTEM REPRESENTATIONS

Establish and maintain service system representations to support capacity and availability management.

Service system representations provide insight into how the service system will behave given specific work volumes and varieties. These insights are used to support decision making about resource allocation, changes to the service system, service agreements, and other aspects of service management and delivery.

For many services, demand fluctuates widely. Managing services in the face of widely fluctuating demand is one of the unique challenges characteristic of services. Depending on the patterns of fluctuation, the representations may focus on small or medium time intervals (e.g., by hour of the day for work-shift scheduling, day of the week, month of the year) or longer time intervals (e.g., seasons of the year, biannually, annually).

Estimated growth of the use of service resources is formulated using collected capacity and availability data, estimated service requirements, and service system representations.

Measurement objectives and specific properties of the service system determine the nature and extent of a service system representation. (The service agreement has a major influence on the measurement objectives.) Experience, historical data, modeling expertise, and current resource use can also influence the nature of a service system representation.

Refer to the Measurement and Analysis process area for more information about establishing measurement objectives and specifying analysis procedures.

Representations can be used to analyze the impact of change requests that are likely to affect availability and capacity. Representations can also be used to characterize the range of future demand that can be met and the impact of required service levels on the service system. Before representations of future behavior or service system performance can be established, descriptions of the normal use of service resources and service system performance must be established.

Examples of service system representations that support capacity and availability management include the following:

- Graphical representations showing a mix of two types of health care provider resources in a hospital with specific constraints and parameters indicating what might be the best allocation of the two resources
- Analysis of waiting lines for bank tellers
- Vehicle scheduling programs
- Simulation modeling of transaction arrival rates against a specific configuration of resources (e.g., bank tellers, network servers)
- Trend analysis of the availability, reliability, and maintainability of service system components
- Impact analysis of service system component failure
- Load testing to generate expected demand on a service system resource and ensure that service system components can perform according to the service agreement
- Fault tree analysis and single point of failure analysis

Service system representations may be established to provide input to support development of the service agreement and descriptions of standard services and service levels.

Refer to the Service Delivery process area for more information about establishing the service agreement.

Refer to the Strategic Service Management process area for more information about establishing standard services.

Service system representations may be established during design of the service system. However, even if great care is taken during the design and development of the service system to ensure that it can meet service requirements over a wide range of operating conditions, service management and delivery must sustain the required levels of service system performance and quality during transition and operation.

Refer to the Service System Development process area for more information about developing service systems.

SSD ADD

Service system representations are maintained throughout the service lifecycle.

Service system representations are generally not the same as the process-performance baselines and models established in Organizational Process Performance (OPP) at levels 4 and 5. Several things distinguish representations from process-performance baselines and models:

- OPP process-performance models and baselines require that statistical techniques be used, that special causes of variation be identified and addressed, and that processes be stable and predictable (i.e., are also statistically managed). Service system representations are not required to have these same attributes.
- Representations established in CAM are not required to be based on data collected from using the organization's set of standard processes.
- The focus of OPP is on process-performance baselines and models. In addition to process data, the focus of CAM's service system representations includes nonprocess data, people, and other parts of the service system, such as infrastructure and automated systems.
- Service system representations are established to support capacity and availability analysis specifically. This scope is narrower than the scope of OPP practices.

See the definition of "statistically managed process" in the glossary.

Refer to the Organizational Process Performance process area for more information about establishing performance baselines and models.

Although not *required* for capacity and availability management, representations provide opportunities to use statistical techniques such as statistical process control. These techniques can be used to quantitatively manage service system performance and quality and to improve service system capability.

Refer to the Quantitative Project Management process area for more information about applying statistical methods to understand variation.

Typical Work Products

1. Representations of resource and service use
2. Representations of service levels
3. Data on the use of resources and services
4. Data on current service levels delivered
5. Thresholds that define exception conditions and breaches

Subpractices

1. Collect measurements on the use of resources and services and the current service levels delivered.

2. Establish and maintain descriptions of the normal use of service resources and service system performance.

   For some services, it may be advisable to establish general systems flow charts to identify the service system and its processes before determining the service system's current capacity, which may require determining the capacity of service system components.

3. Establish and maintain service system representations from collected measurements and analyses.

   For some services, it may be advisable to estimate the capacity of the service system at peak work volumes.

4. Review and get agreement with relevant stakeholders about the descriptions of the normal use of service resources, service system performance, and service system representations.

5. Make available the descriptions of the normal use of service resources, service system performance, and service system representations.

6. Establish and maintain thresholds associated with demand, workload, use of service resources, and service system performance to define exception conditions in the service system and breaches or near breaches of service requirements.

   Thresholds are typically set below the level at which an exception condition or breach of service requirement occurs to allow corrective action to prevent the breach of service requirement, overuse of resources, or poor service system performance.

SG 2 MONITOR AND ANALYZE CAPACITY AND AVAILABILITY

Capacity and availability are monitored and analyzed to manage resources and demand.

The contribution of each service system component to meeting service requirements is analyzed to successfully manage the capacity and availability of services. The efficient use of resources is managed according to the capacity and availability management strategy, which is developed to meet service requirements. It might not be possible for a service organization to influence demand for services, and the requirement to do so is not implied by the phrase "manage resources and demand." Efficient use of resources may include both reactive and proactive responses. Proactive responses are possible in situations in which the service provider can influence demand.

Actual capacity and availability data are monitored regularly. These actual data are also compared regularly with thresholds, descriptions of normal and expected use, and business objectives. These comparisons identify exception conditions in the service system, breaches or near-breaches of service requirements, and changes in the patterns of use of service system resources that may indicate trends. For example, regular monitoring of actual service resource use against estimated service resource use might reveal a pending breach of service requirements.

SP 2.1 MONITOR AND ANALYZE CAPACITY

Monitor and analyze capacity against thresholds.

The use of each service resource is documented as well as the use of each resource by each service (i.e., the extent or degree of use by each service for a given service resource). The impact of service component failures on resources is analyzed.

It may be appropriate for some services to monitor use of surge capacity or "reach-back" resources and determine whether corrective actions are needed, such as adjustments to resources provided, adjustments to thresholds, or adjustments to descriptions of the normal use of service resources and service system performance.

The need for corrective actions may be identified as a result of monitoring and analyzing capacity and availability or in response to service incidents, change requests, changes to service requirements (current and future) or to improve service system performance or prevent breaches of the service agreement.

Refer to the Measurement and Analysis process area for more information about specifying data collection and storage procedures.

Typical Work Products

1. Service resource use data
2. Growth analysis of service use
3. List of resources not used as estimated

Subpractices

1. Monitor the use of service resources against thresholds, descriptions of normal use, and service system performance.

   Refer to the Project Monitoring and Control process area for more information about monitoring project planning parameters.

2. Monitor service response times.

3. Identify breaches of thresholds and exception conditions.

Breaches of thresholds and exception conditions may constitute or indicate an incident.

Refer to the Incident Resolution and Prevention process area for more information about identifying, controlling, and addressing incidents.

Refer to the Service Delivery process area for more information about operating the service system.

4. Determine the corrective action to be taken.

Corrective actions include adjustments to resources and services to prevent performance problems or improve service performance. Adjustments may be automated, performed manually, or both.

Examples of corrective actions include the following:
- Rebalancing workload among resources
- Improving service system processes to allow for greater productivity, efficiency, and effectiveness
- Improving service system design, such as making use of new technologies to allow for greater productivity, efficiency, or effectiveness
- Adding capacity to the service system, such as adding nurses, servers, or phone lines
- Tuning to optimize and improve capacity or service system performance
- Adjusting service requirements
- Improving the use of service resources through demand management techniques

---

Refer to the Service System Development process area for more information about developing service systems.

SSD ADD

Refer to the Project Monitoring and Control process area for more information about managing corrective action to closure.

5. Estimate future changes (either growth or reduction) in the use of resources and services.

Methods and tools for estimating service system behavior include trend analysis, analytical modeling, simulation modeling, baseline models, and application sizing.

Estimates of growth in the use of resources may be based on collected capacity and availability data, estimated service requirements, and service system representations.

6. Store capacity and availability data, specifications, analysis results, and monitoring data.

SP 2.2 MONITOR AND ANALYZE AVAILABILITY

Monitor and analyze availability against targets.

To prevent the failure of service system components and support the availability of the system, the service system must be monitored. At a minimum, availability is monitored. Other "ilities" may be appropriate to monitor depending on the type of service provided. Reliability and maintainability are other "ilities" that may be appropriate to monitor for many types of service systems. Resilience of the service system to service component failure may also be monitored, and the impacts of specific failures on service system availability may be identified.

Typical Work Products

1. Alarm data
2. Availability data
3. Reliability data
4. Maintainability data

Subpractices

1. Monitor availability, reliability, and maintainability against their requirements.
2. Analyze trends in availability, reliability, and maintainability.
   For some services, it may be advisable to perform failure trend analysis as well.
3. Identify breaches of availability, reliability, and maintainability requirements.

   Refer to the Incident Resolution and Prevention process area for more information about identifying, controlling, and addressing incidents.
4. Determine the corrective actions to be taken.

   Refer to the Service Delivery process area for more information about maintaining the service system.

   Refer to the Project Monitoring and Control process area for more information about managing corrective action to closure.

SP 2.3 REPORT CAPACITY AND AVAILABILITY MANAGEMENT DATA

Report capacity and availability management data to relevant stakeholders.

Reports are provided to relevant stakeholders that summarize information about capacity and availability. These reports support monitoring against the service agreement and service reviews. How data are reported strongly influences how much benefit is derived from capacity and availability management.

Refer to the Project Monitoring and Control process area for more information about monitoring the project against the plan.

Service agreements and supplier agreements may define the information to be reported, to whom it should be delivered, and how it is provided (e.g., format, detail, distribution, media). The information should be appropriate to the audience, which means it should be understandable (e.g., not overly technical), and it may need to address multiple perspectives. These perspectives may include business, end user, customer, or service provider perspectives.

Capacity and availability reports may be regular or ad hoc, depending on what is in the service agreement. For some services, reporting can be greatly simplified by the use of databases offering automated reporting features. Organizational reporting standards should be followed, and standard tools and techniques should be used when they exist to support the integration and consolidation of information in the reports.

Refer to the Service Delivery process area for more information about establishing service agreements.

Refer to the Organizational Process Definition process area for more information about establishing standard processes.

Refer to the Supplier Agreement Management process area for more information about establishing supplier agreements.

Availability is often reported as a percentage. In addition to reporting availability, some service providers also report on reliability (e.g., reliability of the service, reliability of service system components) because it is required in the service agreement. The service agreement may also require reporting on maintainability and other "ilities."

Typical Work Products

1. Service system performance reports
2. Service resource use reports
3. Service resource use projections
4. Service availability reports

Subpractices

1. Report the performance and use of resources and services.
2. Report exception conditions in the service system and breaches of service requirements.

3. Report data from monitoring against growth estimates in resource and service use.

4. Report the availability, reliability, and maintainability of resources and services.

CAUSAL ANALYSIS AND RESOLUTION
A Support Process Area at Maturity Level 5

Purpose

The purpose of Causal Analysis and Resolution (CAR) is to identify causes of defects and problems and take action to prevent them from occurring in the future.

Introductory Notes

The Causal Analysis and Resolution process area involves the following activities:

- Identifying and analyzing causes of defects and problems
- Taking actions to remove causes and prevent the occurrence of those types of defects and problems in the future

Causal analysis and resolution improves quality and productivity by preventing the introduction of defects and occurrence of problems. Reliance on detecting defects and problems after they have been introduced is not cost effective. It is more effective to prevent defects and problems by integrating causal analysis and resolution activities into each phase of the project.

Since similar defects and problems may have been previously encountered on other projects or in earlier phases or tasks of the current project, causal analysis and resolution activities are a mechanism for communicating lessons learned among projects.

Types of defects and problems encountered are analyzed to identify trends. Based on an understanding of the defined process and how it is implemented, root causes of defects and problems and future implications of them are determined.

Causal analysis may be performed on problems unrelated to defects. For example, causal analysis may be used to improve coordination and cycle time with one supplier or multiple suppliers.

IN OTHER WORDS

CAR is about getting to the sources of important mistakes and problems and taking effective action to correct them.

WHY DO THE PRACTICES IN CAR?

You won't waste time investigating and solving every defect, but you will tackle the most important ones that affect service delivery. You are more likely to get at causes and not just symptoms. These practices can be applied simply to get some benefit. If you are a high maturity organization, you use quantitative data to figure out what is adversely affecting your performance.

CAR

When it is impractical to perform causal analysis on all defects and problems, targets are selected by tradeoffs on estimated investments and estimated returns of quality, productivity, and cycle time.

A measurement process should already be in place. Already defined measures can be used, though in some instances new measures may be needed to analyze the effects of the process change.

Refer to the Measurement and Analysis process area for more information about aligning measurement and analysis activities and providing measurement results.

Causal Analysis and Resolution activities provide a mechanism for projects to evaluate their processes at the local level and look for improvements that can be implemented.

When improvements are judged to be effective, the information is extended to the organizational level.

Refer to the Organizational Innovation and Deployment process area for more information about selecting and deploying incremental and innovative improvements that measurably improve the organization's processes and technologies.

The informative material in this process area is written assuming that the specific practices are applied to a quantitatively managed process. The specific practices of this process area may be applicable, but with reduced value, if this assumption is not met.

See the definitions of "stable process" and "common cause of process variation" in the glossary.

Related Process Areas

Refer to the Measurement and Analysis process area for more information about aligning measurement and analysis activities and providing measurement results.

Refer to the Organizational Innovation and Deployment process area for more information about selecting and deploying incremental and innovative improvements that measurably improve the organization's processes and technologies.

Refer to the Quantitative Project Management process area for more information about applying statistical methods to understand variation and monitoring performance of the selected subprocesses.

Specific Goal and Practice Summary

SG 1 Determine Causes of Defects and Problems
      SP 1.1   Select Defects and Problems
      SP 1.2   Analyze Causes
SG 2 Address Causes of Defects and Problems
      SP 2.1   Implement Action Proposals
      SP 2.2   Evaluate the Effect of Changes
      SP 2.3   Record Data

Specific Practices by Goal

SG 1   DETERMINE CAUSES OF DEFECTS AND PROBLEMS

Root causes of defects and problems are systematically determined.

A root cause is a source of a defect or problem such that if it is removed, the defect or problem is decreased or removed.

SP 1.1   SELECT DEFECTS AND PROBLEMS

Select defects and problems for analysis.

Typical Work Products

1. Defect and problem data selected for further analysis

Subpractices

1. Gather relevant defect and problem data.

> Examples of relevant defect data include the following:
> - Defects reported by the customer
> - Defects reported by service teams
> - Defects found in service verification

> Examples of relevant problem data include the following:
> - Project management problem reports requiring corrective action
> - Process capability problems
> - Process duration measurements
> - Resource throughput, utilization, or response time measurements
> - Help desk calls, by time and incident category
> - Inadequate availability of the service system

CAR

Refer to the Quantitative Project Management process area for more information about statistical management.

2. Determine the defects and problems to be analyzed further.

When determining which defects and problems to analyze further, consider their impact, their frequency of occurrence, the similarities among them, the cost of analysis, the time and resources needed, safety considerations, etc.

Examples of methods for selecting defects and problems include the following:
- Pareto analysis
- Histograms
- Cause and effects analysis (e.g., design failure mode and effects analysis for the service system being developed, process failure mode and effects analysis for service system development or service delivery)

SP 1.2 ANALYZE CAUSES

Perform causal analysis of selected defects and problems and propose actions to address them.

The purpose of this analysis is to develop solutions to identified defects and problems by analyzing relevant data and producing action proposals for implementation.

Typical Work Products

1. Action proposal
2. Root cause analysis results

Subpractices

1. Conduct causal analysis with those responsible for performing the task.

Causal analysis is performed, typically in meetings, with those who understand the selected defect or problem under study. Those who have the best understanding of the selected defect or problem are typically those responsible for performing the task.

Examples of when to perform causal analysis include the following:
- When a stable subprocess does not meet its specified quality and process-performance objectives
- During the task, if and when problems warrant a causal analysis meeting
- When a work product exhibits an unexpected deviation from its requirements

> *Refer to the Quantitative Project Management process area for more information about monitoring performance of selected subprocesses.*

2. Analyze selected defects and problems to determine their root causes.

    Depending on the type and number of defects and problems, it may make sense to first group them before identifying their root causes.

Examples of methods to determine root causes include the following:
- Cause-and-effect (fishbone) diagrams
- Check sheets

3. Group selected defects and problems based on their root causes.

Examples of cause groups or categories include the following:
- Inadequate training
- Breakdown of communication
- Not accounting for all details of a task
- Making mistakes in manual procedures (e.g., typing)
- Process deficiency

4. Propose and document actions to be taken to prevent the future occurrence of similar defects and problems.

Examples of proposed actions include changes to the following:
- The process in question
- Training
- Tools
- Methods
- Communication
- Work products

Examples of actions include the following:
- Providing training in common problems and techniques for preventing them
- Changing a process so that error-prone steps do not occur
- Automating all or part of a process
- Reordering process activities
- Adding process steps to prevent defects and problems, such as task kickoff meetings to review common defects and problems as well as actions to prevent them

An action proposal usually documents the following:
- Originator of the action proposal
- Description of the defect or problem
- Description of the cause of the defect or problem
- Defect or problem cause category
- Phase when the defect or problem was introduced
- Phase when the defect or problem was identified
- Description of the action proposal
- Action proposal category

SG 2   ADDRESS CAUSES OF DEFECTS AND PROBLEMS

Root causes of defects and problems are systematically addressed to prevent their future occurrence.

Projects operating according to a well-defined process systematically analyze where in the operation problems still occur and implement process changes to eliminate root causes of selected problems.

SP 2.1   IMPLEMENT ACTION PROPOSALS

Implement selected action proposals developed in causal analysis.

Action proposals describe tasks necessary to remove root causes of analyzed defects and problems and avoid their reoccurrence. Only changes that prove to be of value should be considered for broad implementation.

Typical Work Products

1. Action proposals selected for implementation
2. Improvement proposals

Subpractices

1. Analyze action proposals and determine their priorities.

> Criteria for prioritizing action proposals include the following:
> - Implications of not addressing the defect or problem
> - Cost to implement process improvements to prevent the defect or problem
> - Expected impact on quality

2. Select action proposals to be implemented.
3. Create action items for implementing the action proposals.

> Examples of information provided in an action item include the following:
> - Person responsible for implementing it
> - Description of the areas affected by it
> - People who are to be kept informed of its status
> - Next date that status will be reviewed
> - Rationale for key decisions
> - Description of implementation actions
> - Time and cost required to identify the defect or problem and to correct it
> - Estimated cost of not fixing the problem

To implement action proposals, the following tasks must be performed:
- Make assignments
- Coordinate the people doing the work
- Review the results
- Track action items to closure

Experiments may be conducted for particularly complex changes.

> Examples of experiments include the following:
> - Using a temporarily modified process
> - Using a new tool

Action items may be assigned to members of the causal analysis team, members of the project team, or other members of the organization.

4. Identify and remove similar defects and problems that may exist in other processes and work products.

5. Identify and document improvement proposals for the organization's set of standard processes.

> *Refer to the Organizational Innovation and Deployment process area for more information about collecting and analyzing improvement proposals.*

SP 2.2 EVALUATE THE EFFECT OF CHANGES

Evaluate the effect of changes on process performance.

Refer to the Quantitative Project Management process area for more information about selecting measures and analytic techniques.

Once the changed process is deployed across the project, the effect of changes must be evaluated to gather evidence that the process change corrected the problem and improved performance.

Typical Work Products

1. Measures of performance and performance change

Subpractices

1. Measure the change in performance of the project's defined process or of subprocesses as appropriate.

   This subpractice determines whether the selected change has positively influenced process performance and by how much.

An example of a change in the performance of a service would be the change in the cost of delivering the service after a change in the subprocess for integrating revised service system components. This change in performance would be determined through monitoring the delivered service before and after the improvement has been made and comparing these differences statistically (e.g., through a hypothesis test). On a statistical process control chart, this change in performance would be represented by a change in the mean.

---

2. Measure the capability of the project's defined process or of subprocesses as appropriate.

   This subpractice determines whether the selected change has positively influenced the ability of the process to meet its quality and process-performance objectives as determined by relevant stakeholders.

An example of a change in the capability of a service would be a change in the ability to deliver the service so that the resulting service stays within its cost boundaries. This change can be statistically measured by calculating the range in the cost of delivering the service through monitoring before and after the improvement has been made. On a statistical process control chart, this change in cost would be represented by narrowed control limits.

SP 2.3 RECORD DATA

Record causal analysis and resolution data for use across the project and organization.

Data are recorded so that other projects and organizations can make appropriate process changes and achieve similar results.

Record the following:

- Data on defects and problems that were analyzed
- Rationale for decisions
- Action proposals from causal analysis meetings
- Action items resulting from action proposals
- Cost of analysis and resolution activities
- Measures of changes to the performance of the defined process resulting from resolutions

Typical Work Products

1. Causal analysis and resolution records

CONFIGURATION MANAGEMENT
A Support Process Area at Maturity Level 2

Purpose

The purpose of Configuration Management (CM) is to establish and maintain the integrity of work products using configuration identification, configuration control, configuration status accounting, and configuration audits.

Introductory Notes

The Configuration Management process area involves the following activities:

- Identifying the configuration of selected work products that compose baselines at given points in time
- Controlling changes to configuration items
- Building or providing specifications to build work products from the configuration management system
- Maintaining the integrity of baselines
- Providing accurate status and current configuration data to developers, end users, and customers

The work products placed under configuration management include the products that are delivered to the customer, designated internal work products, acquired products, tools, and other items used in creating and describing these work products. (See the definition of "configuration management" in the glossary.)

CM

Examples of work products that may be placed under configuration management include the following:
- Plans
- Process descriptions
- Requirements
- Design data
- Drawings
- Product specifications
- Software
- Compilers
- Product data files
- Product technical publications
- Service agreements
- Authorized versions of controlled software and associated licensing information and documentation
- Repositories of asset information

Acquired products may need to be placed under configuration management by both the supplier and the acquirer. Provisions for conducting configuration management should be established in supplier agreements. Methods to ensure that data are complete and consistent should be established and maintained.

Refer to the Supplier Agreement Management process area for more information about establishing supplier agreements.

Configuration management of work products may be performed at several levels of granularity. Configuration items can be decomposed into configuration components and configuration units. Only the term "configuration item" is used in this process area. Therefore, in these practices, "configuration item" may be interpreted as "configuration component" or "configuration unit" as appropriate. (See the definition of "configuration item" in the glossary.)

Baselines provide a stable basis for the continuing evolution of configuration items.

Baselines are added to the configuration management system as they are developed. Changes to baselines and the release of work products built from the configuration management system are systematically controlled and monitored via the configuration control, change management, and configuration auditing functions of configuration management.

This process area applies not only to configuration management on projects but also to configuration management of organizational work products, such as standards, procedures, and reuse libraries.

Configuration management is focused on the rigorous control of the managerial and technical aspects of work products, including the delivered product or service.

This process area covers the practices for performing the configuration management function and is applicable to all work products that are placed under configuration management.

Related Process Areas

Refer to the Project Monitoring and Control process area for more information about monitoring the project against the plan and managing corrective action to closure.

Refer to the Project Planning process area for more information about developing plans and work breakdown structures, which may be useful for determining configuration items.

Specific Goal and Practice Summary

SG 1 Establish Baselines
  SP 1.1   Identify Configuration Items
  SP 1.2   Establish a Configuration Management System
  SP 1.3   Create or Release Baselines
SG 2 Track and Control Changes
  SP 2.1   Track Change Requests
  SP 2.2   Control Configuration Items
SG 3 Establish Integrity
  SP 3.1   Establish Configuration Management Records
  SP 3.2   Perform Configuration Audits

Specific Practices by Goal

SG 1 ESTABLISH BASELINES

Baselines of identified work products are established.

Specific practices to establish baselines are covered by this specific goal. The specific practices under the Track and Control Changes specific goal serve to maintain the baselines. The specific practices of the Establish Integrity specific goal document and audit the integrity of the baselines.

SP 1.1 *IDENTIFY CONFIGURATION ITEMS*

Identify configuration items, components, and related work products to be placed under configuration management.

Configuration identification is the selection, creation, and specification of the following:

- Products delivered to the customer
- Designated internal work products
- Acquired products
- Tools and other capital assets of the project's work environment
- Other items used in creating and describing these work products

Items under configuration management include requirements specifications and interface documents. Other documents that serve to identify the configuration of the product or service, such as test results, may also be included.

A "configuration item" is an entity designated for configuration management, which may consist of multiple related work products that form a baseline. This logical grouping provides ease of identification and controlled access. The selection of work products for configuration management should be based on criteria established during planning.

Typical Work Products

1. Identified configuration items

Subpractices

1. Select configuration items and work products that compose them based on documented criteria.

Example criteria for selecting configuration items at the appropriate work-product level include the following:
- Work products that may be used by two or more groups
- Work products that are expected to change over time because of either errors or changes in requirements
- Work products that are dependent on each other (i.e., a change in one mandates a change in the others)
- Work products critical to project success

Examples of work products that may be part of a configuration item include the following:

- Process descriptions
- Requirements
- Design
- Test plans and procedures
- Test results
- Interface descriptions
- Drawings
- Source code
- Tools (e.g., compilers)

2. Assign unique identifiers to configuration items.
3. Specify the important characteristics of each configuration item.

Example characteristics of configuration items include author, document or file type, programming language for software code files, and the purpose the configuration item serves.

4. Specify when each configuration item is placed under configuration management.

Example criteria for determining when to place work products under configuration management include the following:

- Stage of the project lifecycle
- When the work product is ready for test
- Degree of control desired on the work product
- Cost and schedule limitations
- Stakeholder requirements

5. Identify the owner responsible for each configuration item.
6. Specify relationships among configuration items.

Incorporating the types of relationships (e.g., parent-child, dependency) that exist among configuration items into the configuration management structure (e.g., configuration management database) assists in managing the effects and impacts of changes.

CM

SP 1.2 ESTABLISH A CONFIGURATION MANAGEMENT SYSTEM

Establish and maintain a configuration management and change management system for controlling work products.

A configuration management system includes the storage media, procedures, and tools for accessing the system. A configuration management system may consist of multiple subsystems with different implementations that are appropriate for each configuration management environment.

In some service domains, CM is focused on document versions and change control.

A change management system includes the storage media, procedures, and tools for recording and accessing change requests.

Typical Work Products

1. Configuration management system with controlled work products
2. Configuration management system access control procedures
3. Change request database

Subpractices

1. Establish a mechanism to manage multiple levels of control.

   The level of control is typically selected based on project objectives, risk, and resources. Control levels may vary in relation to the project lifecycle, type of system under development, and specific project requirements.

   > Example levels of control include the following:
   > - Uncontrolled: Anyone can make changes.
   > - Work-in-progress: Authors control changes.
   > - Released: A designated authority authorizes and controls changes, and relevant stakeholders are notified when changes are made.

   Levels of control can range from informal control that simply tracks changes made when configuration items are being developed to formal configuration control using baselines that can be changed only as part of a formal configuration management process.

2. Provide access control to ensure authorized access to the configuration management system.

3. Store and retrieve configuration items in a configuration management system.

4. Share and transfer configuration items between control levels in the configuration management system.

5. Store and recover archived versions of configuration items.

6. Store, update, and retrieve configuration management records.

7. Create configuration management reports from the configuration management system.

8. Preserve the contents of the configuration management system.

Examples of preservation functions of the configuration management system include the following:
- Backup and restoration of configuration management files
- Archive of configuration management files
- Recovery from configuration management errors

---

9. Revise the configuration management structure as necessary.

SP 1.3 CREATE OR RELEASE BASELINES

Create or release baselines for internal use and for delivery to the customer.

A baseline is a set of work products that has been formally reviewed and approved, that thereafter serves as the basis for further development or delivery, and that can be changed only through change control procedures. A baseline represents the assignment of an identifier to a configuration item or a collection of configuration items and associated entities.

As a product or service evolves, multiple baselines may be used to control development and testing.

Examples of types of baselines include the following:
- Stakeholder requirements
- Identified risks
- Current service levels and resource use
- Operational plan
- Schedules

Typical Work Products

1. Baselines
2. Description of baselines

Subpractices

1. Obtain authorization from the configuration control board (CCB) before creating or releasing baselines of configuration items.
2. Create or release baselines only from configuration items in the configuration management system.
3. Document the set of configuration items that are contained in a baseline.
4. Make the current set of baselines readily available.

SG 2 TRACK AND CONTROL CHANGES

Changes to the work products under configuration management are tracked and controlled.

The specific practices under this specific goal serve to maintain baselines after they are established by specific practices under the Establish Baselines specific goal.

SP 2.1 TRACK CHANGE REQUESTS

Track change requests for configuration items.

Change requests address not only new or changed requirements but also failures and defects in work products.

Change requests are analyzed to determine the impact that the change will have on the work product, related work products, the budget, and the schedule.

Typical Work Products

1. Change requests

Subpractices

1. Initiate and record change requests in the change request database.
2. Analyze the impact of changes and fixes proposed in change requests.

    Changes are evaluated through activities that ensure that they are consistent with all technical and project requirements.

    Changes are evaluated for their impact beyond immediate project or contract requirements. Changes to an item used in multiple products can resolve an immediate issue while causing a problem in other applications.

    Changes are evaluated for their impact on release plans.
3. Categorize and prioritize change requests.

Emergency requests are identified and referred to an emergency authority if appropriate.

Changes are allocated to future baselines.

4. Review change requests to be addressed in the next baseline with relevant stakeholders and get their agreement.

Conduct the change request review with appropriate participants. Record the disposition of each change request and the rationale for the decision, including success criteria, a brief action plan if appropriate, and needs met or unmet by the change. Perform the actions required in the disposition, and report results to relevant stakeholders.

5. Track the status of change requests to closure.

Change requests brought into the system should be handled in an efficient and timely manner. Once a change request has been processed, it is critical to close the request with the appropriate approved action as soon as it is practical. Actions left open result in larger than necessary status lists, which in turn result in added costs and confusion.

SP 2.2 CONTROL CONFIGURATION ITEMS

Control changes to configuration items.

Control is maintained over the configuration of the work product baseline. This control includes tracking the configuration of each configuration item, approving a new configuration if necessary, and updating the baseline.

Typical Work Products

1. Revision history of configuration items
2. Archives of baselines

Subpractices

1. Control changes to configuration items throughout the life of the product or service.
2. Obtain appropriate authorization before changed configuration items are entered into the configuration management system.

For example, authorization may come from the CCB, the project manager, or the customer.

---

3. Check in and check out configuration items in the configuration management system for incorporation of changes in a manner that maintains the correctness and integrity of configuration items.

CM

> Examples of check-in and check-out steps include the following:
> - Confirming that the revisions are authorized
> - Updating the configuration items
> - Archiving the replaced baseline and retrieving the new baseline

4. Perform reviews to ensure that changes have not caused unintended effects on the baselines (e.g., ensure that changes have not compromised the safety or security of the system).

5. Record changes to configuration items and reasons for changes as appropriate.

   If a proposed change to the work product is accepted, a schedule is identified for incorporating the change into the work product and other affected areas.

   Configuration control mechanisms can be tailored to categories of changes. For example, the approval considerations could be less stringent for component changes that do not affect other components.

   Changed configuration items are released after review and approval of configuration changes. Changes are not official until they are released.

SG 3   ESTABLISH INTEGRITY

Integrity of baselines is established and maintained.

The integrity of baselines, established by processes associated with the Establish Baselines specific goal and maintained by processes associated with the Track and Control Changes specific goal, is addressed by the specific practices under this specific goal.

SP 3.1 ESTABLISH CONFIGURATION MANAGEMENT RECORDS

Establish and maintain records describing configuration items.

Typical Work Products

1. Revision history of configuration items
2. Change log
3. Change request records
4. Status of configuration items
5. Differences between baselines

Subpractices

1. Record configuration management actions in sufficient detail so the content and status of each configuration item are known and previous versions can be recovered.

2. Ensure that relevant stakeholders have access to and knowledge of the configuration status of configuration items.

> Examples of activities for communicating configuration status include the following:
> - Providing access permissions to authorized end users
> - Making baseline copies readily available to authorized end users

3. Specify the latest version of baselines.
4. Identify the version of configuration items that constitute a particular baseline.
5. Describe differences between successive baselines.
6. Revise the status and history (i.e., changes and other actions) of each configuration item as necessary.

SP 3.2 PERFORM CONFIGURATION AUDITS

Perform configuration audits to maintain the integrity of configuration baselines.

Configuration audits confirm that the resulting baselines and documentation conform to a specified standard or requirement. Configuration item related records may exist in multiple databases or configuration management systems. In such instances, configuration audits should extend to these other databases as appropriate to ensure accuracy, consistency, and completeness of configuration item information. (See the definition of "configuration audit" in the glossary.)

> Examples of audit types include the following:
> - Functional configuration audits (FCA): Audits conducted to verify that the as-tested functional characteristics of a configuration item have achieved the requirements specified in its functional baseline documentation and that the operational and support documentation is complete and satisfactory.
> - Physical configuration audits (PCA): Audits conducted to verify that the as-built configuration item conforms to the technical documentation that defines it.
> - Configuration management audits: Audits conducted to confirm that configuration management records and configuration items are complete, consistent, and accurate.

Typical Work Products

1. Configuration audit results
2. Action items

Subpractices

1. Assess the integrity of baselines.
2. Confirm that configuration management records correctly identify configuration items.
3. Review the structure and integrity of items in the configuration management system.
4. Confirm the completeness and correctness of items in the configuration management system.

   Completeness and correctness of the configuration management system's content are based on requirements as stated in the plan and the disposition of approved change requests.
5. Confirm compliance with applicable configuration management standards and procedures.
6. Track action items from the audit to closure.

DECISION ANALYSIS AND RESOLUTION
A Support Process Area at Maturity Level 3

Purpose

The purpose of Decision Analysis and Resolution (DAR) is to analyze possible decisions using a formal evaluation process that evaluates identified alternatives against established criteria.

Introductory Notes

The Decision Analysis and Resolution process area involves establishing guidelines to determine which issues should be subject to a formal evaluation process and applying formal evaluation processes to these issues.

A formal evaluation process is a structured approach to evaluating alternative solutions against established criteria to determine a recommended solution.

A formal evaluation process involves the following actions:

- Establishing the criteria for evaluating alternatives
- Identifying alternative solutions
- Selecting methods for evaluating alternatives
- Evaluating alternative solutions using established criteria and methods
- Selecting recommended solutions from alternatives based on evaluation criteria

Rather than using the phrase "alternative solutions to address issues" each time, in this process area, one of two shorter phrases is used: "alternative solutions" or "alternatives."

A formal evaluation process reduces the subjective nature of a decision and provides a higher probability of selecting a solution that meets multiple demands of relevant stakeholders.

IN OTHER WORDS

DAR is about using a formal decision-making process on the decisions that matter most in your business.

WHY DO THE PRACTICES IN DAR?

You will make better decisions. Because the rationale for important decisions is clear, support for these decisions is higher. Over time, everyone is more inclined to trust the decision-making process because it is sensible and visible.

DAR

While the primary application of this process area is to technical concerns, formal evaluation processes can be applied to many non-technical issues, particularly when a project is being planned. Issues that have multiple alternative solutions and evaluation criteria lend themselves to a formal evaluation process.

Typical examples of formal evaluation processes include the following:
- Trade studies of equipment or software
- Comparisons of potential service capabilities to develop

During planning, specific issues requiring a formal evaluation process are identified. Typical issues include selection among architectural or design alternatives, use of reusable or commercial off-the-shelf (COTS) components, supplier selection, engineering support environments or associated tools, test environments, delivery alternatives, and logistics and production. A formal evaluation process can also be used to address a make-or-buy decision, the development of manufacturing processes, the selection of distribution locations, and other decisions.

Guidelines are created for deciding when to use formal evaluation processes to address unplanned issues. Guidelines often suggest using formal evaluation processes when issues are associated with medium- to high-impact risks or when issues affect the ability to achieve project objectives.

Formal evaluation processes can vary in formality, type of criteria, and methods employed. Less formal decisions can be analyzed in a few hours, use few criteria (e.g., effectiveness, cost to implement), and result in a one- or two-page report. More formal decisions may require separate plans, months of effort, meetings to develop and approve criteria, simulations, prototypes, piloting, and extensive documentation.

Both numeric and non-numeric criteria can be used in a formal evaluation process. Numeric criteria use weights to reflect the relative importance of criteria. Non-numeric criteria use a subjective ranking scale (e.g., high, medium, low). More formal decisions may require a full trade study.

A formal evaluation process identifies and evaluates alternative solutions. The eventual selection of a solution may involve iterative activities of identification and evaluation. Portions of identified alternatives may be combined, emerging technologies may change alternatives, and the business situation of suppliers may change during the evaluation period.

A recommended alternative is accompanied by documentation of selected methods, criteria, alternatives, and rationale for the recommendation. The documentation is distributed to relevant stakeholders; it provides a record of the formal evaluation process and rationale, which are useful to other projects that encounter a similar issue.

While some of the decisions made throughout the life of the project involve the use of a formal evaluation process, others do not. As mentioned earlier, guidelines should be established to determine which issues should be subject to a formal evaluation process.

Related Process Areas

Refer to the Integrated Project Management process area for more information about establishing the project's defined process. The project's defined process includes a formal evaluation process for each selected issue and incorporates the use of guidelines for applying a formal evaluation process to unforeseen issues.

Refer to the Risk Management process area for more information about identifying, analyzing, and mitigating risks.

Specific Goal and Practice Summary

SG 1 Evaluate Alternatives
    SP 1.1   Establish Guidelines for Decision Analysis
    SP 1.2   Establish Evaluation Criteria
    SP 1.3   Identify Alternative Solutions
    SP 1.4   Select Evaluation Methods
    SP 1.5   Evaluate Alternatives
    SP 1.6   Select Solutions

Specific Practices by Goal

SG 1 EVALUATE ALTERNATIVES

Decisions are based on an evaluation of alternatives using established criteria.

Issues requiring a formal evaluation process may be identified at any time. The objective should be to identify issues as early as possible to maximize the time available to resolve them.

SP 1.1 ESTABLISH GUIDELINES FOR DECISION ANALYSIS

Establish and maintain guidelines to determine which issues are subject to a formal evaluation process.

Not every decision is significant enough to require a formal evaluation process. The choice between the trivial and the truly important is unclear without explicit guidance. Whether a decision is significant or not is dependent on the project and circumstances and is determined by established guidelines.

Typical guidelines for determining when to require a formal evaluation process include the following:
- A decision is directly related to topics that are medium- or high-impact risk.
- A decision is related to changing work products under configuration management.
- A decision would cause schedule delays over a certain percentage or amount of time.
- A decision affects the ability of the project to achieve its objectives.
- The costs of the formal evaluation process are reasonable when compared to the decision's impact.
- A legal obligation exists during a solicitation.

Refer to the Risk Management process area for more information about evaluating, categorizing, and prioritizing risks.

Examples of when to use a formal evaluation process include the following:
- Selecting elements to include in standard service descriptions
- Selecting, terminating, or renewing suppliers
- Selecting training for project personnel
- Selecting an approach for ongoing support (e.g., disaster recovery, service levels)

Typical Work Products

1. Guidelines for when to apply a formal evaluation process

Subpractices

1. Establish guidelines for when to use a formal evaluation process.
2. Incorporate the use of guidelines into the defined process as appropriate.

    Refer to the Integrated Project Management process area for more information about establishing the project's defined process.

SP 1.2 *Establish Evaluation Criteria*

Establish and maintain criteria for evaluating alternatives, and the relative ranking of these criteria.

Evaluation criteria provide the basis for evaluating alternative solutions. Criteria are ranked so that the highest-ranked criteria exert the most influence on the evaluation.

This process area is referenced by many other process areas in the model, and there are many contexts in which a formal evaluation process can be used. Therefore, in some situations, you may find that criteria have already been defined as part of another process. This specific practice does not suggest that a second development of criteria be conducted.

Document the evaluation criteria to minimize the possibility that decisions will be second guessed or that the reason for making the decision will be forgotten. Decisions based on criteria that are explicitly defined and established remove barriers to stakeholder buy-in.

Typical Work Products

1. Documented evaluation criteria
2. Rankings of criteria importance

Subpractices

1. Define the criteria for evaluating alternative solutions.
   Criteria should be traceable to requirements, scenarios, business case assumptions, business objectives, or other documented sources.

Types of criteria to consider include the following:
- Technology limitations
- Environmental impact
- Risks
- Total ownership and lifecycle costs

---

2. Define the range and scale for ranking the evaluation criteria.
   Scales of relative importance for evaluation criteria can be established with non-numeric values or with formulas that relate the evaluation parameter to a numeric weight.
3. Rank the criteria.
   The criteria are ranked according to the defined range and scale to reflect the needs, objectives, and priorities of the relevant stakeholders.

DAR

4. Assess the criteria and their relative importance.

5. Evolve the evaluation criteria to improve their validity.

6. Document the rationale for the selection and rejection of evaluation criteria.

> Documentation of selection criteria and rationale may be needed to justify solutions or for future reference and use.

SP 1.3 IDENTIFY ALTERNATIVE SOLUTIONS

Identify alternative solutions to address issues.

A wider range of alternatives can surface by soliciting as many stakeholders as practical for input. Input from stakeholders with diverse skills and backgrounds can help teams identify and address assumptions, constraints, and biases. Brainstorming sessions may stimulate innovative alternatives through rapid interaction and feedback.

Sufficient candidate solutions may not be furnished for analysis. As the analysis proceeds, other alternatives should be added to the list of potential candidate solutions. The generation and consideration of multiple alternatives early in a decision analysis and resolution process increases the likelihood that an acceptable decision will be made and that consequences of the decision will be understood.

Typical Work Products

1. Identified alternatives

Subpractices

1. Perform a literature search.

> A literature search can uncover what others have done both inside and outside the organization. Such a search may provide a deeper understanding of the problem, alternatives to consider, barriers to implementation, existing trade studies, and lessons learned from similar decisions.

2. Identify alternatives for consideration in addition to those that may be provided with the issue.

> Evaluation criteria are an effective starting point for identifying alternatives. Evaluation criteria identify priorities of relevant stakeholders and the importance of technical, logistical, or other challenges.
> Combining key attributes of existing alternatives can generate additional and sometimes stronger alternatives.
> Solicit alternatives from relevant stakeholders. Brainstorming sessions, interviews, and working groups can be used effectively to uncover alternatives.

3. Document proposed alternatives.

SP 1.4 SELECT EVALUATION METHODS

Select evaluation methods.

Methods for evaluating alternative solutions against established criteria can range from simulations to the use of probabilistic models and decision theory. These methods should be carefully selected. The level of detail of a method should be commensurate with cost, schedule, performance, and risk impacts.

While many problems may require only one evaluation method, some problems may require multiple methods. For example, simulations may augment a trade study to determine which design alternative best meets a given criterion.

Typical Work Products

1. Selected evaluation methods

Subpractices

1. Select methods based on the purpose for analyzing a decision and on the availability of the information used to support the method.

> For example, the methods used for evaluating a solution when requirements are weakly defined may be different from the methods used when the requirements are well defined.

Typical evaluation methods include the following:
   - Modeling and simulation
   - Engineering studies
   - Manufacturing studies
   - Cost studies
   - Business opportunity studies
   - Surveys
   - Extrapolations based on field experience and prototypes
   - User review and comment
   - Testing
   - Judgment provided by an expert or group of experts (e.g., Delphi Method)

2. Select evaluation methods based on their ability to focus on the issues at hand without being overly influenced by side issues.
   Results of simulations can be skewed by random activities in the solution that are not directly related to the issues at hand.

3. Determine the measures needed to support the evaluation method.
   Consider the impact on cost, schedule, performance, and risks.

DAR

SP 1.5 *EVALUATE ALTERNATIVES*

Evaluate alternative solutions using established criteria and methods.

Evaluating alternative solutions involves analysis, discussion, and review. Iterative cycles of analysis are sometimes necessary. Supporting analyses, experimentation, prototyping, piloting, or simulations may be needed to substantiate scoring and conclusions.

Often, the relative importance of criteria is imprecise, and the total effect on a solution is not apparent until after the analysis is performed. In cases where the resulting scores differ by relatively small amounts, the best selection among alternative solutions may not be clear. Challenges to criteria and assumptions should be encouraged.

Typical Work Products

1. Evaluation results

Subpractices

1. Evaluate proposed alternative solutions using the established evaluation criteria and selected methods.
2. Evaluate assumptions related to the evaluation criteria and the evidence that supports the assumptions.
3. Evaluate whether uncertainty in the values for alternative solutions affects the evaluation, and address these uncertainties as appropriate.
   For instance, if the score can vary between two values, is the difference significant enough to make a difference in the final solution set? Does the variation in score represent a high-impact risk? To address these concerns, simulations may be run, further studies may be performed, or evaluation criteria may be modified, among other things.
4. Perform simulations, modeling, prototypes, and pilots as necessary to exercise the evaluation criteria, methods, and alternative solutions.
   Untested criteria, their relative importance, and supporting data or functions may cause the validity of solutions to be questioned. Criteria and their relative priorities and scales can be tested with trial runs against a set of alternatives. These trial runs of a select set of criteria allow for the evaluation of the cumulative impact of criteria on a solution. If trials reveal problems, different criteria or alternatives might be considered to avoid biases.
5. Consider new alternative solutions, criteria, or methods if proposed alternatives do not test well; repeat evaluations until alternatives do test well.
6. Document the results of the evaluation.
   Document the rationale for the addition of new alternatives or methods and changes to criteria, as well as the results of interim evaluations.

SP 1.6 SELECT SOLUTIONS

Select solutions from alternatives based on evaluation criteria.

Selecting solutions involves weighing results from the evaluation of alternatives. Risks associated with the implementation of solutions must be assessed.

Typical Work Products

1. Recommended solutions to address significant issues

Subpractices

1. Assess the risks associated with implementing the recommended solution.

   Refer to the Risk Management process area for more information about identifying, analyzing, and mitigating risks.

   Decisions must often be made with incomplete information. There can be substantial risk associated with the decision because of having incomplete information.
   When decisions must be made according to a specific schedule, time and resources may not be available for gathering complete information. Consequently, risky decisions made with incomplete information may require reanalysis later. Identified risks should be monitored.

2. Document the results and rationale for the recommended solution.
   It is important to record both why a solution is selected and why another solution was rejected.

INTEGRATED PROJECT MANAGEMENT
A Project Management Process Area at Maturity Level 3

Purpose

The purpose of Integrated Project Management (IPM) is to establish and manage the project and the involvement of relevant stakeholders according to an integrated and defined process that is tailored from the organization's set of standard processes.

Introductory Notes

The term "project" refers to a group of people and resources committed to planning, monitoring, and executing defined processes in a shared endeavor to achieve a set of objectives derived from the goals of the business and (current or future) customers. Obtaining business value from the practices in this and related process areas requires, in part, correctly identifying which endeavors are "projects."

See the introductory notes of the Project Planning process area for more information about the use of the term "project" and the applicability of specific practices that use that term.

Integrated Project Management involves the following activities:

- Establishing the project's defined process at project startup by tailoring the organization's set of standard processes
- Managing the project using the project's defined process
- Establishing the work environment for the project based on the organization's work environment standards
- Establishing integrated teams that are tasked to accomplish project objectives
- Using and contributing to organizational process assets
- Enabling relevant stakeholders' concerns to be identified, considered, and, when appropriate, addressed during the project

IPM

• Ensuring that relevant stakeholders perform their tasks in a coordinated and timely manner (1) to address project requirements, plans, objectives, problems, and risks; (2) to fulfill their commitments; and (3) to identify, track, and resolve coordination issues

The integrated and defined process that is tailored from the organization's set of standard processes is called the project's defined process.

Managing the project's effort, cost, schedule, staffing, risks, and other factors is tied to the tasks of the project's defined process. The implementation and management of the project's defined process are typically described in the project plan. Certain activities may be covered in other plans that affect the project, such as the quality assurance plan, risk management strategy, and the configuration management plan.

Since the defined process for each project is tailored from the organization's set of standard processes, variability among projects is typically reduced, and projects can easily share process assets, data, and lessons learned.

This process area also addresses the coordination of all activities associated with the project such as the following:
• Development activities (e.g., requirements development, design, verification)
• Service activities (e.g., delivery, help desk, operations, customer contact)
• Acquisition activities (e.g., solicitation, agreement monitoring, transition to operations)
• Support activities (e.g., configuration management, documentation, marketing, training)

The working interfaces and interactions among relevant stakeholders internal and external to the project are planned and managed to ensure the quality and integrity of the overall endeavor. Relevant stakeholders participate as appropriate in defining the project's defined process and the project plan. Reviews and exchanges are regularly conducted with relevant stakeholders to ensure that coordination issues receive appropriate attention and that everyone involved with the project is appropriately aware of status, plans, and activities. (See the definition of "relevant stakeholder" in the glossary.) In defining the project's defined process, formal interfaces are created as necessary to ensure that appropriate coordination and collaboration occur.

This process area applies in any organizational structure or approach, including projects that are structured as line organizations, matrix organizations, or integrated teams. The terminology should be appropriately interpreted for the organizational structure in place.

Related Process Areas

Refer to the Service System Development process area for more information about performing peer reviews.

SSD Aᴅᴅ

Refer to the Measurement and Analysis process area for more information about specifying measures and analysis procedures.

Refer to the Organizational Process Definition process area for more information about organizational process assets and work environment standards.

Refer to the Project Monitoring and Control process area for more information about monitoring the project against the plan.

Refer to the Project Planning process area for more information about developing a project plan and planning stakeholder involvement.

Specific Goal and Practice Summary

SG 1 Use the Project's Defined Process
      SP 1.1   Establish the Project's Defined Process
      SP 1.2   Use Organizational Process Assets for Planning Project Activities
      SP 1.3   Establish the Project's Work Environment
      SP 1.4   Integrate Plans
      SP 1.5   Manage the Project Using Integrated Plans
      SP 1.6   Establish Integrated Teams
      SP 1.7   Contribute to Organizational Process Assets
SG 2 Coordinate and Collaborate with Relevant Stakeholders
      SP 2.1   Manage Stakeholder Involvement
      SP 2.2   Manage Dependencies
      SP 2.3   Resolve Coordination Issues

Specific Practices by Goal

SG 1   *Use the Project's Defined Process*

The project is conducted using a defined process tailored from the organization's set of standard processes.

The project's defined process must include those processes from the organization's set of standard processes that address all processes necessary to acquire, develop, maintain, or deliver the product.

IPM

SP 1.1 ESTABLISH THE PROJECT'S DEFINED PROCESS

Establish and maintain the project's defined process from project startup through the life of the project.

Refer to the Organizational Process Definition process area for more information about organizational process assets.

Refer to the Organizational Process Focus process area for more information about deploying organizational process assets and deploying standard processes.

The project's defined process consists of defined processes that form an integrated, coherent lifecycle for the project.

The project's defined process should satisfy the project's contractual requirements, operational needs, opportunities, and constraints. It is designed to provide a best fit for project needs.

A project's defined process is based on the following factors:

- Stakeholder requirements
- Commitments
- Organizational process needs and objectives
- The organization's set of standard processes and tailoring guidelines
- The operational environment
- The business environment
- The service delivery environment

In addition, the description of the project's defined process should be based on the services that the project will deliver, including both standard services that have been tailored for the project and services that are unique to the project.

Establishing the project's defined process at project startup helps to ensure that project staff and stakeholders implement a set of activities needed to efficiently establish an initial set of requirements and plans for the project. As the project progresses, the description of the project's defined process is elaborated and revised to better meet project requirements and the organization's process needs and objectives. Also, as the organization's set of standard processes changes, the project's defined process may need to be revised.

Typical Work Products

1. The project's defined process

Subpractices

1. Select a lifecycle model from those available in organizational process assets.

Examples of project characteristics that could affect the selection of lifecycle models include the following:
- Size of the project
- Project strategy
- Experience and familiarity of staff with implementing the process
- Constraints such as service level and cycle time

---

2. Select standard processes from the organization's set of standard processes that best fit the needs of the project.

    Organizations that define standard services will normally have standard service systems that enable the delivery of those services. Any processes that are components of an organization's relevant standard service system(s) are good candidates to consider when selecting standard processes for a project that will be delivering services.

3. Tailor the organization's set of standard processes and other organizational process assets according to tailoring guidelines to produce the project's defined process.

    Sometimes the available lifecycle models and standard processes are inadequate to meet project needs. In such circumstances, the project must seek approval to deviate from what is required by the organization. Waivers are provided for this purpose.

4. Use other artifacts from the organization's process asset library as appropriate.

Other artifacts may include the following:
- Lessons-learned documents
- Templates
- Example documents
- Estimating models

---

5. Document the project's defined process.

    The project's defined process covers all of the service establishment and delivery activities for the project and its interfaces to relevant stakeholders.

Examples of project activities include the following:
- Project planning
- Project monitoring
- Requirements management
- Supplier management
- Incident management
- Quality assurance
- Risk management
- Decision analysis and resolution
- Service system development and support

---

6. Conduct peer reviews of the project's defined process.

> *Refer to the Service System Development process area for more information about performing peer reviews.*   **SSD ADD**

7. Revise the project's defined process as necessary.

SP 1.2   USE ORGANIZATIONAL PROCESS ASSETS FOR PLANNING PROJECT ACTIVITIES

Use organizational process assets and the measurement repository for estimating and planning project activities.

Refer to the Organizational Process Definition process area for more information about establishing organizational process assets.

Typical Work Products

1. Project estimates
2. Project plans

Subpractices

1. Use the tasks and work products of the project's defined process as a basis for estimating and planning project activities.

   An understanding of the relationships among tasks and work products of the project's defined process and of the roles to be performed by relevant stakeholders is a basis for developing a realistic plan.

2. Use the organization's measurement repository in estimating the project's planning parameters.

   This estimate typically includes the following:
   - Appropriate historical data from this project or similar projects
   - Similarities and differences between the current project and those projects whose historical data will be used

- Independently validated historical data
- Reasoning, assumptions, and rationale used to select the historical data

---

Examples of parameters that are considered for similarities and differences include the following:
- Work product and task attributes
- Application domain
- Service system and service system components
- Operational or delivery environment
- Experience of the people

Examples of data contained in the organization's measurement repository include the following:
- Size of work products or other work product attributes
- Effort
- Cost
- Schedule
- Staffing
- Quality
- Response time
- Service capacity
- Supplier performance

SP 1.3 ESTABLISH THE PROJECT'S WORK ENVIRONMENT

Establish and maintain the project's work environment based on the organization's work environment standards.

An appropriate work environment for a project comprises an infrastructure of facilities, tools, and equipment that people need to perform their jobs effectively in support of business and project objectives. The work environment and its components are maintained at a level of performance and reliability indicated by organizational work environment standards. As required, the project's work environment or some of its components can be developed internally or acquired from external sources.

The project's work environment should encompass all work spaces where the project operates. This work environment includes work spaces not under the direct control or ownership of the organization (e.g., delivering a product or service at a customer site).

Verification and validation of the service system can include both initial and ongoing evaluation of the work environment in which the service is delivered.

> *Refer to the Service System Development process area for more information about preparing for verification and validation.*

Refer to the Establish Work Environment Standards specific practice in the Organizational Process Definition process area for more information about work environment standards.

Typical Work Products

1. Equipment and tools for the project
2. Installation, operation, and maintenance manuals for the project work environment
3. User surveys and results
4. Use, performance, and maintenance records
5. Support services for the project's work environment

Subpractices

1. Plan, design, and install a work environment for the project.

    The critical aspects of the project work environment are, like any other product, requirements driven. Work environment functionality and operations are explored with the same rigor as is done for any other product development project.

It may be necessary to make tradeoffs among performance, costs, and risks. The following are examples of each:
- Performance considerations may include timely communication, safety, security, and maintainability.
- Costs may include capital outlays, training, a support structure; disassembly and disposal of existing environments; and the operation and maintenance of the environment.
- Risks may include workflow and project disruptions.

Examples of equipment and tools include the following:
- Office software
- Decision support software
- Project management tools
- Requirements management tools
- Incident and request management tools
- Test and evaluation equipment

2. Provide ongoing maintenance and operational support for the project's work environment.

   Maintenance and support of the work environment can be accomplished either with capabilities found inside the organization or hired from outside the organization.

Examples of maintenance and support approaches include the following:
- Hiring people to perform maintenance and support
- Training people to perform maintenance and support
- Contracting maintenance and support
- Developing expert users for selected tools

---

3. Maintain the qualification of components of the project's work environment.

   Components include those necessary to support service delivery, software, databases, hardware, tools, test equipment, and appropriate documentation. Qualification of a service delivery environment includes audits of the environment and its components for compliance with safety requirements and regulations. Qualification of software includes appropriate certifications. Hardware and test equipment qualification includes calibration and adjustment records and traceability to calibration standards.

4. Periodically review how well the work environment is meeting project needs and supporting collaboration, and take action as appropriate.

Examples of actions that might be taken include the following:
- Adding new tools
- Acquiring additional networks, equipment, training, and support

---

SP 1.4 INTEGRATE PLANS

Integrate the project plan and other plans that affect the project to describe the project's defined process.

Refer to the Project Planning process area for more information about developing a project plan.

The project plan should include plans for service system development and service delivery as appropriate.

Refer to the Capacity and Availability Management process area for more information about preparing for capacity and availability management.

Refer to the Incident Resolution and Prevention process area for more information about preparing for incident resolution and prevention.

Refer to the Service Continuity process area for more information about establishing service continuity plans.

Refer to the Measurement and Analysis process area for more information about aligning measurement and analysis activities.

Refer to the Organizational Process Definition process area for more information about organizational process assets and, in particular, the organization's measurement repository.

Refer to the Risk Management process area for more information about identifying and analyzing risks.

This specific practice extends the specific practices for establishing and maintaining a project plan to address additional planning activities, such as incorporating the project's defined process, coordinating with relevant stakeholders, using organizational process assets, incorporating plans for peer reviews, and establishing objective entry and exit criteria for tasks.

The development of the project plan should account for current and projected needs, objectives, and requirements of the organization, customer, suppliers, and end users, as appropriate.

Typical Work Products

1. Integrated plans

Subpractices

1. Integrate other plans that affect the project with the project plan.

> Other plans that affect the project plan may include the following:
> - Quality assurance plans
> - Risk management strategy
> - Communication plans
> - Capacity and availability management strategy
> - Service continuity plan
> - Incident management approach

2. Incorporate into the project plan the definitions of measures and measurement activities for managing the project.

Examples of measures that would be incorporated include the following:
- Organization's common set of measures
- Additional project-specific measures

---

3. Identify and analyze product and project interface risks.

Examples of product and project interface risks include the following:
- Incomplete interface descriptions
- Unavailability of tools or test equipment
- Unavailability of COTS components
- Inadequate or ineffective team interfaces
- Inadequate product and service interfaces

---

4. Schedule tasks in a sequence that accounts for critical development and delivery factors and project risks.

Examples of factors considered in scheduling include the following:
- Size and complexity of tasks
- Needs of the customer and end users
- Availability of critical resources
- Availability of key personnel

---

5. Incorporate plans for performing peer reviews on work products of the project's defined process.

> *Refer to the Service System Development process area for more information about performing peer reviews.*

6. Incorporate the training needed to perform the project's defined process in the project's training plans.

   This task typically includes negotiating with the organizational training group on the support they will provide.

7. Establish objective entry and exit criteria to authorize the initiation and completion of tasks described in the work breakdown structure (WBS).

   Refer to the Project Planning process area for more information about establishing a top-level work breakdown structure (WBS).

8. Ensure that the project plan is appropriately compatible with the plans of relevant stakeholders.

Typically the plan and changes to the plan will be reviewed for compatibility.

9. Identify how conflicts will be resolved that arise among relevant stakeholders.

SP 1.5 MANAGE THE PROJECT USING INTEGRATED PLANS

Manage the project using the project plan, other plans that affect the project, and the project's defined process.

Refer to the Organizational Process Definition process area for more information about organizational process assets.

Refer to the Organizational Process Focus process area for more information about establishing organizational process needs, deploying organizational process assets, and deploying standard processes.

Refer to the Project Monitoring and Control process area for more information about monitoring the project against the plan.

Refer to the Risk Management process area for more information about identifying, analyzing, and mitigating risks.

Typical Work Products

1. Work products created by performing the project's defined process
2. Collected measures (i.e., actuals) and status records or reports
3. Revised requirements, plans, and commitments
4. Integrated plans

Subpractices

1. Implement the project's defined process using the organization's process asset library.

This task typically includes the following activities:
- Incorporating artifacts from the organization's process asset library into the project as appropriate
- Using lessons learned from the organization's process asset library to manage the project

---

2. Monitor and control the project's activities and work products using the project's defined process, project plan, and other plans that affect the project.

This task typically includes the following activities:
- Using the defined entry and exit criteria to authorize the initiation and determine the completion of tasks
- Monitoring activities that could significantly affect actual values of the project's planning parameters
- Tracking project planning parameters using measurable thresholds that will trigger investigation and appropriate actions
- Monitoring project interface risks
- Managing external and internal commitments based on plans for tasks and work products of the project's defined process

An understanding of the relationships among tasks and work products of the project's defined process and of the roles to be performed by relevant stakeholders, along with well-defined control mechanisms (e.g., peer reviews), achieves better visibility into project performance and better control of the project.

3. Obtain and analyze selected measurements to manage the project and support organization needs.

Refer to the Measurement and Analysis process area for more information about obtaining and analyzing measurement data.

4. Periodically review and align the project's performance with current and anticipated needs, objectives, and requirements of the organization, customer, and end users, as appropriate.

This review includes alignment with organizational process needs and objectives.

Examples of actions that achieve alignment include the following:
- Accelerating the schedule with appropriate adjustments to other planning parameters and project risks
- Changing requirements in response to a change in market opportunities or customer and end-user needs
- Terminating the project

SP 1.6 ESTABLISH INTEGRATED TEAMS

Establish and maintain integrated teams.

The project is managed using integrated teams that reflect the organizational rules and guidelines for team structuring and forming. The project's shared vision is established prior to establishing the team

IPM

structure, which may be based on the WBS. For small organizations, the whole organization and relevant external stakeholders can be treated as an integrated team.

Refer to the Establish Rules and Guidelines for Integrated Teams specific practice in the Organizational Process Definition process area for more information about establishing and maintaining organizational rules and guidelines for the structure, formation, and operation of integrated teams.

One of the best ways to ensure coordination and collaboration with relevant stakeholders is to include them on an integrated team.

A project may consist of no integrated teams (e.g., a project having only one individual, in which case that individual may possibly be a member of a higher level integrated team), one integrated team (i.e., the whole project team is the integrated team), or many integrated teams. This specific practice applies possibly in the first two instances and certainly in the last instance. Establishing an integrated team is a best practice when team members having complementary skill sets or from different cultures or backgrounds must work together effectively to accomplish a shared objective. It is important to determine at the organizational level the project work to be conducted in integrated teams.

When a project is a service provider, there may be one integrated team responsible for overall service development and maintenance and another team responsible for service delivery. In the case of multiple critical services each requiring a different skill set, the staff associated with each service may form its own integrated team with an objective to ensure the successful and continuing delivery of that service (or timely response to an ad hoc request or incident resolution as appropriate).

In a customer environment that requires coordination among multiple product development or service delivery organizations, it is important to establish an integrated team with representation from all parties that impact overall success. Such representation helps to ensure effective collaboration across these organizations, including the timely resolution of coordination issues.

Typical Work Products

1. Documented shared vision
2. List of team members assigned to each integrated team
3. Integrated team charters
4. Periodic integrated team status reports

Subpractices

1. Establish and maintain the project's shared vision.

    When creating a shared vision, it is critical to understand the interfaces between the project and stakeholders external to the project. The vision should be shared among relevant stakeholders to obtain their agreement and commitment.

2. Establish and maintain the integrated team structure.

    Cost, schedule, project risks, resources, interfaces, the project's defined process, and organizational guidelines are evaluated to establish the basis for defining integrated teams and their responsibilities, authorities, and interrelationships.

3. Establish and maintain each integrated team.

    Establishing and maintaining integrated teams encompasses choosing team leaders and team members and establishing team charters for each team. It also involves providing resources required to accomplish tasks assigned to the team.

4. Periodically evaluate the integrated team structure and composition.

    Integrated teams should be monitored to detect misalignment of work across different teams, mismanaged interfaces, and mismatches of tasks to team members. Take corrective action when performance does not meet expectations.

SP 1.7 CONTRIBUTE TO ORGANIZATIONAL PROCESS ASSETS

Contribute work products, measures, and documented experiences to organizational process assets.

Refer to the Organizational Process Definition process area for more information about organizational process assets, the organization's measurement repository, and the organization's process asset library.

Refer to the Organizational Process Focus process area for more information about incorporating experiences into organizational process assets.

This specific practice addresses collecting information from processes in the project's defined process.

Typical Work Products

1. Proposed improvements to organizational process assets
2. Actual process and product measures collected from the project
3. Documentation (e.g., exemplary process descriptions, plans, training modules, checklists, lessons learned)
4. Process artifacts associated with tailoring and implementing the organization's set of standard processes on the project

IPM

Subpractices

1. Propose improvements to organizational process assets.

2. Store process and product measures in the organization's measurement repository.

   Refer to the Project Monitoring and Control process area for more information about monitoring project planning parameters.

   Refer to the Project Planning process area for more information about planning data management.

These process and product measures typically include the following:
- Planning data
- Replanning data
- Measures

Examples of data recorded by the project include the following:
- Task descriptions
- Assumptions
- Estimates
- Revised estimates
- Definitions of recorded data and measures
- Measures
- Context information that relates the measures to the activities performed and work products produced
- Associated information needed to reconstruct the estimates, assess their reasonableness, and derive estimates for new work

---

3. Submit documentation for possible inclusion in the organization's process asset library.

Examples of documentation include the following:
- Exemplary process descriptions
- Training modules
- Exemplary plans
- Checklists

---

4. Document lessons learned from the project for inclusion in the organization's process asset library.

5. Provide process artifacts associated with tailoring and implementing the organization's set of standard processes in support of the organization's process monitoring activities.

> *Refer to the Monitor the Implementation specific practice in the Organization Process Focus process area for more information about the organization's activities to understand the extent of deployment of standard processes on new and existing projects.*

SG 2 COORDINATE AND COLLABORATE WITH RELEVANT STAKEHOLDERS

Coordination and collaboration between the project and relevant stakeholders are conducted.

SP 2.1 MANAGE STAKEHOLDER INVOLVEMENT

Manage the involvement of relevant stakeholders in the project.

Stakeholder involvement is managed according to the project's integrated and defined process.

The supplier agreement provides the basis for managing supplier involvement in the project. Supplier agreements (e.g., interagency and intercompany agreements, memoranda of understanding, memoranda of agreement) that the project makes with stakeholder organizations, which may be product or service providers or recipients, provide the basis for their involvement. These agreements are particularly important when the project's delivered services must be integrated into a larger service delivery context.

Refer to the Project Planning process area for more information about planning stakeholder involvement and obtaining commitment to the plan.

Typical Work Products

1. Agendas and schedules for collaborative activities
2. Documented issues (e.g., issues with stakeholder and service system requirements, architecture, design)
3. Recommendations for resolving relevant stakeholder issues

Subpractices

1. Coordinate with relevant stakeholders who should participate in project activities.
   The relevant stakeholders should already be identified in the project plan.
2. Ensure work products that are produced to satisfy commitments meet the requirements of the recipients.

SSD ADD

> *Refer to the Service System Development process area for more information about verifying and validating service systems.*

The work products produced to satisfy commitments can be services. This task typically includes the following:

- Reviewing, demonstrating, or testing, as appropriate, each work product produced by relevant stakeholders
- Reviewing, demonstrating, or testing, as appropriate, each work product produced by the project for other projects with representatives of the projects receiving the work product
- Resolving issues related to the acceptance of the work products

3. Develop recommendations and coordinate actions to resolve misunderstandings and problems with requirements.

SP 2.2 MANAGE DEPENDENCIES

Participate with relevant stakeholders to identify, negotiate, and track critical dependencies.

Typical Work Products

1. Defects, issues, and action items resulting from reviews with relevant stakeholders
2. Critical dependencies
3. Commitments to address critical dependencies
4. Status of critical dependencies

Subpractices

1. Conduct reviews with relevant stakeholders.
2. Identify each critical dependency.
3. Establish need dates and plan dates for each critical dependency based on the project schedule.
4. Review and get agreement on commitments to address each critical dependency with those responsible for providing or receiving the work product or performing or receiving the service.
5. Document critical dependencies and commitments.

> Documentation of commitments typically includes the following:
> - Describing the commitment
> - Identifying who made the commitment
> - Identifying who is responsible for satisfying the commitment
> - Specifying when the commitment will be satisfied
> - Specifying the criteria for determining if the commitment has been satisfied

6. Track the critical dependencies and commitments and take corrective action as appropriate.

   Refer to the Project Monitoring and Control process area for more information about monitoring commitments.

> Tracking critical dependencies typically includes the following:
> - Evaluating the effects of late and early completion for impacts on future activities and milestones
> - Resolving actual and potential problems with responsible parties whenever possible
> - Escalating to the appropriate party the actual and potential problems not resolvable by the responsible individual or group

SP 2.3 RESOLVE COORDINATION ISSUES

Resolve issues with relevant stakeholders.

> Examples of coordination issues include the following:
> - Late critical dependencies and commitments
> - Service system requirements and design defects
> - Product-level problems
> - Unavailability of critical resources or personnel

Typical Work Products

1. Relevant stakeholder coordination issues
2. Status of relevant stakeholder coordination issues

IPM

Subpractices

1. Identify and document issues.
2. Communicate issues to relevant stakeholders.
3. Resolve issues with relevant stakeholders.
4. Escalate to appropriate managers those issues not resolvable with relevant stakeholders.
5. Track issues to closure.
6. Communicate with relevant stakeholders on the status and resolution of issues.

INCIDENT RESOLUTION AND PREVENTION
A Service Establishment and Delivery Process Area at Maturity Level 3

Purpose

The purpose of Incident Resolution and Prevention (IRP) is to ensure timely and effective resolution of service incidents and prevention of service incidents as appropriate.

Introductory Notes

The Incident Resolution and Prevention process area involves the following activities:

- Identifying and analyzing service incidents
- Initiating specific actions to address incidents
- Monitoring the status of incidents, tracking progress of incident status, and escalating as necessary
- Identifying and analyzing the underlying causes of incidents
- Identifying workarounds that enable service to continue
- Initiating specific actions to either address the underlying causes of incidents or to provide workarounds
- Communicating the status of incidents to relevant stakeholders
- Validating the complete resolution of incidents with relevant stakeholders

The term "incident" is used to mean "service incident" in this process area and in other areas of the model where the context makes the meaning clear. The term "service incident" is used in the glossary and in other parts of the model to clearly differentiate this specially defined term from the everyday use of the word "incident." (See the definition of "service incident" in the glossary.)

Incidents are events that, if not addressed, eventually may cause the service provider organization to break its service commitments.

Hence, the service provider organization must address incidents in a timely and effective manner according to the terms of the service agreement.

Addressing an incident may include the following activities:

- Removing an underlying cause or causes
- Minimizing the impact of an incident
- Monitoring the condition or series of events causing the incident
- Providing a workaround

Incidents may cause or be indications of interruptions or potential interruptions to a service.

Examples of interruptions to a service include a software application that is down during normal operating hours, an elevator that is stuck, a hotel room that is double booked, and baggage that is lost in an airport.

Examples of potential interruptions to a service include a broken component in resilient equipment, a line with more than three people in it at a counter of a supermarket, and an understaffed call center.

Customer complaints are a special type of potential interruption. A complaint indicates that the customer perceives that a service does not meet his or her expectations, even if the customer is in error about what the agreement calls for. Therefore, complaints should be handled as incidents and are within the scope of the Incident Resolution and Prevention process area.

All incidents have one or more underlying causes, regardless of whether the service provider is aware of the cause. For example, each system outage has an underlying cause, whether it is a memory leak, a corrupt database, or an operator error.

An underlying cause of an incident is a condition or event that contributes to the occurrence of one or more incidents. Not all underlying causes result in incidents immediately. For example, a defect in an infrequently used part of a system may not result in an incident for a long time.

Underlying causes can be any of the following:

- Root causes that are within the service provider's control and can and should be removed

- Positive or negative conditions of a service that may or may not be removed
- Conditions that the service provider cannot change (e.g., weather conditions)

Underlying causes and root causes (as described in the Causal Analysis and Resolution process area) are not synonymous. A root cause is a type of underlying cause that is considered to be fundamental in some sense. We don't normally look for the cause of a root cause, and we normally expect to achieve the greatest reduction in the occurrence of incidents when we address a root cause.

Sometimes, we are unable to address a root cause for practical or budgetary reasons, and so instead we may focus on other nonroot underlying causes. It doesn't always make business sense to remove all underlying causes either. Under some circumstances, addressing incidents with workarounds or simply resolving incidents on a case-by-case basis may be more effective.

Effective practices for incident resolution start with developing a process for addressing incidents with the customers, end users, and other stakeholders who report incidents. Organizations may have both a collection of known incidents, underlying causes of incidents, and workarounds, as well as separate but related activities designed to create the actions for addressing selected incidents and underlying causes. Processing all incidents and analyzing selected incidents and their underlying causes to define approaches to addressing those incidents are two reinforcing activities that may be performed in parallel or in sequence.

Thus, the Incident Resolution and Prevention process area has three specific goals. The Prepare for Incident Resolution and Prevention goal helps to ensure that an approach is established for timely resolution of incidents and effective prevention of incidents when possible. The specific practices of the goal to Identify, Control, and Address Incidents are used to treat and close incidents, often by applying workarounds or other actions defined in the goal to Define Approaches to Address Selected Incidents.

Related Process Areas

Refer to the Capacity and Availability Management process area for more information about monitoring and analyzing capacity and availability.

Refer to the Service Delivery process area for more information about establishing and maintaining service agreements.

Refer to the Causal Analysis and Resolution process area for more information about determining causes of defects and problems.

Refer to the Configuration Management process area for more information about tracking and controlling changes.

Refer to the Project Monitoring and Control process area for more information about providing an understanding of the project's progress so that appropriate corrective actions can be taken when the project's performance deviates significantly from the plan.

Refer to the Risk Management process area for more information about identifying, analyzing, and mitigating risks.

Specific Goal and Practice Summary

SG 1 Prepare for Incident Resolution and Prevention
 SP 1.1 Establish an Approach to Incident Resolution and Prevention
 SP 1.2 Establish an Incident Management System
SG 2 Identify, Control, and Address Incidents
 SP 2.1 Identify and Record Incidents
 SP 2.2 Analyze Incident Data
 SP 2.3 Apply Workarounds to Selected Incidents
 SP 2.4 Address Underlying Causes of Selected Incidents
 SP 2.5 Monitor the Status of Incidents to Closure
 SP 2.6 Communicate the Status of Incidents
SG 3 Define Approaches to Address Selected Incidents
 SP 3.1 Analyze Selected Incident Data
 SP 3.2 Plan Actions to Address Underlying Causes of Selected Incidents
 SP 3.3 Establish Workarounds for Selected Incidents

Specific Practices by Goal

SG 1 *PREPARE FOR INCIDENT RESOLUTION AND PREVENTION*

Preparation for incident resolution and prevention is conducted.

Establish and maintain an approach for ensuring timely and effective resolution and prevention of incidents to ensure that the terms of the service agreement are met.

SP 1.1 *ESTABLISH AN APPROACH TO INCIDENT RESOLUTION AND PREVENTION*

Establish and maintain an approach to incident resolution and prevention.

The approach to incident resolution and prevention describes the organizational functions involved in incident resolution and prevention, the procedures employed, the support tools used, and the assignment of responsibility during the lifecycle of incidents. Such an approach is typically documented.

Often, the amount of time needed to fully address an incident is defined before the start of service delivery and documented in a service agreement.

In many service domains, the approach to incident resolution and prevention involves a function called a "help desk," "service desk," or one of many other names. This function is typically the one that communicates with the customer, accepts incidents, applies workarounds, and addresses incidents. However, this function is not present in all service domains. In addition, other functional groups are routinely included to address incidents as appropriate.

Refer to the Service Delivery process area for more information about establishing and maintaining service agreements.

Typical Work Products

1. Incident management approach
2. Incident criteria

Subpractices

1. Define criteria for determining what an incident is.

   To be able to identify valid incidents, criteria must be defined that enable service providers to determine what is and what is not an incident. Typically, criteria also are defined for differentiating the severity and priority of each incident.

2. Define categories for incidents and criteria for determining which categories an incident belongs to.

   The resolution of incidents is facilitated by having an established set of categories, severity levels, and other criteria for assigning types to incidents. These predetermined criteria can enable prioritization, assignment, and escalation actions quickly and efficiently.

Appropriate incident categories vary according to the service. As an example, IT-related security incident categories could include the following:

- Probes or scans of internal or external systems (e.g., networks, Web applications, mail servers)
- Administrative or privileged (i.e., root) access to accounts, applications, servers networks, etc.
- Distributed denial of service attacks, Web defacements, malicious code (e.g., viruses), etc.
- Insider attacks or other misuse of resources (e.g., password sharing)
- Loss of personally identifiable information

There must be criteria that enable service personnel to quickly and easily identify major incidents.

Examples of incident severity level approaches include the following:
- Critical, high, medium, low
- Numerical scales (e.g., 1–5, with 1 being the highest)

---

3. Describe how responsibility for processing incidents is assigned and transferred.

The description may include the following:
- Who is responsible for addressing underlying causes of incidents
- Who is responsible for monitoring and tracking the status of incidents
- Who is responsible for tracking the progress of actions related to incidents
- Escalation procedures
- How responsibility for all of these elements is assigned and transferred

---

4. Identify one or more mechanisms that customers and end users can use to report incidents.

    These mechanisms must account for how groups and individuals can report incidents.
5. Define methods and secure tools to use for incident management.
6. Describe how to notify all relevant customers and end users who may be affected by a reported incident.

    How to communicate with customers and end users is typically documented in the service agreement.
7. Define criteria for determining severity and priority levels and categories of actions and responses to be taken based on severity and priority levels.

Examples of responses based on severity and priority levels include immediate short-term action, retraining or documentation updates, and deferring responses until later.

---

8. Identify requirements on the amount of time defined for the resolution of incidents in the service agreement.

    Often, the minimum and maximum amounts of time needed to resolve an incident is defined and documented in the service agreement before the start of service delivery.

Refer to the Service Delivery process area for more information about establishing and maintaining service agreements.

9. Document criteria that define when an incident should be closed.

   Not all underlying causes of incidents are addressed, and not all incidents have workarounds either. Incidents should not be closed until the documented criteria are met.

   Often, closure codes are used to classify each incident. These codes are useful when these data are analyzed further.

SP 1.2 ESTABLISH AN INCIDENT MANAGEMENT SYSTEM

Establish and maintain an incident management system for processing and tracking incident information.

An incident management system includes the storage media, procedures, and tools for accessing the incident management system. These storage media, procedures, and tools may be automated but are not required to be automated. For example, storage media might be a filing system where documents are stored. Procedures may be documented on paper, and tools may be hand tools or instruments for performing work without automated help.

A collection of historical data covering addressed incidents, underlying causes of incidents, known approaches to addressing incidents, and workarounds must be available to support incident management.

Typical Work Products

1. An incident management system with controlled work products
2. Access control procedures for the incident management system

Subpractices

1. Ensure that the incident management system allows the escalation and transfer of incidents among groups.

   Incidents may need to be transferred or escalated between different groups because the group that entered the incident may not be best suited for taking action to address it.

2. Ensure that the incident management system allows the storage, update, retrieval, and reporting of incident information that is useful to the resolution and prevention of incidents.

Examples of incident management systems include the following:
- Indexed physical files of customer complaints and resolutions
- Bug or issue tracking software
- Help desk software

3. Maintain the integrity of the incident management system and its contents.

Examples of maintaining the integrity of the incident management system include the following:
- Backing up and restoring incident files
- Archiving incident files
- Recovering from incident errors
- Maintaining security that prevents unauthorized access

---

4. Maintain the incident management system as necessary.

SG 2 IDENTIFY, CONTROL, AND ADDRESS INCIDENTS

Incidents are identified, controlled, and addressed.

The practices that comprise this goal include interaction with those who report incidents and those who are affected by them. The processing and tracking of incident data happens among these practices until the incident is addressed and closed.

Treatment of incidents can include collecting and analyzing data looking for potential incidents or simply waiting for incidents to be reported by end users or customers.

The specific practices of this goal may also depend on the practices in the goal to Define Approaches to Address Selected Incidents. It is often the case that the practices in *that* goal are used to define the approaches used to address selected incidents as called for in the goal to Identify, Control, and Address Incidents.

Often, incidents involve work products that are under configuration management.

Refer to the Configuration Management process area for more information about tracking and controlling changes.

SP 2.1 IDENTIFY AND RECORD INCIDENTS

Identify incidents and record information about them.

Capacity, performance, or availability issues often signal potential incidents.

Refer to the Capacity and Availability Management process area for more information about monitoring and analyzing capacity and availability.

Typical Work Products

1. Incident management record

Subpractices

1. Identify incidents that are in scope.

Examples of how incidents can be identified include the following:
- Incidents reported by the customer to a help desk by phone
- Incidents reported by the end user in a Web form
- Incidents detected by automated detection systems
- Incidents derived from the analysis of anomalies in data collected
- Monitoring and analyzing external sources of information (e.g., RSS feeds, news services, websites)

---

2. Record information about the incident.

When recording information about an incident, record sufficient information to properly support analysis and resolution activities.

Examples of information to record about the incident include the following:
- Name and contact information of the person who reported the incident
- Description of the incident
- Categories the incident belongs to
- Date and time of occurrence and date and time the incident was reported
- The configuration items involved in the incident
- Closure code and information
- Relevant characteristics of the situation in which the incident occurred

---

3. Categorize the incident.

Using the categories established in the approach to incident resolution and prevention, assign the relevant categories to the incident in the incident management system. Communicating with those who reported the incident about its status enables the service provider to confirm incident information early.

SP 2.2 *Analyze Incident Data*

Analyze incident data to determine the best course of action.

The best course of action may be to do nothing, address incidents on a case-by-case basis, provide workarounds for the incidents, remove underlying causes of incidents, educate end users, monitor for indicators of interference with service, or build contingency plans.

Typical Work Products

1. Major incident report
2. Incident assignment report

Subpractices

1. Analyze incident data.

   For known incidents, the analysis may be done by merely selecting the type of incident. For major incidents, a separate incident resolution team may be assembled to analyze the incident.

2. Determine which group is best suited to take action to address the incident.

   Which group is best suited to take action to address the incident may depend on a number of different factors, including the type of incident, locations involved, and severity.

Examples of groups that deal with different types of incidents include the following:
- A healthcare team deals with adverse medical outcomes.
- A network support group handles network connectivity incidents.
- A help desk deals with password-related incidents.

---

3. Determine actions that must be taken to address the incident.

Examples of actions include the following:
- Replacing a broken component
- Training customer, end user, or service delivery personnel
- Releasing an announcement (e.g., public relations release, media response, bulletin, notice to customers or other stakeholders)

---

4. Plan the actions to be taken.

SP 2.3 APPLY WORKAROUNDS TO SELECTED INCIDENTS

Apply workarounds to selected incidents.

Applying workarounds can reduce the impact of incidents. Workarounds can be applied instead of addressing underlying causes of the incident. Or, the workaround can be used temporarily until underlying causes of the incident can be addressed.

It is essential to have a single repository established that contains all known workarounds. This repository can be used to quickly determine the workaround to be used for related incidents.

Typical Work Products

1. Updated incident management record

Subpractices

1. Address the incident using the workaround.
2. Manage the actions until the impact of the incident is at an acceptable level.
3. Record the actions and result.

SP 2.4 ADDRESS UNDERLYING CAUSES OF SELECTED INCIDENTS

Address underlying causes of selected incidents.

After the underlying causes of incidents are identified and analyzed, and action proposals are created using the specific practices of the goal to Define Approaches to Address Selected Incidents, the underlying causes must be addressed.

It is essential to have a single repository established that contains all known incidents, their underlying causes, and approaches to addressing these underlying causes. This repository can be used to quickly determine the causes of related incidents.

Typical Work Products

1. Updated incident management record

Subpractices

1. Address the underlying cause using the action proposal that resulted from the analysis of the incidents' underlying causes.

> *Refer to the Service Delivery process area for more information about maintaining the service system.*

2. Manage the actions until the underlying cause is addressed.
   Managing the actions may include escalating the incidents as appropriate.

> Examples of escalation criteria include the following:
> - When the impact of the incident on the organization or customer is large
> - When addressing the underlying cause of an incident will take considerable time or effort

3. Record the actions and result.

   The actions used to address the incident or its underlying cause and the results of those approaches are recorded in the incident management system to support resolving similar incidents in the future.

SP 2.5 MONITOR THE STATUS OF INCIDENTS TO CLOSURE

Monitor the status of incidents to closure and escalate if necessary.

Throughout the life of the incident, the status of the incident must be recorded, tracked, escalated as necessary, and closed.

Refer to the Project Monitoring and Control process area for more information about providing an understanding of the project's progress so that appropriate corrective actions can be taken when the project's performance deviates significantly from the plan.

Typical Work Products

1. Closed incident management records

Subpractices

1. Document actions and monitor and track the incidents until they meet the terms of the service agreement and satisfy the incident submitter as appropriate.

   The incident should be tracked throughout its life and escalated, as necessary, to ensure its resolution. Monitor the responses to those reporting the incident and how the incident was addressed until it is resolved to the customer's or organization's satisfaction.

2. Review the resolution and confirm the results with relevant stakeholders.

   Confirming that the underlying causes were successfully addressed may involve confirming with the person who reported the incident or others involved in analyzing the incident that the actions taken in fact resulted in the incident no longer occurring. Part of the result of addressing the incident may be the level of customer satisfaction. Now that the incident has been addressed, it must be confirmed that the service again meets the terms of the service agreement.

3. Close incidents that meet the criteria for closure.

SP 2.6 COMMUNICATE THE STATUS OF INCIDENTS

Communicate the status of incidents.

Communication is a critical factor when providing services, especially when incidents occur. Communication with the person who reported the incident and possibly those affected by it should be considered throughout the life of the incident record in the incident management system. Well-informed end users and customers are more understanding and can even be helpful in addressing the incident successfully.

Typically, the results of actions are reviewed with the person who reported the incident to verify that the actions indeed resolved the incident to the satisfaction of the submitter.

Typical Work Products

1. Records of communication with customers and end users

SG 3 DEFINE APPROACHES TO ADDRESS SELECTED INCIDENTS

Approaches to address selected incidents are defined to prevent the future occurrence of incidents or mitigate their impact.

All incidents have one or more underlying causes that trigger their occurrence. Addressing the underlying cause of some incidents may reduce the likelihood or impact of service interference, reduce the workload on the service provider, or improve the level of service. The practices in this goal cover the analysis of incidents to define how to address them. The results of this analysis are fed back to those who control and address incidents.

Underlying causes can be identified for incidents and possible future incidents.

> Examples include analyzing the cause of a delivery error or system outage and monitoring use of software memory to detect memory leaks as soon as possible.

The root cause of an incident is often different from the immediate underlying cause. For example, an incident may be caused by a faulty system component (the underlying cause), while the root cause of the incident is a suboptimal supplier selection process. This process area uses the term "underlying cause" flexibly, ranging from immediate causes or conditions to deeper root causes, to allow for a

range of possible responses from workarounds to prevention of a class of related incidents.

Refer to the Causal Analysis and Resolution process area for more information about determining causes of defects and problems.

SP 3.1 ANALYZE SELECTED INCIDENT DATA

Select and analyze the underlying causes of incidents.

The purpose of conducting causal analysis on incidents is to determine the best course of action to address the incidents so that they don't happen again. Possible courses of action include not addressing the underlying cause and continuing to deal with incidents as they occur or providing a workaround.

Often, analyzing incidents involves work products that are under configuration management.

Refer to the Configuration Management process area for more information about tracking and controlling changes.

Typical Work Products

1. Report of underlying causes of incidents
2. Documented causal analysis activities

Subpractices

1. Identify underlying causes of incidents.

> Examples of approaches to identifying underlying causes of incidents include the following:
> - Analyze incidents reported by customers to a help desk
> - Monitor the service system to identify potential incidents
> - Analyze trends in the use of resources
> - Analyze strengths and weaknesses of the service system
> - Analyze mean times between service system failures and availability
> - Analyze external sources of information, such as alerts, news feeds, and websites

Refer to the Risk Management process area for more information about identifying, analyzing, and mitigating risks.

2. Record information about the underlying causes of an incident or group of incidents.

When recording information about the underlying causes of an incident, record sufficient information to properly support causal analysis

and resolution.

> Examples of information to record include the following:
> - Incidents affected or potentially affected by the underlying cause
> - Configuration items involved
> - Relevant characteristics of the situation in which the incidents did or could occur

3. Conduct causal analysis with the people who are responsible for performing related tasks.

    For underlying causes of major incidents, the analysis may involve assembling a separate team to analyze the underlying cause.

    Refer to the Causal Analysis and Resolution process area for more information about determining causes of defects and problems.

SP 3.2 PLAN ACTIONS TO ADDRESS UNDERLYING CAUSES OF SELECTED INCIDENTS

Identify the underlying causes of selected incidents and create an action proposal to address these causes.

After analysis has determined the underlying causes of incidents, the actions to be taken, if any, are planned. Planning includes determining who will act, when, and how. All of this information is documented in an action proposal. The action proposal is used by those who take action to address the underlying causes of incidents.

Typical Work Products

1. Action proposal
2. Contribution to collection of known approaches to addressing underlying causes of incidents

Subpractices

1. Determine which group is best suited to address the underlying cause.

    Which group is best suited to address the underlying cause may depend on the type of underlying cause, configuration items involved, and the severity of the relevant incidents.

Examples of groups and departments that deal with different types of underlying causes include the following:
- A network support group handles network issues.
- A UNIX server support team deals with server configuration issues.
- Human Resources controls personnel and privacy issues.
- The Legal department controls issues relating to intellectual property, disclosure of information, data loss, etc.
- Public Relations is responsible for issues relating to the reputation of the organization.

2. Determine the actions to be taken to address the underlying cause.
    When analyzing standard incidents, the actions for addressing that standard incident may be documented as a standard action plan. If the incident is not standard, a historical collection of addressed incidents and known errors should be searched to see if the incident is related to others. This data should be maintained to allow this kind of analysis, thus saving time and leveraging effort.

Examples of actions taken to address the underlying cause include the following:
- Replacing a broken component
- Training end users or service delivery staff
- Fixing a software defect
- Not addressing the underlying cause because it is cheaper or less risky to deal with the incidents than address the underlying cause

> *Refer to the Decision Analysis and Resolution process area for more information about analyzing possible decisions using a formal evaluation process that evaluates identified alternatives against established criteria.*

3. Document the actions to be taken in an action proposal.
4. Verify and validate the action proposal to ensure that it effectively addresses the incident.
5. Communicate the action proposal to relevant stakeholders.

SP 3.3 ESTABLISH WORKAROUNDS FOR SELECTED INCIDENTS

Establish and maintain workarounds for selected incidents.

Workarounds are important mechanisms that enable the service to continue in spite of the occurrence of the incident. Therefore, it is important that the workaround be documented and confirmed to be effective before it is used to address incidents with customers and end users.

Typical Work Products

1. Workaround description and instructions
2. Contribution to collection of workarounds for incidents

Subpractices

1. Determine which group is best suited to establish and maintain a workaround.

   Determine which group is best suited to define the workaround, describe the steps involved, and communicate this information appropriately.
2. Plan and document the workaround.
3. Verify and validate the workaround to ensure that it effectively addresses the incident.
4. Communicate the workaround to relevant stakeholders.

MEASUREMENT AND ANALYSIS
A Support Process Area at Maturity Level 2

Purpose

The purpose of Measurement and Analysis (MA) is to develop and sustain a measurement capability used to support management information needs.

CAM calls for measuring and monitoring particular contributors to service performance and quality: capacity and availability. MA is a more general set of measurement practices and can be applied to measure and analyze anything relevant to your business goals.

Introductory Notes

The Measurement and Analysis process area involves the following activities:

- Specifying objectives of measurement and analysis so they are aligned with identified information needs and objectives
- Specifying measures, analysis techniques, and mechanisms for data collection, data storage, reporting, and feedback
- Implementing the collection, storage, analysis, and reporting of data
- Providing objective results that can be used in making informed decisions and taking appropriate corrective action

The integration of measurement and analysis activities into the processes of the project supports the following:

- Objective planning and estimating
- Tracking actual performance against established plans and objectives
- Identifying and resolving process-related issues
- Providing a basis for incorporating measurement into additional processes in the future

The staff required to implement a measurement capability may or may not be employed in a separate organization-wide program. Measurement capability may be integrated into individual projects or other organizational functions (e.g., quality assurance).

The initial focus for measurement activities is at the project level. However, a measurement capability may prove useful for addressing organization- and enterprise-wide information needs. To support this capability, measurement activities should support information needs at multiple levels, including the business, organizational unit, and project to minimize rework as the organization matures.

Projects can store project-specific data and results in a project-specific repository, but when data are to be used widely or are to be analyzed in support of determining data trends or benchmarks, data may reside in the organization's measurement repository.

Measurement and analysis of product components provided by suppliers is essential for effective management of the quality and costs of the project. It is possible, with careful management of supplier agreements, to provide insight into data that support supplier-performance analysis.

Related Process Areas

Refer to the Service System Development process area for more information about developing and analyzing stakeholder requirements.

SSD ADD

Refer to the Organizational Process Definition process area for more information about establishing the organization's measurement repository.

Refer to the Project Monitoring and Control process area for more information about monitoring project planning parameters.

Refer to the Project Planning process area for more information about establishing estimates.

Refer to the Quantitative Project Management process area for more information about applying statistical methods to understand variation.

Specific Goal and Practice Summary

SG 1 Align Measurement and Analysis Activities
  SP 1.1   Establish Measurement Objectives
  SP 1.2   Specify Measures
  SP 1.3   Specify Data Collection and Storage Procedures
  SP 1.4   Specify Analysis Procedures

SG 2 Provide Measurement Results
  SP 2.1   Obtain Measurement Data
  SP 2.2   Analyze Measurement Data
  SP 2.3   Store Data and Results
  SP 2.4   Communicate Results

Specific Practices by Goal

SG 1   ALIGN MEASUREMENT AND ANALYSIS ACTIVITIES

Measurement objectives and activities are aligned with identified information needs and objectives.

The specific practices under this specific goal may be addressed concurrently or in any order:

- When establishing measurement objectives, experts often think ahead about necessary criteria for specifying measures and analysis procedures. They also think concurrently about the constraints imposed by data collection and storage procedures.
- Often it is important to specify the essential analyses to be conducted before attending to details of measurement specification, data collection, or storage.

SP 1.1 ESTABLISH MEASUREMENT OBJECTIVES

Establish and maintain measurement objectives derived from identified information needs and objectives.

Measurement objectives document the purposes for which measurement and analysis are done and specify the kinds of actions that may be taken based on results of data analyses. Measurement objectives can also identify the change in behavior desired as a result of implementing a measurement and analysis activity.

Sources of measurement objectives include management, technical, project, product, and process implementation needs.

Measurement objectives may be constrained by existing processes, available resources, or other measurement considerations. Judgments may need to be made about whether the value of the result is commensurate with resources devoted to doing the work.

Modifications to identified information needs and objectives may, in turn, be indicated as a consequence of the process and results of measurement and analysis.

Sources of information needs and objectives may include the following:
- Project plans
- Project performance monitoring
- Interviews with managers and others who have information needs
- Established management objectives
- Strategic plans
- Business plans
- Formal requirements or contractual obligations
- Recurring or other troublesome management or technical problems
- Experiences of other projects or organizational entities
- External industry benchmarks
- Process improvement plans
- Recurring or other troublesome incidents.

Example measurement objectives include the following:
- Reduce time to delivery
- Reduce total lifecycle costs
- Deliver the specified functionality completely
- Improve prior levels of quality
- Improve prior customer satisfaction ratings
- Maintain and improve relationships between the acquirer and supplier
- Improve the level of stakeholder involvement

Refer to the Service System Development process area for more information about developing and analyzing stakeholder requirements.

SSD A<small>DD</small>

Refer to the Project Monitoring and Control process area for more information about monitoring project planning parameters.

Refer to the Project Planning process area for more information about establishing estimates.

Refer to the Requirements Management process area for more information about maintaining bidirectional traceability among requirements and work products.

Typical Work Products

1. Measurement objectives

Subpractices

1. Document information needs and objectives.

Information needs and objectives are documented to allow traceability to subsequent measurement and analysis activities.

2. Prioritize information needs and objectives.

It may be neither possible nor desirable to subject all initially identified information needs to measurement and analysis. Priorities may also need to be set within the limits of available resources.

3. Document, review, and update measurement objectives.

Carefully consider the purposes and intended uses of measurement and analysis.

The measurement objectives are documented, reviewed by management and other relevant stakeholders, and updated as necessary. Doing so enables traceability to subsequent measurement and analysis activities, and helps to ensure that analyses will properly address identified information needs and objectives.

It is important that users of measurement and analysis results be involved in setting measurement objectives and deciding on plans of action. It may also be appropriate to involve those who provide the measurement data.

4. Provide feedback for refining and clarifying information needs and objectives as necessary.

Identified information needs and objectives may be refined and clarified as a result of setting measurement objectives. Initial descriptions of information needs may be unclear or ambiguous. Conflicts may arise between existing needs and objectives. Precise targets on an already existing measure may be unrealistic.

5. Maintain traceability of measurement objectives to identified information needs and objectives.

There must always be a good answer to the question, "Why are we measuring this?"

Of course, measurement objectives may also change to reflect evolving information needs and objectives.

SP 1.2 SPECIFY MEASURES

Specify measures to address measurement objectives.

Measurement objectives are refined into precise, quantifiable measures.

Measures may be either "base" or "derived." Data for base measures are obtained by direct measurement. Data for derived measures come from other data, typically by combining two or more base measures.

Examples of commonly used base measures include the following:
- Estimates and actual measures of work product size (e.g., number of pages)
- Estimates and actual measures of effort and cost (e.g., number of person hours)
- Quality measures (e.g., number of defects by severity)

Examples of commonly used derived measures include the following:
- Earned value
- Schedule performance index
- Defect density
- Peer review coverage
- Test or verification coverage
- Reliability measures (e.g., mean time to failure)
- Quality measures (e.g., number of defects by severity/total number of defects)

Derived measures typically are expressed as ratios, composite indices, or other aggregate summary measures. They are often more quantitatively reliable and meaningfully interpretable than the base measures used to generate them.

Typical Work Products

1. Specifications of base and derived measures

Subpractices

1. Identify candidate measures based on documented measurement objectives.

   Measurement objectives are refined into measures. Identified candidate measures are categorized and specified by name and unit of measure.

2. Maintain traceability of measures to measurement objectives.

   Interdependencies among candidate measures are identified to enable later data validation and candidate analyses in support of measurement objectives.

3. Identify existing measures that already address measurement objectives.

   Specifications for measures may already exist, perhaps established for other purposes earlier or elsewhere in the organization.

4. Specify operational definitions for measures.

Operational definitions are stated in precise and unambiguous terms. They address two important criteria:

- Communication: What has been measured, how was it measured, what are the units of measure, and what has been included or excluded?
- Repeatability: Can the measurement be repeated, given the same definition, to get the same results?

5. Prioritize, review, and update measures.

Proposed specifications of measures are reviewed for their appropriateness with potential end users and other relevant stakeholders. Priorities are set or changed, and specifications of measures are updated as necessary.

SP 1.3 SPECIFY DATA COLLECTION AND STORAGE PROCEDURES

Specify how measurement data are obtained and stored.

Explicit specification of collection methods helps to ensure that the right data are collected properly. This specification may also help further clarify information needs and measurement objectives.

Proper attention to storage and retrieval procedures helps to ensure that data are available and accessible for future use.

Typical Work Products

1. Data collection and storage procedures
2. Data collection tools

Subpractices

1. Identify existing sources of data that are generated from current work products, processes, or transactions.

   Existing sources of data may have been identified when specifying the measures. Appropriate collection mechanisms may exist whether or not pertinent data have already been collected.

2. Identify measures for which data are needed but are not currently available.

3. Specify how to collect and store the data for each required measure.

   Explicit specifications are made of how, where, and when data will be collected. Procedures for collecting valid data are specified. Data are stored in an accessible manner for analysis. This analysis helps to determine whether data will be saved for possible reanalysis or documentation purposes.

   Specifications may also address other factors that provide information about the context in which the measurement was collected (e.g., time of measurement, age of data) to assist in validating the data for later analyses.

Questions to be considered typically include the following:
- Have the frequency of collection and points in the process where measurements will be made been determined?
- Has the timeline that is required to move measurement results from points of collection to repositories, other databases, or end users been established?
- Who is responsible for obtaining data?
- Who is responsible for data storage, retrieval, and security?
- Have necessary supporting tools been developed or acquired?

---

4. Create data collection mechanisms and process guidance.

   Data collection and storage mechanisms are well integrated with other normal work processes. Data collection mechanisms may include manual or automated forms and templates. Clear, concise guidance on correct procedures is available to those responsible for doing the work. Training is provided as needed to clarify processes required for the collection of complete and accurate data and to minimize the burden on those who must provide and record data.

5. Support automatic collection of data as appropriate and feasible.

   Automated support can aid in collecting more complete and accurate data.

Examples of such automated support include the following:
- Time-stamped activity logs
- Static or dynamic analyses of artifacts

   However, some data cannot be collected without human intervention (e.g., customer satisfaction, other human judgments), and setting up the necessary infrastructure for other automation may be costly.

6. Prioritize, review, and update data collection and storage procedures.

   Proposed procedures are reviewed for their appropriateness and feasibility with those who are responsible for providing, collecting, and storing data. They also may have useful insights about how to improve existing processes or may be able to suggest other useful measures or analyses.

7. Update measures and measurement objectives as necessary.

   Priorities may need to be reset based on the following:
   - The importance of the measures
   - The amount of effort required to obtain the data

   Considerations include whether new forms, tools, or training would be required to obtain the data.

SP 1.4 Specify Analysis Procedures

Specify how measurement data are analyzed and communicated.

Specifying analysis procedures in advance ensures that appropriate analyses will be conducted and reported to address documented measurement objectives (and thereby the information needs and objectives on which they are based). This approach also provides a check that necessary data will, in fact, be collected. Analysis procedures should account for the quality (e.g., age, reliability) of all data that enter into an analysis (whether from the project, organizational measurement repository, or other source). The quality of data should be considered to help select the appropriate analysis procedure and evaluate the results of the analysis.

Typical Work Products

1. Analysis specifications and procedures
2. Data analysis tools

Subpractices

1. Specify and prioritize the analyses to be conducted and the reports to be prepared.

    Early on, pay attention to the analyses to be conducted and to the manner in which results will be reported. These analyses and reports should meet the following criteria:

    - The analyses explicitly address the documented measurement objectives.
    - Presentation of results is clearly understandable by the audiences to whom the results are addressed.

    Priorities may have to be set within available resources.

2. Select appropriate data analysis methods and tools.

Issues to be considered typically include the following:

- Choice of visual display and other presentation techniques (e.g., pie charts, bar charts, histograms, radar charts, line graphs, scatter plots, tables)
- Choice of appropriate descriptive statistics (e.g., arithmetic mean, median, mode)
- Decisions about statistical sampling criteria when it is impossible or unnecessary to examine every data element
- Decisions about how to handle analysis in the presence of missing data elements
- Selection of appropriate analysis tools

Descriptive statistics are typically used in data analysis to do the following:
- Examine distributions of specified measures (e.g., central tendency, extent of variation, data points exhibiting unusual variation)
- Examine interrelationships among specified measures (e.g., comparisons of defects by phase of the product's lifecycle, comparisons of defects by product component)
- Display changes over time

> Refer to the Select Measures and Analytic Techniques specific practice and Apply Statistical Methods to Understand Variation specific practice in the Quantitative Project Management process area for more information about the appropriate use of statistical analysis techniques and understanding variation.

3. Specify administrative procedures for analyzing data and communicating results.

Issues to be considered typically include the following:
- Identifying the persons and groups responsible for analyzing the data and presenting the results
- Determining the timeline to analyze the data and present the results
- Determining the venues for communicating the results (e.g., progress reports, transmittal memos, written reports, staff meetings)

---

4. Review and update the proposed content and format of specified analyses and reports.
   All of the proposed content and format are subject to review and revision, including analytic methods and tools, administrative procedures, and priorities. Relevant stakeholders consulted should include end users, sponsors, data analysts, and data providers.
5. Update measures and measurement objectives as necessary.
   Just as measurement needs drive data analysis, clarification of analysis criteria can affect measurement. Specifications for some measures may be refined further based on specifications established for data analysis procedures. Other measures may prove unnecessary, or a need for additional measures may be recognized.
   Specifying how measures will be analyzed and reported may also suggest the need for refining measurement objectives themselves.
6. Specify criteria for evaluating the utility of analysis results and for evaluating the conduct of measurement and analysis activities.

Criteria for evaluating the utility of the analysis might address the extent to which the following apply:

- The results are provided in a timely manner, understandable, and used for decision making.
- The work does not cost more to perform than is justified by the benefits it provides.

Criteria for evaluating the conduct of the measurement and analysis might include the extent to which the following apply:

- The amount of missing data or the number of flagged inconsistencies is beyond specified thresholds.
- There is selection bias in sampling (e.g., only satisfied end users are surveyed to evaluate end-user satisfaction, only unsuccessful projects are evaluated to determine overall productivity).
- Measurement data are repeatable (e.g., statistically reliable).
- Statistical assumptions have been satisfied (e.g., about the distribution of data, about appropriate measurement scales).

SG 2 PROVIDE MEASUREMENT RESULTS

Measurement results, which address identified information needs and objectives, are provided.

The primary reason for conducting measurement and analysis is to address identified information needs and objectives. Measurement results based on objective evidence can help to monitor performance, fulfill obligations documented in a supplier agreement, make informed management and technical decisions, and enable corrective actions to be taken.

SP 2.1 OBTAIN MEASUREMENT DATA

Obtain specified measurement data.

The data necessary for analysis are obtained and checked for completeness and integrity.

Typical Work Products

1. Base and derived measurement data sets
2. Results of data integrity tests

Subpractices

1. Obtain data for base measures.

   Data are collected as necessary for previously used and newly specified base measures. Existing data are gathered from project records or elsewhere in the organization.

   Note that data that were collected earlier may no longer be available for reuse in existing databases, paper records, or formal repositories.

2. Generate data for derived measures.

   Values are newly calculated for all derived measures.

3. Perform data integrity checks as close to the source of data as possible.

   All measurements are subject to error in specifying or recording data. It is always better to identify these errors and sources of missing data early in the measurement and analysis cycle.

   Checks can include scans for missing data, out-of-bounds data values, and unusual patterns and correlation across measures. It is particularly important to do the following:

   • Test and correct for inconsistency of classifications made by human judgment (i.e., to determine how frequently people make differing classification decisions based on the same information, otherwise known as "inter-coder reliability").

   • Empirically examine the relationships among measures that are used to calculate additional derived measures. Doing so can ensure that important distinctions are not overlooked and that derived measures convey their intended meanings (otherwise known as "criterion validity").

SP 2.2 ANALYZE MEASUREMENT DATA

Analyze and interpret measurement data.

Measurement data are analyzed as planned, additional analyses are conducted as necessary, results are reviewed with relevant stakeholders, and necessary revisions for future analyses are noted.

Typical Work Products

1. Analysis results and draft reports

Subpractices

1. Conduct initial analyses, interpret results, and draw preliminary conclusions.

   The results of data analyses are rarely self evident. Criteria for interpreting results and drawing conclusions should be stated explicitly.

2. Conduct additional measurement and analysis as necessary, and prepare results for presentation.

Results of planned analyses may suggest (or require) additional, unanticipated analyses. In addition, these analyses may identify needs to refine existing measures, to calculate additional derived measures, or even to collect data for additional base measures to properly complete the planned analysis. Similarly, preparing initial results for presentation may identify the need for additional, unanticipated analyses.

3. Review initial results with relevant stakeholders.

It may be appropriate to review initial interpretations of results and the way in which these results are presented before disseminating and communicating them widely.

Reviewing the initial results before their release may prevent needless misunderstandings and lead to improvements in the data analysis and presentation.

Relevant stakeholders with whom reviews may be conducted include intended end users, sponsors, data analysts, and data providers.

4. Refine criteria for future analyses.

Lessons that can improve future efforts are often learned from conducting data analyses and preparing results. Similarly, ways to improve measurement specifications and data collection procedures may become apparent, as may ideas for refining identified information needs and objectives.

SP 2.3 STORE DATA AND RESULTS

Manage and store measurement data, measurement specifications, and analysis results.

Storing measurement-related information enables its timely and cost-effective use as historical data and results. The information also is needed to provide sufficient context for interpretation of data, measurement criteria, and analysis results.

Information stored typically includes the following:
- Measurement plans
- Specifications of measures
- Sets of data that were collected
- Analysis reports and presentations

Stored information contains or refers to other information needed to understand and interpret the measures and to assess them for reasonableness and applicability (e.g., measurement specifications used on different projects when comparing across projects).

Typically, data sets for derived measures can be recalculated and need not be stored. However, it may be appropriate to store summaries based on derived measures (e.g., charts, tables of results, report text).

Interim analysis results need not be stored separately if they can be efficiently reconstructed.

Refer to the Configuration Management process area for more information about establishing a configuration management system.

Refer to the Establish the Organization's Measurement Repository specific practice in the Organizational Process Definition process area for more information about establishing the organization's measurement repository.

Typical Work Products

1. Stored data inventory

Subpractices

1. Review data to ensure their completeness, integrity, accuracy, and currency.
2. Store data according to data storage procedures.
3. Make stored contents available for use only to appropriate groups and personnel.
4. Prevent stored information from being used inappropriately.

Examples of ways to prevent inappropriate use of the data and related information include controlling access to data and educating people on the appropriate use of data.

Examples of inappropriate use of data include the following:
- Disclosure of information provided in confidence
- Faulty interpretations based on incomplete, out-of-context, or otherwise misleading information
- Measures used to improperly evaluate the performance of people or to rank projects
- Impugning the integrity of individuals

SP 2.4 COMMUNICATE RESULTS

Communicate results of measurement and analysis activities to all relevant stakeholders.

The results of the measurement and analysis process are communicated to relevant stakeholders in a timely and usable fashion to support decision making and assist in taking corrective action.

Relevant stakeholders include intended users, sponsors, data analysts, and data providers.

Typical Work Products

1. Delivered reports and related analysis results
2. Contextual information or guidance to help interpret analysis results

Subpractices

1. Keep relevant stakeholders informed of measurement results in a timely manner.

   Measurement results are communicated in time to be used for their intended purposes. Reports are unlikely to be used if they are distributed with little effort to follow up with those who need to know the results.

   To the extent possible and as part of the normal way they do business, users of measurement results are kept personally involved in setting objectives and deciding on plans of action for measurement and analysis. Users are regularly kept informed of progress and interim results.

   Refer to the Project Monitoring and Control process area for more information about conducting progress reviews.

2. Assist relevant stakeholders in understanding results.

   Results are communicated in a clear and concise manner appropriate to relevant stakeholders. Results are understandable, easily interpretable, and clearly tied to identified information needs and objectives.

   The data analyzed are often not self evident to practitioners who are not measurement experts. The communication of results should be clear about the following:
   - How and why base and derived measures were specified
   - How data were obtained
   - How to interpret results based on the data analysis methods used
   - How results address information needs

Examples of actions taken to help others to understand results include the following:
- Discussing the results with relevant stakeholders
- Providing background and explanation in a memo
- Briefing users on results
- Providing training on the appropriate use and understanding of measurement results

ORGANIZATIONAL INNOVATION AND DEPLOYMENT
A Process Management Process Area at Maturity Level 5

Purpose

The purpose of Organizational Innovation and Deployment (OID) is to select and deploy incremental and innovative improvements that measurably improve the organization's processes and technologies. These improvements support the organization's quality and process-performance objectives as derived from the organization's business objectives.

IN OTHER WORDS

OID is about managing your improvements and innovations using a statistical understanding of your process performance.

OID

Introductory Notes

The Organizational Innovation and Deployment process area enables the selection and deployment of improvements that can enhance the organization's ability to meet its quality and process-performance objectives. (See the definition of "quality and process-performance objectives" in the glossary.)

WHY DO THE PRACTICES IN OID?

Once you have mastered statistical management of your processes, you can select and deploy improvements with sophisticated knowledge about how they will affect your work.

The term "improvement," as used in this process area, refers to all ideas (proven and unproven) that would change the organization's processes and technologies to better meet the organization's quality and process-performance objectives.

Processes and technologies, as they apply to a service system, refer to that which is put into place to satisfy service requirements and successfully deliver the service. Therefore, as defined in this process area, processes and technologies make up the components of a service system.

Quality and process-performance objectives that this process area might address include the following:

- Improved product quality (e.g., functionality, performance)
- Increased productivity
- Decreased cycle time
- Greater customer and end-user satisfaction

331

- Shorter development or production time to change functionality, add new features, or adapt to new technologies
- Reduced delivery time
- Reduced time to adapt to new technologies and business needs

Achievement of these objectives depends on the successful establishment of an infrastructure that enables and encourages all people in the organization to propose potential improvements to the organization's processes and technologies. Achievement of these objectives also depends on being able to effectively evaluate and deploy proposed improvements to the organization's processes and technologies. All members of the organization can participate in the organization's process- and technology-improvement activities. Their proposals are systematically gathered and addressed.

Pilots are conducted to evaluate significant changes involving untried, high-risk, or innovative improvements before they are broadly deployed.

Process and technology improvements to be deployed across the organization are selected from process- and technology-improvement proposals based on the following criteria:

- A quantitative understanding of the organization's current quality and process performance
- The organization's quality and process-performance objectives
- Estimates of the improvement in quality and process performance resulting from deploying the process and technology improvements
- Estimated costs of deploying process and technology improvements, and resources and funding available for such deployment

Expected benefits added by the process and technology improvements are weighed against the cost and impact to the organization. Change and stability must be balanced carefully. Change that is too great or too rapid can overwhelm the organization, destroying its investment in organizational learning represented by organizational process assets. Rigid stability can result in stagnation, allowing the changing business environment to erode the organization's business position.

Improvements are deployed as appropriate to new and ongoing projects.

In this process area, the term "process and technology improvements" refers to incremental and innovative improvements to processes and to process or product technologies (including project work environments).

The informative material in this process area is written assuming the specific practices are applied in an organization that has a quantitative understanding of its standard processes and their expected quality and performance in predictable situations. Specific practices of this process area may be applicable, but with reduced value, if this assumption is not met.

The specific practices in this process area complement and extend those found in the Organizational Process Focus process area. The focus of this process area is process improvement based on a quantitative understanding of the organization's set of standard processes and technologies and their expected quality and performance in predictable situations. In the Organizational Process Focus process area, no assumptions are made about the quantitative basis of improvement.

Related Process Areas

Refer to the Decision Analysis and Resolution process area for more information about analyzing possible decisions using a formal evaluation process that evaluates identified alternatives against established criteria.

Refer to the Measurement and Analysis process area for more information about aligning measurement and analysis activities and providing measurement results.

Refer to the Organizational Process Focus process area for more information about planning, implementing, and deploying organizational process improvements based on a thorough understanding of current strengths and weaknesses of the organization's processes and process assets.

Refer to the Organizational Process Performance process area for more information about establishing quality and process-performance objectives, establishing process-performance baselines, and establishing process-performance models.

Refer to the Organizational Training process area for more information about providing necessary training.

OID

Specific Goal and Practice Summary

SG 1 Select Improvements
    SP 1.1   Collect and Analyze Improvement Proposals
    SP 1.2   Identify and Analyze Innovations
    SP 1.3   Pilot Improvements
    SP 1.4   Select Improvements for Deployment
SG 2 Deploy Improvements
    SP 2.1   Plan the Deployment
    SP 2.2   Manage the Deployment
    SP 2.3   Measure Improvement Effects

Specific Practices by Goal

SG 1   SELECT IMPROVEMENTS

Process and technology improvements, which contribute to meeting quality and process-performance objectives, are selected.

SP 1.1   COLLECT AND ANALYZE IMPROVEMENT PROPOSALS

Collect and analyze process- and technology-improvement proposals.

Each process- and technology-improvement proposal must be analyzed.

    Simple process and technology improvements with well-understood benefits and effects will not usually undergo detailed evaluations.

Examples of simple process and technology improvements include the following:
- Add an item to a peer review checklist.
- Combine the technical review and management review for suppliers into a single review.

Typical Work Products

1. Analyzed process- and technology-improvement proposals

Subpractices

1. Collect process- and technology-improvement proposals.
    A process- and technology-improvement proposal documents proposed incremental and innovative improvements to processes and technologies. Managers and staff in the organization as well as customers, end users, and suppliers can submit process- and technology-improvement

proposals. Process and technology improvements may be implemented at the local level before being proposed for the organization.

Examples of sources for process- and technology-improvement proposals include the following:

- Findings and recommendations from process appraisals
- The organization's quality and process-performance objectives
- Analysis of data about customer and end-user problems as well as customer and end-user satisfaction
- Analysis of data about project performance compared to quality and productivity objectives
- Analysis of service system and service delivery performance measures
- Results of process and product benchmarking efforts
- Analysis of data on acceptable quality
- Measured effectiveness of process activities
- Measured effectiveness of project work environments
- Examples of process- and technology-improvement proposals that were successfully adopted elsewhere
- Feedback on previously submitted process- and technology-improvement proposals
- Spontaneous ideas from managers and staff

Refer to the Organizational Process Focus process area for more information incorporating experiences into organizational process assets and managing process improvement proposals.

2. Analyze the costs and benefits of process- and technology-improvement proposals as appropriate.

   Process- and technology-improvement proposals that have a large cost-to-benefit ratio are rejected.

   Criteria for evaluating costs and benefits include the following:

   - Contribution toward meeting the organization's quality and process-performance objectives
   - Effect on mitigating identified project and organizational risks
   - Ability to respond quickly to changes in project requirements, market situations, and the business environment
   - Effect on related processes and associated assets
   - Cost of defining and collecting data that support the measurement and analysis of the process- and technology-improvement proposal
   - Expected life span of the proposal

   Process- and technology-improvement proposals that would not improve the organization's processes are rejected.

   Process-performance models provide insight into the effect of process changes on process capability and performance.

Refer to the Organizational Process Performance process area for more information about establishing process-performance models.

3. Identify the process- and technology-improvement proposals that are innovative.

Innovative improvements are also identified and analyzed in the Identify and Analyze Innovations specific practice.

Whereas this specific practice analyzes proposals that have been passively collected, the purpose of the Identify and Analyze Innovations specific practice is to actively search for and locate innovative improvements. The search primarily involves looking outside the organization.

Innovative improvements are typically identified by reviewing process- and technology-improvement proposals or by actively investigating and monitoring innovations that are in use in other organizations or are documented in research literature. Innovation may be inspired by internal improvement objectives or by the external business environment.

Innovative improvements are typically major changes to the process that represent a break from the old way of doing things (e.g., changing the lifecycle model). Innovative improvements may also include changes in products that support, enhance, or automate the process (e.g., using off-the-shelf products to support the process).

Examples of innovative improvements include additions or major updates to the following:

- Support tools
- Processes or lifecycle models
- Interface standards
- Reusable components
- Management techniques and methodologies
- Quality-improvement techniques and methodologies

---

4. Identify potential barriers and risks to deploying each process- and technology-improvement proposal.

Examples of barriers to deploying process and technology improvements include the following:

- Turf guarding and parochial perspectives
- Unclear or weak business rationale
- Lack of short-term benefits and visible successes
- Unclear picture of what is expected from everyone
- Too many changes at the same time
- Lack of involvement and support from relevant stakeholders

Examples of risk factors that affect the deployment of process and technology improvements include the following:
- Compatibility of the improvement with existing processes, values, and skills of potential end users
- Complexity of the improvement
- Difficulty implementing the improvement
- Ability to demonstrate the value of the improvement before widespread deployment
- Justification for large, up-front investments in areas such as tools and training
- Inability to overcome "technology drag" where the current implementation is used successfully by a large and mature installed base of end users

5. Estimate the cost, effort, and schedule required for deploying each process- and technology-improvement proposal.
6. Select the process- and technology-improvement proposals to be piloted before broadscale deployment.

    Since innovations, by definition, usually represent a major change, most innovative improvements will be piloted.

7. Document results of the evaluation of each process- and technology-improvement proposal.
8. Monitor the status of each process- and technology-improvement proposal.

SP 1.2 IDENTIFY AND ANALYZE INNOVATIONS

Identify and analyze innovative improvements that could increase the organization's quality and process performance.

The specific practice, Collect and Analyze Improvement Proposals, analyzes proposals that are passively collected. The purpose of this specific practice is to actively search for, locate, and analyze innovative improvements. This search primarily involves looking outside the organization.

Typical Work Products

1. Candidate innovative improvements
2. Analysis of proposed innovative improvements

Subpractices

1. Analyze the organization's set of standard processes to determine areas in which innovative improvements would be most helpful.

These analyses are performed to determine which subprocesses are critical to achieving the organization's quality and process-performance objectives and which ones are good candidates to be improved.

2. Investigate innovative improvements that may improve the organization's set of standard processes.

Investigating innovative improvements involves the following activities:

- Systematically maintaining awareness of leading relevant technical work and technology trends
- Periodically searching for commercially available innovative improvements
- Collecting proposals for innovative improvements from projects and the organization
- Systematically reviewing processes and technologies used externally and comparing them to those used in the organization
- Identifying areas in which innovative improvements have been used successfully, and reviewing data and documentation of experience using these improvements
- Identifying improvements that integrate new technology into products and project work environments

3. Analyze potential innovative improvements to understand their effects on process elements and predict their influence on the process.

Process-performance models can provide a basis for analyzing possible effects of changes to process elements.

Refer to the Organizational Process Performance process area for more information about establishing process-performance models.

4. Analyze the costs and benefits of potential innovative improvements.

Innovative improvements that have a large cost-to-benefit ratio are rejected.

5. Create process- and technology-improvement proposals for those innovative improvements that would result in improving the organization's processes or technologies.

6. Select innovative improvements to be piloted before broadscale deployment.

Since innovations, by definition, usually represent a major change, most innovative improvements will be piloted.

7. Document results of evaluations of innovative improvements.

SP 1.3 Pilot Improvements

Pilot process and technology improvements to select which ones to implement.

Pilots are performed to assess new and unproven major changes before they are broadly deployed as appropriate.

The implementation of this specific practice may overlap with the implementation of the Implement Action Proposals specific practice in the Causal Analysis and Resolution process area (e.g., when causal analysis and resolution is implemented organizationally or across multiple projects).

Typical Work Products

1. Pilot evaluation reports
2. Documented lessons learned from pilots

Subpractices

1. Plan the pilots.
   When planning pilots, define quantitative criteria to be used for evaluating pilot results.
2. Review and get relevant stakeholder agreement on plans for pilots.
3. Consult with and assist those performing the pilots.
4. Perform each pilot in an environment that is characteristic of the environment present in a broadscale deployment.
5. Track pilots against their plans.
6. Review and document results of pilots.

Pilot results are evaluated using the quantitative criteria defined during pilot planning. Reviewing and documenting results of pilots usually involves the following activities:

- Deciding whether to terminate the pilot, replan, and continue the pilot, or proceed with deploying the process and technology improvement
- Updating the disposition of process- and technology-improvement proposals associated with the pilot
- Identifying and documenting new process- and technology-improvement proposals as appropriate
- Identifying and documenting lessons learned and problems encountered during the pilot

---

OID

SP 1.4 *SELECT IMPROVEMENTS FOR DEPLOYMENT*

Select process and technology improvements for deployment across the organization.

Selection of process and technology improvements for deployment across the organization is based on quantifiable criteria derived from the organization's quality and process-performance objectives.

Typical Work Products

1. Process and technology improvements selected for deployment

Subpractices

1. Prioritize candidate process and technology improvements for deployment.

   Priority is based on an evaluation of the estimated cost-to-benefit ratio with regard to the quality and process-performance objectives.

   Refer to the Organizational Process Performance process area for more information about establishing quality and process-performance objectives.

2. Select the process and technology improvements to be deployed.

   The selection of process improvements is based on their priorities and available resources.

3. Determine how each process and technology improvement will be deployed.

Examples of where the process and technology improvements may be deployed include the following:
- Organizational process assets
- Project-specific or common work environments
- Organization's service lines
- Organization's capabilities
- Organization's projects
- Organizational groups

---

4. Document results of the selection process.

Results of the selection process usually include the following:
- The selection criteria for candidate improvements
- The disposition of each improvement proposal
- The rationale for the disposition of each improvement proposal
- The assets to be changed for each selected improvement

SG 2   DEPLOY IMPROVEMENTS

Measurable improvements to the organization's processes and technologies are continually and systematically deployed.

SP 2.1   PLAN THE DEPLOYMENT

Establish and maintain plans for deploying selected process and technology improvements.

The plans for deploying selected process and technology improvements may be included in the organization's plan for organizational innovation and deployment, or they may be documented separately.

The implementation of this specific practice complements the Deploy Organizational Process Assets specific practice in the Organizational Process Focus process area and adds the use of quantitative data to guide the deployment and to determine the value of improvements with respect to quality and process-performance objectives.

Refer to the Organizational Process Focus process area for more information about deploying organizational process assets.

This specific practice plans the deployment of selected process and technology improvements. The Plan the Process generic practice addresses comprehensive planning that covers the specific practices in this process area.

Typical Work Products

1. Deployment plans for selected process and technology improvements

Subpractices

1. Determine how each process and technology improvement must be adjusted for organization-wide deployment.

   Process and technology improvements proposed in a limited context (e.g., for a single project) might need to be modified to work across the organization.

2. Determine the changes needed to deploy each process and technology improvement.

> Examples of changes needed to deploy a process and technology improvement include the following:
> - Process descriptions, standards, and procedures
> - Work environments
> - Education and training
> - Skills
> - Existing commitments
> - Existing activities
> - Continuing support to those performing or receiving the service
> - Organizational culture and characteristics

3. Identify strategies that address potential barriers to deploying each process and technology improvement.
4. Establish measures and objectives for determining the value of each process and technology improvement with respect to the organization's quality and process-performance objectives.

> Examples of measures for determining the value of a process and technology improvement include the following:
> - Return on investment
> - Time to recover the cost of the process or technology improvement
> - Measured improvement in the project's or organization's process performance
> - Number and types of project and organizational risks mitigated by the process or technology improvement
> - Average time required to respond to changes in project requirements, market situations, and the business environment

Refer to the Measurement and Analysis process area for more information about aligning measurement and analysis activities and providing measurement results.

5. Document the plans for deploying selected process and technology improvements.
6. Review and get agreement with relevant stakeholders on the plans for deploying selected process and technology improvements.
7. Revise the plans for deploying selected process and technology improvements as necessary.

SP 2.2 MANAGE THE DEPLOYMENT

Manage the deployment of selected process and technology improvements.

The implementation of this specific practice may overlap with the implementation of the Implement Action Proposals specific practice in the Causal Analysis and Resolution process area (e.g., when causal analysis and resolution is implemented organizationally or across multiple projects). The primary difference is that in the Causal Analysis and Resolution process area, planning is done to manage the removal of root causes of defects or problems from the project's defined process. In the Organizational Innovation and Deployment process area, planning is done to manage the deployment of improvements to the organization's processes and technologies that can be quantified against the organization's business objectives.

Typical Work Products

1. Updated training materials (to reflect deployed process and technology improvements)
2. Documented results of process- and technology-improvement deployment activities
3. Revised process- and technology-improvement measures, objectives, priorities, and deployment plans

Subpractices

1. Monitor the deployment of process and technology improvements using the deployment plans.
2. Coordinate the deployment of process and technology improvements across the organization.
   Coordinating deployment includes the following activities:
   - Coordinating activities of projects, support groups, and organizational groups for each process and technology improvement
   - Coordinating activities for deploying related process and technology improvements
3. Quickly deploy process and technology improvements in a controlled and disciplined manner as appropriate.

> Examples of methods for quickly deploying process and technology improvements include the following:
> - Using redlines, process change notices, or other controlled process documentation as interim process descriptions
> - Deploying process and technology improvements incrementally rather than as a single deployment
> - Providing comprehensive consulting to early adopters of the process and technology improvement in lieu of revised formal training

4. Incorporate process and technology improvements into organizational process assets as appropriate.

   Refer to the Organizational Process Definition process area for more information about organizational process assets.

5. Coordinate the deployment of process and technology improvements into the projects' defined processes as appropriate.

   Refer to the Organizational Process Focus process area for more information about deploying organizational process assets and incorporating experiences.

6. Provide consulting as appropriate to support deployment of process and technology improvements.

7. Provide updated training materials to reflect improvements to organizational process assets.

   Refer to the Organizational Training process area for more information about training materials.

8. Confirm that the deployment of all process and technology improvements is completed.

9. Determine whether the ability of the defined process to meet quality and process-performance objectives is adversely affected by the process and technology improvement, and take corrective action as necessary.

   Refer to the Quantitative Project Management process area for more information about quantitatively managing the project's defined process to achieve the project's established quality and process-performance objectives.

10. Document and review results of process- and technology-improvement deployment.

    Documenting and reviewing results includes the following:
    - Identifying and documenting lessons learned
    - Identifying and documenting new process- and technology-improvement proposals
    - Revising process- and technology-improvement measures, objectives, priorities, and deployment plans

SP 2.3 MEASURE IMPROVEMENT EFFECTS

Measure effects of deployed process and technology improvements.

Refer to the Measurement and Analysis process area for more information about aligning measurement and analysis activities and providing measurement results.

The implementation of this specific practice may overlap with the implementation of the Evaluate the Effect of Changes specific practice in the Causal Analysis and Resolution process area (e.g., when causal analysis and resolution is implemented organizationally or across multiple projects).

Typical Work Products

1. Documented measures of the effects resulting from deployed process and technology improvements

Subpractices

1. Measure the actual cost, effort, and schedule for deploying each process and technology improvement.
2. Measure the value of each process and technology improvement.
3. Measure progress toward achieving the organization's quality and process-performance objectives.
4. Analyze progress toward achieving the organization's quality and process-performance objectives, and take corrective action as needed.

   Refer to the Organizational Process Performance process area for more information about establishing quality and process-performance objectives, establishing process-performance baselines, and establishing process-performance models.

5. Store measures in the organization's measurement repository.

OID

ORGANIZATIONAL PROCESS DEFINITION
A Process Management Process Area at Maturity Level 3

Purpose

The purpose of Organizational Process Definition (OPD) is to establish and maintain a usable set of organizational process assets and work environment standards.

Introductory Notes

Organizational process assets enable consistent process performance across the organization and provide a basis for cumulative, long-term benefits to the organization. (See the definition of "organizational process assets" in the glossary.)

The organization's "process asset library" is a collection of items maintained by the organization for use by the organization's people and projects. This collection of items includes descriptions of processes and process elements, descriptions of lifecycle models, process tailoring guidelines, process-related documentation, and data. The organization's process asset library supports organizational learning and process improvement by allowing the sharing of best practices and lessons learned across the organization.

The organization's "set of standard processes" is tailored by projects to create their defined processes. Other organizational process assets are used to support tailoring and implementing defined processes. Work environment standards are used to guide the creation of project work environments.

A "standard process" is composed of other processes (i.e., subprocesses) or process elements. A "process element" is the fundamental (i.e., atomic) unit of process definition that describes activities and tasks to consistently perform work. The process architecture provides rules for connecting the process elements of a standard process. The organization's set of standard processes may include multiple process architectures.

OPD

(See the definitions of "standard process," "process architecture," "subprocess," and "process element" in the glossary.)

Organizational process assets may be organized in many ways, depending on the implementation of the Organizational Process Definition process area. Examples include the following:

- Descriptions of lifecycle models may be part of the organization's set of standard processes, or they may be documented separately.
- The organization's set of standard processes may be stored in the organization's process asset library, or it may be stored separately.
- A single repository may contain both measurements and process-related documentation, or they may be stored separately.

Related Process Areas

Refer to the Strategic Service Management process area for more information about establishing and maintaining standard services in concert with strategic needs and plans.

Refer to the Organizational Process Focus process area for more information about deploying organizational process assets.

Specific Goal and Practice Summary

SG 1 Establish Organizational Process Assets

SP 1.1	Establish Standard Processes
SP 1.2	Establish Lifecycle Model Descriptions
SP 1.3	Establish Tailoring Criteria and Guidelines
SP 1.4	Establish the Organization's Measurement Repository
SP 1.5	Establish the Organization's Process Asset Library
SP 1.6	Establish Work Environment Standards
SP 1.7	Establish Rules and Guidelines for Integrated Teams

Specific Practices by Goal

SG 1   ESTABLISH ORGANIZATIONAL PROCESS ASSETS

A set of organizational process assets is established and maintained.

SP 1.1   ESTABLISH STANDARD PROCESSES

Establish and maintain the organization's set of standard processes.

Standard processes may be defined at multiple levels in an enterprise and they may be related hierarchically. For example, an enterprise may have a set of standard processes that is tailored by individual organizations (e.g., a division, a site) in the enterprise to establish their set of standard processes. The set of standard processes may also be tailored for each of the organization's business areas or product lines. Thus the *organization's set of standard processes* can refer to the standard processes established at the organization level and standard processes that may be established at lower levels, although some organizations may have only one level of standard processes. (See the definitions of "standard process" and "organization's set of standard processes" in the glossary.)

Multiple standard processes may be needed to address the needs of different application domains, lifecycle models, methodologies, and tools. The organization's set of standard processes contains process elements (e.g., a work product size-estimating element) that may be interconnected according to one or more process architectures that describe relationships among process elements.

The organization's set of standard processes typically includes technical, management, administrative, support, and organizational processes.

The organization's set of standard processes should collectively cover all processes needed by the organization and projects, including those addressed by the process areas at maturity level 2.

Typical Work Products

1. Organization's set of standard processes

Subpractices

1. Decompose each standard process into constituent process elements to the detail needed to understand and describe the process.

   Each process element covers a bounded and closely related set of activities. The descriptions of process elements may be templates to be filled in, fragments to be completed, abstractions to be refined, or complete descriptions to be tailored or used unmodified. These elements are described in such detail that the process, when fully defined, can be consistently performed by appropriately trained and skilled people.

Examples of process elements include the following:
- Tailorable incident resolution process
- Template for creating service agreements
- Template for generating work product size estimates
- Description of work product design methodology
- Tailorable peer review methodology
- Template for conducting management reviews

---

2. Specify the critical attributes of each process element.

Examples of critical attributes include the following:
- Process roles
- Applicable standards
- Applicable procedures, methods, tools, and resources
- Process-performance objectives
- Entry criteria
- Inputs
- Product and process measures
- Verification points (e.g., peer reviews)
- Outputs
- Interfaces
- Exit criteria

---

3. Specify relationships among process elements.

Examples of relationships include the following:
- Order of the process elements
- Interfaces among process elements
- Interfaces with external processes
- Interdependencies among process elements

The rules for describing relationships among process elements are referred to as the "process architecture." The process architecture covers essential requirements and guidelines. Detailed specifications of these relationships are covered in descriptions of defined processes that are tailored from the organization's set of standard processes.

4. Ensure that the organization's set of standard processes adheres to applicable policies, standards, and models.

   Adherence to applicable process standards and models is typically demonstrated by developing a mapping from the organization's set of standard processes to relevant process standards and models. This mapping is a useful input to future appraisals.

5. Ensure that the organization's set of standard processes satisfies process needs and objectives of the organization.

   Refer to the Organizational Process Focus process area for more information about establishing organizational process needs.

6. Ensure that there is appropriate integration among processes that are included in the organization's set of standard processes.

7. Document the organization's set of standard processes.

8. Conduct peer reviews on the organization's set of standard processes.

Refer to the Service System Development process area for more information about performing peer reviews.

SSD ADD

9. Revise the organization's set of standard processes as necessary.

SP 1.2 ESTABLISH LIFECYCLE MODEL DESCRIPTIONS

Establish and maintain descriptions of lifecycle models approved for use in the organization.

Lifecycle models may be developed for a variety of customers or in a variety of situations, since one lifecycle model may not be appropriate for all situations. Lifecycle models are often used to define phases of the project. Also, the organization may define different lifecycle models for each type of product and service it delivers.

Typical Work Products

1. Descriptions of lifecycle models

Subpractices

1. Select lifecycle models based on the needs of projects and the organization.

   The selection of a service lifecycle model depends on the characteristics of the services and the environment. Some service providers define lifecycle phases based on their standard service definitions.

OPD

Examples of sets of phases that may comprise a service lifecycle include the following:
- Plan, define, enable, and measure
- Scope definition, planning, execution, and termination
- Strategy, design, transition, operation, and improvement

Often, individual service domains have implicit lifecycles associated with them that involve points of communication, evaluation, and decision. Descriptions of these points may be included in the set of descriptions of lifecycle models approved for use in the organization.

Examples of project lifecycle models used for developing a service system include the following:
- Waterfall
- Spiral
- Evolutionary
- Incremental
- Iterative

---

2. Document descriptions of lifecycle models.

   Lifecycle models may be documented as part of the organization's standard process descriptions, or they may be documented separately.

3. Conduct peer reviews on lifecycle models.

> *Refer to the Service System Development process area for more information about performing peer reviews.*

4. Revise the descriptions of lifecycle models as necessary.

SP 1.3 ESTABLISH TAILORING CRITERIA AND GUIDELINES

Establish and maintain tailoring criteria and guidelines for the organization's set of standard processes.

Tailoring criteria and guidelines describe the following:

- How the organization's set of standard processes and organizational process assets are used to create defined processes
- Requirements that must be satisfied by defined processes (e.g., the subset of organizational process assets that are essential for any defined process)

- Options that can be exercised and criteria for selecting among options
- Procedures that must be followed in performing and documenting process tailoring

---

Examples of reasons for tailoring include the following:
- Adapting the process to a new service or type of customer
- Customizing the process for an application or class of similar applications
- Elaborating the process description so that the resulting defined process can be performed

---

Flexibility in tailoring and defining processes is balanced with ensuring appropriate consistency of processes across the organization. Flexibility is needed to address contextual variables, such as the domain; the nature of the customer; cost, schedule, and quality tradeoffs; the technical difficulty of the work; and the experience of the people implementing the process. Consistency across the organization is needed so that organizational standards, objectives, and strategies are appropriately addressed, and process data and lessons learned can be shared.

Tailoring criteria and guidelines may allow for using a standard process "as is," with no tailoring.

Typical Work Products

1. Tailoring guidelines for the organization's set of standard processes

Subpractices

1. Specify selection criteria and procedures for tailoring the organization's set of standard processes.

Examples of criteria and procedures include the following:
- Criteria for selecting lifecycle models from those approved by the organization
- Criteria for selecting process elements from the organization's set of standard processes
- Procedures for tailoring selected lifecycle models and process elements to accommodate process characteristics and needs

---

OPD

Examples of tailoring include the following:
- Modifying a lifecycle model
- Combining elements of different lifecycle models
- Modifying process elements
- Replacing process elements
- Reordering process elements

---

2. Specify the standards used for documenting defined processes.
3. Specify the procedures used for submitting and obtaining approval of waivers from the organization's set of standard processes.
4. Document tailoring guidelines for the organization's set of standard processes.
5. Conduct peer reviews on the tailoring guidelines.

> *Refer to the Service System Development process area for more information about performing peer reviews.*

SSD ADD

6. Revise tailoring guidelines as necessary.

SP 1.4 ESTABLISH THE ORGANIZATION'S MEASUREMENT REPOSITORY

Establish and maintain the organization's measurement repository.

Refer to the Use Organizational Process Assets for Planning Project Activities specific practice in the Integrated Project Management process area for more information about the use of the organization's measurement repository in planning project activities.

The repository contains both product and process measures related to the organization's set of standard processes. It also contains or refers to information needed to understand and interpret measures and to assess them for reasonableness and applicability. For example, the definitions of measures are used to compare similar measures from different processes.

Typical Work Products

1. Definition of the common set of product and process measures for the organization's set of standard processes
2. Design of the organization's measurement repository
3. Organization's measurement repository (i.e., the repository structure and support environment)
4. Organization's measurement data

Subpractices

1. Determine the organization's needs for storing, retrieving, and analyzing measurements.

2. Define a common set of process and product measures for the organization's set of standard processes.

   Measures in the common set are selected based on the organization's set of standard processes. They are selected for their ability to provide visibility into process performance and to support expected business objectives. The common set of measures may vary for different standard processes.

   Operational definitions for measures specify procedures for collecting valid data and the point in the process where data will be collected.

Examples of classes of commonly used measures include the following:
- Estimates of work product size (e.g., pages)
- Estimates of effort and cost (e.g., person hours)
- Actual measures of size, effort, and cost
- Quality measures (e.g., number of incidents reported)
- Peer review coverage
- Test coverage
- Reliability measures (e.g., mean time to failure)

---

3. Design and implement the measurement repository.

4. Specify procedures for storing, updating, and retrieving measures.

   Refer to the Measurement and Analysis process area for more information about specifying data collection and storage procedures.

5. Conduct peer reviews on definitions of the common set of measures and procedures for storing, updating, and retrieving measures.

   Refer to the Service System Development process area for more information about performing peer reviews.

6. Enter specified measures into the repository.

   Refer to the Measurement and Analysis process area for more information about specifying measures.

7. Make the contents of the measurement repository available for use by the organization and projects as appropriate.

8. Revise the measurement repository, the common set of measures, and procedures as the organization's needs change.

OPD

SSD ADD

Examples of when the common set of measures may need to be revised include the following:
- New processes are added.
- Processes are revised and new measures are needed.
- Finer granularity of data is required.
- Greater visibility into the process is required.
- Measures are retired.

SP 1.5 ESTABLISH THE ORGANIZATION'S PROCESS ASSET LIBRARY

Establish and maintain the organization's process asset library.

Examples of items to be stored in the organization's process asset library include the following:
- Organizational policies
- Process descriptions
- Procedures (e.g., estimating procedure)
- Development plans
- Acquisition plans
- Quality assurance plans
- Training materials
- Process aids (e.g., checklists)
- Lessons-learned reports

Typical Work Products

1. Design of the organization's process asset library
2. The organization's process asset library
3. Selected items to be included in the organization's process asset library
4. The catalog of items in the organization's process asset library

Subpractices

1. Design and implement the organization's process asset library, including the library structure and support environment.
2. Specify criteria for including items in the library.
   Items are selected based primarily on their relationship to the organization's set of standard processes.

3. Specify procedures for storing, updating, and retrieving items.

4. Enter selected items into the library and catalog them for easy reference and retrieval.

5. Make items available for use by projects.

6. Periodically review the use of each item.

7. Revise the organization's process asset library as necessary.

Examples of when the library may need to be revised include the following:
- New items are added.
- Items are retired.
- Current versions of items are changed.

SP 1.6 ESTABLISH WORK ENVIRONMENT STANDARDS

Establish and maintain work environment standards.

Work environment standards allow the organization and projects to benefit from common tools, training, and maintenance as well as cost savings from volume purchases. Work environment standards address the needs of all stakeholders and consider productivity, cost, availability, security, and workplace health, safety, and ergonomic factors. Work environment standards can include guidelines for tailoring and the use of waivers that allow adaptation of the project's work environment to meet needs.

Examples of work environment standards include the following:
- Procedures for the operation, safety, and security of the work environment
- Standard workstation hardware and software
- Standard application software and tailoring guidelines for it
- Standard production and calibration equipment
- Process for requesting and approving tailoring or waivers
- Procedures for the operation, safety, and security of the customer work environment in which the service provider must work

---

Typical Work Products

1. Work environment standards

OPD

Subpractices

1. Evaluate commercially available work environment standards appropriate for the organization.
2. Adopt existing work environment standards and develop new ones to fill gaps based on the organization's process needs and objectives.

SP 1.7 *ESTABLISH RULES AND GUIDELINES FOR INTEGRATED TEAMS*

Establish and maintain organizational rules and guidelines for the structure, formation, and operation of integrated teams.

When establishing rules and guidelines for integrated teams, ensure that they comply with all local and national regulations or laws that may affect the use of integrated teaming.

Operating rules and guidelines for integrated teams define and control how teams are created and how they interact to accomplish objectives. Integrated team members must understand the standards for work and participate according to those standards.

Structuring integrated teams involves defining the number of teams, the type of each team, and how each team relates to the others in the structure. Forming integrated teams involves chartering each team, assigning team members and team leaders, and providing resources to each team to accomplish work.

Typical Work Products

1. Rules and guidelines for structuring and forming integrated teams

Subpractices

1. Establish and maintain empowerment mechanisms to enable timely decision making.

    In a successful teaming environment, clear channels of responsibility and authority must be established. Issues can arise at any level of the organization when integrated teams assume too much or too little authority and when it is unclear who is responsible for making decisions. Documenting and deploying organizational guidelines that clearly define the empowerment of integrated teams can prevent these issues.

2. Establish rules and guidelines for structuring and forming integrated teams.

> Organizational process assets can help the project to structure and implement integrated teams. Such assets may include the following:
> - Team structure guidelines
> - Team formation guidelines
> - Team authority and responsibility guidelines
> - Guidelines for establishing lines of communication, authority, and escalation
> - Team leader selection criteria

3. Define the expectations, rules, and guidelines that guide how integrated teams work collectively.

> These rules and guidelines establish organizational practices for consistency across integrated teams and can include the following:
> - How interfaces among integrated teams are established and maintained
> - How assignments are accepted and transferred
> - How resources and inputs are accessed
> - How work gets done
> - Who checks, reviews, and approves work
> - How work is approved
> - How work is delivered and communicated
> - Who reports to whom
> - What the reporting requirements (e.g., cost, schedule, performance status), measures, and methods are
> - Which progress reporting measures and methods are used

4. Maintain the rules and guidelines for structuring and forming integrated teams.
5. Establish and maintain organizational guidelines to help team members balance their team and home organization responsibilities.

    A "home organization" is the part of the organization to which team members are assigned when they are not on an integrated team. A "home organization" may be called a "functional organization," "home base," "home office," or "direct organization."

OPD

ORGANIZATIONAL PROCESS FOCUS
A Process Management Process Area at Maturity Level 3

Purpose

The purpose of Organizational Process Focus (OPF) is to plan, implement, and deploy organizational process improvements based on a thorough understanding of current strengths and weaknesses of the organization's processes and process assets.

IN OTHER WORDS

OPF is about figuring out your current process strengths and weaknesses, planning what to do to improve, and putting those improvements in place.

Introductory Notes

The organization's processes include all processes used by the organization and its projects. Candidate improvements to the organization's processes and process assets are obtained from various sources, including the measurement of processes, lessons learned in implementing processes, results of process appraisals, results of product and service evaluation activities, results of customer satisfaction evaluation, results of benchmarking against other organizations' processes, and recommendations from other improvement initiatives in the organization.

WHY DO THE PRACTICES IN OPF?

You get a baseline of your current process, keep a focus on the process improvements that align with your business goals, and continue to improve.

Process improvement occurs in the context of the organization's needs and is used to address the organization's objectives. The organization encourages participation in process improvement activities by those who perform the process. The responsibility for facilitating and managing the organization's process improvement activities, including coordinating the participation of others, is typically assigned to a process group. The organization provides the long-term commitment and resources required to sponsor this group and to ensure the effective and timely deployment of improvements.

Careful planning is required to ensure that process improvement efforts across the organization are adequately managed and implemented. Results of the organization's process improvement planning are documented in a process improvement plan.

OPF

The "organization's process improvement plan" addresses appraisal planning, process action planning, pilot planning, and deployment planning. Appraisal plans describe the appraisal timeline and schedule, the scope of the appraisal, resources required to perform the appraisal, the reference model against which the appraisal will be performed, and logistics for the appraisal.

Process action plans usually result from appraisals and document how improvements targeting weaknesses uncovered by an appraisal will be implemented. Sometimes the improvement described in the process action plan should be tested on a small group before deploying it across the organization. In these cases, a pilot plan is generated.

When the improvement is to be deployed, a deployment plan is created. This plan describes when and how the improvement will be deployed across the organization.

Organizational process assets are used to describe, implement, and improve the organization's processes. (See the definition of "organizational process assets" in the glossary.)

Related Process Areas

Refer to the Organizational Process Definition process area for more information about establishing organizational process assets.

Specific Goal and Practice Summary

SG 1 Determine Process Improvement Opportunities
      SP 1.1   Establish Organizational Process Needs
      SP 1.2   Appraise the Organization's Processes
      SP 1.3   Identify the Organization's Process Improvements
SG 2 Plan and Implement Process Actions
      SP 2.1   Establish Process Action Plans
      SP 2.2   Implement Process Action Plans
SG 3 Deploy Organizational Process Assets and Incorporate Experiences
      SP 3.1   Deploy Organizational Process Assets
      SP 3.2   Deploy Standard Processes
      SP 3.3   Monitor the Implementation
      SP 3.4   Incorporate Experiences into Organizational Process Assets

Specific Practices by Goal

SG 1   DETERMINE PROCESS IMPROVEMENT OPPORTUNITIES

Strengths, weaknesses, and improvement opportunities for the organization's processes are identified periodically and as needed.

Strengths, weaknesses, and improvement opportunities may be determined relative to a process standard or model such as a CMMI model or ISO standard. Process improvements should be selected to address the organization's needs.

SP 1.1   ESTABLISH ORGANIZATIONAL PROCESS NEEDS

Establish and maintain the description of process needs and objectives for the organization.

The organization's processes operate in a business context that must be understood. The organization's business objectives, needs, and constraints determine the needs and objectives for the organization's processes. Typically, issues related to customer satisfaction, finance, technology, quality, human resources, and marketing are important process considerations.

The organization's process needs and objectives cover aspects that include the following:
- Characteristics of processes
- Process-performance objectives, such as time-to-market and delivered quality
- Process effectiveness

Typical Work Products

1. The organization's process needs and objectives

Subpractices

1. Identify policies, standards, and business objectives that are applicable to the organization's processes.
2. Examine relevant process standards and models for best practices.
3. Determine the organization's process-performance objectives.
   Process-performance objectives may be expressed in quantitative or qualitative terms.

Refer to the Measurement and Analysis process area for more information about establishing measurement objectives.

Examples of what process-performance objectives may be written to address include the following:
- Customer satisfaction ratings
- Cycle time
- Incident rates
- Productivity

---

4. Define essential characteristics of the organization's processes.

   Essential characteristics of the organization's processes are determined based on the following:
   - Processes currently being used in the organization
   - Standards imposed by the organization
   - Standards commonly imposed by customers of the organization

---

Examples of process characteristics include the following:
- Level of detail
- Process notation
- Granularity

---

5. Document the organization's process needs and objectives.
6. Revise the organization's process needs and objectives as needed.

SP 1.2 APPRAISE THE ORGANIZATION'S PROCESSES

Appraise the organization's processes periodically and as needed to maintain an understanding of their strengths and weaknesses.

Process appraisals may be performed for the following reasons:
- To identify processes to be improved
- To confirm progress and make the benefits of process improvement visible
- To satisfy the needs of a customer-supplier relationship
- To motivate and facilitate buy-in

The buy-in gained during a process appraisal can be eroded significantly if it is not followed by an appraisal-based action plan.

Typical Work Products

1. Plans for the organization's process appraisals
2. Appraisal findings that address strengths and weaknesses of the organization's processes
3. Improvement recommendations for the organization's processes

Subpractices

1. Obtain sponsorship of the process appraisal from senior management.

   Senior management sponsorship includes the commitment to have the organization's managers and staff participate in the process appraisal and to provide resources and funding to analyze and communicate findings of the appraisal.

2. Define the scope of the process appraisal.

   Process appraisals may be performed on the entire organization or may be performed on a smaller part of an organization, such as a single project or business area.

   The scope of the process appraisal addresses the following:
   - Definition of the organization (e.g., sites, business areas) to be covered by the appraisal
   - Identification of the project and support functions that will represent the organization in the appraisal
   - Processes to be appraised

3. Determine the method and criteria to be used for the process appraisal.

   Process appraisals can occur in many forms. They should address the needs and objectives of the organization, which may change over time. For example, the appraisal may be based on a process model, such as a CMMI model, or on a national or international standard, such as ISO 9001 [ISO 2000]. Appraisals may also be based on a benchmark comparison with other organizations in which practices that may contribute to improved performance are identified. The characteristics of the appraisal method may vary, including time and effort, makeup of the appraisal team, and the method and depth of investigation.

4. Plan, schedule, and prepare for the process appraisal.
5. Conduct the process appraisal.
6. Document and deliver the appraisal's activities and findings.

OPF

SP 1.3 *IDENTIFY THE ORGANIZATION'S PROCESS IMPROVEMENTS*

Identify improvements to the organization's processes and process assets.

Typical Work Products

1. Analysis of candidate process improvements
2. Identification of improvements for the organization's processes

Subpractices

1. Determine candidate process improvements.

Candidate process improvements are typically determined by doing the following:

- Measuring processes and analyzing measurement results
- Reviewing processes for effectiveness and suitability
- Assessing customer satisfaction
- Reviewing lessons learned from tailoring the organization's set of standard processes
- Reviewing lessons learned from implementing processes
- Reviewing process improvement proposals submitted by the organization's managers, staff, and other relevant stakeholders
- Soliciting inputs on process improvements from senior management and other leaders in the organization
- Examining results of process appraisals and other process-related reviews
- Reviewing results of other organizational improvement initiatives

---

2. Prioritize candidate process improvements.
    Criteria for prioritization are as follows:
    - Consider the estimated cost and effort to implement the process improvements.
    - Evaluate the expected improvement against the organization's improvement objectives and priorities.
    - Determine the potential barriers to the process improvements and develop strategies for overcoming these barriers.

Examples of techniques to help determine and prioritize possible improvements to be implemented include the following:
- A cost-benefit analysis that compares the estimated cost and effort to implement the process improvements and their associated benefits
- A gap analysis that compares current conditions in the organization with optimal conditions
- Force-field analysis of potential improvements to identify potential barriers and strategies for overcoming those barriers
- Cause-and-effect analyses to provide information on the potential effects of different improvements that can then be compared

3. Identify and document the process improvements to be implemented.
4. Revise the list of planned process improvements to keep it current.

SG 2   PLAN AND IMPLEMENT PROCESS ACTIONS

Process actions that address improvements to the organization's processes and process assets are planned and implemented.

The successful implementation of improvements requires participation in process action planning and implementation by process owners, those performing the process, and support organizations.

SP 2.1   ESTABLISH PROCESS ACTION PLANS

Establish and maintain process action plans to address improvements to the organization's processes and process assets.

Establishing and maintaining process action plans typically involves the following roles:
- Management steering committees that set strategies and oversee process improvement activities
- Process groups that facilitate and manage process improvement activities
- Process action teams that define and implement process actions
- Process owners who manage deployment
- Practitioners who perform the process

This stakeholder involvement helps to obtain buy-in on process improvements and increases the likelihood of effective deployment.

Process action plans are detailed implementation plans. These plans differ from the organization's process improvement plan by targeting improvements that were defined to address weaknesses and that were usually uncovered by appraisals.

Typical Work Products

1. The organization's approved process action plans

Subpractices

1. Identify strategies, approaches, and actions to address identified process improvements.
   New, unproven, and major changes are piloted before they are incorporated into normal use.
2. Establish process action teams to implement actions.
   The teams and people performing the process improvement actions are called "process action teams." Process action teams typically include process owners and those who perform the process.
3. Document process action plans.

Process action plans typically cover the following:
- The process improvement infrastructure
- Process improvement objectives
- Process improvements to be addressed
- Procedures for planning and tracking process actions
- Strategies for piloting and implementing process actions
- Responsibility and authority for implementing process actions
- Resources, schedules, and assignments for implementing process actions
- Methods for determining the effectiveness of process actions
- Risks associated with process action plans

---

4. Review and negotiate process action plans with relevant stakeholders.
5. Review process action plans as necessary.

SP 2.2 IMPLEMENT PROCESS ACTION PLANS

Implement process action plans.

Typical Work Products

1. Commitments among process action teams
2. Status and results of implementing process action plans

3. Plans for pilots

Subpractices

1. Make process action plans readily available to relevant stakeholders.
2. Negotiate and document commitments among process action teams and revise their process action plans as necessary.
3. Track progress and commitments against process action plans.
4. Conduct joint reviews with process action teams and relevant stakeholders to monitor the progress and results of process actions.
5. Plan pilots needed to test selected process improvements.
6. Review the activities and work products of process action teams.
7. Identify, document, and track to closure issues encountered when implementing process action plans.
8. Ensure that results of implementing process action plans satisfy the organization's process improvement objectives.

SG 3   DEPLOY ORGANIZATIONAL PROCESS ASSETS AND INCORPORATE EXPERIENCES

Organizational process assets are deployed across the organization, and process-related experiences are incorporated into organizational process assets.

The specific practices under this specific goal describe ongoing activities. New opportunities to benefit from organizational process assets and changes to them may arise throughout the life of each project. Deployment of standard processes and other organizational process assets must be continually supported in the organization, particularly for new projects at startup.

SP 3.1   DEPLOY ORGANIZATIONAL PROCESS ASSETS

Deploy organizational process assets across the organization.

Deploying organizational process assets or changes to them should be performed in an orderly manner. Some organizational process assets or changes to them may not be appropriate for use in some parts of the organization (e.g., because of stakeholder requirements or the current lifecycle phase being implemented). It is therefore important that those who are or will be executing the process, as well as other organization functions (e.g., training, quality assurance), be involved in deployment as necessary.

Refer to the Organizational Process Definition process area for more information about the deployment of organizational process assets, including the support of the organization's process asset library.

OPF

Typical Work Products

1. Plans for deploying organizational process assets and changes to them across the organization
2. Training materials for deploying organizational process assets and changes to them
3. Documentation of changes to organizational process assets
4. Support materials for deploying organizational process assets and changes to them

Subpractices

1. Deploy organizational process assets across the organization.

Typical activities performed as a part of the deployment of process assets include the following:
- Identifying organizational process assets that should be adopted by those who perform the process
- Determining how organizational process assets are made available (e.g., via a website)
- Identifying how changes to organizational process assets are communicated
- Identifying resources (e.g., methods, tools) needed to support the use of organizational process assets
- Planning the deployment
- Assisting those who use organizational process assets
- Ensuring that training is available for those who use organizational process assets

---

> *Refer to the Organizational Training process area for more information about establishing an organizational training capability.*

2. Document changes to organizational process assets.
   Documenting changes to organizational process assets serves two main purposes:
   - To enable the communication of changes
   - To understand the relationship of changes in the organizational process assets to changes in process performance and results
3. Deploy changes that were made to organizational process assets across the organization.

Typical activities performed as a part of deploying changes include the following:
- Determining which changes are appropriate for those who perform the process
- Planning the deployment
- Arranging for the support needed for the successful transition of changes

4. Provide guidance and consultation on the use of organizational process assets.

SP 3.2 DEPLOY STANDARD PROCESSES

Deploy the organization's set of standard processes to projects at their startup and deploy changes to them as appropriate throughout the life of each project.

It is important that new projects use proven and effective processes to perform critical early activities (e.g., project planning, receiving requirements, obtaining resources).

Projects should also periodically update their defined processes to incorporate the latest changes made to the organization's set of standard processes when it will benefit them. This periodic update helps to ensure that all project activities derive the full benefit of what other projects have learned.

Refer to the Organizational Process Definition process area for more information about standard processes and tailoring guidelines.

Typical Work Products

1. The organization's list of projects and the status of process deployment on each (i.e., existing and planned projects)
2. Guidelines for deploying the organization's set of standard processes on new projects
3. Records of tailoring and implementing the organization's set of standard processes

Subpractices

1. Identify projects in the organization that are starting up.
2. Identify active projects that would benefit from implementing the organization's current set of standard processes.
3. Establish plans to implement the organization's current set of standard processes on the identified projects.

OPF

4. Assist projects in tailoring the organization's set of standard processes to meet their needs.

   Refer to the Integrated Project Management process area for more information about establishing the project's defined process.

5. Maintain records of tailoring and implementing processes on the identified projects.

6. Ensure that the defined processes resulting from process tailoring are incorporated into plans for process-compliance audits.

   Process-compliance audits are objective evaluations of project activities against the project's defined process.

7. As the organization's set of standard processes is updated, identify which projects should implement the changes.

SP 3.3 MONITOR THE IMPLEMENTATION

Monitor the implementation of the organization's set of standard processes and use of process assets on all projects.

By monitoring implementation, the organization ensures that the organization's set of standard processes and other process assets are appropriately deployed to all projects. Monitoring implementation also helps the organization to develop an understanding of the organizational process assets being used and where they are used in the organization. Monitoring also helps to establish a broader context for interpreting and using process and product measures, lessons learned, and improvement information obtained from projects.

Typical Work Products

1. Results of monitoring process implementation on projects
2. Status and results of process-compliance audits
3. Results of reviewing selected process artifacts created as part of process tailoring and implementation

Subpractices

1. Monitor projects' use of the organization's process assets and changes to them.

2. Review selected process artifacts created during the life of each project.

   Reviewing selected process artifacts created during the life of a project ensures that all projects are making appropriate use of the organization's set of standard processes.

3. Review results of process-compliance audits to determine how well the organization's set of standard processes has been deployed.

Refer to the Process and Product Quality Assurance process area for more information about objectively evaluating processes.

4. Identify, document, and track to closure issues related to implementing the organization's set of standard processes.

SP 3.4 INCORPORATE EXPERIENCES INTO ORGANIZATIONAL PROCESS ASSETS

Incorporate process-related work products, measures, and improvement information derived from planning and performing the process into organizational process assets.

Typical Work Products

1. Process improvement proposals
2. Process lessons learned
3. Measurements of organizational process assets
4. Improvement recommendations for organizational process assets
5. Records of the organization's process improvement activities
6. Information on organizational process assets and improvements to them

Subpractices

1. Conduct periodic reviews of the effectiveness and suitability of the organization's set of standard processes and related organizational process assets relative to the organization's business objectives.
2. Obtain feedback about the use of organizational process assets.
3. Derive lessons learned from defining, piloting, implementing, and deploying organizational process assets.
4. Make lessons learned available to people in the organization as appropriate.
   Actions may be necessary to ensure that lessons learned are used appropriately.

OPF

Examples of the inappropriate use of lessons learned include the following:
- Evaluating the performance of people
- Judging process performance or results

Examples of ways to prevent the inappropriate use of lessons learned include the following:
- Controlling access to lessons learned
- Educating people about the appropriate use of lessons learned

5. Analyze measurement data obtained from the use of the organization's common set of measures.

   Refer to the Measurement and Analysis process area for more information about analyzing measurement data.

   Refer to the Organizational Process Definition process area for more information about establishing the organization's measurement repository.

6. Appraise processes, methods, and tools in use in the organization, and develop recommendations for improving organizational process assets.

This appraisal typically includes the following:
- Determining which processes, methods, and tools are of potential use to other parts of the organization
- Appraising the quality and effectiveness of organizational process assets
- Identifying candidate improvements to organizational process assets
- Determining compliance with the organization's set of standard processes and tailoring guidelines

---

7. Make the best of the organization's processes, methods, and tools available to people in the organization as appropriate.

8. Manage process improvement proposals.

   Process improvement proposals can address both process and technology improvements.

The activities for managing process improvement proposals typically include the following:
- Soliciting process improvement proposals
- Collecting process improvement proposals
- Reviewing process improvement proposals
- Selecting the process improvement proposals to be implemented
- Tracking the implementation of process improvement proposals

---

Process improvement proposals are documented as process change requests or problem reports as appropriate.

Some process improvement proposals may be incorporated into the organization's process action plans.

9. Establish and maintain records of the organization's process improvement activities.

ORGANIZATIONAL PROCESS PERFORMANCE
A Process Management Process Area at Maturity Level 4

Purpose

The purpose of Organizational Process Performance (OPP) is to establish and maintain a quantitative understanding of the performance of the organization's set of standard processes in support of achieving quality and process-performance objectives, and to provide process-performance data, baselines, and models to quantitatively manage the organization's projects.

IN OTHER WORDS

OPP is about making sure you understand your process performance and how it affects service quality.

Introductory Notes

Process performance is a measure of actual results achieved by following a process. Process performance is characterized by process measures (e.g., effort, cycle time, defect removal effectiveness) and product measures (e.g., reliability, defect density, capacity, response time, cost).

WHY DO THE PRACTICES IN OPP?

Not only do you know what to expect from your processes, but you also have quantitative objectives for your standard processes. You are able to predict your performance and can use the data you have to quantitatively manage your services. The insight you have into your process performance allows you to adjust to changing conditions.

The common measures for the organization consist of process and product measures that can be used to characterize the actual performance of processes in the organization's individual projects. By analyzing the resulting measurements, a distribution or range of results can be established that characterize the expected performance of the process when used on any individual project.

In this process area, the phrase "quality and process-performance objectives" covers objectives and requirements for product quality, service quality, and process performance. As indicated above, the term "process performance" includes quality; however, to emphasize the importance of quality, the phrase "quality and process-performance objectives" is used rather than just "process-performance objectives."

The expected process performance can be used in establishing the project's quality and process-performance objectives and can be used as a baseline against which actual project performance can be compared. This information is used to quantitatively manage the project.

Each quantitatively managed project, in turn, provides actual performance results that become a part of baseline data for organizational process assets.

Process-performance models are used to represent past and current process performance and to predict future results of the process. For example, the latent defects in the delivered product can be predicted using measurements of defects identified during product verification activities.

When the organization has measures, data, and analytical techniques for critical process, product, and service characteristics, it is able to do the following:

- Determine whether processes are behaving consistently or have stable trends (i.e., are predictable)
- Identify processes in which performance is within natural bounds that are consistent across process implementation teams
- Establish criteria for identifying whether a process or subprocess should be statistically managed, and determine pertinent measures and analytical techniques to be used in such management
- Identify processes that show unusual (e.g., sporadic, unpredictable) behavior
- Identify aspects of processes that can be improved in the organization's set of standard processes
- Identify the implementation of a process that performs best

Related Process Areas

Refer to the Capacity and Availability Management process area for more information about selecting the measures and analytic techniques to be used in managing the capacity and availability of the service system.

Refer to the Strategic Service Management process area for more information about gathering and analyzing data about the capabilities of the organization and the needs of its customers.

Refer to the Measurement and Analysis process area for more information about specifying measures, obtaining measurement data, and analyzing measurement data.

Refer to the Quantitative Project Management process area for more information about quantitatively managing the project, using process-performance models, and establishing trial natural bounds for subprocesses.

Organizational Process Performance **377**

Specific Goal and Practice Summary

SG 1 Establish Performance Baselines and Models
    SP 1.1   Select Processes
    SP 1.2   Establish Process-Performance Measures
    SP 1.3   Establish Quality and Process-Performance Objectives
    SP 1.4   Establish Process-Performance Baselines
    SP 1.5   Establish Process-Performance Models

Specific Practices by Goal

SG 1   ESTABLISH PERFORMANCE BASELINES AND MODELS

Baselines and models, which characterize the expected process performance of the organization's set of standard processes, are established and maintained.

Prior to establishing process-performance baselines and models, it is necessary to determine which processes are suitable to be measured (the Select Processes specific practice), which measures are useful for determining process performance (the Establish Process-Performance Measures specific practice), and the quality and process-performance objectives for those processes (the Establish Quality and Process-Performance Objectives specific practice).

These specific practices are often interrelated and may need to be performed concurrently to select appropriate processes, measures, and quality and process-performance objectives. Often, the selection of one process, measure, or objective will constrain the selection of the others. For example, if a certain process is selected, the measures and objectives for that process may be constrained by the process itself.

SP 1.1 SELECT PROCESSES

Select processes or subprocesses in the organization's set of standard processes to be included in the organization's process-performance analyses.

Refer to the Organizational Process Definition process area for more information about establishing organizational process assets.

The organization's set of standard processes consists of a set of standard processes that, in turn, are composed of subprocesses.

Typically, it will not be possible, useful, or economically justifiable to apply statistical management techniques to all processes or subprocesses of the organization's set of standard processes. Selection of processes or subprocesses is based on the needs and objectives of both the organization and its projects.

Examples of criteria that may be used for the selection of a process or sub-process for the organization's process-performance analysis include the following:
- The relationship of the subprocess to key business objectives
- Current availability of valid historical data relevant to the subprocess
- Current degree of data variability
- Subprocess stability (e.g., stable performance in comparable instances)
- The availability of corporate or commercial information that can be used to build predictive models

---

The existence of project data that indicate that the process or subprocess has been or can be stabilized is a useful criterion that can be used for selecting a process or subprocess.

Typical Work Products

1. List of processes or subprocesses identified for process-performance analyses

SP 1.2 ESTABLISH PROCESS-PERFORMANCE MEASURES

Establish and maintain definitions of measures to be included in the organization's process-performance analyses.

Refer to the Measurement and Analysis process area for more information about specifying measures.

Typical Work Products

1. Definitions of selected measures of process performance

Subpractices

1. Determine which of the organization's business objectives for quality and process performance should be addressed by the measures.
2. Select measures that provide appropriate insight into the organization's quality and process performance.
   The Goal Question Metric paradigm is an approach that can be used to select measures that provide insight into the organization's business objectives.

Examples of criteria used to select measures include the following:
- Relationship of measures to the organization's business objectives
- Coverage that measures provide over the life of the product or service
- Visibility that measures provide into process performance
- Availability of measures
- Extent to which measures are objective
- Frequency at which observations of the measure can be collected
- Extent to which measures are controllable by changes to the process or subprocess
- Extent to which measures represent the users' view of effective process performance

---

3. Incorporate selected measures into the organization's set of common measures.

   Refer to the Organizational Process Definition process area for more information about establishing organizational process assets.

4. Revise the set of measures as necessary.

SP 1.3 ESTABLISH QUALITY AND PROCESS-PERFORMANCE OBJECTIVES

Establish and maintain the organization's quantitative objectives for quality and process performance.

The organization's quality and process-performance objectives should have the following attributes:
- Based on the organization's business objectives
- Based on the past performance of projects
- Gauge process performance in areas such as product quality, productivity, cycle time, or response time
- Account for the inherent variability or natural bounds of the selected process or subprocess

Typical Work Products

1. Organization's quality and process-performance objectives

Subpractices

1. Review the organization's business objectives related to quality and process performance.

Examples of business objectives include the following:
- Achieve a development cycle of a specified duration for a specified release of a product.
- Achieve an average response time less than a specified duration for a specified version of a service.
- Deliver the functionality of the product for a target percentage of estimated cost.
- Decrease the cost of maintenance by a specified percent.
- Increase the availability of a service system component by a specified percent.

2. Define the organization's quantitative objectives for quality and process performance.

Objectives may be established for process or subprocess measurements (e.g., effort, cycle time, defect removal effectiveness) as well as for product measurements (e.g., reliability, defect density) and service measurements (e.g., capacity, response times) as appropriate.

Examples of quality and process-performance objectives include the following:
- Achieve a specified productivity.
- Deliver work products with no more than a specified number of latent defects.
- Shorten time to delivery to a specified percentage of the process-performance baseline.
- Reduce the total lifecycle cost of new and existing products by a percentage.
- Deliver a percentage of the specified product functionality.
- Achieve a specified availability of a service system component.
- Reduce response time by a specified percent.
- Improve service level agreement performance by a specified percent.

3. Define the priorities of the organization's objectives for quality and process performance.
4. Review, negotiate, and obtain commitment to the organization's quality and process-performance objectives and their priorities from relevant stakeholders.
5. Revise the organization's quantitative objectives for quality and process performance as necessary.

> Examples of when the organization's quantitative objectives for quality and process performance may need to be revised include the following:
> - When the organization's business objectives change
> - When the organization's processes change
> - When actual quality and process performance differ significantly from the objectives

SP 1.4 *ESTABLISH PROCESS-PERFORMANCE BASELINES*

Establish and maintain the organization's process-performance baselines.

The organization's process-performance baselines are a measurement of performance for the organization's set of standard processes at various levels of detail as appropriate. The processes include the following:

- Sequence of connected processes
- Processes that cover the entire life of the project
- Processes for developing individual work products

There may be several process-performance baselines to characterize performance for subgroups of the organization.

> Examples of criteria used to categorize subgroups include the following:
> - Product line
> - Line of business
> - Application domain
> - Complexity
> - Team size
> - Work product size
> - Process elements from the organization's set of standard processes

Tailoring of the organization's set of standard processes may significantly affect the comparability of data for inclusion in process-performance baselines. Effects of tailoring should be considered in establishing baselines. Depending on the tailoring allowed, separate performance baselines may exist for each type of tailoring.

Refer to the Quantitative Project Management process area for more information about quantitatively managing the project, using process-performance models, and establishing trial natural bounds for subprocesses.

OPP

Typical Work Products

1. Baseline data on the organization's process performance

Subpractices

1. Collect measurements from the organization's projects.

   The process or subprocess in use when the measurement was taken is recorded to enable appropriate use later.

   Refer to the Measurement and Analysis process area for more information about specifying how measurement data is obtained and stored.

2. Establish and maintain the organization's process-performance baselines from collected measurements and analyses.

   Refer to the Measurement and Analysis process area for more information about aligning measurement and analysis activities and providing measurement results.

   Process-performance baselines are derived by analyzing collected measures to establish a distribution or range of results that characterize the expected performance for selected processes or subprocesses when used on a project in the organization.
   The measurements from stable subprocesses in projects should be used when possible; other data may not be reliable.

3. Review and get agreement with relevant stakeholders about the organization's process-performance baselines.

4. Make the organization's process-performance information available across the organization in the organization's measurement repository.

   The organization's process-performance baselines are used by projects to estimate the natural bounds for process performance.

   Refer to the Organizational Process Definition process area for more information about establishing the organization's measurement repository.

5. Compare the organization's process-performance baselines to associated objectives.

6. Revise the organization's process-performance baselines as necessary.

Examples of when the organization's process-performance baselines may need to be revised include the following:
- When the processes change
- When the organization's results change
- When the organization's needs change
- When suppliers' processes change
- When suppliers change

SP 1.5 ESTABLISH PROCESS-PERFORMANCE MODELS

Establish and maintain process-performance models for the organization's set of standard processes.

Process-performance models are used to estimate or predict the value of a process-performance measure from the values of other process, product, and service measurements. These process-performance models typically use process and product measurements collected throughout the life of the project to estimate progress toward achieving objectives that cannot be measured until later in the project's life.

Process-performance models are used as follows:

- The organization uses them for estimating, analyzing, and predicting the process performance associated with processes in and changes to the organization's set of standard processes.
- The organization uses them to assess the (potential) return on investment for process improvement activities.
- Projects use them for estimating, analyzing, and predicting the process performance of their defined processes.
- Projects use them for selecting processes or subprocesses for use.

These measures and models are defined to provide insight into and to provide the ability to predict critical process and product characteristics that are relevant to business value.

Examples of areas of concern to projects in which models may be useful include the following:
- Schedule and cost
- Reliability
- Defect identification and removal rates
- Defect removal effectiveness
- Latent defect estimation
- Response time
- Project progress
- Combinations of these areas
- Service system availability

Examples of process-performance models include the following:
- System dynamics models
- Reliability growth models
- Complexity models

Refer to the Quantitative Project Management process area for more information about quantitatively managing the project, using process-performance models, and establishing trial natural bounds for subprocesses.

Typical Work Products

1. Process-performance models

Subpractices

1. Establish process-performance models based on the organization's set of standard processes and the organization's process-performance baselines.
2. Calibrate process-performance models based on the organization's past results and current needs.
3. Review process-performance models and get agreement with relevant stakeholders.
4. Support the projects' use of process-performance models.
5. Revise process-performance models as necessary.

Examples of when process-performance models may need to be revised include the following:
- When processes change
- When the organization's results change
- When the organization's needs change

ORGANIZATIONAL TRAINING

A Process Management Process Area at Maturity Level 3

Purpose

The purpose of Organizational Training (OT) is to develop skills and knowledge of people so they can perform their roles effectively and efficiently.

IN OTHER WORDS

OT is about developing the skills and knowledge your people need to deliver superior service.

Introductory Notes

Organizational Training includes training to support the organization's strategic business objectives and to meet the tactical training needs that are common across projects and support groups. Training needs identified by individual projects and support groups are handled at the project and support group level and are outside the scope of the Organizational Training process area. Projects and support groups are responsible for identifying and addressing their training needs.

Refer to the Project Planning process area for more information about planning needed knowledge and skills.

An organizational training program involves the following activities:

- Identifying the training needed by the organization
- Obtaining and providing training to address those needs
- Establishing and maintaining a training capability
- Establishing and maintaining training records
- Assessing training effectiveness

Effective training requires the assessment of needs, planning, instructional design, and appropriate training media (e.g., workbooks, computer software), as well as a repository of training process data. As an organizational process, the main components of training include a managed training development program, documented plans, personnel with appropriate mastery of disciplines and other

WHY DO THE PRACTICES IN OT?

Your people have the skills they need because the right training is available and is constantly coordinated and improved. You don't miss out on business opportunities, because when a service engagement pops up, your training records show you who already has the skills to deliver the desired service, or who can be brought up to speed.

areas of knowledge, and mechanisms for measuring the effectiveness of the training program.

Identifying process training needs is based primarily on the skills required to perform the organization's set of standard processes.

Refer to the Organizational Process Definition process area for more information about standard processes.

Certain skills may be effectively and efficiently imparted through vehicles other than in-class training experiences (e.g., informal mentoring). Other skills require more formalized training vehicles, such as in a classroom, by Web-based training, through guided self study, or via a formalized on-the-job training program. The formal or informal training vehicles employed for each situation should be based on an assessment of the need for training and the performance gap to be addressed. The term "training" used throughout this process area is used broadly to include all of these learning options.

Success in training can be measured by the availability of opportunities to acquire the skills and knowledge needed to perform new and ongoing enterprise activities.

Skills and knowledge may be technical, organizational, or contextual. Technical skills pertain to the ability to use equipment, tools, materials, data, and processes required by a project or process. Organizational skills pertain to behavior within and according to the employee's organization structure, role and responsibilities, and general operating principles and methods. Contextual skills are the self-management, communication, and interpersonal abilities needed to successfully perform in the organizational and social context of the project and support groups.

The phrase "project and support groups" is used frequently in the process area description to indicate an organization-level perspective.

Related Process Areas

Refer to the Decision Analysis and Resolution process area for more information about analyzing possible decisions using a formal evaluation process that evaluates identified alternatives against established criteria.

Refer to the Organizational Process Definition process area for more information about organizational process assets.

Refer to the Project Planning process area for more information about planning needed knowledge and skills.

Specific Goal and Practice Summary

SG 1 Establish an Organizational Training Capability
    SP 1.1   Establish Strategic Training Needs
    SP 1.2   Determine Which Training Needs Are the Responsibility of the Organization
    SP 1.3   Establish an Organizational Training Tactical Plan
    SP 1.4   Establish a Training Capability
SG 2 Provide Necessary Training
    SP 2.1   Deliver Training
    SP 2.2   Establish Training Records
    SP 2.3   Assess Training Effectiveness

Specific Practices by Goal

SG 1   ESTABLISH AN ORGANIZATIONAL TRAINING CAPABILITY

A training capability, which supports the organization's management and technical roles, is established and maintained.

The organization identifies training required to develop the skills and knowledge necessary to perform enterprise activities. Once the needs are identified, a training program addressing those needs is developed.

SP 1.1   ESTABLISH STRATEGIC TRAINING NEEDS

Establish and maintain strategic training needs of the organization.

Strategic training needs address long-term objectives to build a capability by filling significant knowledge gaps, introducing new technologies, or implementing major changes in behavior. Strategic planning typically looks two to five years into the future.

Examples of sources of strategic training needs include the following:
- The organization's standard processes
- The organization's strategic business plan
- The organization's process improvement plan
- Enterprise-level initiatives
- Skill assessments
- Risk analyses
- Acquisition and supplier management

Typical Work Products

1. Training needs
2. Assessment analysis

Subpractices

1. Analyze the organization's strategic business objectives and process improvement plan to identify potential training needs.

2. Document the strategic training needs of the organization.

Examples of categories of training needs include (but are not limited to) the following:
- Process analysis and documentation
- Engineering (e.g., requirements analysis, design, testing, configuration management, quality assurance)
- Service delivery
- Selection and management of suppliers
- Management (e.g., estimating, tracking, risk management)
- Disaster recovery and continuity of operations

---

3. Determine the roles and skills needed to perform the organization's set of standard processes.

4. Document the training needed to perform roles in the organization's set of standard processes.

5. Document the training needed to maintain the safe, secure, and continued operation of the business.

6. Revise the organization's strategic needs and required training as necessary.

SP 1.2 DETERMINE WHICH TRAINING NEEDS ARE THE RESPONSIBILITY OF THE ORGANIZATION

Determine which training needs are the responsibility of the organization and which are left to the individual project or support group.

Refer to the Project Planning process area for more information about planning needed knowledge and skills.

In addition to strategic training needs, organizational training addresses training requirements that are common across projects and support groups. Projects and support groups have the primary responsibility for identifying and addressing their training needs. The organization's training staff is responsible for addressing only common cross-project and support group training needs (e.g., training in work environments common to multiple projects). In some cases, however, the organization's training staff may address additional training needs of projects and support groups, as negotiated with them, in the context of the training resources available and the organization's training priorities.

Typical Work Products

1. Common project and support group training needs
2. Training commitments

Subpractices

1. Analyze the training needs identified by projects and support groups.

    Analysis of project and support group needs is intended to identify common training needs that can be most efficiently addressed organization wide. These needs-analysis activities are used to anticipate future training needs that are first visible at the project and support group level.

2. Negotiate with projects and support groups on how their training needs will be satisfied.

    The support provided by the organization's training staff depends on the training resources available and the organization's training priorities.

Examples of training appropriately performed by the project or support group include the following:

- Training in the application or service domain of the project
- Training in the unique tools and methods used by the project or support group
- Training in safety, security, and human factors

---

3. Document commitments for providing training support to projects and support groups.

SP 1.3 *Establish an Organizational Training Tactical Plan*

Establish and maintain an organizational training tactical plan.

The organizational training tactical plan is the plan to deliver the training that is the responsibility of the organization and is necessary for individuals to perform their roles effectively. This plan addresses the near-term execution of training and is adjusted periodically in response to changes (e.g., in needs, in resources) and to evaluations of effectiveness.

Typical Work Products

1. Organizational training tactical plan

Subpractices

1. Establish the content of the plan.

Organizational training tactical plans typically contain the following:
- Training needs
- Training topics
- Schedules based on training activities and their dependencies
- Methods used for training
- Requirements and quality standards for training materials
- Training tasks, roles, and responsibilities
- Required resources including tools, facilities, environments, staffing, skills, and knowledge

---

2. Establish commitments to the plan.
   Documented commitments by those responsible for implementing and supporting the plan are essential for the plan to be effective.
3. Revise the plan and commitments as necessary.

SP 1.4 ESTABLISH A TRAINING CAPABILITY

Establish and maintain a training capability to address organizational training needs.

Refer to the Decision Analysis and Resolution process area for more information about analyzing possible decisions using a formal evaluation process that evaluates identified alternatives against established criteria.

Typical Work Products

1. Training materials and supporting artifacts

Subpractices

1. Select appropriate approaches to satisfy organizational training needs.
   Many factors may affect the selection of training approaches, including audience-specific knowledge, costs, schedule, and the work environment. Selecting an approach requires consideration of the means to provide skills and knowledge in the most effective way possible given the constraints.

Examples of training approaches include the following:
- Classroom training
- Computer-aided instruction
- Guided self study
- Formal apprenticeship and mentoring programs
- Facilitated videos
- Chalk talks
- Brown bag lunch seminars
- Structured on-the-job training

---

2. Determine whether to develop training materials internally or to acquire them externally.

   Determine the costs and benefits of internal training development and of acquiring training externally.

Example criteria that can be used to determine the most effective mode of knowledge or skill acquisition include the following:
- Performance objectives
- Time available to prepare for project execution
- Business objectives
- Availability of in-house expertise
- Availability of training from external sources

Examples of external sources of training include the following:
- Customer-provided training
- Commercially available training courses
- Academic programs
- Professional conferences
- Seminars

---

3. Develop or obtain training materials.

   Training may be provided by the project, support groups, the organization, or an external organization. The organization's training staff coordinates the acquisition and delivery of training regardless of its source.

Examples of training materials include the following:
- Courses
- Computer-aided instruction
- Videos

4. Develop or obtain qualified instructors.

    To ensure that internal training instructors have the necessary knowledge and training skills, criteria can be defined to identify, develop, and qualify them. In the case of external training, the organization's training staff can investigate how the training provider determines which instructors will deliver the training. This selection of qualified instructors can also be a factor in selecting or continuing to use a training provider.

5. Describe the training in the organization's training curriculum.

Examples of the information provided in training descriptions for each course include the following:
- Topics covered in the training
- Intended audience
- Prerequisites and preparation for participating
- Training objectives
- Length of the training
- Lesson plans
- Completion criteria for the course
- Criteria for granting training waivers

---

6. Revise training materials and supporting artifacts as necessary.

Examples of situations in which training materials and supporting artifacts may need to be revised include the following:
- Training needs change (e.g., when new technology associated with the training topic is available)
- An evaluation of the training identifies the need for change (e.g., evaluations of training effectiveness surveys, training program performance assessments, instructor evaluation forms)

SG 2 PROVIDE NECESSARY TRAINING

Training necessary for individuals to perform their roles effectively is provided.

When selecting people to be trained, the following should be considered:

- Background of the target population of training participants
- Prerequisite background to receive training
- Skills and abilities needed by people to perform their roles

- Need for cross-discipline technical management training for all disciplines, including project management
- Need for managers to have training in appropriate organizational processes
- Need for training in basic principles of all appropriate disciplines or services to support personnel in quality management, configuration management, and other related support functions
- Need to provide competency development for critical functional areas
- Need to maintain competencies and qualifications of personnel to operate and maintain work environments common to multiple projects

SP 2.1 DELIVER TRAINING

Deliver training following the organizational training tactical plan.

Typical Work Products

1. Delivered training course

Subpractices

1. Select those who will receive the training necessary to perform their roles effectively.

   Training is intended to impart knowledge and skills to people performing various roles in the organization. Some people already possess the knowledge and skills required to perform well in their designated roles. Training can be waived for these people, but care should be taken that training waivers are not abused.

2. Schedule the training, including any resources, as necessary (e.g., facilities, instructors).

   Training should be planned and scheduled. Training is provided that has a direct bearing on work performance expectations. Therefore, optimal training occurs in a timely manner with regard to imminent job-performance expectations.

These performance expectations often include the following:
- Training in the use of specialized tools
- Training in procedures that are new to the person who will perform them

---

3. Conduct the training.

   Experienced instructors should conduct the training. When possible, training is conducted in settings that closely resemble actual performance conditions and includes activities to simulate actual work situations. This approach includes integration of tools, methods, and procedures for competency development. Training is tied to work responsibilities so that on-the-job activities or other outside experiences will reinforce the training within a reasonable time after the training was conducted.

4. Track the delivery of training against the plan.

SP 2.2 ESTABLISH TRAINING RECORDS

Establish and maintain records of organizational training.

This practice applies to the training performed at the organizational level. Establishment and maintenance of training records for project- or support-group-sponsored training is the responsibility of each individual project or support group.

Typical Work Products

1. Training records
2. Training updates to the organizational repository

Subpractices

1. Keep records of all students who successfully complete each training course or other approved training activity as well as those who are unsuccessful.
2. Keep records of all staff members who are waived from training.
   The rationale for granting a waiver should be documented, and both the manager responsible and the manager of the excepted individual should approve the waiver.
3. Keep records of all students who successfully complete their required training.
4. Make training records available to the appropriate people for consideration in assignments.
   Training records may be part of a skills matrix developed by the training organization to provide a summary of the experience and education of people, as well as training sponsored by the organization.

SP 2.3 ASSESS TRAINING EFFECTIVENESS

Assess the effectiveness of the organization's training program.

A process should exist to determine the effectiveness of training (i.e., how well training is meeting the organization's needs).

> Examples of methods used to assess training effectiveness include the following:
> - Testing in the training context
> - Post-training surveys of training participants
> - Surveys of manager satisfaction with post-training effects
> - Assessment mechanisms embedded in courseware

Measures may be taken to assess the benefits of training against both the project's and organization's objectives. Particular attention should be paid to the need for various training methods, such as training teams as integral work units. When used, performance objectives should be shared with course participants, unambiguous, observable, and verifiable. The results of the training-effectiveness assessment should be used to revise training materials as described in the Establish a Training Capability specific practice.

Typical Work Products

1. Training-effectiveness surveys
2. Training program performance assessments
3. Instructor evaluation forms
4. Training examinations

Subpractices

1. Assess in-progress or completed projects to determine whether staff knowledge is adequate for performing project tasks.
2. Provide a mechanism for assessing the effectiveness of each training course with respect to established organizational, project, or individual learning (or performance) objectives.
3. Obtain student evaluations of how well training activities met their needs.

PROJECT MONITORING AND CONTROL
A Project Management Process Area at Maturity Level 2

Purpose

The purpose of Project Monitoring and Control (PMC) is to provide an understanding of the project's progress so that appropriate corrective actions can be taken when the project's performance deviates significantly from the plan.

Introductory Notes

A project's documented plan is the basis for monitoring activities, communicating status, and taking corrective action. Progress is primarily determined by comparing actual work product and task attributes, effort, cost, and schedule to the plan at prescribed milestones or control levels in the project schedule or WBS. Appropriate visibility of progress enables timely corrective action to be taken when performance deviates significantly from the plan. A deviation is significant if, when left unresolved, it precludes the project from meeting its objectives.

The term "project plan" is used throughout these practices to refer to the overall plan for controlling the project.

When actual status deviates significantly from expected values, corrective actions are taken as appropriate. These actions may require replanning, which may include revising the original plan, establishing new agreements, or including additional mitigation activities in the current plan.

Related Process Areas

Refer to the Capacity and Availability Management process area for more information about monitoring and analyzing capacity and availability.

Refer to the Measurement and Analysis process area for more information about providing measurement results.

Refer to the Project Planning process area for more information about developing a project plan.

Specific Goal and Practice Summary

SG 1 Monitor the Project Against the Plan
    SP 1.1   Monitor Project Planning Parameters
    SP 1.2   Monitor Commitments
    SP 1.3   Monitor Project Risks
    SP 1.4   Monitor Data Management
    SP 1.5   Monitor Stakeholder Involvement
    SP 1.6   Conduct Progress Reviews
    SP 1.7   Conduct Milestone Reviews
SG 2 Manage Corrective Action to Closure
    SP 2.1   Analyze Issues
    SP 2.2   Take Corrective Action
    SP 2.3   Manage Corrective Actions

Specific Practices by Goal

SG 1   *MONITOR THE PROJECT AGAINST THE PLAN*

Actual performance and progress of the project are monitored against the project plan.

SP 1.1 *MONITOR PROJECT PLANNING PARAMETERS*

Monitor actual values of project planning parameters against the project plan.

Project planning parameters constitute typical indicators of project progress and performance and include attributes of work products and tasks, costs, effort, and schedule. Attributes of the work products and tasks include size, complexity, service level, availability, weight, form, fit, and function.

Parameters to be considered should include the frequency of monitoring. Frequency considerations may include the possible need for monitoring each service request or incident, and possibly even continuous monitoring for continuously delivered services.

Monitoring typically involves measuring actual values of project planning parameters, comparing actual values to estimates in the plan, and identifying significant deviations. Recording actual values of project planning parameters includes recording associated contextual information to help understand measures. An analysis of the impact that significant deviations have on determining the corrective actions to take is handled in specific goal 2 and its specific practices in this process area.

Typical Work Products

1. Records of project performance
2. Records of significant deviations

Subpractices

1. Monitor progress against the schedule.

Progress monitoring typically includes the following:
- Periodically measuring the actual completion of activities and milestones
- Comparing actual completion of activities and milestones against the project plan schedule
- Identifying significant deviations from the project plan budget and schedule estimates

---

2. Monitor the project's cost and expended effort.

Effort and cost monitoring typically includes the following:
- Periodically measuring the actual effort and costs expended and staff assigned
- Comparing actual effort, costs, staffing, and training to the project plan budget and estimates
- Identifying significant deviations from the project plan budget and schedule

---

3. Monitor the attributes of work products and tasks.

> *Refer to the Measurement and Analysis process area for more information about developing and sustaining a measurement capability used to support management information needs.*

> *Refer to the Project Planning process area for more information about establishing estimates of work product and task attributes.*

Monitoring the attributes of work products and tasks typically includes the following:
- Periodically measuring the actual attributes of work products and tasks, such as size, complexity, or service levels (and changes to these attributes)
- Comparing the actual attributes of work products and tasks (and changes to these attributes) to project plan estimates
- Identifying significant deviations from project plan estimates

---

4. Monitor resources provided and used.

Refer to the Capacity and Availability Management process area for more information about monitoring and analyzing capacity.

Refer to the Project Planning process area for more information about planning the project's resources.

Examples of resources include the following:
- Physical facilities
- Computers, peripherals, and software used in design, manufacturing, testing, and operation
- Networks
- Security environment
- Project staff
- Processes

---

5. Monitor the knowledge and skills of project personnel.

Refer to the Project Planning process area for more information about planning needed knowledge and skills.

Monitoring the knowledge and skills of project personnel typically includes the following:
- Periodically measuring the acquisition of knowledge and skills by project personnel
- Comparing actual training obtained to that documented in the project plan
- Identifying significant deviations from estimates in the project plan

---

6. Document significant deviations in project planning parameters.

SP 1.2 MONITOR COMMITMENTS

Monitor commitments against those identified in the project plan.

Typical Work Products

1. Records of commitment reviews

Subpractices

1. Regularly review commitments (both external and internal).
2. Identify commitments that have not been satisfied or are at significant risk of not being satisfied.
3. Document the results of commitment reviews.

SP 1.3 MONITOR PROJECT RISKS

Monitor risks against those identified in the project plan.

Refer to the Project Planning process area for more information about identifying project risks.

Refer to the Risk Management process area for more information about identifying potential problems before they occur so that risk-handling activities can be planned and invoked as needed across the life of the product or project to mitigate adverse impacts on achieving objectives.

Typical Work Products

1. Records of project risk monitoring

Subpractices

1. Periodically review the documentation of risks in the context of the project's current status and circumstances.

> An example risk whose status might change is a threat to the continuity of operations or a change to the average mix of service request types coming from end users. If the risk has become more likely or the possible impact more severe, then corrective action may be necessary.

2. Revise the documentation of risks as additional information becomes available.

   As projects progress (especially those of long duration or continuous operation), new risks arise, and it is important to identify, analyze, and plan the appropriate response (or mitigation) for these new risks. For example, software, equipment, and tools in use may become obsolete; or key personnel may gradually lose skills in areas of particular long-term importance to the project and organization. It is important to identify, analyze, and address these new risks.

3. Communicate the risk status to relevant stakeholders.

Examples of risk status include the following:
- A change in the probability that the risk occurs
- A change in risk priority

SP 1.4 MONITOR DATA MANAGEMENT

Monitor the management of project data against the project plan.

Refer to the Plan Data Management specific practice in the Project Planning process area for more information about identifying types of data to be managed and how to plan for their management.

Data management activities should be monitored to ensure that data management requirements are being satisfied. Depending on the results of monitoring and changes in project requirements, situation, or status, it may be necessary to re-plan the project's data management activities.

Typical Work Products

1. Records of data management

Subpractices

1. Periodically review data management activities against their description in the project plan.

2. Identify and document significant issues and their impacts.

An example of a significant issue is when stakeholders do not have the access to project data they need to fulfill their roles as relevant stakeholders.

---

3. Document results of data management activity reviews.

SP 1.5 MONITOR STAKEHOLDER INVOLVEMENT

Monitor stakeholder involvement against the project plan.

Refer to the Plan Stakeholder Involvement specific practice in the Project Planning process area for more information about identifying relevant stakeholders and planning appropriate involvement with them.

Stakeholder involvement should be monitored to ensure that appropriate interactions occur. Depending on the results of monitoring and changes in project requirements, situation, or status, it may be necessary to re-plan stakeholder involvement.

Typical Work Products

1. Records of stakeholder involvement

Subpractices

1. Periodically review the status of stakeholder involvement.
2. Identify and document significant issues and their impacts.
3. Document the results of stakeholder involvement status reviews.

SP 1.6 CONDUCT PROGRESS REVIEWS

Periodically review the project's progress, performance, and issues.

A "project's progress" is the project's status as viewed at a particular time when the project activities performed so far and their results and impacts are reviewed with relevant stakeholders (especially project representatives and project management) to determine whether there are significant issues or performance shortfalls that must be addressed.

Progress reviews are project reviews to keep stakeholders informed. These project reviews can be informal and may not be specified explicitly in project plans.

Typical Work Products

1. Documented project review results

Subpractices

1. Regularly communicate status on assigned activities and work products to relevant stakeholders.

   Managers, staff members, customers, end users, suppliers, and other relevant stakeholders are included in reviews as appropriate.

2. Review the results of collecting and analyzing measures for controlling the project.

> The measurements reviewed include those collected for service parameter measures identified in project planning (e.g., availability, number of users) and may include those collected for measures of customer satisfaction.

> *Refer to the Measurement and Analysis process area for more information about aligning measurement and analysis activities and providing measurement results.*

3. Identify and document significant issues and deviations from the plan.

4. Document change requests and problems identified in work products and processes.

> *Refer to the Configuration Management process area for more information about tracking and controlling changes.*

5. Document the results of reviews.

6. Track change requests and problem reports to closure.

SP 1.7 CONDUCT MILESTONE REVIEWS

Review the project's accomplishments and results at selected project milestones.

Refer to the Measurement and Analysis process area for more information about providing measurement results.

Refer to the Project Planning process area for more information about identifying major milestones.

Milestones are preplanned events or times at which a thorough review of status is conducted to understand how well stakeholder requirements are being met. (If the project includes a developmental milestone, then the review is conducted to ensure that the assumptions and requirements associated with that milestone are being met.) Milestones may be associated with the overall project or a particular service type or instance. Milestones can thus be event based or calendar based.

Milestone reviews are planned during project planning and are typically formal reviews.

Progress reviews and milestone reviews need not be held separately. A single review can address the intent of both. For example, a single preplanned review can evaluate progress, issues, and performance up through a planned time period (or milestone) against the plan's expectations.

Typical Work Products

1. Documented milestone review results

Subpractices

1. Conduct milestone reviews with relevant stakeholders at meaningful points in the project's schedule, such as the completion of selected stages.

   Managers, staff members, customers, end users, suppliers, and other relevant stakeholders are included in milestone reviews as appropriate.

2. Review commitments, the plan, status, and risks of the project.

   The reviews may include an analysis of measurements collected for customer satisfaction.

3. Identify and document significant issues and their impacts.

4. Document results of the review, action items, and decisions.

5. Track action items to closure.

SG 2 MANAGE CORRECTIVE ACTION TO CLOSURE

Corrective actions are managed to closure when the project's performance or results deviate significantly from the plan.

SP 2.1 ANALYZE ISSUES

Collect and analyze issues and determine corrective actions necessary to address them.

This analysis is performed for a different purpose and generally on different issues than the analysis performed as part of incident analysis, problem analysis, or change request analysis. However, the same or a similar mechanism may be used to analyze each of these types of issues and to manage them to closure. How best to implement a common solution for their analysis and management to closure depends on the risk of failing to handle each appropriately and the costs incurred by alternative solutions.

Typical Work Products

1. List of issues requiring corrective actions

Subpractices

1. Gather issues for analysis.

   Issues are collected from reviews and the execution of other processes.

Examples of issues to be gathered include the following:
- Issues discovered when performing verification and validation activities
- Significant deviations in project planning parameters from estimates in the project plan
- Commitments (either internal or external) that have not been satisfied
- Significant changes in risk status
- Data access, collection, privacy, or security issues
- Stakeholder representation or involvement issues
- Repetitive deviations that accumulate before becoming significant, but whose resolution should be addressed
- Product, tool, or environment transition assumptions (or other customer or supplier commitments) that have not been achieved

2. Analyze issues to determine the need for corrective action.

> *Refer to the Project Planning process area for more information about corrective action criteria.*

Corrective action is required when the issue, if left unresolved, may prevent the project from meeting its objectives.

SP 2.2 TAKE CORRECTIVE ACTION

Take corrective action on identified issues.

Typical Work Products

1. Corrective action plans

Subpractices

1. Determine and document the appropriate actions needed to address identified issues.

> *Refer to the Project Planning process area for more information about developing a project plan.*

Examples of potential actions include the following:
- Modifying the statement of work
- Modifying requirements
- Revising estimates and plans
- Renegotiating commitments
- Adding resources
- Changing processes
- Revising project risks

2. Review and get agreement with relevant stakeholders on the actions to be taken.
3. Negotiate changes to internal and external commitments.

SP 2.3 MANAGE CORRECTIVE ACTIONS

Manage corrective actions to closure.

Typical Work Products

1. Corrective action results

Subpractices

1. Monitor corrective actions for their completion.

    Refer to the Incident Resolution and Prevention process area for more information about monitoring the status of incidents to closure.

2. Analyze results of corrective actions to determine the effectiveness of the corrective actions.
3. Determine and document appropriate actions to correct deviations from planned results from performing corrective actions.

    Lessons learned as a result of taking corrective action can be inputs to planning and risk management processes.

PROJECT PLANNING
A Project Management Process Area at Maturity Level 2

Purpose

The purpose of Project Planning (PP) is to establish and maintain plans that define project activities.

Introductory Notes

In CMMI, the term "project" is given a broad definition so that the practices that use that term (e.g., in the Project Management process areas) have appropriately broad applicability. The term "project" refers to a group of people and resources committed to planning, monitoring, and executing defined processes in a shared endeavor to achieve a set of objectives. These objectives include (or may be derived from) the goals of the business but will also include goals associated with customers, though there may not yet be any customers identified (or service agreements in place) when the project is initiated.

The definition above of "project" includes those endeavors that have an intended termination (e.g., developing a product, delivering services under a service agreement with a specified end date) as well as those that an organization does not intend to terminate (e.g., providing health care, providing fire safety services in a community). Some people are unaccustomed to this broad interpretation of the term "project" and may habitually restrict its use to only those kinds of endeavors with a defined end point. However, the process areas, goals, and practices in CMMI for *perpetual* endeavors overlap completely with those needed for traditional projects. Therefore, CMMI models use the single term "project" to encompass both types of endeavors as a way of avoiding unnecessary distinctions and duplication among model components.

PP

A project can be composed of multiple projects, in which case the CMMI project-related practices apply to the projects at these lower levels as well, though they may be implemented less formally as the level of their application moves to an individual team and as the risk of failure decreases.

The term "organization" refers to a higher level of management that provides policies, resources, standard processes, and other support to several projects. Obtaining business value from the practices in this and related process areas requires, in part, correctly identifying which endeavors are *projects*. (See the definitions of "project" and "organization" in the glossary.)

One of the keys to effectively managing a project is project planning. The Project Planning process area involves the following activities:

* Developing the project plan
* Interacting with stakeholders appropriately
* Getting commitment to the plan
* Maintaining the plan

Planning includes estimating the attributes of work products and tasks, determining the resources needed, negotiating commitments, producing a schedule, and identifying and analyzing project risks. Iterating through these activities may be necessary to establish the project plan. The project plan provides the basis for performing and controlling project activities that address commitments with the project's customer.

The project plan is usually revised as the project progresses to address changes in requirements and commitments, inaccurate estimates, corrective actions, and process changes. Specific practices describing both planning and replanning are contained in this process area.

The term "project plan" is used throughout this process area to refer to the overall plan for controlling the project.

Projects that respond to service requests generated over time by end users may require an entire level of detailed and frequently revised plans for resource-to-task allocation and task queue management (e.g., the assignment of repair jobs in a maintenance shop). These low-level operating plans may be considered a detailed extension of the overall project plan.

PROJECT PLANNING FOR SERVICE DELIVERY

If you're in one of the many service provider organizations that doesn't typically structure its work into projects, you may wonder how any of these project planning goals and practices will be useful to you. Even if you've read and accepted the discussion of the term *project* in the section Important CMMI-SVC Concepts in Chapter 1, you may have some difficulty with the idea of project planning. Here is one interpretation that may help you to gain advantage from the practices in this process area. How does project planning help with effective service delivery?

This question is best answered by working from the bottom up. At the lowest level of planning, a service delivery project needs to allocate and schedule resources *operationally* in response to a varying stream of service requests and incidents. The focus at this level is on how to plan and manage the next task, which may have just materialized.

Some types of projects may have settled on an initial set of continuing service requests up front in a service agreement, but even in these cases, new requests may arise, and incidents still need to be dealt with in any event. This type of operational planning is constructed as needed through the use of the project's request management and incident management systems (which may be a single integrated system) and their related processes. These operational plans rely on a well-specified set of available resources to respond to requests and incidents; the extent and availability of those resources over time are specified by a project plan.

The focus of project planning in a services context is therefore a level above task-focused operational planning at the level of an entire project (e.g., for one or more closely related service agreements). Project planning for service delivery establishes and estimates overall project scope, resources, and costs; allocates and schedules specific resources to various service delivery functions (e.g., shift schedules); outlines how other projectwide issues will be handled (e.g., data management and risk management); coordinates these plans with other plans; and gets appropriate commitment from those who will actually be performing or supporting the work.

When the scope of a project is a single service agreement with a single customer, most service requests are known at the start of the project, or the operational tempo of the project is low (i.e., there are few incidents or new service requests over time), project planning and operational planning might be handled more effectively as a single integrated activity. In any event, effective operational planning for service delivery depends on effective project planning to establish a stable service management framework.

Continues

Another use for project planning in a services context is when an organization needs to perform a major activity not specifically related to individual service requests or incidents. For example, creating and rolling out a major new or modified service system for service delivery may be managed as a project of its own, or as part of an existing service delivery project. (Remember that a single "project" can have parts that are projects themselves.) Other examples of these kinds of projects include creating, deploying, and using a new customer survey system to gather data needed to define standard services; and establishing a new customer awareness program through a major marketing campaign.

Related Process Areas

Refer to the Capacity and Availability Management process area for more information about ensuring effective service system performance and ensuring that resources are provided and used effectively to support service requirements.

Refer to the Service Delivery process area for more information about preparing for service system operations.

Refer to the Service System Development process area for more information about developing and analyzing stakeholder requirements and developing service systems.

SSD ADD

Refer to the Strategic Service Management process area for more information about gathering and analyzing data about the strategic needs and capabilities of the organization.

Refer to the Measurement and Analysis process area for more information about specifying measures.

Refer to the Requirements Management process area for more information about managing changes to requirements as they evolve during the project.

Refer to the Risk Management process area for more information about identifying, analyzing, and mitigating risks.

Specific Goal and Practice Summary

SG 1 Establish Estimates
- SP 1.1 Establish the Project Strategy
- SP 1.2 Estimate the Scope of the Project
- SP 1.3 Establish Estimates of Work Product and Task Attributes
- SP 1.4 Define Project Lifecycle Phases
- SP 1.5 Estimate Effort and Cost

SG 2 Develop a Project Plan
  SP 2.1 Establish the Budget and Schedule
  SP 2.2 Identify Project Risks
  SP 2.3 Plan Data Management
  SP 2.4 Plan the Project's Resources
  SP 2.5 Plan Needed Knowledge and Skills
  SP 2.6 Plan Stakeholder Involvement
  SP 2.7 Establish the Project Plan
SG 3 Obtain Commitment to the Plan
  SP 3.1 Review Plans That Affect the Project
  SP 3.2 Reconcile Work and Resource Levels
  SP 3.3 Obtain Plan Commitment

Specific Practices by Goal

SG 1 ESTABLISH ESTIMATES

Estimates of project planning parameters are established and maintained.

Project planning parameters include all information needed by the project to perform necessary planning, organizing, staffing, directing, coordinating, reporting, and budgeting.

Estimates of planning parameters should have a sound basis to instill confidence that plans based on these estimates are capable of supporting project objectives.

Factors to consider when estimating these parameters include the following:

- The project strategy
- Project requirements, including product requirements, requirements imposed by the organization, requirements imposed by the customer, and other requirements that impact the project
- The scope of the project
- Identified tasks and work products
- Identified services and service levels
- How incidents and requests are to be handled
- The selected project lifecycle model (e.g., waterfall, incremental, spiral)
- Attributes of work products and tasks (e.g., size, complexity)
- The schedule
- Models or historical data used for converting attributes of work products and tasks into labor hours and costs
- The methodology (e.g., models, data, algorithms) used to determine needed material, skills, labor hours, and cost

---

PP

Documentation of the estimating rationale and supporting data is needed for stakeholder review and commitment to the plan and for maintenance of the plan as the project progresses.

SP 1.1 ESTABLISH THE PROJECT STRATEGY

Establish and maintain the project strategy.

The project strategy provides the business framework for planning and managing the project. The strategy includes consideration of the following factors at an appropriate level of abstraction:

- The objectives and constraints for the project
- Possible approaches to meeting those objectives and constraints
- The resources (e.g., skills, environment, tools, new technologies) that will be needed
- Risks associated with these factors and how they are addressed

The project strategy typically takes a long-term view of a project, reflects its entire scope, considers long-term risks, and addresses the roles to be played by multiple stakeholders, including suppliers, the customer, and other projects.

The project strategy may play various roles, but typically and initially, it serves as the basis for senior management approving a project and committing resources to it. As project planning proceeds, and the solution, processes, resources, and risks are explored and developed, the project strategy may need to be revised.

For a short-duration project, a project strategy may not be developed or only developed once, in which case it is replaced by the project plan as the project progresses and more detailed planning becomes possible.

For a long-duration project, the strategy plays a continuing role in helping to maintain a long-term view of the project and its rationale, touching on various elements of the project plan but at a higher level of abstraction; whereas the project plan will typically reflect a much lower level of detail over a shorter time horizon.

A project strategy may initially be created by the organization or by prospective project personnel perhaps in collaboration with potential customers and suppliers, or some other combination of parties with a strategic business view of the prospects for the project.

The project strategy may include a top-level description of the services to be provided, the approach to developing the service system, and the approach to service delivery as appropriate.

Typical Work Products

1. Project strategy

Subpractices

1. Identify the objectives of the project and the capabilities it intends to provide.

    The organization may maintain an overall business strategy in which the project plays a role in establishing capabilities needed by the organization. The project-related objectives and capabilities described in this subpractice may be derived from such considerations for the overall business, but will tend to have a specific or near-term set of objectives and capabilities.

    Refer to the Strategic Service Management process area for more information about establishing and maintaining standard services in concert with strategic needs and plans.

2. Identify the approach used to achieve the objectives or provide the capabilities.

    There will often be both an approach to developing the infrastructure needed to deliver services (i.e., technical approach) and an approach to delivery that accounts for customer satisfaction, skill levels needed, skill levels available, costs, and risks.

    Refer to the Service Delivery process area for more information about establishing the service delivery approach.

3. Document business considerations.

    Business considerations include potential costs and benefits, intellectual property, competitive climate, aging of the industry and impact on long-term needs and profit margins, core competencies of the organization to be enhanced, core competencies needed from other parties, and future trends in society, trade, and technology.

4. Identify major resource needs.

    A review of the project approach helps to identify categories of resources needed by the project and the suppliers of these resources (e.g., other business groups within the organization, specific functional groups, human resources, intellectual property experts, the legal department, the marketing department, business partners, external suppliers).

    Refer to the Capacity and Availability Management process area for more information about ensuring effective service system performance and ensuring that resources are provided and used effectively to support service requirements.

5. Identify stakeholders that will play major roles in the project.

The Plan Stakeholder Involvement specific practice provides a more detailed, though perhaps shorter term, consideration of which stakeholders to involve in the project and in what way.

The project approach may be able to leverage external stakeholders (e.g., existing and potential customers and business partners) to provide some of the needed resources.

6. Identify the agreement types to be used.

   To be successful, the project must establish agreements with its major stakeholders. The nature of those agreements is determined, in part, by considering each party's needs, objectives, expectations, constraints, and risks. The types of agreements selected should be part of business considerations and thus help answer how various parties will share in the risks, costs, and benefits of the project.

7. Identify risks and how those risks may be allocated to various stakeholders.

   The Identify Project Risks specific practice in this process area provides a more detailed, though perhaps shorter term, consideration of the risks that the project may encounter.

8. Identify the approach used to maintain safety and security in the project.

   Attention to safety and security should be present in all major planning activities (e.g., those related to project objectives, resources, risks, and stakeholders) but this subpractice suggests taking a holistic view and focus on safety and security issues and risks, and the activities the project might take to address them.

9. Review the project strategy with senior management and obtain its agreement.

   Review the project strategy from the following key business perspectives:
   - Are these objectives the right ones?
   - Is the approach feasible?
   - Is this strategy an appropriate allocation of the organization's resources for a prolonged period of time?
   - What is the return on investment?
   - What opportunities open up as a result of this strategy?
   - Will the organization be subjected to excessive risk?
   - What roles might some not-yet-identified major stakeholders play in project success?
   - How might customers, suppliers, and competitors react?

10. Revise the project strategy as necessary.

    Depending on the duration of the project, it may be necessary to refine the project strategy to reflect changes in the objectives, approach, availability of resources, market conditions, customer needs, process and product technologies, etc.

SP 1.2 ESTIMATE THE SCOPE OF THE PROJECT

Establish a top-level work breakdown structure (WBS) to estimate the scope of the project.

The WBS evolves with the project. Initially, a top-level WBS can serve to structure initial estimating. The development of a WBS divides the overall project into an interconnected set of manageable components.

Typically, the WBS is a product, work product, or task-oriented structure that provides a scheme for identifying and organizing the logical units of work to be managed, which are called "work packages." The WBS provides a reference and organizational mechanism for assigning effort, schedule, and responsibility and is used as the underlying framework to plan, organize, and control the work done on the project.

The activities in a WBS may be organized in different ways but are typically scoped by time or duration and address both service system development and maintenance as well as service delivery as appropriate. Some of the services identified may be continuously delivered; others may be in response to ad hoc requests. Both are specified in a (possibly future) service agreement.

Activities may be further organized along one or more dimensions. For example, in the case of product maintenance, we could further distinguish activities according to those persisting through the end of the life of the product (from product delivery through product disposal), activities related to managing and executing the service agreement, and activities related to an individual incident or service request.

Typical Work Products

1. Task descriptions
2. Work package descriptions
3. WBS

Subpractices

1. Develop a WBS based on the project strategy.
    The WBS provides a scheme for organizing the project's work. The WBS should permit the identification of the following items:
    - Risks and their mitigation tasks
    - Tasks for deliverables and supporting activities
    - Tasks for skill and knowledge acquisition

- Tasks for the development of needed support plans, such as configuration management, quality assurance, and verification plans
- Tasks for the integration and management of nondevelopmental items

2. Define the work packages in sufficient detail so that estimates of project tasks, responsibilities, and schedule can be specified.

   The top-level WBS is intended to help gauge the project work effort for tasks and organizational roles and responsibilities. The amount of detail in the WBS at this level helps in developing realistic schedules, thereby minimizing the need for management reserve.

3. Identify products and product components to be externally acquired.

   Refer to the Supplier Agreement Management process area for more information about managing the acquisition of products and services from suppliers.

4. Identify work products to be reused.

SP 1.3 ESTABLISH ESTIMATES OF WORK PRODUCT AND TASK ATTRIBUTES

Establish and maintain estimates of work product and task attributes.

The estimate of size is the primary input to many models used to estimate effort, cost, and schedule. Models can also be based on other attributes, such as service level, connectivity, complexity, availability, and structure.

Examples of tasks for which size measures are made include the following:
- Service system development and delivery
- Service system monitoring
- Preventative maintenance or repair
- Training in operations
- Incident management and resolution
- Monitoring for and addressing obsolescence
- Updating equipment and supplies used by service teams
- Logistical support
- Facilities maintenance
- System disposal

> Examples of size measures include the following:
> - Number of requirements
> - Number and complexity of interfaces
> - Number of risk items
> - Volume of data
> - Number of service levels
> - Availability of services, by service level (e.g., turnaround time, operational availability ratio, number of calls the help desk should be able to handle per hour)
> - Number of stakeholders affected by a service level

The estimates should be consistent with project requirements to determine the project's effort, cost, and schedule. A relative level of difficulty or complexity should be assigned for each size attribute.

Typical Work Products

1. Size and complexity of tasks and work products
2. Estimating models
3. Attribute estimates

Subpractices

1. Use appropriate methods to determine the attributes of the work products and tasks to be used to estimate resource requirements.
   Methods for determining size and complexity should be based on validated models or historical data.
   The methods for determining attributes evolve as the understanding of the relationship of service development and delivery characteristics to attributes increases.
2. Estimate the attributes of work products and tasks.

SP 1.4 *DEFINE PROJECT LIFECYCLE PHASES*

Define project lifecycle phases on which to scope the planning effort.

The determination of a project's lifecycle phases provides for planned periods of evaluation and decision making. These periods are normally defined to support logical decision points at which the appropriateness of continued reliance on the project plan and strategy is determined and significant commitments are made concerning resources. Such points provide planned events at which project course corrections and determinations of future scope and cost can be made.

Understanding the project lifecycle is crucial in determining the scope of the planning effort and the timing of initial planning, as well as the timing and criteria (critical milestones) for replanning.

The selection of a lifecycle for development and delivery of services will depend on the characteristics of the services and their environment. Some service providers will define phases based on their standard service definitions.

Refer to the Strategic Service Management process area for more information about establishing standard services.

Often, individual services have implicit lifecycles associated with them that involve points of communication, evaluation, and decision and should be considered when estimating what is required to support delivery of such a service.

Typical Work Products

1. Project lifecycle phases

SP 1.5 ESTIMATE EFFORT AND COST

Estimate the project's effort and cost for work products and tasks based on estimation rationale.

Estimates of effort and cost are generally based on results of analysis using models or historical data applied to size, activities, and other planning parameters. Confidence in these estimates is based on rationale for the selected model and the nature of the data. There may be occasions when available historical data do not apply, such as when efforts are unprecedented or when the type of task does not fit available models. An effort is unprecedented if the organization has no experience with such a product.

Typical Work Products

1. Estimation rationale
2. Project effort estimates
3. Project cost estimates

Subpractices

1. Collect models or historical data to be used to transform the attributes of work products and tasks into estimates of labor hours and costs.
   Many parametric models have been developed to help estimate cost and schedule. The use of these models as the sole source of estimation is not recommended, because these models are based on historical project data that may or may not be pertinent to the project. Multiple models and methods can be used to ensure a high level of confidence in the estimate.

Historical data should include the cost, effort, and schedule data from previously executed projects and appropriate scaling data to account for differing sizes and complexity.

2. Include supporting infrastructure needs when estimating effort and cost.

   The supporting infrastructure includes resources needed from a development and sustainment perspective for the product.

   Consider the infrastructure resource needs in the development environment, the test environment, the production environment, the target environment, or any appropriate combination of these environments when estimating effort and cost.

Examples of infrastructure resources include the following:
- Critical computer resources
- Tools with which service teams will be equipped
- Facilities, machinery, and equipment

---

3. Estimate effort and cost using models and historical data.

Effort and cost inputs used for estimating typically include the following:
- Estimates provided by an expert or group of experts (e.g., Delphi Method)
- Risks, including the extent to which the effort is unprecedented
- Critical competencies and roles needed to perform the work
- Service and service system requirements
- Product and product component requirements
- Project strategy
- WBS
- Size estimates of work products, tasks, and anticipated changes
- Cost of externally acquired products
- Selected project lifecycle model and processes
- Lifecycle cost estimates
- Capability of tools provided
- Skill levels of managers and staff needed to perform the work
- Knowledge, skill, and training needs
- Facilities needed (e.g., for developing and maintaining the service system and for service delivery)
- Capability of manufacturing processes
- Travel
- Level of security required for tasks, work products, personnel, and the work environment
- Service agreements for call centers and warranty work
- Direct labor and overhead

SG 2 *DEVELOP A PROJECT PLAN*

A project plan is established and maintained as the basis for managing the project.

A project plan is a formal, approved document used to manage and control the execution of the project. It is based on project requirements and established estimates.

The project plan should consider all phases of the project lifecycle. Project planning should ensure that all plans affecting the project are consistent with the overall project plan.

SP 2.1 *ESTABLISH THE BUDGET AND SCHEDULE*

Establish and maintain the project's budget and schedule.

The project's budget and schedule are based on developed estimates and ensure that budget allocation, task complexity, and task dependencies are appropriately addressed.

Event-driven, resource-limited schedules have proven to be effective in dealing with project risk. Identifying accomplishments to be demonstrated before initiation of an event provides some flexibility in the timing of the event, a common understanding of what is expected, a better vision of the state of the project, and a more accurate status of the project's tasks.

The subpractices and typical work products of this specific practice should be interpreted both at the overall project level and within each service type as appropriate. That is, individual service requests (e.g., to repair a piece of equipment in a remote facility, transport a package to a destination) may have individual milestones, task dependencies, resource allocations, and scheduling constraints that should be considered together and in coordination with the larger project's budgeting and scheduling activities.

Typical Work Products

1. Project schedules
2. Schedule dependencies
3. Project budget

Subpractices

1. Identify major milestones.

   Milestones are preplanned events or points in time at which a thorough review of status is conducted to understand how well stakeholder requirements are being met. (If the project includes a developmental milestone, then the review is conducted to ensure that the assumptions and requirements associated with that milestone are being met.) Milestones may be associated with the overall project or a particular service type or instance. Milestones can thus be event based or calendar based. If calendar based, once agreed, milestone dates are often difficult to change.

2. Identify schedule assumptions.

   When schedules are initially developed, it is common to make assumptions about the duration of certain activities. These assumptions are frequently made on items for which little if any estimation data are available. Identifying these assumptions provides insight into the level of confidence (i.e., uncertainties) in the overall schedule.

3. Identify constraints.

   Factors that limit the flexibility of management options should be identified as early as possible. The examination of the attributes of work products and tasks often brings these issues to the surface. Such attributes can include task duration, resources, inputs, and outputs.

4. Identify task dependencies.

   Frequently, the tasks for a project or service can be accomplished in some ordered sequence that minimizes the duration. This sequencing involves the identification of predecessor and successor tasks to determine optimal ordering.

Examples of tools that can help determine optimal ordering of task activities include the following:
- Critical Path Method (CPM)
- Program Evaluation and Review Technique (PERT)
- Resource-limited scheduling

---

5. Define the budget and schedule.

PP

Establishing and maintaining the project's budget and schedule typically includes the following:
- Defining the committed or expected availability of resources and facilities
- Determining the time phasing of activities
- Determining a breakout of subordinate schedules
- Defining dependencies among activities (predecessor or successor relationships)
- Defining schedule activities and milestones to support project monitoring and control
- Identifying milestones for the delivery of products to the customer
- Defining activities of appropriate duration
- Defining milestones of appropriate time separation
- Defining a management reserve based on the confidence level in meeting the schedule and budget
- Using appropriate historical data to verify the schedule
- Defining incremental funding requirements
- Documenting project assumptions and rationale

---

6. Establish corrective action criteria.

   Criteria are established for determining what constitutes a significant deviation from the project plan. A basis for gauging issues and problems is necessary to determine when corrective action should be taken. Corrective actions may require replanning, which may include revising the original plan, establishing new agreements, or including mitigation activities in the current plan.

   Criteria for corrective action are based on the project objectives identified in the project strategy and are typically stated in terms of process, product, and service level measures. The criteria trace back to specific stakeholder needs and threshold values for project success. The project plan defines when (e.g., under what circumstances, with what frequency) the criteria will be applied and by whom.

SP 2.2 IDENTIFY PROJECT RISKS

Identify and analyze project risks.

Refer to the Monitor Project Risks specific practice in the Project Monitoring and Control process area for more information about risk monitoring activities.

Refer to the Risk Management process area for more information about identifying potential problems before they occur so that risk-handling activities can be planned and invoked as needed across the life of the product or project to mitigate adverse impacts on achieving objectives.

Risks are identified or discovered and analyzed to support project planning. This specific practice should be extended to all plans that affect the project to ensure that appropriate interfacing is taking place among all relevant stakeholders on identified risks.

Project planning risk identification and analysis typically include the following:

- Identifying risks
- Analyzing risks to determine the impact, probability of occurrence, and time frame in which problems are likely to occur
- Prioritizing risks

Typical Work Products

1. Identified risks
2. Risk impacts and probability of occurrence
3. Risk priorities

Subpractices

1. Identify risks.

   The identification of risks involves the identification of potential issues, hazards, threats, vulnerabilities, and so on that could negatively affect work efforts and plans. Risks must be identified and described in an understandable way before they can be analyzed. When identifying risks, it is a good idea to use a standard method for defining risks. Risk identification and analysis tools can be used to help identify possible problems.

Examples of risk identification and analysis tools include the following:

- Risk taxonomies
- Risk assessments
- Checklists
- Structured interviews
- Brainstorming
- Performance models
- Cost models
- Network analysis
- Quality factor analysis

Examples of risks include the following:
- Change of mission
- Change of customer or end user
- Change of project strategy
- Change in the availability of a needed facility
- Equipment, tool, and part obsolescence
- Defects
- Lost skills
- Supplier failures
- Service interruptions

---

2. Document risks.
3. Review and obtain agreement with relevant stakeholders on the completeness and correctness of documented risks.
4. Revise risks as appropriate.

Examples of when identified risks may need to be revised include the following:
- When new risks are identified
- When risks become problems
- When risks are retired
- When project circumstances change significantly

SP 2.3   PLAN DATA MANAGEMENT

Plan for the management of project data.

Data are forms of documentation required to support a project in all of its areas (e.g., administration, engineering, configuration management, finance, logistics, quality, safety, manufacturing, procurement). The data can take any form (e.g., reports, manuals, notebooks, charts, drawings, specifications, files, correspondence). The data may exist in any medium (e.g., printed or drawn on various materials, photographs, electronic, or multimedia).

Data may be deliverable (e.g., items identified by a project's contract data requirements), or data may be nondeliverable (e.g., informal data, trade studies, analyses, internal meeting minutes, internal design review documentation, lessons learned, or action items). Distribution can take many forms, including electronic transmission.

Data requirements for the project should be established for both data items to be created and their content and form, based on a common or standard set of data requirements. Uniform content and format requirements for data items facilitate understanding of data content and help with consistent management of data resources.

The reason for collecting each document should be clear. This task includes the analysis and verification of project deliverables and non-deliverables, data requirements, and customer-supplied data. Often, data are collected with no clear understanding of how they will be used. Data are costly and should be collected only when needed.

Typical Work Products

1. Data management plan
2. Master list of managed data
3. Data content and format description
4. Lists of data requirements for acquirers and suppliers
5. Privacy requirements
6. Security requirements
7. Security procedures
8. Mechanisms for data retrieval, reproduction, and distribution
9. Schedule for the collection of project data
10. List of project data to be collected

Subpractices

1. Establish requirements and procedures to ensure privacy and the security of data.

   Not everyone will have the need or clearance necessary to access project data. Procedures must be established to identify who has access to which data as well as when they have access to which data. Requirements and procedures may cover service staff who will have the responsibility for the security of data under the terms of a service agreement.

2. Establish a mechanism to archive data and to access archived data.

   Accessed information should be in an understandable form (e.g., electronic or computer output from a database) or represented as originally generated.

3. Determine the project data to be identified, collected, and distributed.

4. Determine the requirements for providing access to and distribution of data to stakeholders.

A review of other elements of the project plan may help to determine who requires access to or receipt of project data as well as which data are involved.

5. Decide which project data and plans require version control or more stringent levels of configuration control and establish mechanisms to ensure project data are controlled.

SP 2.4 PLAN THE PROJECT'S RESOURCES

Plan for necessary resources to perform the project.

Defining project resources (e.g., labor, equipment, materials, methods) and quantities needed to perform project activities builds on initial estimates and provides additional information that can be applied to expand the WBS used to manage the project.

The top-level WBS developed earlier as an estimation mechanism is typically expanded by decomposing these top levels into work packages that represent single work units that can be separately assigned, performed, and tracked. This subdivision is done to distribute management responsibility and provide better management control.

Each work package in the WBS should be assigned a unique identifier (e.g., number) to permit tracking. A WBS can be based on requirements, activities, work products, services, or a combination of these items. A dictionary that describes the work for each work package in the WBS should accompany the work breakdown structure.

Typical Work Products

1. Work packages
2. WBS task dictionary
3. Staffing requirements based on project size and scope
4. Critical facilities and equipment list
5. Process and workflow definitions and diagrams
6. Project administration requirements list
7. Status reporting templates

Subpractices

1. Determine process requirements.
   The processes used to manage a project must be identified, defined, and coordinated with all relevant stakeholders to ensure efficient operations during project execution.
2. Determine requirements for communication mechanisms.
   These requirements address the kinds of mechanisms to be used for communicating with customers, end users, service provider personnel,

and other stakeholders during service delivery. Such requirements are derived, in part, from process requirements, service agreements, and the project strategy.

Communication mechanisms may be created during service system development and must be regularly reviewed, tailored, and possibly supplemented to meet ongoing service delivery needs.

> *Refer to the Service System Development process area for more information about developing service systems.* **SSD ADD**

3. Determine staffing requirements.

   The staffing of a project depends on the decomposition of project requirements into tasks, roles, and responsibilities for accomplishing project requirements as laid out in the work packages of the WBS. Staffing requirements must consider the knowledge and skills required for each identified position as defined in the Plan Needed Knowledge and Skills specific practice.

   Refer to the Capacity and Availability Management process area for more information about ensuring effective service system performance and ensuring that resources are provided and used effectively to support service requirements.

4. Determine facility, equipment, and component requirements.

   Most projects are unique in some way and require a set of unique assets to accomplish project objectives. The determination and acquisition of these assets in a timely manner are crucial to project success. It is best to identify lead-time items early to determine how they will be addressed. Even when required assets are not unique, compiling a list of all facilities, equipment, and parts (e.g., number of computers for the personnel working on the project, software applications, office space) provides insight into aspects of the scope of an effort that are often overlooked.

5. Determine other continuing resource requirements.

   Beyond determining processes, reporting templates, staffing, facilities, and equipment, there may be a continuing need for other types of resources to effectively carry out project activities, including the following:

   - Consumables (e.g., electricity, office supplies)
   - Access to intellectual property
   - Access to transportation (for people and equipment)

   The requirements for such resources are derived from the requirements found in (existing and future) agreements (e.g., customer agreements, service agreements, supplier agreements), the project's strategic approach, and the need to manage and maintain the project's operations for a period of time.

SP 2.5 *PLAN NEEDED KNOWLEDGE AND SKILLS*

Plan for knowledge and skills needed to perform the project.

Refer to the Organizational Training process area for more information about developing skills and knowledge of people so that they perform their roles effectively and efficiently.

Knowledge delivery to projects involves training project personnel and acquiring knowledge from outside sources.

Staffing requirements are dependent on the knowledge and skills available to support the execution of the project.

Planning for training addresses the knowledge and skills required by project members and support personnel to perform their tasks. Knowledge and skill needs can be derived from project risk.

> For example, if the project is providing a service whose successful delivery requires detailed familiarity with a piece of complicated equipment, planning for training ensures that personnel assigned to the project have the appropriate expertise with such equipment or provides training for the project team in those areas.

Training can also include orientation in the project's processes and the domain knowledge required to execute project tasks. The project may also identify and plan for the knowledge and skills needed by its suppliers. Planning includes ensuring that costs and funding sources to pay for training are available and lead times are sufficient to obtain funding and training.

For long-duration and continuous-operation projects, the knowledge and skills needed will evolve as the following occur:

- Project personnel rotate in and out of the project (or from one service type to another)
- The technology used in the service system or an individual service changes
- The processes and technology used in the development or customer environments change

> For example, a change in project personnel creates the need to determine the knowledge and skills needed by new project members. New knowledge and skills are needed during different phases of the project (or as new services or service levels are added). Planning for needed knowledge and skills should address these sources of change.

Refer to the Service System Transition process area for more information about preparing for service system transition and preparing stakeholders for changes.

Typical Work Products

1. Inventory of skill needs
2. Staffing and new-hire plans
3. Databases (e.g., skills, training)
4. Training plans

Subpractices

1. Identify the knowledge and skills needed to perform the project.
2. Assess the knowledge and skills available.
3. Select mechanisms for providing needed knowledge and skills.

Example mechanisms include the following:
- In-house training (both organizational and project)
- External training
- Staffing and new hires
- External skill acquisition

> The choice of in-house training or outsourced training for needed knowledge and skills is determined by the availability of training expertise, the project's schedule, and business objectives.

4. Incorporate selected mechanisms into the project plan.

SP 2.6 PLAN STAKEHOLDER INVOLVEMENT

Plan the involvement of identified stakeholders.

Stakeholders are identified from all phases of the project lifecycle by identifying the people and functions that should be represented in the project and describing their relevance and the degree of interaction for project activities. A two-dimensional matrix with stakeholders along one axis and project activities along the other axis is a convenient format for accomplishing this identification. Relevance of the stakeholder to the activity in a particular project phase and the amount of interaction expected would be shown at the intersection of the project phase activity axis and the stakeholder axis.

For inputs of stakeholders to be useful, careful selection of relevant stakeholders is necessary. For each major activity, identify stakeholders who are affected by the activity and those who have expertise that is needed to conduct the activity. This list of relevant stakeholders will probably change as the project moves through phases of the project lifecycle. It is important, however, to ensure that relevant stakeholders in the latter phases of the lifecycle have early input to requirements and design decisions that affect them.

Example relevant stakeholders may include project members, management, suppliers, customers, end users, the organization's product line team, and other providers of related products and services with which the project must coordinate.

Refer to the Service Delivery process area for more information about establishing service agreements.

Examples of the type of material that should be included in a plan for stakeholder interaction include the following:
- List of all relevant stakeholders
- Rationale for stakeholder involvement
- Roles and responsibilities of relevant stakeholders with respect to the project by project lifecycle phase
- Relationships among stakeholders
- Relative importance of the stakeholder to the success of the project by project lifecycle phase
- Resources (e.g., training, materials, time, funding) needed to ensure stakeholder interaction
- Schedule for the phasing of stakeholder interaction

Implementing this specific practice relies on shared or exchanged information with the previous Plan Needed Knowledge and Skills specific practice.

Typical Work Products

1. Stakeholder involvement plan

SP 2.7 ESTABLISH THE PROJECT PLAN

Establish and maintain the overall project plan.

A documented plan that addresses all relevant planning items is necessary to achieve the mutual understanding, commitment, and performance of individuals, groups, and organizations that must execute or support the plans.

The plan generated for the project defines all aspects of the effort, tying together the following in a logical manner:

- Project lifecycle considerations
- Project tasks
- Budgets and schedules
- Milestones
- Data management
- Risk identification
- Resource and skill requirements
- Stakeholder identification and interaction

Infrastructure descriptions include responsibility and authority relationships for project staff, management, and support organizations.

Typical Work Products

1. Overall project plan

Subpractices

1. Document the project plan.

    Projects may consist of other, lower level projects. A project may consist of a service system development project and a service delivery project. A service delivery project may consist of several services that may benefit from separate planning and the practices of this process area. See the introductory notes for additional comments about the applicability of the specific practices in this process area to projects. When projects consist of other projects, the overall project plan should include or reference the project plans of the lower level projects, and all related plans should be compatible and appropriately support one another.

2. Include, reference, and reconcile the results of planning activities as appropriate.

    To gain the support of relevant stakeholders, the project plan should document a realistic and sensible approach to meeting their needs, expectations, and constraints. Such a plan requires various planning elements to be reasonably complete and consistent (at least until the next plan revision, which may be weeks or months away).

    If implemented appropriately, the specific practices of this process area address the Plan the Process generic practice as applied to other project-related process areas within the scope of the process improvement effort, but otherwise the results of implementing that generic practice should also be considered in this subpractice.

3. Review the project plan with relevant stakeholders and get their agreement.

The specific practices of the next specific goal, Obtain Commitment to the Plan, describe activities to help ensure the project plan describes a realistic approach for meeting the needs, expectations, and constraints of relevant stakeholders and to help ensure that these relevant stakeholders will fulfill their roles as described in the project plan, including the provision of resources and other forms of support during project execution.

4. Revise the project plan as necessary.

In general, when revising the project plan, it may be necessary to repeat many of the planning activities described in this process area to help ensure that relevant stakeholder commitments to the plan are maintained.

SG 3 OBTAIN COMMITMENT TO THE PLAN

Commitments to the project plan are established and maintained.

To be effective, plans require commitment by those responsible for implementing and supporting the plan.

SP 3.1 REVIEW PLANS THAT AFFECT THE PROJECT

Review all plans that affect the project to understand project commitments.

Plans developed in other process areas typically contain information similar to that called for in the overall project plan. These plans may provide additional detailed guidance and should be compatible with and support the overall project plan to indicate who has the authority, responsibility, accountability, and control. All plans that affect the project should be reviewed to ensure that they contain a common understanding of the scope, objectives, roles, and relationships that are required for the project to be successful. Many of these plans are described by the Plan the Process generic practice.

Typical Work Products

1. Record of the reviews of plans that affect the project

SP 3.2 RECONCILE WORK AND RESOURCE LEVELS

Adjust the project plan to reconcile available and estimated resources.

To establish a project that is feasible, obtain commitment from relevant stakeholders and reconcile differences between estimates and available resources. Reconciliation is typically accomplished by modifying or deferring requirements, negotiating more resources, finding ways to increase productivity, outsourcing, adjusting the staff skill mix, or revising all plans that affect the project or its schedules.

Typical Work Products

1. Revised methods and corresponding estimating parameters (e.g., better tools, the use of off-the-shelf components)
2. Renegotiated budgets
3. Revised schedules
4. Revised requirements list
5. Renegotiated stakeholder agreements

SP 3.3 OBTAIN PLAN COMMITMENT

Obtain commitment from relevant stakeholders responsible for performing and supporting plan execution.

Obtaining commitment involves interaction among all relevant stakeholders, both internal and external to the project. The individual or group making a commitment should have confidence that the work can be performed within cost, schedule, and performance constraints. Often, a provisional commitment is adequate to allow the effort to begin and to permit research to be performed to increase confidence to the appropriate level needed to obtain a full commitment.

Typical Work Products

1. Documented requests for commitments
2. Documented commitments

Subpractices

1. Identify needed support and negotiate commitments with relevant stakeholders.

   The WBS can be used as a checklist for ensuring that commitments are obtained for all tasks.

   The plan for stakeholder interaction should identify all parties from whom commitment should be obtained.

2. Document all organizational commitments, both full and provisional, ensuring the appropriate level of signatories.

   Commitments must be documented to ensure a consistent mutual understanding and for project tracking and maintenance. Provisional commitments should be accompanied by a description of risks associated with the relationship.

3. Review internal commitments with senior management as appropriate.

4. Review external commitments with senior management as appropriate.

   Management may have the necessary insight and authority to reduce risks associated with external commitments.

5. Identify commitments regarding interfaces between project elements and other projects and organizational units so that these commitments can be monitored.

   Well-defined interface specifications form the basis for commitments.

PROCESS AND PRODUCT QUALITY ASSURANCE
A Support Process Area at Maturity Level 2

Purpose

The purpose of Process and Product Quality Assurance (PPQA) is to provide staff and management with objective insight into processes and associated work products.

Introductory Notes

The Process and Product Quality Assurance process area involves the following activities:

- Objectively evaluating performed processes and work products against applicable process descriptions, standards, and procedures
- Identifying and documenting noncompliance issues
- Providing feedback to project staff and managers on the results of quality assurance activities
- Ensuring that noncompliance issues are addressed

The Process and Product Quality Assurance process area supports the delivery of high-quality products by providing project staff and managers at all levels with appropriate visibility into, and feedback on, processes and associated work products throughout the life of the project.

The practices in the Process and Product Quality Assurance process area ensure that planned processes are implemented, while the practices in the Service System Development process area ensure that specified requirements are satisfied. These two process areas may on occasion address the same work product but from different perspectives. Projects should take advantage of the overlap to minimize duplication of effort while taking care to maintain separate perspectives.

PPQA

Objectivity in process and product quality assurance evaluations is critical to the success of the project. (See the definition of "objectively evaluate" in the glossary.) Objectivity is achieved by both independence and the use of criteria. A combination of methods providing evaluations against criteria by those not producing the work product is often used. Less formal methods can be used to provide broad day-to-day coverage. More formal methods can be used periodically to ensure objectivity.

Examples of ways to perform objective evaluations include the following:
- Formal audits by organizationally separate quality assurance organizations
- Peer reviews, which may be performed at various levels of formality
- In-depth review of work at the place it is performed (i.e., desk audits)
- Distributed review and comment of work products

Traditionally, a quality assurance group that is independent of the project provides objectivity. However, another approach may be appropriate in some organizations to implement the process and product quality assurance role without that kind of independence.

For example, in an organization with an open, quality-oriented culture, the process and product quality assurance role may be performed, partially or completely, by peers, and the quality assurance function may be embedded in the process. For small organizations, this embedded approach might be the most feasible approach.

If quality assurance is embedded in the process, several issues must be addressed to ensure objectivity. Everyone performing quality assurance activities should be trained. Those performing quality assurance activities for a work product should be separate from those directly involved in developing or maintaining the work product. An independent reporting channel to the appropriate level of organizational management must be available so that noncompliance issues can be escalated as necessary.

> For example, when implementing peer reviews as an objective evaluation method, the following issues must be addressed:
> - Members are trained and roles are assigned for people attending the peer reviews.
> - A member of the peer review who did not produce this work product is assigned to perform the quality assurance role.
> - Checklists are available to support the quality assurance activity.
> - Defects are recorded as part of the peer review report and are tracked and escalated outside the project when necessary.

Quality assurance should begin in the early phases of a project to establish plans, processes, standards, and procedures that will add value to the project and satisfy the requirements of the project and organizational policies. Those performing quality assurance participate in establishing plans, processes, standards, and procedures to ensure that they fit project needs and that they will be usable for performing quality assurance evaluations. In addition, processes and associated work products to be evaluated during the project are designated. This designation may be based on sampling or on objective criteria that are consistent with organizational policies, project requirements, and project needs.

When noncompliance issues are identified, they are first addressed in the project and resolved there if possible. Noncompliance issues that cannot be resolved in the project are escalated to an appropriate level of management for resolution.

This process area applies primarily to evaluations of project activities and work products, but it also applies to other activities and work products, such as training organizational support groups. For these activities and work products, the term "project" should be appropriately interpreted.

Related Process Areas

Refer to the Service System Development process area for more information about verifying selected service system components against their specified requirements.

SSD ADD

PPQA

Specific Goal and Practice Summary

SG 1 Objectively Evaluate Processes and Work Products
    SP 1.1   Objectively Evaluate Processes
    SP 1.2   Objectively Evaluate Work Products
SG 2 Provide Objective Insight
    SP 2.1   Communicate and Ensure the Resolution of Noncompliance Issues
    SP 2.2   Establish Records

Specific Practices by Goal

SG 1   OBJECTIVELY EVALUATE PROCESSES AND WORK PRODUCTS

Adherence of the performed process and associated work products to applicable process descriptions, standards, and procedures is objectively evaluated.

SP 1.1 OBJECTIVELY EVALUATE PROCESSES

Objectively evaluate designated performed processes against applicable process descriptions, standards, and procedures.

Objectivity in quality assurance evaluations is critical to the success of the project. A description of the quality assurance reporting chain and how it ensures objectivity should be defined.

Typical Work Products

1. Evaluation reports
2. Noncompliance reports
3. Corrective actions

Subpractices

1. Promote an environment (created as part of project management) that encourages employee participation in identifying and reporting quality issues.
2. Establish and maintain clearly stated criteria for evaluations.
    The intent of this subpractice is to provide criteria, based on business needs such as the following:
    • What will be evaluated
    • When or how often a process will be evaluated
    • How the evaluation will be conducted
    • Who must be involved in the evaluation
3. Use the stated criteria to evaluate performed processes for adherence to process descriptions, standards, and procedures.

4. Identify each noncompliance found during the evaluation.

5. Identify lessons learned that could improve processes for future products.

SP 1.2 OBJECTIVELY EVALUATE WORK PRODUCTS

Objectively evaluate designated work products against applicable process descriptions, standards, and procedures.

Typical Work Products

1. Evaluation reports
2. Noncompliance reports
3. Corrective actions

Subpractices

1. Select work products to be evaluated based on documented sampling criteria if sampling is used.

   Work products may include services produced by a process whether the recipient of the service is internal or external to the project or organization.

2. Establish and maintain clearly stated criteria for the evaluation of selected work products.

   The intent of this subpractice is to provide criteria, based on business needs, such as the following:
   - What will be evaluated during the evaluation of a work product
   - When or how often a work product will be evaluated
   - How the evaluation will be conducted
   - Who must be involved in the evaluation

3. Use the stated criteria during evaluations of selected work products.

4. Evaluate selected work products at selected periods in their lifetime as appropriate, including before and during delivery to the customer.

5. Perform in-progress or incremental evaluations of selected work products against process descriptions, standards, and procedures.

   If a service to be evaluated has a process description, then SP 1.1 covers the evaluation of that service against its process description. This specific practice would then instead focus on the service itself—its results, its impacts, etc.

6. Identify each case of noncompliance found during evaluations.

7. Identify lessons learned that could improve processes for future products.

PPQA

SG 2 *Provide Objective Insight*

Noncompliance issues are objectively tracked and communicated, and resolution is ensured.

SP 2.1 *Communicate and Ensure the Resolution of Noncompliance Issues*

Communicate quality issues and ensure the resolution of noncompliance issues with the staff and managers.

Noncompliance issues are problems identified in evaluations that reflect a lack of adherence to applicable standards, process descriptions, or procedures. The status of noncompliance issues provides an indication of quality trends. Quality issues include noncompliance issues and trend analysis results.

When noncompliance issues cannot be resolved in the project, use established escalation mechanisms to ensure that the appropriate level of management can resolve the issue. Track noncompliance issues to resolution.

Typical Work Products

1. Corrective action reports
2. Evaluation reports
3. Quality trends

Subpractices

1. Resolve each noncompliance with the appropriate members of the staff if possible.
2. Document noncompliance issues when they cannot be resolved in the project.

> Examples of ways to resolve a noncompliance in the project include the following:
> - Fixing the noncompliance
> - Changing the process descriptions, standards, or procedures that were violated
> - Obtaining a waiver to cover the noncompliance

3. Escalate noncompliance issues that cannot be resolved in the project to the appropriate level of management designated to receive and act on noncompliance issues.
4. Analyze noncompliance issues to see if there are quality trends that can be identified and addressed.

5. Ensure that relevant stakeholders are aware of results of evaluations and quality trends in a timely manner.

6. Periodically review open noncompliance issues and trends with the manager designated to receive and act on noncompliance issues.

7. Track noncompliance issues to resolution.

SP 2.2 ESTABLISH RECORDS

Establish and maintain records of quality assurance activities.

Typical Work Products

1. Evaluation logs
2. Quality assurance reports
3. Status reports of corrective actions
4. Reports of quality trends

Subpractices

1. Record process and product quality assurance activities in sufficient detail so that status and results are known.

2. Revise the status and history of quality assurance activities as necessary.

QUANTITATIVE PROJECT MANAGEMENT
A Project Management Process Area at Maturity Level 4

Purpose

The purpose of Quantitative Project Management (QPM) is to quantitatively manage the project's defined process to achieve the project's established quality and process-performance objectives.

IN OTHER WORDS

QPM is about managing service to quantitative process and performance objectives.

Introductory Notes

The Quantitative Project Management process area involves the following activities:

WHY DO THE PRACTICES IN QPM?

You have confidence in your estimates and your ability to predict service performance. You make the most of all the measurement you do to understand variations in your performance and take the right corrective actions when needed.

- Establishing and maintaining the project's quality and process-performance objectives
- Identifying suitable subprocesses that compose the project's defined process based on historical stability and capability data found in process-performance baselines or models
- Selecting subprocesses within the project's defined process to be statistically managed
- Monitoring the project to determine whether the project's objectives for quality and process performance are being satisfied and to identify appropriate corrective action
- Selecting measures and analytic techniques to be used in statistically managing selected subprocesses
- Establishing and maintaining an understanding of the variation of selected subprocesses using selected measures and analytic techniques
- Monitoring the performance of selected subprocesses to determine whether they are capable of satisfying their quality and process-performance objectives, and identifying corrective action
- Recording statistical and quality management data in the organization's measurement repository

QPM

The quality and process-performance objectives, measures, and baselines identified here are developed as described in the Organizational Process Performance process area. Subsequently, the results of performing the processes associated with the Quantitative Project Management process area (e.g., measures, measurement data) become part of the organizational process assets referred to in the Organizational Process Performance process area.

To effectively address the specific practices in this process area, the organization must have already established a set of standard processes and related organizational process assets, such as the organization's measurement repository and the organization's process asset library for use by each project in establishing its defined process.

The project's defined process is a set of subprocesses that form an integrated and coherent framework for project activities. It is established, in part, through selecting and tailoring processes from the organization's set of standard processes. (See the definition of "defined process" in the glossary.)

The project should ensure that supplier effort and progress measurements are made available. Establishing effective relationships with suppliers is also important to the successful implementation of this process area's specific practices.

Process performance is a measure of actual process results achieved. Process performance is characterized by both process measures (e.g., effort, cycle time, defect removal efficiency) and product measures (e.g., reliability, defect density, response time).

Subprocesses are defined components of a larger defined process. For example, a typical organization's service system development process may be defined in terms of subprocesses, such as requirements development, design, build, test, and peer review. The subprocesses themselves may be further decomposed as necessary into other subprocesses and process elements.

An essential element of quantitative management is having confidence in estimates (i.e., being able to predict the extent to which the project can fulfill its quality and process-performance objectives). Subprocesses to be statistically managed are chosen based on identified needs for predictable performance. (See the definitions of "statistically managed process," "quality and process-performance objectives," and "quantitatively managed process" in the glossary.)

Another essential element of quantitative management is understanding the nature and extent of the variation experienced in process performance and recognizing when the project's actual performance may not be adequate to achieve the project's quality and process-performance objectives.

Statistical management involves statistical thinking and the correct use of a variety of statistical techniques, such as run charts, control charts, confidence intervals, prediction intervals, and tests of hypotheses. Quantitative management uses data from statistical management to help the project predict whether it will be able to achieve its quality and process-performance objectives and identify what corrective action should be taken.

This process area applies to managing a project, but the concepts found here also apply to managing other groups and functions. Applying these concepts to managing other groups and functions may not necessarily contribute to achieving the organization's business objectives but may help these groups and functions control their processes.

Examples of other groups and functions that could benefit from using this process area include the following:
- Quality assurance
- Process definition and improvement
- Effort reporting
- Customer complaint handling
- Problem tracking and reporting

Related Process Areas

Refer to the Capacity and Availability Management process area for more information about ensuring effective service system performance and ensuring that resources are provided and used effectively to support service requirements.

Refer to the Strategic Service Management process area for more information about establishing and maintaining standard services in concert with strategic needs and plans.

Refer to the Causal Analysis and Resolution process area for more information about identifying causes of defects and problems and taking action to prevent them from occurring in the future.

Refer to the Integrated Project Management process area for more information about establishing and maintaining the project's defined process.

Refer to the Measurement and Analysis process area for more information about aligning measurement and analysis activities and providing measurement results.

QPM

Refer to the Organizational Innovation and Deployment process area for more information about selecting and deploying incremental and innovative improvements that measurably improve the organization's processes and technologies.

Refer to the Organizational Process Definition process area for more information about establishing organizational process assets.

Refer to the Organizational Process Performance process area for more information about establishing and maintaining a quantitative understanding of the performance of the organization's set of standard processes in support of achieving quality and process-performance objectives, and to provide process-performance data, baselines, and models to quantitatively manage the organization's projects.

Refer to the Project Monitoring and Control process area for more information about monitoring and controlling the project and taking corrective action.

Specific Goal and Practice Summary

SG 1 Quantitatively Manage the Project

    SP 1.1   Establish the Project's Objectives

    SP 1.2   Compose the Defined Process

    SP 1.3   Select Subprocesses to Be Statistically Managed

    SP 1.4   Manage Project Performance

SG 2 Statistically Manage Subprocess Performance

    SP 2.1   Select Measures and Analytic Techniques

    SP 2.2   Apply Statistical Methods to Understand Variation

    SP 2.3   Monitor the Performance of Selected Subprocesses

    SP 2.4   Record Statistical Management Data

Specific Practices by Goal

SG 1   QUANTITATIVELY MANAGE THE PROJECT

The project is quantitatively managed using quality and process-performance objectives.

SP 1.1 ESTABLISH THE PROJECT'S OBJECTIVES

Establish and maintain the project's quality and process-performance objectives.

When establishing the project's quality and process-performance objectives, it is often useful to think ahead about which processes from the organization's set of standard processes will be included in the project's defined process and what the historical data indicate regarding their process performance. These considerations will help in establishing realistic objectives for the project. Later, as the project's actual performance becomes known and more predictable, objectives may need to be revised.

Typical Work Products

1. The project's quality and process-performance objectives

Subpractices

1. Review the organization's objectives for quality and process performance.

   The intent of this review is to ensure that the project understands the broader business context in which the project must operate. The project's objectives for quality and process performance are developed in the context of these overarching organizational objectives.

   Refer to the Organizational Process Performance process area for more information about establishing quality and process-performance objectives.

2. Identify the quality and process-performance needs and priorities of the customer, suppliers, end users, and other relevant stakeholders.

> Examples of quality and process-performance attributes for which needs and priorities might be identified include the following:
> - Duration
> - Response time
> - Availability
> - Reliability
> - Service continuity
> - Predictability

3. Identify how quality and process performance is to be measured.

   Consider whether measures established by the organization are adequate for assessing progress in fulfilling customer, end-user, and other stakeholder needs and priorities. It may be necessary to supplement these measures with additional ones.

> Examples of measurable quality attributes include the following:
> - Mean time between failures
> - Number and severity of customer complaints
> - Availability
> - Response time (of service performance)

Examples of measurable process-performance attributes include the following:

- Cycle time
- Percentage of rework time
- Compliance to service level agreements

> *Refer to the Measurement and Analysis process area for more information about specifying measures.*

4. Define and document measurable quality and process-performance objectives for the project.

   Defining and documenting objectives for the project involve the following:

   - Incorporating the organization's quality and process-performance objectives
   - Writing objectives that reflect the quality and process-performance needs and priorities of the customer, end users, and other stakeholders and the way these objectives should be measured

5. Derive interim objectives for each lifecycle phase as appropriate to monitor progress toward achieving the project's objectives.

An example of a method to predict future results of a process is the use of process-performance models to predict latent defects in the delivered product using interim measures of defects identified during product verification activities (e.g., peer reviews, testing).

---

6. Resolve conflicts among the project's quality and process-performance objectives (e.g., if one objective cannot be achieved without compromising another).

   Resolving conflicts involves the following activities:

   - Setting relative priorities for objectives
   - Considering alternative objectives in light of long-term business strategies as well as short-term needs
   - Involving the customer, end users, senior management, project management, and other relevant stakeholders in tradeoff decisions
   - Revising objectives as necessary to reflect results of conflict resolution

7. Establish traceability to the project's quality and process-performance objectives from their sources.

Examples of sources of objectives include the following:
- Requirements
- The organization's quality and process-performance objectives
- The customer's quality and process-performance objectives
- Business objectives
- Discussions with customers and potential customers
- Market surveys

An example of a method to identify and trace these needs and priorities is Quality Function Deployment (QFD).

8. Define and negotiate quality and process-performance objectives for suppliers.

   Refer to the Supplier Agreement Management process area for more information about establishing supplier agreements.

9. Revise the project's quality and process-performance objectives as necessary.

SP 1.2 COMPOSE THE DEFINED PROCESS

Select subprocesses that compose the project's defined process based on historical stability and capability data.

Refer to the Integrated Project Management process area for more information about establishing and maintaining the project's defined process.

Refer to the Organizational Process Definition process area for more information about the organization's process asset library.

Refer to the Organizational Process Performance process area for more information about establishing performance baselines and models.

Subprocesses are identified from process elements in the organization's set of standard processes and process artifacts in the organization's process asset library.

Typical Work Products

1. Criteria used to identify which subprocesses are valid candidates for inclusion in the project's defined process
2. Candidate subprocesses for inclusion in the project's defined process
3. Subprocesses to be included in the project's defined process
4. Identified risks when selected subprocesses lack a process-performance history

Subpractices

1. Establish the criteria to use in identifying which subprocesses are valid candidates for use.

> Identification may be based on the following:
> - Quality and process-performance objectives
> - Existence of process-performance data
> - Product line standards
> - Project lifecycle models
> - Stakeholder requirements
> - Laws and regulations

2. Determine whether subprocesses that are to be statistically managed and were obtained from organizational process assets are suitable for statistical management.

   A subprocess may be more suitable for statistical management if it has a history of the following:
   - Stable performance in previous comparable instances
   - Process-performance data that satisfy the project's quality and process-performance objectives

   Historical data are primarily obtained from the organization's process-performance baselines. However, these data may not be available for all subprocesses.

3. Analyze the interaction of subprocesses to understand relationships among subprocesses and measured attributes of the subprocesses.

> Examples of analysis techniques include system dynamics models and simulations.

4. Identify the risk when no subprocess is available that is known to be capable of satisfying quality and process-performance objectives (i.e., no capable subprocess is available or the capability of the subprocess is not known).

   Even when a subprocess has not been selected to be statistically managed, historical data and process-performance models may indicate that the subprocess is not capable of satisfying quality and process-performance objectives.

   Refer to the Risk Management process area for more information about identifying and analyzing risks.

SP 1.3 SELECT SUBPROCESSES TO BE STATISTICALLY MANAGED

Select subprocesses of the project's defined process to be statistically managed.

Selecting subprocesses to be statistically managed is often a concurrent and iterative process of identifying applicable project and organization quality and process-performance objectives, selecting subprocesses, and identifying process and product attributes to measure and control. Often the selection of a process, quality and process-performance objective, or measurable attribute will constrain the selection of the other two. For example, if a particular process is selected, measurable attributes and quality and process-performance objectives may be constrained by that process.

Typical Work Products

1. Quality and process-performance objectives to be addressed by statistical management
2. Criteria used to select which subprocesses will be statistically managed
3. Subprocesses to be statistically managed
4. Identified process and product attributes of selected subprocesses that should be measured and controlled

Subpractices

1. Identify which of the project's quality and process-performance objectives will be statistically managed.
2. Identify criteria to be used in selecting subprocesses that are the main contributors to achieving identified quality and process-performance objectives and for which predictable performance is important.

> Examples of sources for criteria used in selecting subprocesses include the following:
> - Stakeholder requirements related to quality and process performance
> - Quality and process-performance objectives established by the customer
> - Quality and process-performance objectives established by the organization
> - The organization's performance baselines and models
> - Stable performance of the subprocess on other projects
> - Laws and regulations

3. Select subprocesses to be statistically managed using selection criteria.

> It may not be possible to statistically manage some subprocesses (e.g., where new subprocesses and technologies are being piloted). In other cases, it may not be economically justifiable to apply statistical techniques to certain subprocesses.

4. Identify product and process attributes of selected subprocesses to be measured and controlled.

Examples of product and process attributes include the following:
- Percentage compliance to the service level agreement
- Response time

SP 1.4 MANAGE PROJECT PERFORMANCE

Monitor the project to determine whether the project's objectives for quality and process performance will be satisfied, and identify corrective action as appropriate.

Refer to the Measurement and Analysis process area for more information about obtaining and analyzing measurement data.

A prerequisite for such a determination is that the selected subprocesses of the project's defined process are statistically managed and their process capability is understood. Specific practices of specific goal 2 provide detail on statistically managing selected subprocesses.

Typical Work Products

1. Estimates (i.e., predictions) of the achievement of the project's quality and process-performance objectives
2. Documentation of risks in achieving the project's quality and process-performance objectives
3. Documentation of actions needed to address deficiencies in achieving project objectives

Subpractices

1. Periodically review the performance and capability of each subprocess selected to be statistically managed to appraise progress toward achieving the project's quality and process-performance objectives.

The process capability of each selected subprocess is determined with respect to that subprocess' established quality and process-performance objectives. These objectives are derived from the project's quality and process-performance objectives, which are defined for the project as a whole.

2. Periodically review actual results achieved against established interim objectives for each phase of the project lifecycle to appraise progress toward achieving the project's quality and process-performance objectives.

3. Track supplier results for achieving their quality and process-performance objectives.

4. Use process-performance models calibrated with obtained measures of critical attributes to estimate progress toward achieving the project's quality and process-performance objectives.

    Process-performance models are used to estimate progress toward achieving objectives that cannot be measured until a future phase in the project lifecycle. An example is the use of process-performance models to forecast frequency of downtime using interim measures of mean time to repair.

    Refer to the Organizational Process Performance process area for more information about establishing process-performance models.

    Calibration of process-performance models is based on the results obtained from performing the previous subpractices.

5. Identify and manage risks associated with achieving the project's quality and process-performance objectives.

    Refer to the Risk Management process area for more information about identifying, analyzing, and mitigating risks.

Example sources of risks include the following:
- Inadequate stability and capability data in the organization's measurement repository
- Subprocesses having inadequate performance or capability
- Suppliers not achieving their quality and process-performance objectives
- Lack of visibility into supplier capability
- Inaccuracies in the organization's process-performance models for predicting future performance
- Deficiencies in predicted process performance (estimated progress)
- Other identified risks associated with identified deficiencies

---

6. Determine and document actions needed to address deficiencies in achieving the project's quality and process-performance objectives.

QPM

The intent of these actions is to plan and deploy the right set of activities, resources, and schedule to place the project back on a path toward achieving its objectives.

Examples of actions that can be taken to address deficiencies in achieving the project's objectives include the following:

- Changing quality and process-performance objectives so that they are within the expected range of the project's defined process
- Improving the implementation of the project's defined process to reduce its normal variability (Reducing variability may bring the project's performance within the objectives without having to move the mean.)
- Adopting new subprocesses and technologies that have the potential for satisfying objectives and managing associated risks
- Identifying the risk and risk mitigation strategies for deficiencies
- Terminating the project

Refer to the Project Monitoring and Control process area for more information about managing corrective action to closure.

SG 2 STATISTICALLY MANAGE SUBPROCESS PERFORMANCE

The performance of selected subprocesses within the project's defined process is statistically managed.

This specific goal describes an activity critical to achieving the Quantitatively Manage the Project specific goal of this process area. The specific practices under this specific goal describe how to statistically manage subprocesses whose selection was described in specific practices under specific goal 1. When selected subprocesses are statistically managed, their capability to achieve their objectives can be determined. By these means, it is possible to predict whether the project will be able to achieve its objectives, which is crucial to quantitatively managing the project.

SP 2.1 SELECT MEASURES AND ANALYTIC TECHNIQUES

Select measures and analytic techniques to be used in statistically managing selected subprocesses.

Refer to the Measurement and Analysis process area for more information about aligning measurement and analysis activities and providing measurement results.

Typical Work Products

1. Definitions of measures and analytic techniques to be used to statistically manage subprocesses
2. Operational definitions of measures, their collection points in subprocesses, and how the integrity of measures will be determined
3. Traceability of measures back to the project's quality and process-performance objectives
4. Instrumented organizational support environment that supports automatic data collection

Subpractices

1. Identify common measures from the organizational process assets that support statistical management.

   Refer to the Organizational Process Definition process area for more information about defining a common set of process and product measures for the organization's set of standard processes.

   Refer to the Organizational Process Performance process area for more information about common measures.

   Product lines or other stratification criteria may categorize common measures.

2. Identify additional measures that may be needed for this instance to cover critical product and process attributes of the selected subprocesses.

   In some cases, measures may be research oriented. Such measures should be explicitly identified.

3. Identify the measures that are appropriate for statistical management.

   Critical criteria for selecting statistical management measures include the following:
   - Controllable (e.g., Can a measure's values be changed by changing how the subprocess is implemented?)
   - Adequate performance indicator (e.g., Is the measure a good indicator of how well the subprocess is performing relative to the objectives of interest?)

Examples of subprocess measures include the following:
- Requirements volatility
- Ratios of estimated to measured values of planning parameters (e.g., size, cost, schedule)
- Effectiveness of training (e.g., percent of planned training completed, test scores)

QPM

4. Specify the operational definitions of measures, their collection points in subprocesses, and how the integrity of measures will be determined.

Operational definitions are stated in precise and unambiguous terms. They address two important criteria:
- Communication: What has been measured, how it was measured, what are the units of measure, and what has been included or excluded?
- Repeatability: Can the measurement be repeated, given the same definition, to get the same results?

5. Analyze the relationship of identified measures to the objectives of the organization and its projects, and derive objectives that state target measures or ranges to be met for each measured attribute of each selected subprocess.

6. Instrument the organizational or project support environment to support collection, derivation, and analysis of statistical measures.

This instrumentation is based on the following:
- Description of the organization's set of standard processes
- Description of the project's defined process
- Capabilities of the organizational or project support environment

7. Identify appropriate statistical analysis techniques that are expected to be useful in statistically managing the selected subprocesses.

The concept of *one size fits all* does not apply to statistical analysis techniques. What makes a particular technique appropriate is not just the type of measures but, more important, how the measures will be used and whether the situation warrants applying that technique. The appropriateness of the selection may need to be reviewed from time to time.

Examples of statistical analysis techniques are given in the next specific practice.

8. Revise measures and statistical analysis techniques as necessary.

SP 2.2 APPLY STATISTICAL METHODS TO UNDERSTAND VARIATION

Establish and maintain an understanding of the variation of selected subprocesses using selected measures and analytic techniques.

Refer to the Measurement and Analysis process area for more information about aligning measurement and analysis activities and providing measurement results.

Understanding variation is achieved, in part, by collecting and analyzing process and product measures so that special causes of variation can be identified and addressed to achieve predictable performance.

A special cause of process variation is characterized by an unexpected change in process performance. Special causes are also known as "assignable causes" because they can be identified, analyzed, and addressed to prevent recurrence.

The identification of special causes of variation is based on departures from the system of common causes of variation. These departures can be identified by the presence of extreme values or other identifiable patterns in data collected from the subprocess or associated work products. Typically, knowledge of variation and insight about potential sources of anomalous patterns is needed to detect special causes of variation.

Sources of anomalous patterns of variation may include the following:
- Lack of process compliance
- Undistinguished influences of multiple underlying subprocesses on the data
- Ordering or timing of activities within the subprocess
- Uncontrolled inputs to the subprocess
- Environmental changes during subprocess execution
- Schedule pressure
- Inappropriate sampling or grouping of data

Typical Work Products

1. Collected measurements
2. Natural bounds of process performance for each measured attribute of each selected subprocess
3. Process performance compared to the natural bounds of process performance for each measured attribute of each selected subprocess

Subpractices

1. Establish trial natural bounds for subprocesses having suitable historical performance data.

   Refer to the Organizational Process Performance process area for more information about establishing process-performance baselines.

   Natural bounds of an attribute are the range within which variation normally occurs. All processes show some variation in process and product measures each time they are executed. The issue is whether this variation is due to common causes of variation in the normal performance of the process or to some special cause that can and should be identified and removed.

When a subprocess is initially executed, suitable data for establishing trial natural bounds are sometimes available from prior instances of the subprocess or comparable subprocesses, process-performance baselines, or process-performance models. Typically, these data are contained in the organization's measurement repository. As the subprocess is executed, data specific to that instance are collected and used to update and replace the trial natural bounds. However, if the subprocess has been materially tailored or if conditions are materially different from those in previous instantiations, data in the repository may not be relevant and should not be used.

In some cases, there may be no comparable historical data (e.g., when introducing a new subprocess, when entering a new application domain, when significant changes have been made to the subprocess). In such cases, trial natural bounds will have to be made from early process data of this subprocess. These trial natural bounds must then be refined and updated as subprocess execution continues.

Examples of criteria for determining whether data are comparable include the following:
- Standard services and service lines
- Application domain
- Work product and task attributes
- Service system attributes (e.g., size, complexity, number of stakeholders)

---

2. Collect data, as defined by selected measures, on subprocesses as they execute.
3. Calculate the natural bounds of process performance for each measured attribute.

Examples of statistical techniques for calculating natural bounds include the following:
- Control charts
- Confidence intervals (for parameters of distributions)
- Prediction intervals (for future outcomes)

---

4. Identify special causes of variation.

An example of a criterion for detecting a special cause of process variation in a control chart is a data point that falls outside 3-sigma control limits.

The criteria for detecting special causes of variation are based on statistical theory and experience and depend on economic justification. As criteria are added, special causes are more likely to be identified if they are present, but the likelihood of false alarms also increases.

5. Analyze special causes of process variation to determine the reasons why the anomaly occurred.

Examples of techniques for analyzing the reasons for special causes of variation include the following:
- Cause-and-effect (i.e., fishbone) diagrams
- Designed experiments
- Control charts (applied to subprocess inputs or lower level subprocesses)
- Subgrouping (i.e., analyzing the same data segregated into smaller groups based on an understanding of how the subprocess was implemented facilitates isolation of special causes)

Some anomalies may simply be extremes of the underlying distribution rather than problems. Those implementing a subprocess are usually the ones best able to analyze and understand special causes of variation.

6. Determine the corrective action to be taken when special causes of variation are identified.

Removing a special cause of process variation does not change the underlying subprocess. It addresses an error or condition in the execution of the subprocess.

Refer to the Project Monitoring and Control process area for more information about managing corrective action to closure.

7. Recalculate natural bounds for each measured attribute of the selected subprocesses as necessary.

Recalculating the (statistically estimated) natural bounds is based on measured values that signify that the subprocess has changed. It is not based on expectations or arbitrary decisions.

QPM

Examples of when natural bounds may need to be recalculated include the following:
- There are incremental improvements to the subprocess
- New tools are deployed for the subprocess
- A new subprocess is deployed
- The collected measures suggest that the subprocess mean has permanently shifted or subprocess variation has permanently changed

SP 2.3 MONITOR THE PERFORMANCE OF SELECTED SUBPROCESSES

Monitor the performance of selected subprocesses to determine their capability to satisfy their quality and process-performance objectives, and identify corrective action as necessary.

The intent of this specific practice is to do the following:

- Statistically determine process behavior expected from the subprocess
- Appraise the probability that the subprocess will meet its quality and process-performance objectives
- Identify the corrective action to be taken based on a statistical analysis of process-performance data

> Corrective actions may include renegotiating affected project objectives, identifying and implementing alternative subprocesses, or identifying and measuring lower level subprocesses to achieve greater detail in performance data.

These actions are intended to help the project use a more capable process. (See the definition of "capable process" in the glossary.)

A prerequisite for comparing the capability of a selected subprocess against its quality and process-performance objectives is that the measured attributes of the subprocess indicate that its performance is stable and predictable.

Process capability is analyzed for those subprocesses and measured attributes for which (derived) objectives are established. Not all subprocesses or measured attributes that are statistically managed are analyzed regarding process capability.

Historical data may be inadequate for initially determining whether the subprocess is capable. It also is possible that the estimated natural bounds for subprocess performance may shift away from quality and process-performance objectives. In either case, statistical control implies monitoring capability as well as stability.

Typical Work Products

1. Natural bounds of process performance for each selected subprocess compared to its established (derived) objectives
2. The process capability of each subprocess
3. The actions needed to address deficiencies in the process capability of each subprocess

Subpractices

1. Compare quality and process-performance objectives to the natural bounds of the measured attribute.

    This comparison provides an appraisal of the process capability for each measured attribute of a subprocess. These comparisons can be displayed graphically in ways that relate the estimated natural bounds to the objectives or as process capability indices, which summarize the relationship of objectives to natural bounds.

2. Monitor changes in quality and process-performance objectives and the process capability of the selected subprocess.

3. Identify and document deficiencies in subprocess capability.

4. Determine and document actions needed to address deficiencies in subprocess capability.

Examples of actions that can be taken when the performance of a selected subprocess does not satisfy its objectives include the following:

- Rederiving quality and process-performance objectives for each selected subprocess so that they can be met given the performance of the selected subprocess
- Improving the implementation of the existing subprocess to reduce its normal variability (Reducing variability may bring natural bounds within the objectives without having to move the mean.)
- Adopting new process elements, subprocesses, and technologies that have the potential to satisfy objectives and manage associated risks
- Identifying risks and risk mitigation strategies for each deficiency in subprocess capability

---

Refer to the Project Monitoring and Control process area for more information about managing corrective action to closure.

SP 2.4 RECORD STATISTICAL MANAGEMENT DATA

Record statistical and quality management data in the organization's measurement repository.

Refer to the Measurement and Analysis process area for more information about aligning measurement and analysis activities and providing measurement results.

Refer to the Organizational Process Definition process area for more information about the organization's measurement repository.

Typical Work Products

1. Statistical and quality management data recorded in the organization's measurement repository

REQUIREMENTS MANAGEMENT
A Project Management Process Area at Maturity Level 2

Purpose

The purpose of Requirements Management (REQM) is to manage requirements of the project's products and product components and to identify inconsistencies between those requirements and the project's plans and work products.

Introductory Notes

Requirements management processes manage all requirements received or generated by the project, including both technical and nontechnical requirements as well as requirements levied on the project by the organization.

In particular, all requirements that the customer and service provider have approved are addressed in the Requirements Management process area.

Throughout the process areas, where the terms "product" and "product component" are used, their intended meanings also encompass services, service systems, and their components.

The written agreement can take the form of a service level agreement (SLA), performance work statement (PWS), statement of objectives (SOO), statement of work (SOW), or other type of agreement. The written agreement may be part of a contract, a memorandum of agreement, an approved requirements document, or some other form.

The written agreement may have to be established while service provision is ongoing. The intent of Requirements Management is to repeat the service agreement process during the service period to support a positive relationship between the service provider and the customer while meeting the needs of both. Requirements management processes should encourage open communication without retribution.

The customer may be internal or external to the service provider's organization.

Sources and considerations for service requirements include mission-related performance goals and objectives (found in strategic plans and employee performance plans), monitoring capability, current performance levels and service levels, constraints identified during selection of design solutions, and requirements derived from designing the service system (e.g., reliability, maintainability, availability, supportability, safety and health, mission operations, lifecycle cost, obsolescence management).

Other considerations affecting service requirements may stem from the customer's agreements with other suppliers (e.g., the customer's underpinning contracts, operational level agreements, memoranda of agreement, subcontracts).

The project takes appropriate steps to ensure that the set of approved requirements is managed to support the planning and execution needs of the project. When a project receives requirements from an approved requirements provider, these requirements are reviewed with the requirements provider to resolve issues and prevent misunderstanding before requirements are incorporated into project plans. Once the requirements provider and the requirements receiver reach an agreement, commitment to the requirements is obtained from project participants. The project manages changes to requirements as they evolve and identifies inconsistencies that occur among plans, work products, and requirements.

Part of managing requirements is documenting requirements changes and their rationale and maintaining bidirectional traceability between source requirements and all product and product component requirements. (See the definition of "bidirectional traceability" in the glossary.)

All projects have requirements. In the case of maintenance activities, changes are based on changes to the existing requirements, design, or implementation. The requirements changes, if any, might be documented in change requests from the customer or users, or they might take the form of new requirements received from the requirements development process. Regardless of their source or form, the maintenance activities that are driven by changes to requirements are managed accordingly.

BIDIRECTIONAL TRACEABILITY

Many service provider organizations don't address bidirectional traceability adequately, and the impact can be significant. When well implemented, bidirectional traceability can save you from failing to address critical customer needs on the one hand and wasting resources on the other hand. How does it create this double benefit?

The essence of bidirectional traceability is that it ties everything back to your fundamental service requirements, which identify your customer's priority needs. Your customer's initial expression of their needs (or *your* initial expression of their needs when you are defining a standard service) may have varying degrees of specificity and completeness. Once you have an initial set of these needs refined into service requirements (which may already have been expressed that way in a service agreement), these initial requirements can serve as the basis for scoping much of the work you do. Every derived service requirement, service system requirement, feature, process, skill, tool, test procedure—in short, everything you need to create or use to meet the initial requirements—should be linked directly or indirectly back to these initial requirements. You can even link individual service requests back to initial service requirements (again, directly or indirectly).

The establishment and management of these links allows you to ensure that every initial requirement can be supported by your service system, that the service system itself is complete, and that there are no "holes" in its design, implementation, verification, or validation. (This also requires you to develop your service system in a disciplined way. See the Service System Development process area for guidance on that subject.) The links also allow you to ensure that you are not wastefully creating capabilities or providing services that your customers do not actually require.

By the way, if you find that some customers are repeatedly requesting services that are *not* linkable to your initial service requirements, you may have discovered a requirements defect. If you treat these instances as incidents, the analytical and planning practices of the Incident Resolution and Prevention process area may lead you to an effective solution. For example, you might work with your customer to improve their understanding and awareness of what the service agreement covers, or even to revise the service agreement to begin to cover what were previously unspecified requirements.

Related Process Areas

Refer to the Service System Development process area for more information about developing and analyzing stakeholder requirements.

SSD ADD

Refer to the Strategic Service Management process area for more information about establishing and maintaining standard services in concert with strategic needs and plans.

Refer to the Configuration Management process area for more information about establishing baselines and tracking and controlling changes.

Refer to the Project Monitoring and Control process area for more information about monitoring the project against the plan and managing corrective action to closure.

Refer to the Project Planning process area for more information about establishing and maintaining plans that define project activities.

Refer to the Risk Management process area for more information about identifying and analyzing risks.

Specific Goal and Practice Summary

SG 1 Manage Requirements
    SP 1.1   Understand Requirements
    SP 1.2   Obtain Commitment to Requirements
    SP 1.3   Manage Requirements Changes
    SP 1.4   Maintain Bidirectional Traceability of Requirements
    SP 1.5   Identify Inconsistencies Between Project Work and Requirements

Specific Practices by Goal

SG 1   MANAGE REQUIREMENTS

Requirements are managed and inconsistencies with project plans and work products are identified.

The project maintains a current and approved set of requirements over the life of the project by doing the following:

- Managing all changes to requirements
- Maintaining relationships among requirements, project plans, and work products
- Identifying inconsistencies among requirements, project plans, and work products
- Taking corrective action

If the Service Delivery, Strategic Service Management, or Incident Resolution and Prevention process areas are implemented, their processes will generate stakeholder requirements that will also be managed by requirements management processes.

Refer to the Project Monitoring and Control process area for more information about managing corrective action to closure.

SP 1.1 UNDERSTAND REQUIREMENTS

Develop an understanding with the requirements providers on the meaning of the requirements.

As the project matures and requirements are derived, all activities or disciplines will receive requirements. To avoid requirements creep, criteria are established to designate appropriate channels or official sources from which to receive requirements. Those receiving requirements conduct analyses of them with the provider to ensure that a compatible, shared understanding is reached on the meaning of requirements. The result of these analyses and dialog is a set of approved requirements.

Typical Work Products

1. Lists of criteria for distinguishing appropriate requirements providers
2. Criteria for evaluation and acceptance of requirements
3. Results of analyses against criteria
4. A set of approved requirements

Subpractices

1. Establish criteria for distinguishing appropriate requirements providers.
2. Establish objective criteria for the evaluation and acceptance of requirements.

> *Refer to the Service System Development process area for more information about analyzing and validating requirements.*

SSD ADD

Lack of evaluation and acceptance criteria often results in inadequate verification, costly rework, or customer rejection.

REQM

Examples of evaluation and acceptance criteria include the following:
- Clearly and properly stated
- Complete
- Consistent with one another
- Uniquely identified
- Appropriate to implement
- Verifiable (i.e., testable)
- Traceable
- Achievable with current or planned capability

---

3. Analyze requirements to ensure that established criteria are met.
4. Reach an understanding of requirements with requirements providers so that project participants can commit to them.

SP 1.2 OBTAIN COMMITMENT TO REQUIREMENTS

Obtain commitment to requirements from project participants.

Refer to the Project Monitoring and Control process area for more information about monitoring commitments.

The previous specific practice dealt with reaching an understanding with requirements providers. This specific practice deals with agreements and commitments among those who must carry out activities necessary to implement requirements. Requirements evolve throughout the project. As requirements evolve, this specific practice ensures that project participants commit to the current and approved requirements and the resulting changes in project plans, activities, and work products.

Typical Work Products

1. Requirements impact assessments
2. Documented commitments to requirements and requirements changes

Subpractices

1. Assess the impact of requirements on existing commitments.
   The impact on the project participants should be evaluated when the requirements change or at the start of a new requirement.
2. Negotiate and record commitments.
   Changes to existing commitments should be negotiated before project participants commit to a new requirement or requirement change.

SP 1.3 MANAGE REQUIREMENTS CHANGES

Manage changes to requirements as they evolve during the project.

Refer to the Configuration Management process area for more information about tracking and controlling changes.

Requirements change for a variety of reasons (e.g., breaches of service levels). As needs change and as work proceeds, changes may have to be made to existing requirements. It is essential to manage these additions and changes efficiently and effectively. To effectively analyze the impact of changes, it is necessary that the source of each requirement is known and the rationale for the change is documented. The project may, however, want to track appropriate measures of requirements volatility to judge whether new or revised controls are necessary.

Typical Work Products

1. Requirements status
2. Requirements database
3. Requirements decision database

Subpractices

1. Document all requirements and requirements changes that are given to or generated by the project.
2. Maintain a requirements change history, including the rationale for changes.
   Maintaining the change history helps to track requirements volatility.
3. Evaluate the impact of requirement changes from the standpoint of relevant stakeholders.
4. Make requirements and change data available to the project.

SP 1.4 MAINTAIN BIDIRECTIONAL TRACEABILITY OF REQUIREMENTS

Maintain bidirectional traceability among requirements and work products.

The intent of this specific practice is to maintain the bidirectional traceability of requirements. (See the definition of "bidirectional traceability" in the glossary.) When requirements are managed well, traceability can be established from a source requirement to its lower level requirements and from those lower level requirements back to their source requirements. Such bidirectional traceability helps to determine whether all source requirements have been completely addressed and whether all lower level requirements can be traced to a valid source.

REQM

Requirements traceability can also cover relationships to other entities, such as intermediate and final work products, changes in design documentation, and test plans. Traceability can cover horizontal relationships, such as across interfaces, as well as vertical relationships. Traceability is particularly needed when assessing the impact of requirements changes on project activities and work products.

In a service environment, you should be able to trace stakeholder requirements to the elements of the delivered service and supporting service system that were developed from those requirements or other requirements derived from stakeholder requirements. Conversely, elements of the delivered service and supporting service system should be traceable back to the stakeholder requirements they meet.

Such bidirectional traceability is not always automated. It can be done manually using spreadsheets, databases, and other common tools.

Examples of what aspects of traceability to consider include the following:
- Scope of traceability: the boundaries within which traceability is needed
- Definition of traceability of service: the service elements that need logical relationships
- Type of traceability: when horizontal and vertical traceability is needed
- Integrated service environment: the scope of traceability applied in an organization in which tangible products or product elements are integral elements of services and services are the primary focus of the organization

---

Typical Work Products

1. Requirements traceability matrix
2. Requirements tracking system

Subpractices

1. Maintain requirements traceability to ensure that the source of lower level (i.e., derived) requirements is documented.
2. Maintain requirements traceability from a requirement to its derived requirements and allocation to functions, interfaces, objects, people, processes, and work products.
3. Generate a requirements traceability matrix.

   A traceability matrix might have the list of stakeholder requirements and derived requirements on one axis. The other axis might list all of the components of the service system, including people and consumables. The intersections of the rows and columns would indicate where a particular requirement applies to the parts of the service system.

SP 1.5 IDENTIFY INCONSISTENCIES BETWEEN PROJECT WORK AND REQUIREMENTS

Identify inconsistencies between the project plans and work products and the requirements.

Refer to the Project Monitoring and Control process area for more information about monitoring the project against the plan.

This specific practice finds inconsistencies between requirements and project plans and work products and initiates corrective actions to resolve them.

Typical Work Products

1. Documentation of inconsistencies between requirements and project plans and work products, including sources and conditions
2. Corrective actions

Subpractices

1. Review project plans, activities, and work products for consistency with requirements and changes made to them.
2. Identify the source of the inconsistency.
3. Identify changes that must be made to plans and work products resulting from changes to the requirements baseline.
4. Initiate corrective actions.

RISK MANAGEMENT

A Project Management Process Area at Maturity Level 3

Purpose

The purpose of Risk Management (RSKM) is to identify potential problems before they occur so that risk-handling activities can be planned and invoked as needed across the life of the product or project to mitigate adverse impacts on achieving objectives.

IN OTHER WORDS

RSKM is about supporting the success of your service mission by anticipating problems and how you will handle them—before they occur.

Introductory Notes

Risk management is a continuous, forward-looking process that is an important part of project management. Risk management should address issues that could endanger achievement of critical objectives. A continuous risk management approach effectively anticipates and mitigates risks that may have a critical impact on a project.

WHY DO THE PRACTICES IN RSKM?

You can avoid costs, customer dissatisfaction, harm to your reputation, service failures, and even loss of health and life by thinking about what can go wrong and what you can do to prevent or respond to problems.

Effective risk management includes early and aggressive risk identification through collaboration and the involvement of relevant stakeholders as described in the stakeholder involvement plan addressed in the Project Planning process area. Strong leadership across all relevant stakeholders is needed to establish an environment for free and open disclosure and discussion of risk.

Risk management must consider both internal and external sources of cost, schedule, performance, and other risks. Early and aggressive detection of risk is important because it is typically easier, less costly, and less disruptive to make changes and correct work efforts during the earlier, rather than the later, phases of the project.

Industry standards can help when determining how to prevent or mitigate specific risks commonly found in a particular industry. Certain risks can be proactively managed or mitigated by reviewing industry best practices and lessons learned.

Risk management can be divided into three parts:

- Defining a risk management strategy
- Identifying and analyzing risks
- Handling identified risks, including the implementation of risk mitigation plans as needed

As represented in the Project Planning and Project Monitoring and Control process areas, organizations initially may focus on risk identification for awareness, and react to the realization of these risks as they occur. The Risk Management process area describes an evolution of these specific practices to systematically plan, anticipate, and mitigate risks to proactively minimize their impact on the project.

Although the primary emphasis of the Risk Management process area is on the project, these concepts can also be applied to manage organizational risks.

Related Process Areas

Refer to the Service Continuity process area for more information about establishing and maintaining plans to ensure continuity of services during and following any significant disruption of normal operations.

Refer to the Decision Analysis and Resolution process area for more information about analyzing possible decisions using a formal evaluation process that evaluates identified alternatives against established criteria.

Refer to the Project Monitoring and Control process area for more information about monitoring project risks.

Refer to the Project Planning process area for more information about identifying project risks and planning stakeholder involvement.

Specific Goal and Practice Summary

SG 1 Prepare for Risk Management
    SP 1.1   Determine Risk Sources and Categories
    SP 1.2   Define Risk Parameters
    SP 1.3   Establish a Risk Management Strategy
SG 2 Identify and Analyze Risks
    SP 2.1   Identify Risks
    SP 2.2   Evaluate, Categorize, and Prioritize Risks
SG 3 Mitigate Risks
    SP 3.1   Develop Risk Mitigation Plans
    SP 3.2   Implement Risk Mitigation Plans

Specific Practices by Goal

SG 1 PREPARE FOR RISK MANAGEMENT

Preparation for risk management is conducted.

Prepare for risk management by establishing and maintaining a strategy for identifying, analyzing, and mitigating risks. Typically, this strategy is documented in a risk management plan. The risk management strategy addresses specific actions and the management approach used to apply and control the risk management program. The strategy typically includes identifying sources of risk, the scheme used to categorize risks, and parameters used to evaluate, bound, and control risks for effective handling.

SP 1.1 DETERMINE RISK SOURCES AND CATEGORIES

Determine risk sources and categories.

Identifying risk sources provides a basis for systematically examining changing situations over time to uncover circumstances that impact the ability of the project to meet its objectives. Risk sources are both internal and external to the project. As the project progresses, additional sources of risk may be identified. Establishing categories for risks provides a mechanism for collecting and organizing risks as well as ensuring appropriate scrutiny and management attention to risks that can have serious consequences on meeting project objectives.

Typical Work Products

1. Risk source lists (external and internal)
2. Risk categories list

Subpractices

1. Determine risk sources.

   Risk sources are fundamental drivers that cause risks in a project or organization. There are many sources of risks, both internal and external to a project. Risk sources identify where risks may originate.

> Typical internal and external risk sources include the following:
> - Uncertain requirements
> - Unprecedented efforts (i.e., estimates unavailable)
> - Infeasible design
> - Unavailable technology
> - Unrealistic schedule estimates or allocation
> - Inadequate staffing and skills
> - Cost or funding issues
> - Uncertain or inadequate subcontractor capability
> - Uncertain or inadequate supplier capability
> - Inadequate communication with actual or potential customers or with their representatives
> - Disruptions to the continuity of operations

Many of these sources of risk are accepted without adequately planning for them. Early identification of both internal and external sources of risk can lead to early identification of risks. Risk mitigation plans can then be implemented early in the project to preclude occurrence of risks or reduce consequences of their occurrence.

2. Determine risk categories.

   Risk categories are "bins" used for collecting and organizing risks. Identifying risk categories aids the future consolidation of activities in risk mitigation plans.

> The following factors may be considered when determining risk categories:
> - Phases of the project's lifecycle model
> - Types of processes used
> - Types of products used
> - Project management risks (e.g., contract risks, budget risks, schedule risks, resource risks, performance risks, supportability risks)

A risk taxonomy can be used to provide a framework for determining risk sources and categories.

SP 1.2 DEFINE RISK PARAMETERS

Define parameters used to analyze and categorize risks and to control the risk management effort.

Parameters for evaluating, categorizing, and prioritizing risks include the following:

- Risk likelihood (i.e., probability of risk occurrence)
- Risk consequence (i.e., impact and severity of risk occurrence)
- Thresholds to trigger management activities

Risk parameters are used to provide common and consistent criteria for comparing risks to be managed. Without these parameters, it is difficult to gauge the severity of an unwanted change caused by a risk and to prioritize the actions required for risk mitigation planning.

Projects should document the parameters used to analyze and categorize risks so that they are available for reference throughout the life of the project because circumstances change over time. Using these parameters, risks can easily be recategorized and analyzed when changes occur.

The project may use techniques such as failure mode and effects analysis (FMEA) to examine risks of potential failures in the service system or in selected service delivery processes. Such techniques may help to provide discipline in working with risk parameters.

Typical Work Products

1. Risk evaluation, categorization, and prioritization criteria
2. Risk management requirements (e.g., control and approval levels, reassessment intervals)

Subpractices

1. Define consistent criteria for evaluating and quantifying risk likelihood and severity levels.

   Consistently used criteria (e.g., bounds on likelihood or severity levels) allow impacts of different risks to be commonly understood, to receive the appropriate level of scrutiny, and to obtain the management attention warranted. In managing dissimilar risks (e.g., personnel safety versus environmental pollution), it is important to ensure consistency in the end result. (For example, a high-impact risk of environmental pollution is as important as a high-impact risk to personnel safety.) One way of providing a common basis for comparing dissimilar risks is risk monetization.

2. Define thresholds for each risk category.

   For each risk category, thresholds can be established to determine acceptability or unacceptability of risks, prioritization of risks, or triggers for management action.

Examples of thresholds include the following:
- Project-wide thresholds could be established to involve senior management when product costs exceed 10 percent of the target cost or when cost performance indices (CPIs) fall below 0.95.
- Schedule thresholds could be established to involve senior management when schedule performance indices (SPIs) fall below 0.95.
- Performance thresholds could be established to involve senior management when specified key items (e.g., processor utilization, average response times) exceed 125 percent of the intended design.

For each identified risk, establish points at which aggressive risk monitoring is employed or to signal the implementation of risk mitigation plans. These points can be redefined later in the project as necessary.

3. Define bounds on the extent to which thresholds are applied against or within a category.

There are few limits to which risks can be assessed in either a quantitative or qualitative fashion. Definition of bounds (or boundary conditions) can be used to help define the extent of the risk management effort and avoid excessive resource expenditures. Bounds may include the exclusion of a risk source from a category. These bounds can also exclude conditions that occur below a given frequency.

SP 1.3 *Establish a Risk Management Strategy*

Establish and maintain the strategy to be used for risk management.

A comprehensive risk management strategy addresses items such as the following:

- The scope of the risk management effort
- Methods and tools to be used for risk identification, risk analysis, risk mitigation, risk monitoring, and communication
- Project-specific sources of risks
- How risks are to be organized, categorized, compared, and consolidated
- Parameters used for taking action on identified risks, including likelihood, consequence, and thresholds
- Risk mitigation techniques to be used, such as prototyping, piloting, simulation, alternative designs, or evolutionary development
- The definition of risk measures used to monitor the status of risks
- Time intervals for risk monitoring or reassessment

The risk management strategy should be guided by a common vision of success that describes desired future project outcomes in terms of the product delivered, its cost, and its fitness for the task. The risk management strategy is often documented in a risk management plan for the organization or project. This strategy is reviewed with relevant stakeholders to promote commitment and understanding.

A risk management strategy should be developed early in the project, so that relevant risks are identified and managed proactively. Early identification and assessment of critical risks allows the project to formulate risk handling approaches and adjust project definition and allocation of resources based on critical risks.

Typical Work Products

1. Project risk management strategy

SG 2   IDENTIFY AND ANALYZE RISKS

Risks are identified and analyzed to determine their relative importance.

The degree of risk affects the resources assigned to handle the risk and the timing of when appropriate management attention is required.

Risk analysis entails identifying risks from identified internal and external sources and evaluating each identified risk to determine its likelihood and consequences. Risk categorization, based on an evaluation against established risk categories and criteria developed for the risk management strategy, provides information needed for risk handling. Related risks may be grouped to enable efficient handling and effective use of risk management resources.

SP 2.1   IDENTIFY RISKS

Identify and document risks.

Identifying potential issues, hazards, threats, and vulnerabilities that could negatively affect work efforts or plans is the basis for sound and successful risk management. Risks must be identified and described understandably before they can be analyzed and managed properly. Risks are documented in a concise statement that includes the context, conditions, and consequences of risk occurrence.

Risk identification should be an organized, thorough approach to seek out probable or realistic risks that may affect achieving objectives. To be effective, risk identification should not attempt to address every possible event regardless of how improbable it may be. Using categories and parameters developed in the risk management strategy and identified sources of risk can provide the discipline and streamlining appropriate for risk identification. Identified risks form a baseline for initiating risk management activities. Risks should be reviewed periodically to reexamine possible sources of risk and changing conditions to uncover sources and risks previously overlooked or nonexistent when the risk management strategy was last updated.

Risk identification focuses on identifying risks, not placement of blame. The results of risk identification activities should never be used by management to evaluate the performance of individuals.

There are many methods used for identifying risks. Typical identification methods include the following:

- Examine each element of the project work breakdown structure.
- Conduct a risk assessment using a risk taxonomy.
- Interview subject matter experts.
- Review risk management efforts from similar products.
- Examine lessons-learned documents or databases.
- Examine design specifications and agreement requirements.

Typical Work Products

1. List of identified risks, including the context, conditions, and consequences of risk occurrence

Subpractices

1. Identify the risks associated with cost, schedule, and performance.
   Cost, schedule, and performance risks should be examined to the extent that they impact project objectives. Potential risks may be discovered that are outside the scope of project objectives but vital to customer interests. For example, risks in development costs, product acquisition costs, cost of spare (or replacement) products, and product disposition (or disposal) costs have design implications.
   The customer may not have considered the full cost of supporting a fielded product or using a delivered service. The customer should be informed of such risks, but actively managing those risks may not be necessary. Mechanisms for making such decisions should be examined at project and organization levels and put in place if deemed appropriate, especially for risks that impact the project's ability to verify and validate the product.

In addition to the cost risks identified above, other cost risks may include those associated with funding levels, funding estimates, and distributed budgets. Risks associated with service agreements, such as supplier dependencies, customer processes, and unrealistic service levels, also should be considered.

Schedule risks may include risks associated with planned activities, key events, and milestones.

Performance risks may include risks associated with the following:
- Requirements
- Service interruptions
- Meeting service levels
- Impacts of customer processes
- Analysis and design
- Application of new technology
- Physical size
- Shape
- Weight
- Manufacturing and fabrication
- Functional performance and operation
- Verification
- Validation
- Performance maintenance attributes

Performance maintenance attributes are those characteristics that enable an in-use product or service to provide required performance, such as maintaining safety and security performance.

There are other risks that do not fall into cost, schedule, or performance categories.

Examples of these other risks include those related to the following:
- Strikes
- Dependency on customer-provided resources (e.g., equipment, facilities)
- Operational resiliency
- Dependencies on suppliers
- Diminishing sources of supply
- Technology cycle time
- Competition
- Overreliance on key personnel

RSKM

2. Review environmental elements that may impact the project.

   Risks to a project that frequently are missed include those supposedly outside the scope of the project (i.e., the project does not control whether they occur but can mitigate their impact). These risks include weather or natural disasters, political changes, and telecommunications failures.

3. Review all elements of the work breakdown structure as part of identifying risks to help ensure that all aspects of the work effort have been considered.

4. Review all elements of the project plan as part of identifying risks to help ensure that all aspects of the project have been considered.

   Refer to the Project Planning process area for more information about identifying project risks.

5. Document the context, conditions, and potential consequences of each risk.

   Risk statements are typically documented in a standard format that contains the risk context, conditions, and consequences of occurrence. The risk context provides additional information about the risk, such as the relative time frame of the risk, the circumstances or conditions surrounding the risk that has brought about the concern, and any doubt or uncertainty.

6. Identify the relevant stakeholders associated with each risk.

SP 2.2 *EVALUATE, CATEGORIZE, AND PRIORITIZE RISKS*

Evaluate and categorize each identified risk using defined risk categories and parameters, and determine its relative priority.

The evaluation of risks is needed to assign a relative importance to each identified risk and is used in determining when appropriate management attention is required. Often, it is useful to aggregate risks based on their interrelationships and develop options at an aggregate level. When an aggregate risk is formed by a rollup of lower level risks, care must be taken to ensure that important lower-level risks are not ignored.

Collectively, the activities of risk evaluation, categorization, and prioritization are sometimes called a "risk assessment," or "risk analysis."

Typical Work Products

1. List of risks and their assigned priority

Subpractices

1. Evaluate identified risks using defined risk parameters.

Each risk is evaluated and assigned values according to defined risk parameters, which may include likelihood, consequence (i.e., severity or impact), and thresholds. The assigned risk parameter values can be integrated to produce additional measures, such as risk exposure, which can be used to prioritize risks for handling.

Often, a scale with three to five values is used to evaluate both likelihood and consequence.

Likelihood, for example, can be categorized as remote, unlikely, likely, highly likely, or nearly certain.

Example categories for consequence include the following:
- Low
- Medium
- High
- Negligible
- Marginal
- Significant
- Critical
- Catastrophic

Probability values are frequently used to quantify likelihood. Consequences are generally related to cost, schedule, environmental impact, or human measures (e.g., labor hours lost, severity of injury).

Risk evaluation is often a difficult and time-consuming task. Specific expertise or group techniques may be needed to assess risks and gain confidence in the prioritization. In addition, priorities may require reevaluation as time progresses. To provide a basis for comparing the impact of the realization of identified risks, consequences of the risks can be monetized.

2. Categorize and group risks according to defined risk categories.

   Risks are categorized into defined risk categories, providing a means to review them according to their source, taxonomy, or project component. Related or equivalent risks may be grouped for efficient handling. The cause-and-effect relationships between related risks are documented.

3. Prioritize risks for mitigation.

   A relative priority is determined for each risk based on assigned risk parameters. Clear criteria should be used to determine risk priority. Risk prioritization helps to determine the most effective areas to which resources for risks mitigation can be applied with the greatest positive impact on the project.

SG 3 *MITIGATE RISKS*

Risks are handled and mitigated as appropriate to reduce adverse impacts on achieving objectives.

The steps in handling risks include developing risk-handling options, monitoring risks, and performing risk-handling activities when defined thresholds are exceeded. Risk mitigation plans are developed and implemented for selected risks to proactively reduce the potential impact of risk occurrence. Risk mitigation planning can also include contingency plans to deal with the impact of selected risks that may occur despite attempts to mitigate them. Risk parameters used to trigger risk-handling activities are defined by the risk management strategy.

SP 3.1 *DEVELOP RISK MITIGATION PLANS*

Develop a risk mitigation plan for the most important risks to the project as defined by the risk management strategy.

A critical component of risk mitigation planning is developing alternative courses of action, workarounds, and fallback positions, and a recommended course of action for each critical risk. The risk mitigation plan for a given risk includes techniques and methods used to avoid, reduce, and control the probability of risk occurrence; the extent of damage incurred should the risk occur (sometimes called a "contingency plan"); or both. Risks are monitored and when they exceed established thresholds, risk mitigation plans are deployed to return the impacted effort to an acceptable risk level. If the risk cannot be mitigated, a contingency plan can be invoked. Both risk mitigation and contingency plans often are generated only for selected risks for which consequences of the risks are high or unacceptable. Other risks may be accepted and simply monitored.

Options for handling risks typically include alternatives such as the following:

- Risk avoidance: changing or lowering requirements while still meeting user needs
- Risk control: taking active steps to minimize risks
- Risk transfer: reallocating requirements to lower risks
- Risk monitoring: watching and periodically reevaluating the risk for changes in assigned risk parameters
- Risk acceptance: acknowledging risk but not taking action

Often, especially for high-impact risks, more than one approach to handling a risk should be generated.

> For example, in the case of an event that disrupts the continuity of operations, approaches to risk management can include establishing the following:
> - Resource reserves to respond to disruptive events
> - Lists of available back-up equipment
> - Back-up of key personnel
> - Plans for testing emergency response systems
> - Posted procedures for emergencies
> - Disseminated lists of key contacts and information resources for emergencies

In many cases, risks are accepted or watched. Risk acceptance is usually done when the risk is judged too low for formal mitigation or when there appears to be no viable way to reduce the risk. If a risk is accepted, the rationale for this decision should be documented. Risks are watched when there is an objectively defined, verifiable, and documented threshold of performance, time, or risk exposure (i.e., the combination of likelihood and consequence) that will trigger risk mitigation planning or invoke a contingency plan.

Refer to the Decision Analysis and Resolution process area for more information about evaluating alternatives and selecting solutions.

Adequate consideration should be given early to technology demonstrations, models, simulations, pilots, and prototypes as part of risk mitigation planning.

Typical Work Products

1. Documented handling options for each identified risk
2. Risk mitigation plans
3. Contingency plans
4. List of those responsible for tracking and addressing each risk

Subpractices

1. Determine the levels and thresholds that define when a risk becomes unacceptable and triggers the execution of a risk mitigation plan or contingency plan.

   Risk level (derived using a risk model) is a measure combining the uncertainty of reaching an objective with the consequences of failing to reach the objective.

Risk levels and thresholds that bound planned or acceptable perform-ance must be clearly understood and defined to provide a means with which risk can be understood. Proper categorization of risk is essen-tial for ensuring an appropriate priority based on severity and the associated management response. There may be multiple thresholds employed to initiate varying levels of management response. Typi-cally, thresholds for the execution of risk mitigation plans are set to engage before the execution of contingency plans.

2. Identify the person or group responsible for addressing each risk.

3. Determine the costs and benefits of implementing the risk mitiga-tion plan for each risk.

    Risk mitigation activities should be examined for benefits they pro-vide versus resources they will expend. Just like any other design activity, alternative plans may need to be developed and costs and benefits of each alternative assessed. The most appropriate plan is selected for implementation.

4. Develop an overall risk mitigation plan for the project to orchestrate the implementation of individual risk mitigation and contingency plans.

    The complete set of risk mitigation plans may not be affordable. A tradeoff analysis should be performed to prioritize risk mitigation plans for implementation.

5. Develop contingency plans for selected critical risks in the event their impacts are realized.

    Risk mitigation plans are developed and implemented as needed to proactively reduce risks before they become problems. Despite best efforts, some risks may be unavoidable and will become problems that impact the project. Contingency plans can be developed for criti-cal risks to describe actions a project may take to deal with the occur-rence of this impact. The intent is to define a proactive plan for handling the risk. Either the risk is reduced (mitigation) or addressed (contingency). In either event, the risk is managed.

    Some risk management literature may consider contingency plans a synonym or subset of risk mitigation plans. These plans also may be addressed together as risk handling or risk action plans.

SP 3.2 IMPLEMENT RISK MITIGATION PLANS

Monitor the status of each risk periodically and implement the risk mitigation plan as appropriate.

To effectively control and manage risks during the work effort, follow a proactive program to regularly monitor risks and the status and results of risk-handling actions. The risk management strategy defines the intervals at which risk status should be revisited. This activity may result in the discovery of new risks or new risk-handling options that can require replanning and reassessment. In either event, acceptability thresholds associated with the risk should be compared to the risk status to determine the need for implementing a risk mitigation plan.

Typical Work Products

1. Updated lists of risk status
2. Updated assessments of risk likelihood, consequence, and thresholds
3. Updated list of risk-handling options
4. Updated list of actions taken to handle risks
5. Risk mitigation plans of risk-handling options
6. Updated list of actions taken to handle risks
7. Risk mitigation plans

Subpractices

1. Monitor risk status.

   After a risk mitigation plan is initiated, the risk is still monitored. Thresholds are assessed to check for the potential execution of a contingency plan.
   A mechanism for monitoring should be employed.

2. Provide a method for tracking open risk-handling action items to closure.

   Refer to the Project Monitoring and Control process area for more information about managing corrective action to closure.

3. Invoke selected risk-handling options when monitored risks exceed defined thresholds.

   Often, risk handling is only performed for risks judged to be *high* and *medium*. The risk-handling strategy for a given risk may include techniques and methods to avoid, reduce, and control the likelihood of the risk or the extent of damage incurred should the risk (i.e., anticipated event or situation) occur or both. In this context, risk handling includes both risk mitigation plans and contingency plans.
   Risk-handling techniques are developed to avoid, reduce, and control adverse impact to project objectives and to bring about acceptable outcomes in light of probable impacts. Actions generated to handle a risk require proper resource loading and scheduling in plans and baseline schedules. This replanning must closely consider the effects on adjacent or dependent work initiatives or activities.

4. Establish a schedule or period of performance for each risk-handling activity that includes a start date and anticipated completion date.

5. Provide a continued commitment of resources for each plan to allow the successful execution of risk-handling activities.

6. Collect performance measures on risk-handling activities.

SUPPLIER AGREEMENT MANAGEMENT
A Project Management Process Area at Maturity Level 2

Purpose

The purpose of Supplier Agreement Management (SAM) is to manage the acquisition of products and services from suppliers.

Introductory Notes

The scope of this process area addresses the acquisition of products, services, and product and service components that can be delivered to the project's customer or included in a service system. This process area's practices may also be used for other purposes that benefit the project (e.g., purchasing consumables).

Throughout the process areas, where the terms "product" and "product component" are used, their intended meanings also encompass services, service systems, and their components.

The Supplier Agreement Management process area involves the following activities:

- Determining the type of acquisition
- Selecting suppliers
- Establishing and maintaining agreements with suppliers
- Executing supplier agreements
- Monitoring selected supplier processes
- Evaluating selected supplier work products
- Accepting delivery of acquired products
- Ensuring successful transition of acquired products to the project

Examples of both tangible and intangible products that may be acquired by the project to become part of a service delivered to the customer or to become part of the service system include the following:

- Maintenance of a specialized piece of equipment through a service level agreement with an external supplier as part of a facility maintenance service
- User training for a service, where the training is performed by an internal supplier as part of an operating level agreement (OLA)
- Nursing services at a hospital supplied through an outsourcing agreement
- Meals and refreshments at a conference supplied through a catering contract
- Communications equipment that is purchased and delivered by a purchasing agent on receipt of an order
- Gasoline to be sold at a gas station
- Automobiles to be delivered by a delivery service as ordered
- Automated teller machines at a bank
- Components of a Web-based search engine
- Airplanes at an airline
- Automobiles at a car rental outlet

Typically, the products to be acquired by the project are determined during the early stages of planning and development of the service system.

This process area does not directly address arrangements in which the supplier is integrated into the project team and uses the same processes and reports to the same management as the project team members (e.g., integrated teams). Typically, these situations are handled by other processes or functions (e.g., project management processes, processes or functions external to the project), though some of the specific practices of this process area may be useful in managing the supplier agreement.

This process area typically is not implemented to address arrangements in which the supplier is also the project's customer. These situations usually are handled by either informal agreements with the customer or by specification of the customer-furnished items in the overall service agreement that the project has with the customer. In the latter case, some of the specific practices of this process area may be useful in managing the service agreement, although others may not, due to the fundamentally different relationship that exists with a customer as opposed to an ordinary supplier.

Suppliers may take many forms depending on business needs, including in-house vendors (i.e., vendors that are in the same organization but are external to the project), fabrication departments, and commercial vendors. (See the definition of "supplier" in the glossary.)

A supplier agreement is established to manage the relationship between the organization and the supplier. A supplier agreement is any written agreement between the organization (representing the project) and the supplier. This agreement may be a contract, license, service level agreement, or memorandum of agreement. The acquired product is delivered to the project from the supplier according to the supplier agreement. (See the definition of "supplier agreement" in the glossary.)

Related Process Areas

Refer to the Service System Development process area for more information about developing and analyzing stakeholder requirements and developing service systems.

SSD ADD

Refer to the Project Monitoring and Control process area for more information about monitoring the project against the plan and managing corrective action to closure.

Refer to the Requirements Management process area for more information about maintaining bidirectional traceability of requirements.

Specific Goal and Practice Summary

SG 1 Establish Supplier Agreements
- SP 1.1   Determine Acquisition Type
- SP 1.2   Select Suppliers
- SP 1.3   Establish Supplier Agreements

SG 2 Satisfy Supplier Agreements
- SP 2.1   Execute the Supplier Agreement
- SP 2.2   Monitor Selected Supplier Processes
- SP 2.3   Evaluate Selected Supplier Work Products
- SP 2.4   Accept the Acquired Product
- SP 2.5   Ensure Transition of Products

Specific Practices by Goal

SG 1 ESTABLISH SUPPLIER AGREEMENTS

Agreements with the suppliers are established and maintained.

SP 1.1 DETERMINE ACQUISITION TYPE

Determine the type of acquisition for each product or product component to be acquired.

Many different types of acquisitions can be used to acquire products and product components that can be used by the project.

Examples of types of acquisitions include the following:
- Purchasing COTS products
- Obtaining products through a supplier agreement
- Obtaining products from an in-house vendor
- Obtaining services from another part of the business enterprise
- Obtaining products from the customer
- Combining some of the above (e.g., contracting for a modification to a COTS product, having another part of the business enterprise co-develop products with an external supplier)

If acquiring COTS products, care in evaluating and selecting these products and the supplier may be critical to the project. Aspects to consider in the selection decision include proprietary issues and the availability of the products.

Typical Work Products

1. List of the acquisition types that will be used for all products and product components to be acquired

SP 1.2 SELECT SUPPLIERS

Select suppliers based on an evaluation of their ability to meet the specified requirements and established criteria.

Refer to the Service System Development process area for more information about developing and analyzing stakeholder requirements.

SSD ADD

Refer to the Decision Analysis and Resolution process area for more information about analyzing possible decisions using a formal evaluation process that evaluates identified alternatives against established criteria.

Criteria should be established to address factors that are important to the project.

Examples of factors that may be important to the project include the following:

- Geographical location of the supplier
- Supplier's performance records on similar work
- Engineering capabilities
- Staff and facilities available to perform the work
- Prior experience in similar situations
- Customer satisfaction with similar products delivered by the supplier

---

Typical Work Products

1. Market studies
2. List of candidate suppliers
3. Preferred supplier list
4. Trade study or other record of evaluation criteria, advantages and disadvantages of candidate suppliers, and rationale for selection of suppliers
5. Solicitation materials and requirements

Subpractices

1. Establish and document criteria for evaluating potential suppliers.
2. Identify potential suppliers and distribute solicitation material and requirements to them.

   A proactive manner of performing this activity is to conduct market research to identify potential sources of candidate products to be acquired.
3. Evaluate proposals according to evaluation criteria.
4. Evaluate risks associated with each proposed supplier.

   Refer to the Risk Management process area for more information about identifying and evaluating risks.
5. Evaluate proposed suppliers' ability to perform the work.

Examples of methods used to evaluate the proposed supplier's ability to perform the work include the following:
- Evaluation of prior experience in similar applications
- Evaluation of customer satisfaction with similar products provided
- Evaluation of prior performance on similar work
- Evaluation of management capabilities
- Capability evaluations
- Evaluation of staff available to perform the work
- Evaluation of available facilities and resources
- Evaluation of the project's ability to work with the proposed supplier
- Evaluation of the impact of candidate COTS products on the project's plan and commitments

When COTS products are being evaluated, consider the following:
- Cost of the COTS products
- Cost and effort to incorporate the COTS products into the project
- Security requirements
- Benefits and impacts that may result from future product releases

Future releases of the COTS product may provide additional features that support planned or anticipated enhancements for the project, but may result in the supplier discontinuing support of its current release.

6. Select the supplier.

SP 1.3 ESTABLISH SUPPLIER AGREEMENTS

Establish and maintain supplier agreements.

A supplier agreement is any written agreement between the organization (representing the project) and the supplier. This agreement may be a contract, license, service level agreement, or memorandum of agreement.

The content of the supplier agreement should specify the reviews, monitoring, evaluations, and acceptance tests to be performed, if such activities are appropriate to the acquisition or product being acquired.

An acquired service may be delivered directly to the service provider's customer or end user. The content of the supplier agreement for such an acquired service should also specify whether the acceptance process will be performed before, during, or after supplier delivery. If the supplier will continuously or repeatedly deliver the service to the customer, the content should also specify when or how often the acceptance process will be performed (e.g., every time the service is delivered, at specified or random times on a subset of the service deliveries).

Supplier agreements between independent legal entities are typically reviewed by legal or contract advisors prior to approval.

Supplier agreements should address the expected end of service, early end of service, and transition of service as appropriate.

Typical Work Products

1. Statements of work
2. Contracts
3. Memoranda of agreement
4. Licensing agreement

Subpractices

1. Revise the requirements (e.g., product requirements, service level requirements) to be fulfilled by the supplier to reflect negotiations with the supplier when necessary.

> *Refer to the Service System Development process area for more information about developing and analyzing stakeholder requirements.*

> *Refer to the Requirements Management process area for more information about managing requirements.*

2. Document what the project will provide to the supplier.
   Include the following:
   - Project-furnished facilities
   - Documentation
   - Services
3. Document the supplier agreement.
   The supplier agreement should include a statement of work, a specification, terms and conditions, a list of deliverables, a schedule, a budget, and a defined acceptance process.

This subpractice typically includes the following tasks:

- Establishing the statement of work, specification, terms and conditions, list of deliverables, schedule, budget, and acceptance process
- Identifying who from the project and supplier are responsible and authorized to make changes to the supplier agreement
- Identifying how requirements changes and changes to the supplier agreement are to be determined, communicated, and addressed
- Identifying standards and procedures that will be followed
- Identifying critical dependencies between the project and the supplier
- Identifying the type and depth of project oversight of the supplier, including selection of processes to be monitored and work products to be evaluated (and the corresponding procedures and evaluation criteria to be used)
- Identifying the types of reviews that will be conducted with the supplier
- Identifying the supplier's responsibilities for ongoing maintenance and support of the acquired products
- Identifying warranty, ownership, and rights of use for the acquired products
- Identifying acceptance criteria
- Identifying specific requirements, scope, level of service, and communication processes to be provided by the suppliers
- Aligning subcontract service level agreements with contractor's service level agreements
- Ensuring that risk handling responsibilities are flowed down to suppliers as appropriate
- Reviewing the legal aspects of the supplier agreement if necessary to ensure compliance and enforceability

---

In some cases, selection of COTS products may require a supplier agreement in addition to the agreements in the product's license. Examples of what could be covered in an agreement with a COTS supplier include the following:

- Discounts for large quantity purchases
- Coverage of relevant stakeholders under the licensing agreement, including project suppliers, team members, and the project's customer
- Plans for future enhancements
- On-site support, such as responses to queries and problem reports
- Additional capabilities that are not in the product
- Maintenance support, including support after the product is withdrawn from general availability

4. Periodically review the supplier agreement to ensure that it accurately reflects the project's relationship with the supplier and current risks and market conditions.

5. Ensure that all parties to the supplier agreement understand and agree to all requirements before implementing the agreement or any changes.

6. Revise the supplier agreement as necessary to reflect changes to the supplier's processes or work products.

7. Revise the project's plans and commitments, including changes to the project's processes or work products, as necessary to reflect the supplier agreement.

> *Refer to the Project Monitoring and Control process area for more information about monitoring commitments.*

SG 2 SATISFY SUPPLIER AGREEMENTS

Agreements with suppliers are satisfied by both the project and the supplier.

SP 2.1 EXECUTE THE SUPPLIER AGREEMENT

Perform activities with the supplier as specified in the supplier agreement.

Refer to the Project Monitoring and Control process area for more information about monitoring the project against the plan and managing corrective action to closure.

Typical Work Products

1. Supplier progress reports and performance measures
2. Supplier review materials and reports
3. Action items tracked to closure
4. Product and documentation deliveries

Subpractices

1. Monitor supplier progress and performance (e.g., schedule, effort, cost, technical performance) as defined in the supplier agreement.

2. Conduct reviews with the supplier as specified in the supplier agreement.

   > *Refer to the Project Monitoring and Control process area for more information about conducting milestone reviews and progress reviews.*

   Reviews cover both formal and informal reviews and include the following steps:
   • Preparing for the review
   • Ensuring that relevant stakeholders participate

- Conducting the review
- Identifying, documenting, and tracking all action items to closure
- Preparing and distributing to the relevant stakeholders a summary report of the review

3. Conduct technical reviews with the supplier as defined in the supplier agreement.

Technical reviews typically include the following:
- Providing the supplier with visibility into the needs and desires of the project's customers and end users as appropriate
- Reviewing the supplier's technical activities and verifying that the supplier's interpretation and implementation of the requirements are consistent with the project's interpretation
- Ensuring that technical commitments are being met and that technical issues are communicated and resolved in a timely manner
- Obtaining technical information about the supplier's products
- Providing appropriate technical information and support to the supplier
- Evaluating the supplier's delivery of services against targets in service agreements (e.g., service level agreements, operating level agreements)

---

4. Conduct management reviews with the supplier as defined in the supplier agreement.

Management reviews typically include the following:
- Reviewing critical dependencies
- Reviewing project risks involving the supplier
- Reviewing schedule and budget
- Reviewing the supplier's compliance with legal and regulatory requirements

---

Technical and management reviews may be coordinated and held jointly.

5. Use the results of reviews to improve the supplier's performance and to establish and nurture long-term relationships with preferred suppliers.

Possible sources for improvements to the supplier's performance or the organization-supplier relationship may come from analyzing the results of technical and management reviews as well as a comprehensive review that ensures alignment of business needs and contractual obligations. A comprehensive review of supplier agreements is held periodically to ensure alignment of business needs and contractual obligations. Improvements identified during these reviews may be recorded and included in an improvement plan.

6. Monitor risks involving the supplier, and take corrective action as necessary.

Refer to the Risk Management process area for more information about identifying and analyzing risks.

Examples of sources of risks to monitor include the following:
- Supplier's ability to continue effective delivery
- Supplier's viability
- Items covered by nondisclosure agreements
- Contract terms and conditions
- Availability of alternative suppliers

SP 2.2 MONITOR SELECTED SUPPLIER PROCESSES

Select, monitor, and analyze processes used by the supplier.

Supplier processes that are critical to the success of the project (e.g., due to complexity, due to importance) should be monitored. The selection of processes to monitor must consider the impact of the supplier's processes on the project.

On larger projects with significant subcontracts, monitoring key processes is expected. For smaller, less critical components, the selection process may determine that monitoring is not appropriate. Between these extremes, the overall risk should be considered in selecting processes to be monitored.

The processes selected for monitoring should include service system development, project management (including risk management and contracting), and support processes critical to successful project performance.

Monitoring, if not performed with adequate care, can at one extreme be invasive and burdensome or at the other extreme be uninformative and ineffective. Monitoring should be sufficient to detect issues as early as possible that may affect the supplier's ability to satisfy the requirements of the supplier agreement.

Once data are obtained from monitoring selected supplier processes, they are analyzed to determine whether there are serious issues.

Documenting the roles and relationships between the project and its suppliers helps to ensure that effective monitoring and management of suppliers can be accomplished.

Typical Work Products

1. List of processes selected for monitoring or rationale for nonselection
2. Activity reports
3. Performance reports
4. Performance curves
5. Discrepancy reports

Subpractices

1. Identify the supplier processes that are critical to the success of the project.
2. Monitor the selected supplier's processes for compliance with requirements of the supplier agreement.
3. Analyze the results of monitoring the selected processes to detect issues as early as possible that may affect the supplier's ability to satisfy the requirements of the supplier agreement.

    Trend analysis can rely on internal and external data.
4. Determine and document actions needed to resolve detected issues.

    Refer to the Project Monitoring and Control process area for more information about managing corrective action to closure.

SP 2.3 *EVALUATE SELECTED SUPPLIER WORK PRODUCTS*

Select and evaluate work products from the supplier.

The scope of this specific practice is limited to suppliers providing the project with some risk due to complexity or criticality. The intent of this specific practice is to evaluate selected work products produced by the supplier to help detect issues as early as possible that may affect the supplier's ability to satisfy the requirements of the supplier agreement.

The work products selected for evaluation should include critical products, product components, and work products that provide insight into quality issues as early as possible. In situations of low risk, it may not be necessary to select any work products for evaluation.

Typical Work Products

1. List of work products selected for evaluation or rationale for non-selection
2. Activity reports
3. Discrepancy reports

Subpractices

1. Identify the work products that are critical to the success of the project and that should be evaluated to help detect issues early.

Examples of supplier work products that may be critical to the success of the project include the following:
- Requirements
- Analyses
- Architecture
- Documentation
- Service staffing plans
- Service procedures

---

2. Evaluate the selected work products.

    Work products are evaluated to ensure the following as appropriate:
    - Derived requirements are traceable to higher level requirements
    - The architecture is feasible and will satisfy future product growth and reuse needs.
    - Documentation that will be used to operate and support the product or service is adequate.
    - Work products are consistent with one another.
    - Products and product components (e.g., custom-made products, off-the-shelf products) can be integrated.
    - Service staffing plans are feasible.
    - Service procedures are complete.
3. Determine and document actions needed to address deficiencies identified in the evaluations.

    Refer to the Project Monitoring and Control process area for more information about managing corrective action to closure.

SP 2.4 *ACCEPT THE ACQUIRED PRODUCT*

Ensure that the supplier agreement is satisfied before accepting the acquired product.

An acceptance process involving appropriate activities, such as acceptance reviews, tests, and configuration audits, should be completed before accepting the product as defined in the supplier agreement.

When acquiring a service that will be delivered directly to the service provider's customer or end user, this practice may be implemented before, during, or after delivery of the service to the customer or end user. Potentially, you may implement this specific practice more than once.

Typical Work Products

1. Acceptance procedures
2. Acceptance review or test results
3. Discrepancy reports or corrective action plans

Subpractices

1. Define the acceptance procedures.
2. Review and obtain agreement from relevant stakeholders on the acceptance procedures before the acceptance review or test.
3. Verify that the acquired products satisfy their requirements.

Examples of verifying that an acquired service satisfies its requirements include the following:
- Piloting the service and comparing the results against its service level agreement or operating level agreement
- Inspecting the supplier's service system to verify that it meets its requirements
- Monitoring the supplier's delivery (or deliveries) of the service to the customer against the requirements in the supplier agreement

---

Refer to the Service System Development process area for more information about verifying and validating service systems.

SSD ADD

4. Confirm that the nontechnical commitments associated with the acquired products are satisfied.
   This confirmation may include confirming that the appropriate license, warranty, ownership, use, and support or maintenance agreements are in place and that all supporting materials are received.

5. Document the results of the acceptance review or test.

Examples of documenting the results of an acceptance review of a service include the following:
- A report assessing the results of piloting the service
- A report evaluating the results of inspecting the supplier's service system
- A completed checklist recording the results of monitoring the supplier's delivery (or deliveries) of the service to the customer

---

6. Establish an action plan, and obtain supplier agreement to take action to correct acquired products that do not pass their acceptance review or test.

7. Track action items to closure.

   Refer to the Project Monitoring and Control process area for more information about tracking corrective action to closure.

SP 2.5 ENSURE TRANSITION OF PRODUCTS

Ensure the transition of acquired products from the supplier to the project as appropriate.

Before the acquired product is transferred to the project, customer, or end user, appropriate planning and evaluation should occur to ensure a smooth transition. The use of "as appropriate" in this specific practice refers to the fact that the transition of products is not applicable to those acquired products that are services, because they cannot be stored. Therefore, in a service context, this practice applies only to products that are not services.

Refer to the Service System Development process area for more information about integrating service system components.

SSD ADD

Typical Work Products

1. Transition plans
2. Training reports
3. Support and maintenance reports
4. Descriptions of how ongoing support obligations, such as warranties and licenses, will be satisfied

SAM

Subpractices

1. Ensure that there are facilities to receive, store, integrate, and maintain the acquired products, as appropriate.

2. Ensure that appropriate training is provided for those involved in receiving, storing, integrating, and maintaining acquired products.

3. Ensure that acquired products are stored, distributed, and integrated according to the terms and conditions specified in the supplier agreement or license.

SERVICE CONTINUITY
A Project Management Process Area at Maturity Level 3

Purpose

The purpose of Service Continuity (SCON) is to establish and maintain plans to ensure continuity of services during and following any significant disruption of normal operations.

IN OTHER WORDS

SCON is about being ready to recover from a disaster and get back to delivering your service.

Introductory Notes

Service continuity is the process of preparing mitigation for significant disruptions to service delivery so that delivery can continue or resume, although perhaps in a degraded fashion. These practices describe how to prepare service systems and the resources they depend on to help ensure that a minimum critical level of service can continue if a significant risk is realized. Part of service continuity is identifying which services cannot be disrupted and which can be disrupted and for what amount of time.

WHY DO THE PRACTICES IN SCON?

The consequences of hurricane Katrina and 9/11 are proof for service businesses that those who prepare for disaster are better able to recover and stay in business.

The Service Continuity process area builds on the practices in the Risk Management process area. The Risk Management process area describes a general systematic approach to identifying and mitigating all risks to proactively minimize their impact on the project. Service continuity practices are a specialization of risk management that focuses on dealing with significant disruptions of normal operations. If risk management has been implemented, some of the resulting capability may be used to provide for more effective service continuity. However, generic risk management does not guarantee that service continuity is accomplished. Therefore, the specific practices of the Service Continuity process area are required in addition to those of the Risk Management process area.

Service Continuity can be applied at both the organization level and the project level. Therefore, the use of the term "organization" in this process area can apply to a project or the organization as appropriate.

507

SCON

Typically, service disruption is a situation that involves an event (or sequence of events) that make it virtually impossible for a service provider to conduct business as usual.

Examples of such events include the following:
- Disruptions to infrastructure, such as significant equipment malfunctions and building collapse
- Natural disasters, such as hurricanes, tornados, and earthquakes
- Human events, such as civil unrest and acts of terrorism

A service provider may only have a short period of time in which to recover and resume providing services.

The Service Continuity process area covers developing, testing, and maintaining a service continuity plan. First, the following must be identified:

- The essential functions that support the services the organization has agreed to deliver
- The resources that are required to deliver services
- The potential hazards or threats to these resources
- The susceptibility of the service provider to the effects of each hazard or threat
- The potential impact of each threat on service continuity

This information is used to develop a service continuity plan that, in the event of a disruption, enables the organization to resume service delivery. Creating the service continuity plan typically involves the following three activities conducted after the information listed above has been collected. All of these activities, including the collection of information, are repeated periodically to keep the plan current:

- Documenting the service continuity plan based on the information previously collected
- Documenting the tests to validate the service continuity plan
- Documenting the training materials and training delivery methods for carrying out the service continuity plan

Finally, service continuity plans must be validated. Because it is unwise to wait until an emergency occurs to first execute the service continuity plan, personnel who will perform the procedures in the service continuity plan must be trained in how to perform these procedures. In addition, periodic tests must be conducted to determine whether the service continuity plan would be effective in an actual emergency or significant disruption and what changes to the plan are needed to enable the organization to continue to deliver service reliably.

SERVICE CONTINUITY

If you've read and understood the Risk Management process area, you may wonder why service continuity requires its own process area. Isn't service continuity just a special kind of risk management? And if so, isn't it already covered by the Risk Management process area? If service continuity is *not* a kind of risk management, what is it all about? Disaster recovery?

In fact, service continuity as described in this process area *is* a type of risk management, one that focuses on risks that are so catastrophic or overwhelming that they can potentially bring an organization to a complete halt for extended periods of time and at a minimum will severely cripple the full spectrum of its operations. Service continuity goals and practices help to ensure that the most critical services can continue to be delivered in some form in spite of such major disruptions.

Service continuity needs its own process area because the Risk Management process area is completely agnostic with respect to the selection of risks that projects and organizations choose to address and mitigate. Because the probabilities of many types of major disasters are so low, and because most of them have causes that are outside any form of control by a service provider (and in some cases, are even outside the realm of predictability), it is quite possible for projects and organizations to perform reasonable risk management without addressing potential major disasters at all.

The CMMI for Services model team felt that such a blind spot would be unacceptable for any sufficiently mature (level 3) service provider organization. The specific goals and practices of the Service Continuity process area are necessary to be certain that the risks of major disasters are not overlooked and that appropriate types of mitigations are established, trained for, verified, and validated. In fact, the depth of service continuity preparation necessarily goes far beyond the types of mitigations required for routine risk management. Separate goals and practices are needed to ensure that mature service providers have made these necessary preparations.

Related Process Areas

Refer to the Service Delivery process area for more information about delivering services.

Refer to the Decision Analysis and Resolution process area for more information about evaluating alternatives.

Refer to the Organizational Training process area for more information about delivering training.

Refer to the Project Planning process area for more information about developing a project plan.

Refer to the Risk Management process area for more information about identifying and analyzing risks.

Specific Goal and Practice Summary

SG 1 Identify Essential Service Dependencies
    SP 1.1   Identify and Prioritize Essential Functions
    SP 1.2   Identify and Prioritize Essential Resources
SG 2 Prepare for Service Continuity
    SP 2.1   Establish Service Continuity Plans
    SP 2.2   Establish Service Continuity Training
    SP 2.3   Provide and Evaluate Service Continuity Training
SG 3 Verify and Validate the Service Continuity Plan
    SP 3.1   Prepare for the Verification and Validation of the Service Continuity Plan
    SP 3.2   Verify and Validate the Service Continuity Plan
    SP 3.3   Analyze Results of Verification and Validation

Specific Practices by Goal

SG 1 *IDENTIFY ESSENTIAL SERVICE DEPENDENCIES*

The essential functions and resources on which services depend are identified and documented.

The first step in service continuity planning is to identify and prioritize essential services so that a plan can be created that enables these services to be provided during an emergency.

The second step is to identify and document the functions and resources on which these services depend. Essential functions may include manual processes, automated processes, end-user activities, and service delivery activities themselves whether prescheduled or a result of on-the-fly service request management.

Identified and prioritized services, functions, and resources are effectively the requirements for service continuity and can be managed as such.

Refer to the Requirements Management process area for more information about managing requirements.

SP 1.1 IDENTIFY AND PRIORITIZE ESSENTIAL FUNCTIONS

Identify and prioritize the essential functions that must be performed to ensure service continuity.

To identify essential functions, an intimate understanding of all service system operations is required. Although many functions are important, not every activity performed is an essential function that must be sustained in an emergency or significant disruption of services.

The priorities of essential functions should reflect which services can be disrupted and for what period of time (i.e., long *versus* short disruption). Understanding which services are critical drives which essential functions are required to provide critical services.

Establishing correct priorities requires involvement of a wide range of stakeholders.

Refer to the Integrated Project Management process area for more information about coordinating and collaborating with relevant stakeholders.

Typical Work Products

1. A business impact analysis

Subpractices

1. Identify and prioritize the essential services of the organization.
2. Identify the essential functions on which services rely.
3. Analyze the criticality of providing those functions and the impact to services if the essential functions cannot be performed.

    Refer to the Decision Analysis and Resolution process area for more information about analyzing possible decisions using a formal evaluation process that evaluates identified alternatives against established criteria.

4. Prioritize the list of essential functions that must be provided despite a significant disruption.

SP 1.2 *IDENTIFY AND PRIORITIZE ESSENTIAL RESOURCES*

Identify and prioritize the essential resources required to ensure service continuity.

Essential resources are resources necessary to the continued functioning or reconstitution of services during and after an emergency. These resources are typically unique and hard to replace. Essential resources therefore include key personnel as well as essential assets, data, and systems. Essential resources may need to be protected. Suitable substitutes may need to be provisioned in advance. In the case of data, backups and archives may need to be established.

Many organizations make the mistake of identifying systems, personnel, and infrastructure inside the organization while overlooking resources outside the organization on which service continuity also depends. Resources that are commonly overlooked include consumables and vital records (e.g., documents describing legal or financial obligations).

Essential resources may be identified through analyses of the following:

- Delivery of services
- Functions essential to service continuity
- In-service agreements, supplier agreements, and standard service definitions
- Dependencies among service system components, relevant stakeholders, and the delivery environment

Common resource dependencies include information and data sources from both inside and outside the organization and the key personnel who make decisions regarding the service delivery or who are significant contributors to performing service delivery tasks.

Refer to the Integrated Project Management process area for more information about coordinating and collaborating with relevant stakeholders.

Essential resources generally fall into one of the following categories:

- Emergency operating resources (e.g., key personnel, equipment, consumables) necessary to resume disrupted services
- Legal and financial resources (e.g., contractual documents) that are essential to protect the rights and interests of the organization and individuals directly affected by the emergency

Refer to the Plan Data Management specific practice in the Project Planning process area for more information about data management activities.

Typical Work Products

1. Orders of succession
2. Delegations of authority
3. Directory of critical personnel with contact information
4. Data and systems required to support identified essential service functions
5. Records of service agreements and contracts
6. Records of legal operating charters (e.g., articles of incorporation, authorization by local, state, or national government agencies)
7. Personnel benefit balances, payroll, and insurance records
8. List of internal and external resources required
9. List of dependencies and interdependencies of resources

Subpractices

1. Identify and document internal and external dependencies.
2. Identify and document key personnel and their roles in relation to service delivery.
3. Identify and document organizational and relevant stakeholder responsibilities.
4. Identify and document resources required by essential functions to ensure continuity.
5. Prioritize resources based on an evaluation of impact from their loss or from lack of access.
6. Ensure that safety provisions are made for personnel, both internal and external, within the delivery environment and for organizational supporting functions.
7. Ensure that records and databases are protected, accessible, and usable in an emergency.

SG 2 PREPARE FOR SERVICE CONTINUITY

Preparations are made for service continuity.

Preparing for service continuity involves creating a plan, delivering training to execute the plan, and putting resources into place such as back up sites or systems.

Not all services must be resumed immediately following a disruption. The service continuity plan identifies those services that must be resumed and the priority sequence for recovery of those services.

In addition, training to execute the service continuity plan must be developed and delivered to those who may have to implement the plan.

Refer to the Integrated Project Management process area for more information about integrating plans.

Refer to the Project Planning process area for more information about developing a project plan.

SP 2.1 ESTABLISH SERVICE CONTINUITY PLANS

Establish and maintain service continuity plans that enable the organization to resume performing essential functions.

A service continuity plan provides explicit guidance to the organization in the event of a significant disruption to normal operations. An organization may maintain multiple plans covering different types of disruptions or different types of services. Conversely, there may be need for only one service continuity plan.

Typical Work Products

1. Formal statement of who has the authority to initiate and execute the service continuity plan
2. List of communication mechanisms needed to initiate the execution of the service continuity plan
3. List of threats and vulnerabilities that could impede the ability of the organization to deliver services
4. List of alternate resources and locations that support the organization's essential functions
5. Documentation of the recovery sequence
6. List of key personnel's roles and responsibilities
7. List of stakeholders and the methods used for communicating with them
8. Documented methods for handling security-related material, as appropriate

Subpractices

1. Identify and document threats and vulnerabilities to ongoing service delivery.

    Information on threats and vulnerabilities is usually developed in other processes and activities and used as an input to the service continuity plan. In the service continuity plan, the events, threats, and vulnerabilities most likely to lead to enacting the plan are recorded. Different actions may be planned for categories of events. Risk information gathered about individual services may also be an input to this portion of the plan.

Refer to the Risk Management process area for more information about identifying, analyzing, and mitigating risks.

2. Document the service continuity plan.
3. Review the service continuity plan with relevant stakeholders.

Refer to the Service System Development process area for more information about performing peer reviews.

SSD ADD

4. Ensure that secure storage and access methods exist for the service continuity plan and critical information and functions needed to implement the plan.
5. Ensure that vital data and systems are adequately protected.
   Addressing the protection of vital data and systems may include developing additional service system components.

Refer to the Service System Development process area for more information about developing service systems.

SSD ADD

6. Document the acceptable service level agreed to by the customer for when a shift between the normal delivery environment and the recovery environment (e.g., site affected by disruption, alternate site) is necessary.
   Document the acceptable service levels for various outage scenarios (e.g., site, city, country).
7. Plan for returning to normal working conditions.
8. Develop procedures for implementing the service continuity plan.
9. Revise the service continuity plan as necessary.

Examples of when the service continuity plan may need to be revised include the following:
- There are major changes to the services being delivered.
- Essential functions or infrastructure change.
- Key dependencies on resources, both internal and external, change.
- Feedback from training warrants change.
- Preparing for verification and validation of the service continuity plan identifies changes that are needed.
- Results of verification and validation warrant change.
- The delivery environment changes.
- New significant threats or vulnerabilities have been identified.

SCON

SP 2.2 *ESTABLISH SERVICE CONTINUITY TRAINING*

Establish and maintain training for service continuity.

Training the personnel who will be involved in executing the service continuity increases the probability of success in the event that the plan must be executed. It may be appropriate to include the customer and end user in service continuity training.

Examples of when customers and end users should be considered include the following:
- Situations in which the customer and end user are colocated with the service provider and could be affected by the same events causing the service provider to initiate its service continuity plan
- Situations in which a change required by executing a service continuity plan may affect the customer's or end user's way of doing business

---

Examples of the types of staff to be trained include the following:
- Personnel who respond to service requests
- Personnel who provide infrastructure support (e.g., information technology, utilities)
- End users
- Suppliers
- Selected project and organization managers and staff

Examples of service continuity training methods include the following:
- Role playing
- Scenario-based training
- Classroom instruction
- Group discussions

Typical Work Products

1. Service continuity training material

Subpractices

1. Develop a strategy for conducting service continuity training.
2. Develop and document service continuity training for each category of threat and vulnerability to service delivery.
3. Review service continuity training material with relevant stakeholders.

> *Refer to the Service System Development process area for more information about performing peer reviews.*

4. Revise the training material as needed to reflect changes in the service continuity plan and feedback on training effectiveness.

SP 2.3 PROVIDE AND EVALUATE SERVICE CONTINUITY TRAINING

Provide and evaluate training in the execution of the service continuity plan.

Training provides instruction to personnel who might have to participate in executing the service continuity plan in the event of a significant disruption. In addition, training provides a mechanism for gathering feedback on whether the service continuity plan should be updated or clarified.

Refer to the Organizational Training process area for more information about providing necessary training.

Typical Work Products

1. Training records
2. Evaluations of training effectiveness by students and training specialists
3. Suggested improvements to the service continuity plan

Subpractices

1. Deliver training that covers the execution of the service continuity plan to appropriate personnel.
2. Maintain records of those who successfully complete service continuity training.
3. Solicit feedback on how well service continuity training prepared those who will execute the service continuity plan.
4. Analyze training feedback and document suggested improvements to the service continuity plan and service continuity training.

SG 3 VERIFY AND VALIDATE THE SERVICE CONTINUITY PLAN

The service continuity plan is verified and validated.

Verifying and validating the service continuity plan helps to ensure preparedness for various threats and vulnerabilities before a significant disruption occurs. This practice enables reviews, tests, and demonstrations to be conducted in a relatively benign environment.

Accomplishing verification and validation includes selecting appropriate methods, conducting verification and validation, and analyzing results.

Examples of verification methods include the following:
- Inspections
- Peer reviews
- Audits
- Walkthroughs
- Analyses
- Simulations
- Testing
- Demonstrations

Examples of validation methods include the following:
- Discussions with end users, perhaps in the context of a formal review
- Prototype demonstrations
- Functional demonstrations (e.g., testing a backup file system, exercising an alternative communication network to coordinate service delivery, switching to manual processes)
- Pilots of training materials
- Tests of the service system and its components by end users and other relevant stakeholders

---

The Service System Development process area contains practices that focus on verifying and validating service system components and services. The guidance found there may be useful when implementing verification and validation of service continuity plans.

Refer to the Service System Development process area for more information about verifying selected service system components against their specified requirements.

SSD ADD

SP 3.1 PREPARE FOR THE VERIFICATION AND VALIDATION OF THE SERVICE CONTINUITY PLAN

Prepare for the verification and validation of the service continuity plan.

Verification and validation should be conducted on a periodic and event-driven basis. Typically, the verification and validation of the service continuity plan is performed periodically (e.g., annually).

However, when there are major changes to the service system or to the delivery environment, the service continuity plan should be reviewed or tested to confirm that the service continuity plan is still correct and current.

Typical Work Products

1. Verification and validation plan for ensuring service continuity
2. Evaluation methods used for verification and validation
3. Description of environments necessary to conduct verification and validation
4. Verification and validation procedures
5. Criteria for what constitutes successful verification and validation

Subpractices

1. Develop a plan for conducting service continuity verification and validation.

   The strategy for conducting service continuity verification and validation documents the requirements for verification and validation and addresses the key principles, activities, resources, and environments required for effective verification and validation of the service continuity plan.

   Verification and validation is not a one-time event. The strategy should address the frequency with which verification and validation should be performed.

The plan for conducting verification and validation of the service continuity plan typically includes the following:
- Strategy used for conducting verification and validation
- Categories of threats and vulnerabilities to be evaluated
- Essential functions and resources to be verified and validated for each category
- Methods to evaluate the adequacy of preparation
- Environments needed to support verification and validation
- Schedule of activities to conduct verification and validation
- Assigned resources

---

2. Review with relevant stakeholders the verification and validation plan, including evaluation methods and the environments and other resources that will be needed.

   Stakeholders must understand and agree to the verification and validation strategy, methods, activities, environments, and resources.

SCON

3. Determine the procedures and criteria for verification and validation of the service continuity plan.

   Procedures and criteria are used to ensure that the elements of the service continuity plan are correct, effective, and current relative to the categories of threats and vulnerabilities.

4. Identify changes to the service continuity plan from the preparation for verification and validation.

SP 3.2 VERIFY AND VALIDATE THE SERVICE CONTINUITY PLAN

Verify and validate the service continuity plan.

Verification and validation is conducted according to the defined plan, methods, and procedures to confirm that the service continuity plan is complete, reasonable, and effective.

Typical Work Products

1. Roster of personnel and stakeholders involved in service continuity verification and validation
2. Results of service continuity plan verification and validation

Subpractices

1. Prepare the environment to conduct verification and validation.
2. Conduct verification and validation of the service continuity plan.
3. Record the results of verification and validation activities.

SP 3.3 ANALYZE RESULTS OF VERIFICATION AND VALIDATION

Analyze the results of validation and verification activities.

Results of service continuity plan verification and validation are analyzed against defined verification and validation criteria. Analysis reports identify elements to improve in the service continuity plan and identify problems with verification and validation methods, environments, procedures, and criteria.

Typical Work Products

1. Verification and validation analysis reports
2. Improvement recommendations for the service continuity plan
3. Verification and validation improvement recommendations

Subpractices

1. Compare actual to expected results of service continuity plan verification and validation.

2. Evaluate whether restoration to agreed service levels or some other planned state was achieved.

3. Document recommendations for improving the service continuity plan.

4. Document recommended improvements to the verification and validation of the service continuity plan.

5. Collect improvement proposals for services or service system components as appropriate based on the analyses of results.

6. Provide information on how defects can be resolved (including verification methods, criteria, and the verification environment) and initiate corrective action.

> *Refer to the Project Monitoring and Control process area for more information about managing corrective action to closure.*

SERVICE DELIVERY

A Service Establishment and Delivery Process Area at Maturity Level 2

Purpose

The purpose of Service Delivery (SD) is to deliver services in accordance with service agreements.

Introductory Notes

The Service Delivery process area focuses on the following:

- Establishing and maintaining service agreements
- Preparing and maintaining a service delivery approach
- Preparing for service delivery
- Delivering services
- Receiving and processing service requests
- Maintaining service systems

Service delivery covers establishing and maintaining a written agreement with customers. A "service agreement" describes the service to be delivered to the customer, service level targets, and responsibilities of the service provider, customer, and end user, as appropriate.

A service agreement may cover multiple services or multiple customers. It can take the form of a service level agreement (SLA), performance work statement (PWS), statement of objectives (SOO), statement of work (SOW), or other type of agreement. The service agreement may be part of a contract, a memorandum of agreement, an approved requirements document, or some other document. For simple cases, it may be nothing more than a printed menu of services and prices.

The Service Delivery process area supports a positive relationship between the service provider and its customers and end users while

IN OTHER WORDS

SD is about setting up agreements, taking care of service requests, and operating the service system.

WHY DO THE PRACTICES IN SD?

You and your customer have the same expectation, your services are consistent and cost-effective, and customers know how to make requests.

The service delivery approach can be a more operational view of the material in SP 1.1 in PP: Establish the Project Strategy.

SD

meeting the needs of all three. Service delivery processes should encourage open communication without the assignment of blame. The primary focus is on satisfying the documented needs of end users.

A "customer" is a party (i.e., individual, project, or organization) responsible for accepting the service or for authorizing payment. Customers identify their needs for services, buy services, and define and agree to service level targets. Customers may be internal or external to the service provider's organization and may or may not be the same as end users, who are the ultimate beneficiaries of service delivery.

In addition to establishing service agreements, the Service Delivery process area includes practices for preparing for service delivery as well as for operating, monitoring, and maintaining the service system. Service delivery is accomplished through the operation of the service system in response to service requests, which are communications from customers or end users that identify a need to deliver an agreed service. These requests are made within the context of an accepted service agreement.

There are two types of service requests:

- Those that are specified on a continuous or scheduled basis as determined by service agreements
- Those that are identified over time by customers or end users as their needs develop on an ad hoc basis

---

Examples of ad hoc requests include the following:
- Requesting a custom-made query on a database as part of a systems management service
- Calling for a package pickup as part of a package delivery service
- Identifying a broken component of a maintained system as part of a maintenance service
- Requesting a health check as part of a health program

Whatever the nature of a specific service request, it should be recorded, tracked, and resolved through some type of request management system. This approach helps to ensure that all service requests are fulfilled to meet service agreements. The response to service requests also encompasses performing any needed low-level planning as a detailed extension of broader project planning activities.

Related Process Areas

Refer to the Service System Development process area for more information about analyzing, designing, developing, integrating, verifying, and validating service systems, including service system components, to satisfy existing or anticipated service agreements.

Refer to the Service System Transition process area for more information about deploying new or significantly changed service system components while managing their effect on ongoing service delivery.

Refer to the Configuration Management process area for more information about establishing baselines and tracking and controlling changes.

Refer to the Project Monitoring and Control process area for more information about monitoring the project against the plan.

Specific Goal and Practice Summary

SG 1 Establish Service Agreements
    SP 1.1   Analyze Existing Agreements and Service Data
    SP 1.2   Establish the Service Agreement
SG 2 Prepare for Service Delivery
    SP 2.1   Establish the Service Delivery Approach
    SP 2.2   Prepare for Service System Operations
    SP 2.3   Establish a Request Management System
SG 3 Deliver Services
    SP 3.1   Receive and Process Service Requests
    SP 3.2   Operate the Service System
    SP 3.3   Maintain the Service System

Specific Practices by Goal

SG 1   ESTABLISH SERVICE AGREEMENTS

Service agreements are established and maintained.

The service agreement between a service provider and a customer is established and maintained. An ongoing collaborative approach to the activities described in this process area encourages a culture that supports service quality improvement in contrast to a culture that focuses on blame and disputing small details of agreements.

The service agreement should be established prior to the start of service delivery. Over time, the service agreement may be revised based on service delivery results (e.g., to reflect needed changes to services delivered, service level targets, or the responsibilities of the service provider or customer).

To succeed in maintaining collaboration between the service provider and customer, it is important to define the responsibilities of both parties. It is also important to set realistic expectations for service levels, which requires defining measurable, achievable service levels.

When standard service definitions and baseline service delivery data are available at the organizational level, the service provider should use that information as a basis for establishing and tailoring agreements.

> *Refer to the Service System Development process area for more information about developing and analyzing stakeholder requirements.*

SSD ADD

Refer to the Strategic Service Management process area for more information about establishing and maintaining standard services in concert with strategic needs and plans.

Refer to the Project Monitoring and Control process area for more information about monitoring commitments.

SP 1.1 ANALYZE EXISTING AGREEMENTS AND SERVICE DATA

Analyze existing service agreements and service data to prepare for expected new agreements.

This practice considers the complete context in which requirements are being established. Customer goals, supplier constraints, service provider concerns, and existing service delivery data and definitions (e.g., performance data, service levels, baselines, resource use, monitoring capabilities, service catalogs, standard service lines) are included in this analysis.

The analysis of existing agreements and service data is an activity that is repeatedly executed during the service agreement's life. The service agreement is not a static artifact. It is dynamic and must be adjustable because the ongoing analysis of service data and agreements may identify changes over time.

Typical Work Products

1. Customer descriptions of plans, goals, and service needs
2. Results of customer and end-user satisfaction surveys and questionnaires
3. Results of assessments of provider capability to meet customer needs

Subpractices

1. Review available customer and end-user need data.

   It is important to obtain an understanding of the customer and end-user perceptions of service prior to establishing the service agreement. These perceptions may include customer objectives that are not directly expressed as service requirements.

Examples of sources of customer and end-user need data include the following:
- Face-to-face or telephone interviews
- Customer-supplied plans and goals outlining their expected use of services
- Statements of work and related solicitation materials
- Customer and end-user survey results

   Refer to the Strategic Service Management process area for more information about gathering and analyzing relevant data.

2. Review concerns of service delivery and support personnel.

   Prior to establishing the service agreement, it is important to obtain an understanding of the perspectives of the service delivery and support personnel who work with customers and end users. These personnel are ultimately responsible for ensuring that service delivery meets requirements. They also have unique operational insight into the potential impacts of new agreements. This information may be collected through face-to-face or telephone interviews, or through other methods of soliciting employee feedback (e.g., staff meetings, e-mail, surveys).

3. Review existing service agreements and supplier agreements.

Reviewing existing agreements includes the following:
- Considering the impact of the customer's supplier agreements on the achievement of the requested service
- Reviewing the requested service requirements against standard service definitions if they exist
- Reviewing existing service level agreements and supplier agreements (e.g., operational level agreements, underpinning contracts) for their ability to meet identified service requirements

---

4. Review available current service data and service system designs.

   Existing service data (e.g., performance data, service levels, baselines, incident histories, data from capacity and availability management) and capabilities (e.g., monitoring capabilities) are reviewed. Available industry benchmarks or other published data may be used, especially in the case of service requirements not previously addressed by the provider.

Refer to the Capacity and Availability Management process area for more information about monitoring and analyzing capacity and availability.

Refer to the Incident Resolution and Prevention process area for more information about identifying, controlling, and addressing incidents.

Refer to the Service System Development process area for more information about developing the design of the service system.   **SSD ADD**

5. Analyze the capability to supply requested services.
    Consider the overall approach to how the requested service delivery will be accomplished.

> Approaches to service delivery include the following make-buy-reuse approaches:
> - By using the resources of an existing service system
> - By modifying or creating a service system to meet new requirements
> - By outsourcing some services or service system components to external suppliers

Refer to the Capacity and Availability Management process area for more information about ensuring effective service system performance and ensuring that resources are provided and used effectively to support service requirements.

Refer to the Service System Development process area for more information about developing service systems.   **SSD ADD**

Refer to the Supplier Agreement Management process area for more information about managing the acquisition of products and services from suppliers.

SP 1.2 ESTABLISH THE SERVICE AGREEMENT

Establish and maintain the service agreement.

Depending on the service type, market, and the nature of the service provider's business model, the initial form of a service agreement may be determined by either the customer or the service provider. There may be different types of content in the agreement that must be established by one party or the other, or that must be jointly negotiated.

The service agreement should cover all terms, conditions, and commitments that are necessary for ongoing successful service delivery, including commitments for which customers and end users are responsible when appropriate.

Examples of items in a service agreement include the following:
- Service types, levels, and measures
- Service availability
- Service acceptance and quality criteria
- Acceptable impact on customer and end-user activities
- Risk and contingency identification
- Intellectual property considerations
- Customer and end-user roles and responsibilities
- Customer-supplied resources
- Expected cost, payment, and funding schedules
- Security and safety considerations

Refer to the Strategic Service Management process area for more information about establishing properties of standard services and service levels.

Typical Work Products

1. Service agreement

Subpractices

1. Define the structure and format of the service agreement.

    It is important to define a structure for the service agreement that will meet the needs of the customer and service provider. The structure of the service agreement complements or reflects the critical attributes, categories, and structure or hierarchy of standard service definitions if they exist.

Examples of structures to consider include the following:
- Service based: The service agreement is organized around a service (e.g., providing corporate e-mail) and may cover several different customers.
- Customer based: The service agreement is organized around a customer and may cover several services for that customer.

In some service contexts (e.g., government contracting), customers provide considerable detail on their expectations for the structure and format of a service agreement. In those situations, this subpractice amounts to developing an understanding of the customer's expectations and the range of allowable tailoring of the agreement's structure and format.

2. Define, negotiate, and obtain agreement on a draft service agreement.
3. Publish the service agreement and make it available to service providers, customers, and end users, as appropriate.
4. Review and revise the service agreement on a periodic and event-driven basis as appropriate.

SG 2 PREPARE FOR SERVICE DELIVERY

Preparation for service delivery is conducted.

Preparing for service delivery involves developing a detailed approach for receiving and processing service requests and for delivering services specified in the service agreements. The approach includes identifying and integrating the required service delivery activities, ensuring that service systems are ready for service delivery in the appropriate service delivery environments, and ensuring that requisite consumables are on hand.

SP 2.1 ESTABLISH THE SERVICE DELIVERY APPROACH

Establish and maintain the approach to be used for service delivery and service system operations.

The service delivery approach identifies and describes resources, processes, and interfaces that are essential to successful service delivery over time.

A service delivery approach addresses how the following activities should be carried out:

- Delivering services in accordance with an established schedule
- Preparing and updating the schedule for daily operations
- Making and transferring assignments for performing service delivery operations
- Communicating appropriate information to operations staff, management, customers, and end users
- Using methods and tools for performing service delivery operations
- Assigning and transferring responsibility for resolving requests
- Assigning and transferring responsibility for monitoring the status of requests and for tracking the progress of actions related to requests
- Enabling customers and end users to submit requests
- Categorizing requests
- Using methods and tools for request management
- Collecting, distributing, and analyzing performance data

A mature project or organization treats these items as components of a defined service system and develops them during a rigorous set of service system development practices.

Refer to the Capacity and Availability Management process area for more information about ensuring effective service system performance and ensuring that resources are provided and used effectively to support service requirements.

Refer to the Service System Development process area for more information about analyzing, designing, developing, integrating, verifying, and validating service systems, including service system components, to satisfy existing or anticipated service agreements.

SSD ADD

Refer to the Project Planning process area for more information about developing a project plan.

Typical Work Products

1. Service delivery approach (i.e., approach to request management and service system operations)
2. Contact and roster lists
3. Service request criteria
4. Internal status reporting templates (e.g., dashboards)
5. External status reporting templates (e.g., service request completion notices)

Subpractices

1. Define criteria for determining service requests.

    To be able to identify valid service requests, criteria must be defined that enable service providers to determine what is and what is not a service request. In addition, there are typically criteria for differentiating the priority of a service request and its associated impact.

2. Define categories for service requests and criteria for categorizing service requests.

    The fulfillment of service requests is facilitated by having an established set of categories. These predetermined categories can enable appropriate and efficient assignment of resources.

Examples of service request categories include the following:
- Administrative service request (e.g., set up new user, change passwords, restore backup files)
- Software request (e.g., install a software package, upgrade a software package)
- Lab request (e.g., radiology analysis, blood analysis)
- Oversized package delivery
- Billing inquiry

SD

3. Describe how responsibility for processing service requests is assigned and transferred.

The description may include the following:
- Who is responsible for addressing the request
- Who is responsible for monitoring and tracking the status of the request
- Who is responsible for tracking the progress of actions related to the request
- How responsibility for all of these activities is assigned and transferred

---

4. Identify one or more mechanisms that customers and end users can use to submit service requests.

   These mechanisms must account for how groups and individuals can submit requests, such as through telephone support, paper forms (mailed or delivered in person), and electronic forms submitted through Web pages.

5. Identify requirements on the amount of time defined for the fulfillment of service requests in the service agreement.

   Often, the agreed minimum and maximum amount of time needed for fulfillment of service requests is documented in the service agreement before the start of service delivery.

6. Determine the resource requirements for service delivery as required.

   Resource requirements are generated by service agreements, by the need to respond to foreseeable service incidents and requests, and by the need to maintain service systems so that service delivery can continue over time. These resources may include personnel, consumables, and any other resources that must be controlled to ensure that service is delivered in accordance with service agreements.

   Refer to the Capacity and Availability Management process area for more information about ensuring effective service system performance and ensuring that resources are provided and used effectively to support service requirements.

7. Review, refine, or enhance stakeholder communication mechanisms (e.g., notices, status reports, dashboards) as necessary.

   Methods and tools for communicating with customers, end users, service provider personnel, and other relevant stakeholders during the course of service delivery are components of a complete service system. These methods and tools (e.g., contact lists) may be created during service system development, but they should be reviewed regularly, tailored, and possibly supplemented to meet ongoing service delivery needs.

> *Refer to the Service System Development process area for more information about developing service systems.*

8. Document the service delivery approach.

9. Review and get agreement with relevant stakeholders on the approach for delivering each separately identifiable service.

   Information presented to stakeholders about the approach should be in terms that they can understand. The review should allow them to identify concerns about the approach.

10. Revise the approach for delivering services as necessary.

SP 2.2 PREPARE FOR SERVICE SYSTEM OPERATIONS

Confirm the readiness of the service system to enable the delivery of services.

Ensure that the appropriate service system components (e.g., tools, consumables, people, processes, procedures) are ready for service system operations. Service systems may require that consumables be acquired to enable consistent service delivery. Confirming the ongoing readiness for service delivery is not a one-time practice. These activities should be performed repeatedly as needed by the overall service delivery approach, even when the service system is not changing.

Refer to the Service System Transition process area for more information about deploying new or significantly changed service system components while managing their effect on ongoing service delivery.

Typical Work Products

1. Monitoring tool thresholds validation report
2. Operating procedures validation report
3. Consumables (e.g., paper media, magnetic media) validation report
4. Logs of consumable acquisition and use
5. Service delivery logs and receipts
6. Results from demonstrated service system operation

Subpractices

1. Confirm that the appropriate service system's components and tools are operational.

Examples of service system tools include the following:
- Monitoring tools
- System management tools
- Tracking systems
- Presentation tools
- Log files
- Analysis tools
- Online knowledge management tools
- Virus scanning tools
- Database management tools

---

2. Evaluate the results of confirming service system component readiness, and determine what corrective action is needed.

    Depending on the situation, any deficiencies or issues that are uncovered should be treated as service incidents.

    Refer to the Incident Resolution and Prevention process area for more information about identifying, controlling, and addressing incidents.

3. Review the service level requirements in the service agreements, and ensure that proper thresholds are set in service system monitoring tools.

4. Develop, review, or refine service delivery procedures.

    Detailed processes, standard operating procedures, or work instructions may be created during service system development, but they must be reviewed regularly, tailored, and possibly supplemented to meet ongoing service delivery needs.

    Refer to the Service System Development process area for more information about developing service systems.

5. Ensure that necessary resources are available for performing service delivery activities and tasks.

    Service delivery activities and tasks may include the following: operating, monitoring, and repairing service system components; supporting users of the service system; and acquiring and replacing service system components.

6. Prepare and update detailed job execution and monitoring schedules for delivering services as requested.

7. Provide orientation to incoming service delivery and support personnel on current service delivery operations during personnel changes.

    Whenever there is a change of personnel involved in service delivery (e.g., a staff rotation at a shift change), incoming personnel are oriented on the current state of operations to ensure that ongoing service delivery is not interrupted.

8. Ensure that any necessary consumables are available for service delivery.

Procedures are documented for replenishing consumables and replacing or upgrading infrastructure components. As necessary, acquire and inspect service system consumables according to documented procedures.

SP 2.3 ESTABLISH A REQUEST MANAGEMENT SYSTEM

Establish and maintain a request management system for processing and tracking request information.

A request management system includes the storage media, procedures, and tools for accessing the request management system. These storage media, procedures, and tools may be automated but are not required to be. For example, storage media might be a filing system where documents are stored. Procedures may be documented on paper, and tools may be hand tools or instruments for performing work without automated help.

Service requests are often submitted through a service desk or help desk function.

Typical Work Products

1. A request management system with controlled work products
2. Access control procedures for the request management system

Subpractices

1. Ensure that the request management system allows the reassignment and transfer of requests among groups.

Requests may need to be transferred between different groups because the group that entered the request may not be best suited for taking action to address it.

2. Ensure that the request management system allows the storage, update, and retrieval of request management information.

Examples of request management systems include the following:
- Help desk
- Ticket tracking
- Service log books
- Task status boards

---

3. Ensure that the request management system enables data reporting that is useful to the fulfillment of requests.

4. Maintain the integrity of the request management system and its contents.

Examples of maintaining the integrity of the request management system include the following:

- Backing up and restoring request records
- Archiving request records
- Maintaining security that prevents unauthorized access

---

5. Maintain the request management system as necessary.

SG 3 DELIVER SERVICES

Services are delivered in accordance with service agreements.

Services are delivered continuously and in response to service requests in accordance with service agreements. This delivery is accomplished through operation of the service system, which must be kept in operation or returned to operation as needed in spite of the occurrence of service incidents. The service system is also subject to varying needs for maintenance.

Refer to the Incident Resolution and Prevention process area for more information about identifying, controlling, and addressing incidents.

SP 3.1 RECEIVE AND PROCESS SERVICE REQUESTS

Receive and process service requests in accordance with service agreements.

Service requests may be submitted through various mechanisms (e.g., Web forms, phone calls). Some requests may also be identified in service agreements, especially those for continuous or repeatedly scheduled services. The receipt and processing of all service requests should be coordinated through an established request management system.

Typical Work Products

1. Request management record
2. Action proposal
3. Customer satisfaction data
4. End user receipts confirming request fulfillment

Subpractices

1. Receive service requests and ensure that each request is within the scope of the service agreement.

Examples of receiving service requests include the following:
- Service requests submitted by the customer or end user by use of a Web form
- Service requests submitted by the customer or end user by calling the help desk or service desk

---

In organizations that use a help desk function, service requests are usually submitted to such a function.

2. Record information about the service request.

When recording service request information, include sufficient information to properly support the analysis and resolution of the service request.

Examples of service request information to record include the following:
- Name and contact information of the person who submitted the service request
- Description of the service request
- Categories the service request belongs to
- Date and time the service request was submitted
- The configuration items involved in the request
- Closure code and information

---

3. Categorize and analyze the service request.

Using the categories established in the approach to service delivery, assign the relevant categories to the service request in the request management system. For some service requests, the request analysis may be completed by merely selecting the type of service request. For other service requests (e.g., upgrade operating system software), it may be necessary to assemble a special team to analyze the request.

Examples of when to perform request analysis include the following:
- When the impact of the request on the organization or customer is large
- When resolving a service request will take considerable time or effort

---

4. Determine which resources are required to resolve the service request.

Which individuals, groups, and other resources are best suited may depend on the type of service request, locations involved, and impact on the organization or customer.

5. Determine actions that must be taken to satisfy the service request.

Using the categories established in the approach to service delivery, determine the appropriate actions to perform. In some cases, the categories themselves may have predetermined actions associated with them.

Examples of actions include the following:
- Answering a customer inquiry
- Repairing items (as part of a maintenance service)
- Training an end user
- Providing new consumables or tools

---

6. Plan the actions further as appropriate.

Perform additional scheduling and other planning required to guide the actions that have been selected. When analyzing standard service requests, the actions for resolving a standard service request may be documented in a standard action plan.

7. Monitor the status of service requests as appropriate until they are fulfilled as described in the service agreement.

Throughout the life of the service request, the status of the request must be recorded, tracked, transferred as necessary, and closed.

Refer to the Project Monitoring and Control process area for more information about monitoring the project against the plan.

8. Review service request status and resolution, and confirm results with relevant stakeholders.

Communication is a critical factor when providing services. Communication with the person who requested the service and possibly other stakeholders affected by it should be considered throughout the life of the service request in the request management system. Usually, the result of relevant actions taken should be reviewed with the person who submitted the service request to verify that the actions fulfilled the service request to the satisfaction of the submitter.

In organizations that use a help desk function, the status of service requests is communicated to relevant stakeholders by the help desk.

9. Close the service request and record the actions taken and results.

The actions performed to fulfill the service request and the result of performing the actions are recorded in the request management system to support satisfying similar service requests in future situations.

SP 3.2 OPERATE THE SERVICE SYSTEM

Operate the service system to deliver services in accordance with service agreements.

This practice encompasses performing the activities necessary to operate the service system to deliver services based on the agreed service delivery approach. Operation means the integrated performance of a service system and use of its processes and other resources by service provider personnel to deliver services to end users.

Typical Work Products

1. List of services delivered
2. Service logs
3. Performance reports and dashboards
4. Log of corrective actions
5. Customer satisfaction data
6. Request management database record

Subpractices

1. Operate service system components according to service system procedures.

   Operating service system components may include starting or stopping them, providing input to them, controlling them, or handling output from them, as appropriate.

2. Perform operations support activities (e.g., revise thresholds).

3. Manage the critical dependencies and paths of the service delivery schedules according to operating procedures.

   Management of some service delivery activities can be adequately covered by project management and measurement and analysis activities, especially for service requests identified directly in service agreements.

4. Manage and control the security of service delivery.

   Security can include monitoring for security breaches, ensuring that vulnerabilities are corrected, and controlling access to services.

   When delivering services, the service systems should ensure that only approved services as specified in the service agreement are delivered to authorized personnel.

5. Perform low-level monitoring of service system components using monitoring and data collection tools as appropriate.

   Some monitoring of service system operation can be adequately covered by project-level monitoring and control or measurement and analysis. However, some services may require monitoring and data collection at the level of individual service requests or continuously within the scope of a single service request. Such low-level monitoring may require its own tools to handle data collection, analysis, and reporting appropriately. These tools are often automated.

6. As appropriate, perform the activities needed to fulfill service requests or resolve service incidents according to the service agreement.

   Throughout the life of a service request or service incident, its status must be recorded, tracked, escalated as necessary, and closed. The appropriate resolution of an incident may be a simple operational procedure (e.g., restarting a failed service system component), or it may involve some degree of service system maintenance.

   Refer to the Incident Resolution and Prevention process area for more information about identifying, controlling, and addressing incidents.

   Refer to the Project Monitoring and Control process area for more information about monitoring the project against the plan.

7. Communicate the status of service requests until closed.

8. Collect customer satisfaction information immediately after services are delivered or service requests are fulfilled.

SP 3.3 MAINTAIN THE SERVICE SYSTEM

Maintain the service system to ensure the continuation of service delivery.

Operational service systems must be maintained to ensure a continuing capability to deliver services in accordance with service agreements over time. This practice may encompass a variety of types of maintenance, including the following:

- Corrective maintenance (i.e., correcting and repairing components that degrade the operational capability of the service system)
- Preventive maintenance (i.e., preventing service incidents and defects from occurring through preplanned activities)
- Adaptive maintenance (i.e., adapting the service system to a changing or different service delivery environment)
- Perfective maintenance (i.e., developing or acquiring additional or improved operational capability of the service system)

Corrective maintenance may be performed to address service incidents or to resolve their underlying causes.

Depending on the type and scope of actual instances of service system maintenance, other process areas may contribute practices that are relevant to accomplishing this effort, especially for any maintenance that has the following characteristics:

- Represents a change to the requirements or design of the service system (e.g., perfective maintenance)
- Entails significant risks to implement changes required by maintenance activities

Maintenance can be performed on any portion of a service system, including consumables, processes, and people. The maintenance of people as service system components is often accomplished through training, although other methods may be appropriate as well (e.g., transferring personnel to roles that better match their skills).

Refer to the Service System Development process area for more information about developing and analyzing stakeholder requirements. **SSD ADD**

Refer to the Service System Transition process area for more information about preparing for service system transition.

Refer to the Configuration Management process area for more information about tracking and controlling changes.

Typical Work Products

1. Corrective or preventive maintenance change requests
2. Maintenance notifications
3. Preventive maintenance schedules

Subpractices

1. Review maintenance requests and prioritize requests based on criteria identified when establishing the service delivery approach.

    Significant maintenance activities—ones that result in changes to the requirements or design of the service system—benefit from Service System Development practices as well. **SSD ADD**

2. Analyze impacts on service systems and services delivery.
3. Develop a plan to implement maintenance.
    Nonroutine maintenance requests should be scheduled into agreed maintenance slots to ensure that the availability of services is not adversely impacted.
4. Release maintenance notifications to relevant stakeholders.
5. Update service system documentation as appropriate.

SD

6. Implement and test corrective or preventive maintenance according to the plan and operating procedures.

   Testing should be performed outside the service delivery environment when appropriate. Significant maintenance changes to a service system should apply Service System Transition practices as well.

7. Submit maintenance documentation and configuration changes to a configuration management repository.

SERVICE SYSTEM DEVELOPMENT
A Service Establishment and Delivery Process Area at Maturity Level 3

Purpose

The purpose of Service System Development (SSD) is to analyze, design, develop, integrate, verify, and validate service systems, including service system components, to satisfy existing or anticipated service agreements.

Introductory Notes

The Service System Development process area is applicable to all aspects of a service system. It applies to new service systems as well as changes to existing service systems.

A "service system" is an integrated and interdependent combination of service system components that satisfies stakeholder requirements.

A "service system component" is a process, work product, person, consumable, or customer or other resource required for a service system to deliver value. Service system components may include components owned by the customer or a third party.

A "service system consumable" is anything usable by the service provider that ceases to be available or becomes permanently changed by its use during the delivery of a service.

The people who are considered service system components are those who perform tasks as part of the service system, including provider staff and end users, to enable the system to operate and thereby deliver services.

See the definitions of "service system," "service system component," "service system consumable," and "work product" in the glossary.

Organizations that wish to improve and appraise their product development processes should rely on the complete CMMI-DEV model, which specifically focuses on development as an area of interest.

IN OTHER WORDS

SSD is about making sure you have everything you need to deliver the services, including people, processes, consumables, and equipment.

Remember that "system" does not mean an IT system; we intend the more general definition of system: a regularly interacting or interdependent group of items forming a unified whole.

It is common for service businesses to already have a service system in place for services already in their portfolio. If you do, the practices in SSD are used to confirm and make adjustments as needed.

WHY DO THE PRACTICES IN SSD?

You anticipate service requirements and avoid costly changes. The service system does what is required for both the service provider and the customer.

**WHY IS SSD
AN ADDITION?**

We intended this option to be user friendly for the large range of service types covered by CMMI-SVC. Very large, complex services may use the Engineering PAs of CMMI-DEV instead. Very small, simple services need not use SSD at all.

If SSD is too much, you can find service system help with small, simple services in the following two places in the model:

- The example box in SD SP 2.1 for what to include in the service delivery approach

- SP 1.3 in IPM, Establish the Project's Work Environment

Service provider organizations may also choose to use the CMMI-DEV model as the basis for improving and appraising their service system development processes. This use of the CMMI-DEV model is preferred for organizations that are already experienced with CMMI-DEV and for those that must develop large-scale, complex service systems.

However, the Service System Development process area offers an alternative means of achieving somewhat similar ends by covering requirements development as well as service system development, integration, verification, and validation in a single process area. Using SSD may be preferred by service provider organizations that are new to CMMI, especially those that are developing simple services with relatively few components and interfaces. Even organizations that use the CMMI-DEV model for service system development may wish to refer to the Service System Development process area for helpful guidance on applying development practices to service system components, such as people, processes, and consumables.

It is especially important to remember that the components of some service systems may be limited to people and the processes they perform. In those and similar contexts in which service systems are fairly simple, exercise care when interpreting the specific practices of this process area so that the implementations that result provide business value to the service provider organization.

The service system development process is driven by service and service system requirements that are collected from various sources, such as service agreements and defects and problems identified during both service delivery and incident resolution and prevention processes.

The Service System Development process area focuses on the following activities:

- Collecting, coordinating, analyzing, validating, and allocating stakeholder requirements for service systems
- Evaluating and selecting from alternative service system solutions
- Designing and building or composing (as needed), integrating, and documenting service systems that meet requirements
- Verifying and validating service systems to confirm that they satisfy their intended requirements and will satisfy customer and end-user expectations during actual service delivery

SSD ADDITION

Related Process Areas

Refer to the Service Delivery process area for more information about maintaining the service system.

Refer to the Service System Transition process area for more information about deploying the service system.

Refer to the Strategic Service Management process area for more information about establishing standard services.

Refer to the Decision Analysis and Resolution process area for more information about analyzing possible decisions using a formal evaluation process that evaluates identified alternatives against established criteria.

Refer to the Organizational Innovation and Deployment process area for more information about selecting and deploying incremental and innovative improvements.

Refer to the Requirements Management process area for more information about managing requirements.

Specific Goal and Practice Summary

SG 1 Develop and Analyze Stakeholder Requirements
    SP 1.1   Develop Stakeholder Requirements
    SP 1.2   Develop Service System Requirements
    SP 1.3   Analyze and Validate Requirements
SG 2 Develop Service Systems
    SP 2.1   Select Service System Solutions
    SP 2.2   Develop the Design
    SP 2.3   Ensure Interface Compatibility
    SP 2.4   Implement the Service System Design
    SP 2.5   Integrate Service System Components
SG 3 Verify and Validate Service Systems
    SP 3.1   Prepare for Verification and Validation
    SP 3.2   Perform Peer Reviews
    SP 3.3   Verify Selected Service System Components
    SP 3.4   Validate the Service System

SSD Addition

Specific Practices by Goal

SG 1   DEVELOP AND ANALYZE STAKEHOLDER REQUIREMENTS

Stakeholder needs, expectations, constraints, and interfaces are collected, analyzed, and transformed into validated service system requirements.

SSD

This goal covers the transformation of collected stakeholder needs, expectations, and constraints into requirements that can be used to develop a service system that enables service delivery.

Needs are collected from sources that may include service agreements, standard defined services, organizational policies, and communication with end users, customers, and other relevant stakeholders. These service needs may define stakeholder expectations of what is to be delivered, specify particular levels or grades of service, or identify constraints on how, when, how often, or to whom services are to be delivered. These needs, expectations, and constraints in turn may need to be analyzed and elaborated to identify needed details of delivered services not considered by the original sources. The result is a set of stakeholder requirements specified in the language of service system developers, not in the language of those who submitted the requirements.

For example, a customer might establish a requirement to "maintain the equipment listed in Table 25 in working order" with additional details of availability rates, average repair times, and other service levels. However, this requirement may also imply a need for a variety of specialized subservices, such as diagnostics, field support, and preventive maintenance, each with its own implied subservice requirements. These refinements may not be of interest or even visible to the original stakeholders, but their full specification is needed to identify everything that a service system must do to meet the service delivery requirements.

As service requirements are analyzed and elaborated, they eventually yield derived service system requirements, which define and constrain what the service system must accomplish to ensure that the required service is delivered. For example, if the service has a response time requirement, the service system must have derived requirements that enable it to support that response time.

The process of developing and analyzing requirements may involve multiple iterations that include all relevant stakeholders in communicating requirements and their ramifications so that everyone agrees on a consistent defined set of requirements for the service system. Changes may be driven by changes to stakeholder expectations or by new needs discovered during subsequent service system development activities, service system transition, or service delivery. Since needs often change throughout the life of the project, the development and analysis of requirements should rarely be considered a one-time process.

SSD ADDITION

As with all requirements, appropriate steps are taken to ensure that the approved set of service and service system requirements is effectively managed to support development of the service and service system.

Refer to the Requirements Management process area for more information about managing requirements changes.

SP 1.1 DEVELOP STAKEHOLDER REQUIREMENTS

Collect and transform stakeholder needs, expectations, constraints, and interfaces into stakeholder requirements.

The needs of relevant stakeholders (e.g., customers, end users, suppliers, builders, testers, manufacturers, logistics support personnel, service delivery personnel) are the basis for determining stakeholder requirements. Stakeholder needs, expectations, constraints, interfaces, operational concepts, and service concepts are analyzed, harmonized, refined, and elaborated for translation into a set of stakeholder requirements.

Requirements collected from customers and end users of the service to be delivered are documented in the service agreement. These requirements are also used to derive requirements for the service system. These derived requirements are combined with other requirements collected for the service system to result in the complete set of stakeholder requirements.

Refer to the Service Delivery process area for more information about analyzing existing agreements and service data.

These stakeholder requirements should be stated in language that the stakeholders can understand yet precise enough for the needs of those developing the service or service system.

Examples of stakeholder requirements include the following:
- Operations requirements
- Customer delivery requirements
- Monitoring requirements
- Instrumentation requirements
- Documentation requirements
- Operating level agreement requirements
- Requirements from agreements with other stakeholders

SSD ADDITION

SSD

Typical Work Products

1. Customer requirements
2. End-user requirements
3. Customer and end-user constraints on the conduct of verification and validation
4. Staffing level constraints

Subpractices

1. Engage relevant stakeholders using methods for eliciting needs, expectations, constraints, and external interfaces.

   Eliciting goes beyond collecting requirements by proactively identifying additional requirements not explicitly provided by customers through surveys, analyses of customer satisfaction data, prototypes, simulations, etc.

2. Transform stakeholder needs, expectations, constraints, and interfaces into stakeholder requirements.

   The various inputs from relevant stakeholders must be consolidated, missing information must be obtained, and conflicts must be resolved in documenting the recognized set of stakeholder requirements.

3. Define constraints for verification and validation.

SP 1.2   DEVELOP SERVICE SYSTEM REQUIREMENTS

Refine and elaborate stakeholder requirements to develop service system requirements.

Stakeholder requirements are analyzed in conjunction with the development of the operational concept to derive more detailed and precise sets of requirements called "derived requirements." These requirements address all aspects of the service system associated with service delivery, including work products, services, processes, consumables, and customer and other resources.

See the definition of "operational concept" in the glossary.

Derived requirements arise from constraints, consideration of issues implied but not explicitly stated in the stakeholder requirements baseline, and factors introduced by the selected service system architecture, the design, the developer's unique business considerations, and strategic priorities, including industry market trends. The extent and depth of derived requirements vary with the complexity of the service system needed to meet stakeholder requirements.

SSD ADDITION

Refer to the Strategic Service Management process area for more information about establishing standard services.

In some service contexts, derived requirements may be as simple as identification and quantification of required resources. For complex service systems with many types of components and interfaces, the initial requirements are reexamined through iterative refinement into lower level sets of more detailed requirements that parallel the functional architecture as the preferred solution is refined.

Typical Work Products

1. Derived requirements with relationships and priorities
2. Service requirements
3. Service system requirements
4. Requirement allocations
5. Design constraints
6. Interface requirements
7. Skill-level requirements

Subpractices

1. Develop requirements and express them in the terms necessary for service and service system design.
2. Derive requirements that result from solution selections and design decisions.
3. Establish and maintain relationships among requirements for consideration during change management and requirements allocation.
   Relationships among requirements can aid in design and in evaluating the impact of changes.
4. Allocate the requirements to service system components.
   Relationships include dependencies in which a change in one requirement may affect other requirements.
5. Identify interfaces both external and internal to the service system.
6. Develop requirements for the identified interfaces.

SP 1.3 ANALYZE AND VALIDATE REQUIREMENTS

Analyze and validate requirements, and define required service system functionality.

Requirements analyses are performed to determine the impact the intended service delivery environment will have on the ability to satisfy the stakeholders' needs, expectations, constraints, and interfaces.

Depending on the service delivery context, factors such as feasibility, mission needs, cost constraints, end-user heterogeneity, potential market size, and procurement strategy must be taken into account. A definition of required functionality is also established. All specific methods of service delivery are considered and a timeline analysis is generated for time-critical sequencing of functions.

The objectives of the analyses are to determine candidate requirements for service system concepts that will satisfy stakeholder needs, expectations, and constraints, and then to translate these concepts into comprehensive service system requirements. In parallel with this activity, the parameters used to evaluate the effectiveness of service delivery are determined based on customer and end-user input and the preliminary service delivery concept.

Requirements are validated by working with relevant stakeholders to increase the probability that the resulting service system will deliver services as intended in the expected delivery environment.

Typical Work Products

1. Operational concepts, use cases, activity diagrams, and timeline scenarios
2. Service system and service system component installation, training, operational, maintenance, support, and disposal concepts
3. New requirements
4. Functional architecture
5. Requirements defects reports and proposed changes to resolve
6. Assessment of risks related to requirements
7. Record of analysis methods and results

Subpractices

1. Develop operational concepts and scenarios that include functionality, performance, maintenance, support, and disposal as appropriate.

    Identify and develop scenarios consistent with the level of detail in the stakeholder needs, expectations, and constraints in which the proposed service system is expected to operate.

    Operational concept and scenario development is an iterative process. Reviews of operational concepts and scenarios should be held periodically to ensure that they agree with the requirements. The review may be in the form of a walkthrough.

SSD ADDITION

2. Develop a detailed operational concept that defines the interaction of the service system, end users, and the environment and that satisfies operational, maintenance, support, and disposal needs.

3. Establish and maintain a definition of required functionality.
   The definition of functionality, also referred to as "functional analysis," is the description of what the service system is designed to do. The definition of functionality can include actions, sequence, inputs, outputs, or other information that communicates the manner in which the service system will operate.

4. Analyze requirements to ensure that they are necessary, sufficient, and balance stakeholder needs and constraints.
   As requirements are defined, their relationship to higher level requirements and the higher level defined functionality must be understood. One of the other actions is to determine which key requirements will be used to track progress.

5. Validate requirements to ensure that the resulting service system will perform as intended in the user's environment

SG 2 *DEVELOP SERVICE SYSTEMS*

Service system components are selected, designed, implemented, and integrated.

A service system can encompass work products, processes, people, consumables, and customer and other resources.

An important and often-overlooked component of service systems is the human aspect. People who perform tasks as part of a service system enable the system to operate, and both provider staff and end users may fill this role. For example, a service system that processes incoming calls for a service must have available trained staff that can receive the calls and process them appropriately using the other components of the service system. In another example, end users of an insurance service may need to follow a prescribed claims process to receive service benefits from the service system.

A consumable is anything usable by the service provider that ceases to be available or becomes permanently changed because of its use during the delivery of a service. An example is gasoline for a transportation service system that uses gasoline-powered vehicles. Even service systems that are comprised primarily of people and manual processes often use consumables such as office supplies. The role of consumables in service systems should always be considered.

SSD ADDITION

SSD

This goal focuses on the following activities:

- Evaluating and selecting solutions that potentially satisfy an appropriate set of requirements
- Developing detailed designs for the selected solutions (detailed enough to implement the design as a service system)
- Implementing the designs of service system components as needed
- Integrating the service system so that its functions can be verified and validated

Typically, these activities overlap, recur, and support one another. Some level of design, at times fairly detailed, may be needed to select solutions. Prototypes, pilots, and stand-alone functional tests may be used as a means of gaining sufficient knowledge to develop a complete set of requirements or to select from among available alternatives.

From a people perspective, designs may be skill-level specifications and staffing plans, and prototypes or pilots may try out different staffing plans to determine which one works best under certain conditions. From a consumables perspective, designs may be specifications of necessary consumable characteristics and quantities. Some consumables may even require implementation. For example, specific paper forms may need to be designed and printed to test them as part of the service system later.

Development processes are implemented repeatedly on a service system as needed to respond to changes in requirements, or to problems uncovered during verification, validation, transition, or delivery. For example, some questions that are raised by verification and validation processes may be resolved by requirements development processes. Recursion and iteration of these processes enable the project to ensure quality in all service system components before it begins to deliver services to end users.

SP 2.1 SELECT SERVICE SYSTEM SOLUTIONS

Select service system solutions from alternative solutions.

Alternative solutions and their relative merits are considered in advance of selecting a solution. Key requirements, design issues, and constraints are established for use in alternative solution analysis. Architectural features that provide a foundation for service system improvement and evolution are considered.

SSD ADDITION

Refer to the Decision Analysis and Resolution process area for more information about analyzing possible decisions using a formal evaluation formal evaluation process that evaluates identified alternatives against established criteria.

A potentially ineffective approach to implementing this practice is to generate solutions that are based on only the way services have been delivered in the past. It is important to consider alternatives that represent different ways of allocating and performing necessary functions (e.g., manual versus automated processes, end user versus service delivery personnel responsibilities, prescheduled versus on-the-fly service request management).

Components of the service system, including service delivery and support functions, may be allocated to external suppliers. As a result, prospective supplier agreements are investigated. The use of externally supplied components is considered relative to cost, schedule, performance, and risk. Externally supplied alternatives may be used with or without modification. Sometimes, such items may require modifications to aspects such as interfaces or a customization of some of their features to better meet service or service system requirements.

Refer to the Supplier Agreement Management process area for more information about managing the acquisition of products and services from suppliers.

Typical Work Products

1. Alternative solution screening criteria
2. Selection criteria
3. Service system component selection decisions and rationale
4. Documented relationships between requirements and service system components
5. Documented solutions, evaluations, and rationale

Subpractices

1. Establish defined criteria for selection.
2. Develop alternative solutions.
3. Select the service system solutions that best satisfy the criteria established.

    Selecting service system solutions that best satisfy the criteria is the basis for allocating requirements to the different aspects of the service system. Lower level requirements are generated from the selected alternative and used to develop the design of service system components. Interface requirements among service system components are described (primarily functionally).

SP 2.2 DEVELOP THE DESIGN

Develop designs for the service system and service system components.

The term "design" in this practice refers to the definition of the service system's components and their intended set of relationships; these components will collectively interact in intended ways to achieve actual service delivery.

Service system designs must provide the appropriate content not only for implementation but also for other aspects of the service system lifecycle, such as modification, transition and rollout, maintenance, sustainment, and service delivery. The design documentation provides a reference to support mutual understanding of the design by relevant stakeholders and supports making future changes to the design both during development and in subsequent phases of the lifecycle.

A complete design description is documented in a "design package" that includes a full range of features and parameters, including functions, interfaces, operating thresholds, manufacturing and service process characteristics (e.g., which functions are automated versus manually performed), and other parameters. Established design standards (e.g., checklists, templates, process frameworks) form the basis for achieving a high degree of definition and completeness in design documentation.

SSD ADDITION

Examples of other service-related work products include the following:
- Descriptions of roles, responsibilities, authorities, accountabilities, and skills of people required to deliver the service
- Functional use cases describing roles and activities of service participants
- Designs or templates for manuals, paper forms, training materials, and guides for end users, operators, and administrators

"Designing people" in this context means specifying the skills and skill levels necessary to accomplish needed tasks and may include appropriate staffing levels as well as training needs (if training is necessary to achieve needed skill levels).

"Designing consumables" in this context means specifying the consumable properties and characteristics necessary to support service delivery as well as resource utilization estimates for service system operation.

Typical Work Products

1. Service system architecture
2. Service system component and consumable designs
3. Skill descriptions and details of the staffing solution (e.g., allocated from available staff, hired as permanent or temporary staff)
4. Interface design specifications and control documents
5. Criteria for design and service system component reuse
6. Results of make-or-buy analyses

Subpractices

1. Develop a design for the service system.
2. Ensure that the design adheres to allocated requirements.
3. Document the design.
4. Design interfaces for the service system components using established criteria.

   The criteria for interfaces frequently reflect critical parameters that must be defined, or at least investigated, to ascertain their applicability. These parameters are often peculiar to a given type of service system and are often associated with safety, security, durability, and mission-critical characteristics. Carefully determine which processes should be automated or partially automated and which processes should be performed manually.

5. Evaluate whether the components of the service system should be developed, purchased, or reused based on established criteria.

SP 2.3 ENSURE INTERFACE COMPATIBILITY

Manage internal and external interface definitions, designs, and changes for service systems.

Many integration problems arise from unknown or uncontrolled aspects of both internal and external interfaces. Effective management of interface requirements, specifications, and designs helps to ensure that implemented interfaces will be complete and compatible.

In the context of service systems, interfaces can be broadly characterized according to one of four major groups:

- Person-to-person interfaces are those that represent direct or indirect communication between two or more people, any of whom might be service provider personnel or end users. For example, a call script, which defines how a help desk operator should interact with an end user, defines a direct person-to-person interface. Log books and instructional signage are examples of indirect person-to-person interfaces.

- Person-to-component interfaces are those that encompass interactions between a person and one or more service system components. These interfaces can include both graphical user interfaces for automated components (e.g., software applications) and operator control mechanisms for automated, partially automated, and nonautomated components (e.g., equipment, vehicles).
- Component-to-component interfaces are those that do not include direct human interaction. The interfaces of many interactions between automated components belong to this group, but other possibilities exist, such as specifications constraining the physical mating of two components (e.g., a delivery truck, a loading dock).
- Compound interfaces are those that merge or layer together interfaces from more than one of the other three groups. For example, an online help system with "live" chat support might have a compound interface built on an integrated combination of person-to-person, person-to-component, and component-to-component interfaces.

Interfaces can also be characterized as external or internal interfaces. "External interfaces" are interactions among components of the service system and any other entity external to the service system, including people, organizations, and systems. Internal interfaces can include the interactions among the staff, teams, and functions of the service-provider organization. "Internal interfaces" can also include interaction between the staff or end users and service system components.

Examples of user interface work products include the following:
- Customer interaction scripts
- Reporting types and frequency
- Application program interfaces

Typical Work Products

1. Categories of interfaces with lists of interfaces per category
2. Table or mapping of interface relationships among service system components and the external environment

SSD Addition

3. List of agreed interfaces defined for each pair of service system components when applicable

4. Reports from meetings of the interface control working group

5. Action items for updating interfaces

6. Updated interface description or agreement

Subpractices

1. Review interface descriptions for coverage and completeness.

   The interface descriptions should be reviewed with relevant stake-holders to avoid misinterpretations, reduce delays, and prevent the development of interfaces that do not work properly.

2. Manage internal and external interface definitions, designs, and changes for service system components.

SP 2.4 IMPLEMENT THE SERVICE SYSTEM DESIGN

Implement the service system design.

The term "implement" in this practice refers to the actual creation of designed components of the service system in a form that can subsequently be integrated, verified, and validated. "Implement" does not refer to putting the service system into place in the delivery environment. That deployment process occurs later, during service system transition.

In some cases, consumables and people (e.g., provider staff) may be "implemented." For example, specialized paper forms may need to be printed. The "implementation" of people may involve hiring new staff or putting into place a new organizational or team structure to handle new kinds of responsibilities. Such new structures should be integrated, verified, and validated prior to the start of service transition.

Refer to the Service System Transition process area for more information about deploying the service system.

Service system components are implemented from previously established designs and interfaces. The implementation may include stand-alone testing of service system components and usually includes the development of any necessary training materials for staff and end users.

SSD ADDITION

SSD

Example activities during implementation include the following:
- Interface compatibility is confirmed.
- Software is coded.
- Training materials are developed.
- Electrical and mechanical parts are fabricated.
- Procedures that implement process designs are written.
- Facilities are constructed.
- Supplier agreements are established.
- Personnel are hired or transferred.
- Organizational and team structures are established.
- Custom consumables are produced (e.g., disposable packaging materials).

Typical Work Products

1. Implemented service system components
2. Training materials
3. User, operator, and maintenance manuals
4. Procedure descriptions
5. Records of new hires and staff transfers
6. Records of communications about organizational changes

Subpractices

1. Use effective methods to implement the service system design.
2. Adhere to applicable standards and criteria.
3. Conduct peer reviews of selected service system components.
4. Perform standalone testing of service system components as appropriate.
5. Revise the service system as necessary.

SP 2.5 *INTEGRATE SERVICE SYSTEM COMPONENTS*

Assemble and integrate implemented service system components into a verifiable service system.

Integration of the service system should proceed according to a planned integration sequence and available procedures. Before integration, each service system component should be verified for compliance with its interface requirements. Service system components that are manual processes should be performed while making appropriate use of any other necessary service system components to verify compliance with requirements.

SSD ADDITION

During integration, subordinate components are combined into larger, more complex service system assemblies, and more complete service delivery functions are performed. These combined service system assemblies are checked for correct interoperation. This process continues until service system integration is complete. During this process, if problems are identified, the problems are documented and corrective actions are initiated.

Some service systems may require assembly with customer or end-user resources to complete full integration. When these resources are available under the terms of a service agreement, they should be incorporated as appropriate in integration activities. When such resources are not available from customers and end users, substitute equivalent resources may be employed temporarily to enable full service system integration.

Typical Work Products

1. Service system integration sequence with rationale
2. Documented and verified environment for service system integration
3. Service system integration procedures and criteria
4. Exception reports
5. Assembled service system components
6. Interface evaluation reports
7. Service system integration summary reports
8. Staffing plans that show the sequence of where and when staff members are provided

Subpractices

1. Ensure the readiness of the integration environment.
2. Confirm that each service system component required for integration has been properly identified and functions according to its description, and that all interfaces comply with their interface descriptions.
3. Evaluate the assembled service system for interface compatibility, functionality, and performance.

SG 3   VERIFY AND VALIDATE SERVICE SYSTEMS

Selected service system components and services are verified and validated to ensure correct service delivery.

Some service providers refer to all verification and validation as "testing." However, in CMMI, "testing" is considered a specific

SSD ADDITION

SSD

method used for verification or validation. Verification and validation are described separately in this process area to ensure that both aspects are treated adequately.

Examples of verification methods include the following:
- Inspections
- Peer reviews
- Audits
- Walkthroughs
- Analyses
- Simulations
- Testing
- Demonstrations

Examples of validation methods include the following:
- Discussions with users, perhaps in the context of a formal review
- Prototype demonstrations
- Functional presentations (e.g., service delivery run-throughs, end-user interface demonstrations)
- Pilots of training materials
- Tests of services and service system components by end users and other relevant stakeholders

---

Verification practices include verification preparation, conduct of verification, and identification of corrective action. Verification includes testing of the service system and selected service system components against all selected requirements, including existing service agreements, service requirements, and service system requirements.

Examples of service system components that may be verified and validated include the following:
- People
- Processes
- Equipment
- Software
- Consumables

SSD ADDITION

Validation demonstrates that the service system, as developed, will deliver services as intended. Verification addresses whether the service system properly reflects the specified requirements. In other words, verification ensures that "you built it right." Validation ensures that "you built the right thing."

Validation activities use approaches similar to verification (e.g., test, analysis, inspection, demonstration, simulation). These activities focus on ensuring that the service system enables the delivery of services as intended in the expected delivery environment. End users and other relevant stakeholders are usually involved in validation activities. Both validation and verification activities often run concurrently and may use portions of the same environment. Validation and verification activities can take place repeatedly in multiple phases of the service system development process.

SP 3.1 PREPARE FOR VERIFICATION AND VALIDATION

Establish and maintain an approach and an environment for verification and validation.

Preparation is necessary to ensure that verification provisions are embedded in service and service system requirements, designs, developmental plans, and schedules. Verification encompasses selection, inspection, testing, analysis, and demonstration of all service system components, including work products, processes, and consumable resources.

Similar preparation activities are necessary for validation to be meaningful and successful. These activities include selecting services and service system components and establishing and maintaining the validation environment, procedures, and criteria. It is particularly important to involve end users and front-line service delivery personnel in validation activities because their perspectives on successful service delivery can vary significantly from one another and from service system developers.

Typical Work Products

1. Lists of the service system components selected for verification and validation
2. Verification and validation methods for each selected component
3. Verification and validation environment
4. Verification and validation procedures
5. Verification and validation criteria

SSD ADDITION

SSD

Subpractices

1. Select the components to be verified and validated and the verification and validation methods that will be used for each.

   Service system components are selected based on their contribution to meeting project objectives and requirements and to addressing project risks.

2. Establish and maintain the environments needed to support verification and validation.

3. Establish and maintain verification and validation procedures and criteria for selected service system components.

SP 3.2 PERFORM PEER REVIEWS

Perform peer reviews on selected service system components.

Peer reviews involve a methodical examination of service system components by the producers' peers to identify defects for removal and to recommend changes.

A peer review is an important and effective verification method implemented via inspections, structured walkthroughs, or a number of other collegial review methods.

Typical Work Products

1. Peer review schedule
2. Peer review checklist
3. Entry and exit criteria for service system components and work products
4. Criteria for requiring another peer review
5. Peer review training material
6. Service system components selected for peer review
7. Peer review results, including issues and action items
8. Peer review data

Subpractices

1. Determine what type of peer review will be conducted.

Examples of types of peer reviews include the following:
- Inspections
- Structured walkthroughs
- Active reviews

SSD ADDITION

2. Establish and maintain peer review procedures and criteria for the selected service system components and work products.

3. Define requirements for the peer review.
   Peer reviews should address the following guidelines:
   - The preparation must be sufficient.
   - The conduct must be managed and controlled.
   - Consistent and sufficient data must be recorded.
   - Action items must be recorded.

Examples of requirements for peer reviews include the following:
- Data collection
- Entry and exit criteria
- Criteria for requiring another peer review

---

4. Establish and maintain checklists to ensure that service system components and work products are reviewed consistently.

Examples of items addressed by checklists include the following:
- Rules of construction
- Design guidelines
- Completeness
- Correctness
- Maintainability
- Common defect types

Checklists are modified as necessary to address the specific type of work product and peer review. Peers of checklist developers and potential users review the checklists.

5. Develop a detailed peer review schedule, including dates for peer review training and for when materials for peer reviews will be available.

6. Prepare for the peer review.

Preparation activities for peer reviews typically include the following:
- Identifying the staff who will be invited to participate in the peer review of each service system component or work product
- Identifying the key reviewers who must participate in the peer review
- Preparing and updating the materials to be used during the peer reviews, such as checklists and review criteria

---

SSD ADDITION

SSD

7. Ensure that the service system component or work product satisfies the peer review entry criteria, and make the component or work product available for review to participants early enough to enable them to adequately prepare for the peer review.

8. Assign roles for the peer review as appropriate.

> Examples of roles include the following:
> - Leader
> - Reader
> - Recorder
> - Author

9. Conduct peer reviews on selected service system components and work products, and identify issues resulting from the peer review.

    One purpose of conducting a peer review is to find and remove defects early. Peer reviews are performed incrementally as service system components and work products are being developed.

    Peer reviews may be performed on key work products of specification, design, test, and implementation activities and specific planning work products. Peer reviews may be performed on personnel staffing plans, competency descriptions, organizational structure, and other people-oriented aspects of a service system. However, they should be used to review individual performance and competency with caution and should be employed only in coordination with other methods of individual evaluation that the organization already has in place.

    When issues arise during a peer review, they should be communicated to the primary developer or manager of the service system component or work product for correction.

10. Conduct an additional peer review if the defined criteria indicate the need.

11. Ensure that exit criteria for the peer review are satisfied.

12. Record and store data related to the preparation, conduct, and results of peer reviews.

    Typical data are service system component or work product name, composition of the peer review team, type of peer review, preparation time per reviewer, length of the review meeting, number of defects found, type and origin of defect, and so on. Additional information on the service system component or work product being peer reviewed may be collected.

    Protect the data to ensure that peer review data are not used inappropriately. The purpose of peer reviews is to verify proper development and identify defects to ensure greater quality, not to provide

SSD ADDITION

reasons for disciplining personnel or publicly criticizing performance. Failure to protect peer review data properly can ultimately
compromise the effectiveness of peer reviews by leading participants
to be less than fully candid about their evaluations.

13. Analyze peer review data.

Examples of peer review data that can be analyzed include the following:
- Actual preparation time or rate versus expected time or rate
- Actual number of defects versus expected number of defects
- Types of defects detected
- Causes of defects
- Defect resolution impact

SP 3.3 VERIFY SELECTED SERVICE SYSTEM COMPONENTS

Verify selected service system components against their specified requirements.

The verification methods, procedures, criteria, and environment are
used to verify the selected service system and any associated maintenance, training, and support processes. Verification activities should
be performed throughout the service system lifecycle.

Typical Work Products

1. Verification results and logs
2. Verification reports
3. Analysis report (e.g., statistics on performance, causal analysis of
   nonconformance, comparison of the behavior between the real
   service system and models, trends)
4. Trouble reports
5. Change requests for verification methods, criteria, and the environment

Subpractices

1. Perform verification of selected service system components and
   work products against their requirements.
2. Record the results of verification activities.
3. Identify action items resulting from the verification of service system components and work products.
4. Document the "as-run" verification method and deviations from the
   available methods and procedures discovered during its performance.
5. Analyze and record the results of all verification activities.

SSD ADDITION

SSD

SP 3.4 *VALIDATE THE SERVICE SYSTEM*

Validate the service system to ensure that it is suitable for use in the intended delivery environment and meets stakeholder expectations.

The validation methods, procedures, and criteria are used to validate selected services, service system components, and any associated maintenance, training, and support processes using the appropriate validation environment. Validation activities are performed throughout the service system lifecycle. It is particularly important to involve actual end users and front-line service delivery personnel in validation activities because their perspectives on successful service delivery can vary significantly from each other and from service system developers.

Validation must take place in an environment that provides enough similarities to the delivery environment to ensure that validation actually occurs. The delivery environment is the complete set of circumstances and conditions under which services are actually delivered in accordance with service agreements. Sometimes validation may be effectively performed in a simulated environment, but in other contexts it can be performed only in a portion of the delivery environment. In those latter cases, care must be taken to ensure that validation activities do not perturb ongoing service activities to the point of risking failures of agreed service delivery.

See the definition of "delivery environment" in the glossary.

Typical Work Products

1. Validation reports and results
2. Validation cross-reference matrix
3. Validation deficiency reports and other issues
4. Change requests for validation methods, criteria, and the environment
5. User acceptance (i.e., sign off) for service delivery validation
6. Focus group reports

Subpractices

1. Perform functional and nonfunctional validation on selected service system components to ensure that they are suitable for use in their intended delivery environment.

   The validation methods, procedures, criteria, and environment are used to validate the selected service system components and any associated maintenance, training, and support services.

2. Analyze the results of validation activities.

The data resulting from validation tests, inspections, demonstrations, or evaluations are analyzed against defined validation criteria. Analysis reports indicate whether the needs were met. In the case of deficiencies, these reports document the degree of success or failure and categorize probable cause of failure. The collected test, inspection, or review results are compared with established criteria to determine whether to proceed or to address requirements or design issues.

SSD Addition

VERIFICATION AND VALIDATION

How do you make sure that your service system works properly and delivers services that your customers actually need? If you still think that "working properly" and "delivering actually needed services" mean the same thing, keep reading. The distinction is familiar to some people but is foreign to most.

When you verify your service system, you are checking that it satisfies all your service requirements. These include all the derived requirements for services, subservices, service system components, and interfaces, as well as the initial requirements derived from service agreements or standard service definitions. Verification can be performed by testing, but many other methods are available and may be appropriate for different situations, including inspections, peer reviews, prototyping, piloting, and modeling and simulation. The important thing to remember about verification is that it can *only* tell you if the service system satisfies all the expressed requirements. *Your service system can meet all of its expressed requirements and still fail to satisfy end users.*

A common way this can occur is through a requirements defect, in which one or more of the initial service requirements are ambiguous, incorrectly specified, outright wrong, or completely missing. If initial service requirements are specified well, derived requirements may have been developed inadequately. You may also have customers or end users with conflicting requirements that are not fully reflected in the initial requirements statements or that are fully expressed but without sufficient guidance for prioritizing requirements or otherwise resolving the conflicts.

Too often, these types of issues come to light only when a service system is actually delivering services to end users. Fixing a requirements defect after a service system has been built can be expensive at best and can create a good deal of customer ill will at worst.

Continues

SSD

Validation practices help to keep these problems from occurring, by making sure that customers and end users are involved throughout service system development. (The distinction between customers and end users is important here, because they often have a different perspective on service requirements.) The model states, "Validation demonstrates that the service system, as developed, will deliver services as intended." What it fails to state explicitly, and what needs some reinforcement, is that the focus is on delivering services as intended *by the customer and the end user.* If the service system does only what the service provider organization intends, that may not be good enough.

Both verification and validation are important for service system development, but of the two, validation is probably the greater challenge for the project. Validation makes the project dependent on both input from and cooperation by customers and end users, and this dependency adds risks and management complications.

Also, because services are intangible by definition and cannot be stored, validating the actual delivery of services requires a service system to be operational in a way that can legitimately deliver real value to real end users. For some projects, performing this level of validation before a service system is fully deployed can be difficult. Piloting a new or modified service system with a sample group of informed and willing end users is one method of validating it, and piloting can even work in situations with high-impact risks (e.g., controlled clinical testing of a new medical procedure).

But piloting often requires extra resources to be set aside from ongoing service delivery that may simply be unavailable for some organizations. In these cases, a project may be able to complete final validation of service delivery only *after* a new or changed service system is partially or fully deployed. Customer and end-user feedback can always be solicited at that point to help with validation.

However you handle it, validation is *not* something you want to skip over simply because it can create difficulties for your project. If you do, you risk running into much greater challenges in the long run.

SERVICE SYSTEM TRANSITION
A *Service Establishment and Delivery Process Area at Maturity Level 3*

Purpose

The purpose of Service System Transition (SST) is to deploy new or significantly changed service system components while managing their effect on ongoing service delivery.

Introductory Notes

The Service System Transition process area addresses all aspects of planning, communicating, managing, deploying, and confirming that service system components effectively make the transition to the delivery environment. The scope of this process area covers both new components and significant changes to existing components.

"Significant" is defined as a change that introduces unacceptable risk that the service system will not meet its objectives. Although these practices center on the transition of service system components, the transition of an entire service system (i.e., an interdependent and integrated collection of components) can also be managed using these practices.

In this process area, the term "transition" refers to the comprehensive process of preparing for, executing, and confirming a deployment of service system components to a fully operational state while maintaining service delivery. The term "deploy" or "deployment" is more specific and refers to the activity of moving service system components into the delivery environment. In some domains, a deployment is also called a "roll-out."

Deployments generally fall into one of three categories:

- New installation
- Replacement
- Retirement

SST

Transition planning ensures that relevant stakeholders are properly informed of upcoming changes. Preparing for transition also encompasses compatibility evaluations of the to-be service system within the current delivery environment as constrained by existing service agreements and ongoing service delivery activities. Impacts on a service system that will be replaced or phased out over time by a new service system are considered. Impacts on service systems that share interfaces or resources with a new one are also considered, as are impacts on service continuity.

Critical aspects of service system transition include the following:

- Configuration control of service system components
- Management of internal and external interfaces
- Deployment of service system components into the delivery environment
- Stakeholder acceptance of new or revised service system components
- Management of impacts of the transition

Emergency changes to a service system may be made when approved by a designated authority according to established policies. The normal, expected order of service system transition processes may be altered to accommodate the unique needs of an emergency situation, but all relevant processes should eventually be completed once the situation returns to normal. This approach allows any unanticipated impacts associated with emergency changes to be identified and addressed.

Related Process Areas

Refer to the Incident Resolution and Prevention process area for more information about identifying, controlling, and addressing incidents.

Refer to the Service Continuity process area for more information about establishing and maintaining plans to ensure continuity of services during and following any significant disruption of normal operations.

Refer to the Service Delivery process area for more information about operating the service system.

Refer to the Service System Development process area for more information about analyzing, designing, developing, integrating, verifying, and validating service systems, including service system components, to satisfy existing or anticipated service agreements.

SSD ADD

Refer to the Causal Analysis and Resolution process area for more information about identifying causes of defects and problems and taking action to prevent them from occurring in the future.

Refer to the Configuration Management process area for more information about tracking and controlling changes.

Specific Goal and Practice Summary

SG 1 Prepare for Service System Transition
    SP 1.1   Analyze Service System Transition Needs
    SP 1.2   Develop Service System Transition Plans
    SP 1.3   Prepare Stakeholders for Changes
SG 2 Deploy the Service System
    SP 2.1   Deploy Service System Components
    SP 2.2   Assess and Control the Impacts of the Transition

Specific Practices by Goal

SG 1   PREPARE FOR SERVICE SYSTEM TRANSITION

Preparation for service system transition is conducted.

Thorough planning enables a smooth transition of service system components into the delivery environment. Compatibility analysis is critical to this preparation and is addressed within this goal. Additionally, proactive, well-thought-out transition plans with accompanying notification and training strategies clarify the transition, thus eliciting buy-in from relevant stakeholders.

As part of preparing for service system transition, review the operational concepts and scenarios for the service system, and tailor them as necessary to help ensure that planning is sufficiently thorough. Also review the criteria for service system acceptance to ensure that the service system meets those criteria.

The practices that address this goal should begin while new or changed service system components are still under development. By doing so, the needs and constraints for transition can be considered during the component's development.

SP 1.1 ANALYZE SERVICE SYSTEM TRANSITION NEEDS

Analyze the functionality and compatibility of the current and future service systems to minimize impact on service delivery.

The purpose of this practice is to identify and mitigate issues associated with the transition. This identification and mitigation is accomplished in part by analyzing how the current (as-is) service system will be affected by the changes anticipated for the post-transition (to-be) service system.

The transition of new or modified service system components affects the service delivery environment. Some of these effects may have been anticipated during the development of the service system.

Similarly, ongoing service delivery activities (if any), ad hoc service requests, and environmental circumstances may lead to deployment failure if the constraints they impose are not considered. Actual deployment of new or changed service delivery capabilities may need to be phased in over time because of these constraints. The service system design may need to be adjusted to make the transition feasible. Consequently, this practice should be conducted in parallel with service system development practices and should continue throughout transition to an operational state.

Refer to the Service Delivery process area for more information about preparing for service system operations.

Refer to the Service System Development process area for more information about developing service systems, including ensuring interface compatibility.

SSD ADD

Typical Work Products

1. Compatibility analysis of current and post-transition service systems
2. Issues to be addressed and risks to be mitigated associated with the transition

Subpractices

1. Establish a baseline of the current service system, if it has not been done previously.

   Refer to the Configuration Management process area for more information about establishing baselines.

2. Analyze the current service system as it operates within the current delivery environment.

   In some cases, documentation and operational concepts may exist for the current service system. These documentation and operational concepts can be used to better understand current operations. If the current service system is undocumented or does not exist, elicit as much input as possible from relevant stakeholders regarding current operations.

3. Analyze the service system components that are proposed for transition (e.g., the post-transition or to-be service system) for potential compatibility, functionality, or interface issues.

This analysis should use development documentation for the proposed service system components. This documentation can include operational concepts, scenarios, design documents, and workflow diagrams.

If necessary, define procedures to ensure service system compatibility prior to actual deployment. These procedures may reuse applicable verification and validation methods employed during service system development, but they should also account for additional real-world constraints that are in place once service system transition begins. Depending on the complexity of the service system and the risks associated with the transition, these procedures may range from a simple analysis and resolution of potential compatibility issues to a formal test and evaluation regimen.

4. Identify and mitigate potential issues.

   Refer to the Risk Management process area for more information about mitigating risks.

SP 1.2 DEVELOP SERVICE SYSTEM TRANSITION PLANS

Establish and maintain plans for specific transitions of the service system.

For each specific transition of the service system, a plan is established that encompasses all activities from accepting service system components to resolution of impacts on users and the delivery environment. A transition plan should identify all activities and resources that are required for a specific transition.

The following should be included in transition plans when appropriate:

- Identification of service system components ready for transition
- Deployment type (e.g., new, replacement, retirement)
- Acquisition approach
- Installation and integration of service system components within the delivery environment
- Phasing of deployment over time that satisfies operational dependencies between service system components
- Deployment acceptance criteria
- Resource constraints and restrictions
- Initial provisioning of consumables
- Rollback (or backout) procedures to "undo" the transition and restore the delivery environment to its former stable operating status
- Training of service delivery and support personnel
- Communication of transition status and service changes to relevant stakeholders

The depth of a transition plan should be appropriate for the type of transition and the criticality of the components going through transition. For example, the transition of new business-critical components may require detailed plans and schedules, risk assessment, deployment back-out procedures, and a formal review of planning materials by relevant stakeholders. Less significant transitions, such as retirement of an outdated service, may need less planning rigor.

If similar transitions were performed in the past, the results of their post-deployment reviews should be considered during transition planning. This information can speed up the planning process and help identify issues that might otherwise be overlooked.

Refer to the Project Planning process area for more information about developing a project plan.

Typical Work Products

1. Plans for service system transition

Subpractices

1. Define the deployment approach for each specific service system transition.

    Consider the type of deployment (e.g., new installation, replacement, retirement) when defining an approach, taking into account that a transition may include a combination of these types of deployments. Consider priorities and constraints of relevant stakeholders.

    Also define a rollback or backout strategy in the event that a deployment is unsuccessful and the service system must be restored to its former state. Include criteria for what constitutes a successful deployment versus when to back out changes.

    If a service system is being retired, address topics such as user notification, error handling, archival methods, demolition, and recycling.

2. Determine the cost, resources, and schedule required for transition of the service system to a new or changed operational state.

    Schedule transition activities in a way that balances work and available resources against customer and end-user needs, including the need to have time to prepare for and conduct the transition. When appropriate, use actual data from similar transitions to estimate cost, resources, and schedule.

3. Identify relevant stakeholders for transition activities.

    When identifying transition stakeholders and defining their roles and responsibilities, be sure to consider outsourced stakeholders.

4. Develop a service system transition plan.

    Based on the deployment approach and estimates for a transition, document a plan for the transition.

5. Obtain stakeholder commitment to the plan.
   Ensure that the service system transition plan is reviewed by relevant stakeholders to obtain buy-in. Respond to review comments.

6. Establish a baseline of the transition plan.

7. If new or significantly changed essential functions are part of a transition, ensure that the service continuity plan is refreshed to include the new functionality.

   Refer to the Service Continuity process area for more information about establishing service continuity plans.

   Refer to the Integrated Project Management process area for more information about integrating plans and coordinating and collaborating with relevant stakeholders.

SP 1.3 PREPARE STAKEHOLDERS FOR CHANGES

Prepare relevant stakeholders for changes in services and service systems.

This practice ensures that the service system transition is not impaired because of failure to prepare relevant stakeholders for all of the changes caused by introducing new or modified service system components. Relevant stakeholders should always include customers, end users, provider personnel, senior management, external suppliers, and anyone else who has a need to become aware of expected changes.

Typical Work Products

1. Transition notification strategy
2. Transition training strategy

Subpractices

1. Establish and maintain a transition notification strategy.

2. Implement the notification strategy to keep relevant stakeholders informed about scheduled changes in services and service availability during the transition.
   Ensure that the notification strategy addresses how rollback or backout will be communicated, if appropriate.

3. Establish and maintain a transition training strategy.
   The transition training strategy may encompass a broad range of orientation and training activities involving customers, end users, service delivery and support personnel, managers, and senior leadership, as appropriate. The transition training strategy should also encompass activities that ensure the effectiveness of the training after it has been provided, such as testing, piloting, or surveys.

SST

Examples of information that should be incorporated in orientation and training include the following:
- New or changed services and how to request them
- Procedures and tools for customer and end-user feedback
- Procedures and tools for maintenance, tuning, and end-user support
- Use of tools selected for service delivery
- Design of the service system
- Anticipated operating thresholds
- Procedures and tools for service system scheduling, monitoring, and resource management
- Procedures for handling service incidents that occur during transition

---

4. Implement the training strategy.

Refer to the Organizational Training process area for more information about establishing an organizational training tactical plan.

SG 2   DEPLOY THE SERVICE SYSTEM

The service system is deployed to the delivery environment.

This goal focuses on obtaining service system components (from the configuration control authority when appropriate) and installing and integrating them into the delivery environment. This process is conducted according to the tactical plan for service system transition.

Deployment may cause both planned and unplanned effects on service system operation. Identifying, assessing, and controlling these effects is an essential part of achieving a successful deployment.

SP 2.1   DEPLOY SERVICE SYSTEM COMPONENTS

Systematically deploy service system components into the delivery environment based on transition planning.

The preparation for transition, including the tactical plan for service system transition, is used to guide the deployment.

Typical Work Products

1. Installation records
2. Deployment evaluation artifacts

Subpractices

1. Confirm that service system components to be deployed are placed under configuration control as appropriate.

Refer to the Configuration Management process area for more information about establishing baselines.

2. Install the service system into the delivery environment.
   This subpractice involves packaging, distributing, integrating, and installing service system components into the delivery environment. Installation and integration details should be included in the tactical plan for service system transition.

3. Validate service system components in the delivery environment.
   Ensure that the deployed components operate as expected. Operational scenarios and procedures can be used to evaluate the new or modified service system. Deployment acceptance criteria, which were defined as part of the tactical plan for transition, may need to be revised as part of this evaluation.

   Refer to the Service Delivery process area for more information about preparing for service system operations.

   Refer to the Service System Development process area for more information about verifying and validating service systems.

   SSD ADD

4. In the case of service system component retirement, archive the service system components appropriately and remove them from the delivery environment.
   Ensure that interfaces with the retired service system components are adequately handled.

SP 2.2 ASSESS AND CONTROL THE IMPACTS OF THE TRANSITION

Assess the impacts of the transition on stakeholders and service delivery, and take appropriate corrective action.

Transition activities extend past installation of new service system components in the delivery environment. The service provider must ensure that service operations are not adversely affected by recent changes.

Often, this assessment period may extend through several iterations of the new functionality to help ensure that unintended effects are not realized. For example, in the medical domain, a pediatric clinic may implement specific services to support parents of children with special needs. Services could include a facilitated parents' group, centralized therapy sessions, and educational guidance. Assessing the impacts of these new service system changes would require gathering input from families with children of various ages and diagnoses. It may take some time to gather these data and ensure that the new services are positively affecting relevant stakeholders.

SST

Additionally, this practice ensures that a deployment does not degrade other aspects of the service system or service delivery in general. Unanticipated impacts are addressed in a timely manner and as detailed in the tactical plan for transition. Back-out plans may be implemented as needed based on adverse system impacts.

Refer to the Incident Resolution and Prevention process area for more information about identifying, controlling, and addressing incidents to closure.

Typical Work Products

1. Post deployment review
2. Deployment assessment artifacts

Subpractices

1. Use data gathering methods to obtain input from relevant stakeholders about the deployment.

Examples of data gathering methods include the following:
- Survey
- Comments box
- Web-based input form
---

2. Proactively communicate information about deployment impacts. Communication should be handled as determined by the tactical plan for service system transition and should, at a minimum, include confirming with relevant stakeholders that a transition has completed successfully.

Multiple communication vehicles can be used to ensure that relevant stakeholders are made aware of deployment issues:
- Email notification
- Embedded system notifications
- Frequently asked questions (FAQ) documentation
- Visible signage in the delivery environment
- Meetings
---

3. For significant impacts, refer to the tactical plan for details about how and when deployment backout or rollback should be performed.
4. Continue to assess and control impacts until deployment issues are resolved.

Impacts that potentially or actually interfere with service delivery are service incidents that should be handled through the project's incident management system.

5. Conduct a post-deployment review.

This review identifies, collects, and documents lessons learned from the deployment. This information may be useful both for current service system operation and for future transitions. Relevant stakeholders should be included to address questions such as the following:

- Is the new functionality operating effectively?
- Have other aspects of the service system been degraded?
- Have stakeholders been negatively affected?
- Has the new functionality of the service system been thoroughly evaluated through sufficient use?

STRATEGIC SERVICE MANAGEMENT
A Service Establishment and Delivery Process Area at Maturity Level 3

Purpose

The purpose of Strategic Service Management (STSM) is to establish and maintain standard services in concert with strategic needs and plans.

Introductory Notes

The Strategic Service Management process area involves the following activities:

- Analyzing capabilities and needs for services that span multiple customers and agreements
- Establishing and maintaining standard services, service levels, and descriptions that reflect these capabilities and needs

Strategic service management processes improve alignment between the set of services offered by a service provider organization and its strategic business objectives. If the organization is small or has a narrow focus, the standard services may consist of a single service or small related group of services. Larger organizations may have a more complex set of standard services.

Active analysis of customer and competitor data, market trends and opportunities, and organizational characteristics such as capabilities and strengths yield information that the organization uses to establish standard services. Standard services are one enabler of consistent service performance across the organization. The objective of this process area is not to manage individual services but to get the information needed to make effective strategic decisions about the set of standard services the organization maintains.

Standard services provide a basis for making the most of the service provider organization's capabilities to meet its business objectives.

IN OTHER WORDS

STSM is about portfolio management or deciding what services you should be providing, making them standard, and letting people know about them.

WHY DO THE PRACTICES IN STSM?

Because you have standard services, developing new services is faster and cheaper. You can increase business capture and market share. You and your customers agree about what you have to offer.

These standard services are like templates for services you offer more than once. They may include things such as lifecycle options and suppliers you may use when offering that service. The new SP in PP, Establish the Project Strategy, is a practice that makes the standard service more particular for the agreement you are contemplating. You may tailor the lifecycle, and perhaps you need an additional supplier for this instance of the service.

SP 2.1 in SD, which calls for developing your service delivery approach, is used to make more tactical decisions (how to schedule the additional supplier staff, for example).

Standard services may also improve service quality, business capture, and satisfaction of both customers and end users while reducing costs, errors, and time to develop and deliver services. Standard service levels are a key component of standard services. Service levels make expectations and responsibilities clear, specific, and measurable between the service organization and the customer.

In this process area, when customer needs are mentioned, end-user needs are also implied. The needs of the customer and end user may differ. Both are critical when collecting and analyzing data to develop standard services and understand strategic needs and plans.

Standard services are typically described in a service catalog that is oriented to the information needs of customers. In addition, standard service descriptions oriented to the needs of the service provider organization's personnel may be maintained.

Attention to satisfaction with and use of current services allows the organization to adjust or correct some services and may contribute to planning for future services. The organization may also identify requirements for new service systems or changes to existing systems. These systems may support single or multiple customers.

The specific practices in this process area complement those in Organizational Process Definition, Organizational Process Focus, and Organizational Process Performance. In OPD, OPF, and OPP, the organization defines, improves, and quantitatively understands its standard processes. In contrast, the broader focus of STSM is on services rather than only on service system components that may be processes.

STANDARD PROCESSES, STANDARD SERVICES, AND SERVICE LEVELS

It's easy to forget that services and processes are distinct things, and when that happens, it becomes easy to lump standard services together with standard processes. They are not equivalent. Remember that a service is a type of product, and it is the *result* of performing a process. Services are results, and processes are sets of activities. The service of being transported from one city to another at the time you have chosen is not the same as the complicated process required to deliver that service.

This distinction carries over into the terms *standard process* and *standard service*. Standard processes describe the common elements of processes used throughout an organization, and they are the central focus of several other process areas in the model (OPF, OPD, and OPP). Standard services are common sets of services that are requested by customers and delivered to end users. Once it has been tailored and implemented, a single standard process might be associated with multiple standard services (e.g., a standard training process that delivers distinct courses of instruction), or it might support a single standard service having one or more service levels.

Distinct service levels represent varying defined degrees of magnitude, degree, or quality for the same overall service, as well as possible additional subservices to be included in the overall service. The gold, silver, and bronze service levels for a typical travel rewards program are a familiar example of this type of distinction. The choice of what service levels to make available and how to define them should be determined by an analysis of the priority needs of major customers or customer groups versus the business needs and strategic direction of the service provider organization.

From another perspective, standard services and service levels may be delivered with or without the existence of standard processes (although the latter approach is likely to be riskier and more difficult). Therefore, no matter how you look at them, standard processes and standard services are truly separable and different. The Strategic Service Management process area focuses on defining your standard services and service levels in ways that make the most business sense.

Related Process Areas

Refer to the Incident Resolution and Prevention process area for more information about monitoring the status of incidents.

Refer to the Service Delivery process area for more information about delivering services.

Refer to the Service System Development process area for more information about developing and analyzing stakeholder requirements.

SSD ADD

Refer to the Organizational Process Definition process area for more information about establishing standard processes.

Refer to the Project Monitoring and Control process area for more information about monitoring the project against the plan.

Refer to the Requirements Management process area for more information about developing an understanding with requirements providers on the meaning of the requirements.

Specific Goal and Practice Summary

SG 1 Establish Strategic Needs and Plans for Standard Services
  SP 1.1   Gather and Analyze Relevant Data
  SP 1.2   Establish Plans for Standard Services
SG 2 Establish Standard Services
  SP 2.1   Establish Properties of Standard Services and Service Levels
  SP 2.2   Establish Descriptions of Standard Services

Specific Practices by Goal

SG 1   ESTABLISH STRATEGIC NEEDS AND PLANS FOR STANDARD SERVICES

Strategic needs and plans for standard services are established and maintained.

"Strategic needs" are conditions or objectives in the organization, often driven by factors in the environment. An organization may need to increase revenue, profitability, or market share. Customers may need a different or new set of services or expect a change in an organization's service offerings based on what competitors are providing or based on shifts in their own objectives. The organization considers the range of needs in light of its capabilities, makes decisions about which objectives to pursue, and reflects these needs and objectives in plans for standard services.

In many organizations, strategic planning information can be proprietary, sensitive, and subject to nondisclosure requirements or other controls. Anyone participating in developing plans for standard services should exercise care in complying with controls to protect sensitive strategic information.

SP 1.1   GATHER AND ANALYZE RELEVANT DATA

Gather and analyze data about the strategic needs and capabilities of the organization.

The organization gathers and analyzes data that can help with planning the standard services that the organization will establish and maintain. The appropriate data may vary for different services, market segments, and organizational characteristics, such as size. The data will offer insights into both the organization's capabilities and the needs of its market, including customers and end users.

Examples of sources and techniques for gathering and analyzing relevant data include the following:

- Business plans
- Market research
- Surveys
- Business intelligence
- Data from service reviews and account management
- Service use trends and patterns
- Customer complaints and compliments
- Service incident and request patterns
- Breaches of service levels
- Competitor data
- Trade studies
- Plans
- Strategic planning techniques, such as strengths, weaknesses, opportunities, and threats (SWOT)
- Core competence analysis
- Scenario planning

Typical Work Products

1. Analyzed data on the organization's capabilities
2. Analyzed data on strategic needs
3. Descriptions of the organization's capabilities
4. Descriptions of strategic needs

Subpractices

1. Gather and analyze data on the organization's capabilities.
2. Gather and analyze data on the organization's strategic needs.
3. Describe the organization's capabilities and strategic needs.
4. Communicate the descriptions to relevant stakeholders.

SP 1.2 ESTABLISH PLANS FOR STANDARD SERVICES

Establish and maintain plans for standard services.

Standard service planning translates information about the organization's capabilities and strategic needs into decisions about standard services. Plans for standard services reflect actions needed to balance capabilities of the organization; strategic needs, including the needs of customers and end users; and the conditions of the competitive market.

Typical Work Products

1. Descriptions of strategic business objectives
2. Prospective service descriptions
3. Analysis of service system needs
4. Decision or approval packages for selected services
5. Plans for standard services

Subpractices

1. Confirm strategic business objectives.

   Strategic business objectives for a service organization may be explicit and available. If they are not, the planners executing this activity document their understanding of the implicit goals as part of their planning. This understanding should be reviewed and approved by senior management.

2. Recommend requirements for standard services based on strategic business objectives, the organization's capabilities, and strategic needs.

3. Identify needed actions on standard services.

   Needed actions may include development of new standard services, revision or improvement of current standard services, or retirement of standard services. A known failure mode in managing services is inattention to managing the obsolescence of services. Standard services that no longer fit the needs of the organization's customer or the current capabilities of the organization should be retired or altered so that they do fit. The organization should set priorities and decide on the phasing of actions as appropriate.

   Refer to the Organizational Innovation and Deployment process area for more information about selecting improvements.

   Refer to the Project Monitoring and Control process area for more information about managing corrective action to closure.

   New or changed standard services may require new or changed service systems. These service systems may support single or multiple customers and single or multiple standard services.

4. Review and get agreement from relevant stakeholders on the standard services to be established and maintained.

STANDARD SERVICE PLANS, PROJECT STRATEGIES, AND SERVICE DELIVERY APPROACHES

In the Project Planning process area, the model states that a project strategy "provides the business framework for planning and managing the project." What does this mean, and how does it differ from a service delivery approach (outlined in the Service Delivery process area) and a plan for standard services (outlined here in Strategic Service Management)? Isn't there a lot of overlap?

The terminology *can* be confusing, but it is possible to sort out the differences. One way to understand these differences is to work from the top down. A plan for standard services spans the business needs of the entire organization and the full range of its current or desired future customers. It is *organizationally strategic*, with a long-term perspective that goes beyond any one project. The plan at this level outlines what new standard services or changes to existing standard services are needed over time (including retirement), how they should be prioritized, and what fundamental business objectives they should satisfy.

At the project level, the practice of establishing a project strategy tailors a standard service (if available) or outlines a service (if no appropriate standard one is available) to meet the needs of one or more *anticipated* service agreements. (Remember that a single project can encompass multiple service agreements with different customers.) The project strategy lays out overall constraints, service types, types of delivery approaches, types of resources, and types of risks to be handled by that project alone.

Before the project can actually be planned (which will then allow it to have specific resources allocated for service delivery processes at certain times), additional details must be developed, but these depend on the existence of *actual* service agreements. Once a service agreement has been established and service requirements are determined, an operational service delivery approach can be fleshed out in detail from the project strategy. This approach can vary significantly for different service agreements or may be consistent (with tailorable variations) for standard services. In either case, the service delivery approach provides enough additional operational detail to allow subsequent service project planning to be meaningful.

SG 2 ESTABLISH STANDARD SERVICES

A set of standard services is established and maintained.

SP 2.1 ESTABLISH PROPERTIES OF STANDARD SERVICES AND SERVICE LEVELS

Establish and maintain properties of the organization's set of standard services and service levels.

Multiple standard services and service levels may be required to address the needs of different customers, units of the organization, markets, or application domains. In addition to establishing standard services, services may be grouped into service lines when the size and complexity of the set of services warrant further organization. The organization develops standard processes to deliver standard services.

Refer to the Organizational Process Definition process area for more information about establishing standard processes.

Typical Work Products

1. Critical attributes of standard services
2. Organization's set of standard service levels
3. Templates for service level agreements (SLAs)
4. Tailoring criteria
5. Common and variable parts of standard services
6. Grouping of services into service lines

Subpractices

1. Select standard services.

    The selected standard services must adhere to organizational policies, standards, and models.

2. Specify the critical attributes of each service.

Examples of critical attributes include the following:
- Features and benefits
- Available service levels and categories
- Costs
- Current users
- Intended users
- Service components
- Service delivery system
- Related services

---

3. Determine common and variable parts of standard services.

    Variable parts of a standard service may be assigned categories and parameters. Standard service levels may represent some of the degrees of variability in standard services.

Examples of allowable variations include the following:
- Pricing
- Subservice providers
- Criteria for using customer components

---

4. Organize services into service lines as needed.

   This organization of services into service lines may include ensuring an appropriate integration among services.

5. Define service levels.

   Defined service levels make the levels of service that are offered specific and measurable. Service levels may help to balance cost and demand for services and make roles and responsibilities between the service provider and user clear.

   Determining service levels includes the following service requirements:

   - The maximum acceptable continuous period of lost service
   - The maximum acceptable period of degraded service
   - Acceptable degraded service levels during the period of service recovery
   - Redundancy requirements

   Standard service levels may be reflected in standard SLAs or templates for SLAs.

Service level information includes the following:
- Provider and user responsibilities
- Availability of the service
- Agreed service hours and exceptions
- Anticipated service volume
- Response times for service incidents and requests
- Performance or quality targets
- Key measures to monitor
- Reporting and escalation procedures
- Consequences of failure to achieve a service level
- Variations available (e.g., "gold" service)

---

6. Establish tailoring criteria as appropriate.

   The organization uses knowledge of variability in customer needs to develop tailoring options that limit risk and improve customer satisfaction and time to market while maintaining consistency across the organization.

   The tailoring criteria and guidelines describe the following:

   - How the organization's set of standard services are used to guide the development of individual services
   - Mandatory requirements that must be satisfied by the defined services
   - Options that can be exercised and criteria for selecting among the options
   - Procedures that must be followed in performing and documenting tailoring

---

Examples of tailoring criteria and procedures include the following:
- Criteria for selecting standard services from those approved by the organization
- Criteria for selecting service components from the organization's set of standard services
- Procedures for tailoring the selected services and service components to accommodate specific needs

---

Examples of tailoring actions include the following:
- Modifying a service level
- Combining components of different services
- Modifying service components
- Replacing service components
- Reordering service components

Examples of reasons for tailoring include the following:
- Adapting the service for a new customer need or work environment
- Customizing the service for a specific use or class of similar uses

---

SP 2.2 ESTABLISH DESCRIPTIONS OF STANDARD SERVICES

Establish and maintain descriptions of the organization's defined standard services.

Establishing the properties of standard services is not sufficient. These properties must also be packaged into specific descriptions. In addition to a set of descriptions used by the service provider, a separate version is typically needed for customer use. A common failure mode with the use of standard services is that they are defined and described to meet the needs of some personnel in the service-provider organization but not described in a manner that is effective and appropriate for all intended users of standard services. For successful use, standard services must be appropriately described for the full range of intended users of the descriptions.

Typical Work Products

1. Descriptions of services
2. Service catalog or menu
3. Adjunct materials, such as instructions for delivery staff, sales force instructions, proposal and pricing information, and contracting information

Subpractices

1. Develop the descriptions of standard services for all relevant users.
   Additional materials related to the standard services may also be
   developed if they do not already exist. These materials can include
   information for those developing specific services, service-delivery
   staff, or sales and other business staff.

2. Conduct peer reviews on the descriptions with relevant stakeholders.
   Customer and end-user representatives may be included in these peer
   reviews to ensure that the descriptions meet their information needs

3. Revise the descriptions as necessary.

4. Store the descriptions in a location and medium where all intended
   users have access.

   To be effective, standard service descriptions must be available and
   accessible in a consistent location that encourages use by the full
   range of intended users. The location may be a large, complex online
   site or a single sheet of paper, depending on the characteristics of the
   services and organization.

   While the catalog or menu of services is often in an electronic format,
   many organizations also produce a paper version. Adjunct materials
   may be stored along with the descriptions, such as the tailoring
   guidelines or instructions for the delivery staff, sales force, proposal
   authors, and contract specialists. Variants of the service catalog or
   menu may be required for customers and staff of the service provider
   organization.

Examples of locations for a standard service repository include the following:

- Configuration management database
- Web pages
- Document portfolio or library
- Process asset library

PART THREE

The Appendices
and Glossary

REFERENCES

Ahern 2005 Ahern, Dennis M.; Armstrong, Jim; Clouse, Aaron; Ferguson, Jack R.; Hayes, Will; & Nidiffer, Kenneth E. *CMMI SCAMPI Distilled: Appraisals for Process Improvement.* Boston, MA: Addison-Wesley, 2005.

Anderson 2008 Anderson, David; Dalton, Jeff; Glazer, Hillel; Konrad, Mike; and Shrum, Sandy. *CMMI or Agile: Why Not Embrace Both! (CMU/SEI-2008-TN-003).* Pittsburgh, PA: Software Engineering Institute, Carnegie Mellon University, November 2008. www.sei.cmu.edu/library/abstracts/reports/08tn003.cfm.

Bernard 2005 Bernard, Tom; Gallagher, Brian; Bate, Roger; & Wilson, Hal. *CMMI Acquisition Module, Version 1.1. (CMU/SEI-2005-TR-011, ADA441245).* Pittsburgh, PA: Software Engineering Institute, Carnegie Mellon University, May 2005. www.sei.cmu.edu/library/abstracts/reports/05tr011.cfm.

Crosby 1979 Crosby, Philip B. *Quality Is Free: The Art of Making Quality Certain.* New York: McGraw-Hill, 1979.

Curtis 2001 Curtis, Bill; Hefley, William E.; & Miller, Sally A. *The People Capability Maturity Model: Guidelines for Improving the Workforce.* Boston, MA: Addison-Wesley, 2001.

Deming 1986 Deming, W. Edwards. *Out of the Crisis.* Cambridge, MA: MIT Press, 1986.

Dodson 2006 Dodson, Kathryn M.; Hofmann, Hubert F.; Ramani, Gowri S.; & Yedlin, Deborah K. *Adapting CMMI for Acquisition Organizations: A Preliminary Report (CMU/SEI-2006-SR-005, ADA453524).* Pittsburgh, PA: Software Engineering Institute, Carnegie Mellon University, June 2006. www.sei.cmu.edu/library/abstracts/reports/06sr005.cfm.

EIA 2002 Electronic Industries Alliance. *Systems Engineering Capability Model (EIA/IS-731.1).* Washington, DC, 2002.

EIA 2003 Electronic Industries Alliance. *EIA Interim Standard: Systems Engineering (EIA/IS-632).* Washington, DC, 2003.

EIA 2002 Government Electronics and Information Technology Alliance. *Earned Value Management Systems (ANSI/EIA-748).* New York, NY, 2002. webstore.ansi.org/RecordData.aspx?sku=ANSI%2FEIA-748-B.

Gibson 2006 Gibson, Diane L.; Goldenson, Dennis R.; & Kost, Keith. *Performance Results of CMMI-Based Process Improvement (CMU/SEI-2006-TR-004, ADA454687).* Pittsburgh, PA: Software Engineering Institute, Carnegie Mellon University, August 2006. www.sei.cmu.edu/library/abstracts/reports/06tr004.cfm.

Humphrey 1989 Humphrey, Watts S. *Managing the Software Process.* Boston, MA: Addison-Wesley, 1989.

IEEE 1991 Institute of Electrical and Electronics Engineers. *IEEE Standard Computer Dictionary: A Compilation of IEEE Standard Computer Glossaries.* New York, NY: IEEE, 1991.

ISO 1995 International Organization for Standardization and International Electrotechnical Commission. *ISO/IEC TR 12207 Information Technology—Software Life Cycle Processes,* 1995. www.webstore.ansi.org/RecordDetail.aspx?sku=IEEE+Std+12207-2008.

ISO 2000 International Organization for Standardization. *ISO 9001, Quality Management Systems—Requirements,* 2000. www.iso.org/iso/en/CatalogueDetailPage.CatalogueDetail?CSNUMBER=21823&ICS1=3&ICS2=120&ICS3=10.

ISO 2002a International Organization for Standardization and International Electrotechnical Commission. *ISO/IEC 15288 Systems Engineering—System Life Cycle Processes,* 2002. www.jtc1-sc7.org/.

ISO 2002b International Organization for Standardization and International Electrotechnical Commission. *ISO/IEC 15939 Software and Systems Engineering—Measurement Process,* 2002. www.jtc1-sc7.org/.

ISO 2005 International Organization for Standardization and International Electrotechnical Commission. *ISO/IEC 20000-1 Information Technology—Service Management, Part 1: Specification; ISO/IEC 20000-2 Information Technology—Service Management, Part 2: Code of Practice,* 2005.
www.iso.org/iso/iso_catalogue/catalogue_tc/catalogue_detail.htm
?csnumber=41333.

ISO 2006 International Organization for Standardization and International Electrotechnical Commission. *ISO/IEC TR 15504 Information Technology—Software Process Assessment Part 1: Concepts and Vocabulary, Part 2: Performing an Assessment, Part 3: Guidance on Performing an Assessment, Part 4: Guidance on Use for Process Improvement and Process Capability Determination, Part 5: An Exemplar Process Assessment Model,* 2003-2006.
www.iso.org/iso/search.htm?qt=15504&published=true&active_
tab=standards.

IT Governance 2005 IT Governance Institute. *CobiT 4.0.* Rolling Meadows, IL: IT Governance Institute, 2005.
www.isaca.org/Content/NavigationMenu/Members_and_Leaders/COBIT6/Obtain_COBIT/Obtain_COBIT.htm.

Juran 1988 Juran, Joseph M. *Juran on Planning for Quality.* New York: Macmillan, 1988.

McFeeley 1996 McFeeley, Robert. *IDEAL: A User's Guide for Software Process Improvement (CMU/SEI-96-HB-001, ADA305472).* Pittsburgh, PA: Software Engineering Institute, Carnegie Mellon University, February 1996.
www.sei.cmu.edu/library/abstracts/reports/96hb001.cfm.

Office of Government Commerce 2007a Office of Government Commerce. *ITIL: Continual Service Improvement.* London, UK: Office of Government Commerce, 2007.

Office of Government Commerce 2007b Office of Government Commerce. *ITIL: Service Design.* London, UK: Office of Government Commerce, 2007.

Office of Government Commerce 2007c Office of Government Commerce. *ITIL: Service Operation.* London, UK: Office of Government Commerce, 2007.

Office of Government Commerce 2007d Office of Government Commerce. *ITIL: Service Strategy*. London, UK: Office of Government Commerce, 2007.

Office of Government Commerce 2007e Office of Government Commerce. *ITIL: Service Transition*. London, UK: Office of Government Commerce, 2007.

SEI 1995 Software Engineering Institute. *The Capability Maturity Model: Guidelines for Improving the Software Process*. Reading, MA: Addison-Wesley, 1995.

SEI 2002 Software Engineering Institute. *Software Acquisition Capability Maturity Model (SA-CMM) Version 1.03 (CMU/SEI-2002-TR-010, ADA399794)*. Pittsburgh, PA: Software Engineering Institute, Carnegie Mellon University, March 2002. www.sei.cmu.edu/library/abstracts/reports/02tr010.cfm.

SEI 2006a CMMI Product Team. *CMMI for Development, Version 1.2 (CMU/SEI-2006-TR-008, ADA455858)*. Pittsburgh, PA: Software Engineering Institute, Carnegie Mellon University, August 2006. www.sei.cmu.edu/library/abstracts/reports/06tr008.cfm.

SEI 2006b SCAMPI Upgrade Team. *Standard CMMI Appraisal Method for Process Improvement (SCAMPI) A, Version 1.2: Method Definition Document (CMU/SEI-2006-HB-002)*. Pittsburgh, PA: Software Engineering Institute, Carnegie Mellon University, August 2006. www.sei.cmu.edu/library/abstracts/reports/06hb002.cfm.

SEI 2006c SCAMPI Upgrade Team. *Appraisal Requirements for CMMI, Version 1.2 (ARC, V1.2) (CMU/SEI-2006-TR-011, ADA454612)*. Pittsburgh, PA: Software Engineering Institute, Carnegie Mellon University, August 2006. www.sei.cmu.edu/library/abstracts/reports/06tr011002.cfm.

SEI 2007 CMMI Guidebook for Acquirers Team. *Understanding and Leveraging a Supplier's CMMI Efforts: A Guidebook for Acquirers (CMU/SEI-2007-TR-004)*. Pittsburgh, PA: Software Engineering Institute, Carnegie Mellon University, March 2007. www.sei.cmu.edu/library/abstracts/reports/07tr004.cfm.

SEI 2009 CMMI Product Team. *CMMI for Services, Version 1.2 (CMU/SEI-2009-TR-001)*. Pittsburgh, PA: Software Engineering Institute, Carnegie Mellon University, February 2009. www.sei.cmu.edu/library/abstracts/reports/09tr001.cfm.

Sheard 1996 Sheard, Sarah A. Twelve Systems Engineering Roles, Software Productivity Consortium, NRP, Inc. 1996. http://www.incose.org/educationcareers/PDF/12-roles.pdf.

Shewhart 1931 Shewhart, Walter A. *Economic Control of Quality of Manufactured Product*. New York: Van Nostrand, 1931.

APPENDIX B

ACRONYMS

ARC Appraisal Requirements for CMMI

CAM Capacity and Availability Management (process area)

CAR Causal Analysis and Resolution (process area)

CCB configuration control board

CL capability level

CM Configuration Management (process area)

CMM Capability Maturity Model

CMMI Capability Maturity Model Integration

CMMI-ACQ CMMI for Acquisition

CMMI-DEV CMMI for Development

CMMI-SVC CMMI for Services

CPM critical path method

CobiT Control Objectives for Information and related Technology

COTS commercial off the shelf

CPM critical path method

DAR Decision Analysis and Resolution (process area)

DoD Department of Defense

EIA Electronic Industries Alliance

EIA/IS Electronic Industries Alliance/Interim Standard

FCA functional configuration audit

GG generic goal

GP generic practice

IBM International Business Machines

IDEAL Initiating, Diagnosing, Establishing, Acting, Learning

IEEE Institute of Electrical and Electronics Engineers

IPD-CMM Integrated Product Development Capability Maturity Model

IPM Integrated Project Management (process area)

IRP Incident Resolution and Prevention (process area)

ISO International Organization for Standardization

ISO/IEC International Organization for Standardization and International Electrotechnical Commission

IT information technology

ITIL Information Technology Infrastructure Library

ITSCMM Information Technology Services Capability Maturity Model

MA Measurement and Analysis (process area)

MDD Method Definition Document

ML maturity level

OID Organizational Innovation and Deployment (process area)

OPD Organizational Process Definition (process area)

OPF Organizational Process Focus (process area)

OPP Organizational Process Performance (process area)

OT Organizational Training (process area)

PCA physical configuration audit

P-CMM People Capability Maturity Model

PA process area

PAL process asset library

PERT Program Evaluation and Review Technique

PMC Project Monitoring and Control (process area)

PP Project Planning (process area)

PPQA Process and Product Quality Assurance (process area)

PWS performance work statement

QA quality assurance

QFD Quality Function Deployment

QPM Quantitative Project Management (process area)

REQM Requirements Management (process area)

RSKM Risk Management (process area)

SCAMPI Standard CMMI Appraisal Method for Process Improvement

SCON Service Continuity (process area)

SD Service Delivery (process area)

SEI Software Engineering Institute

SG specific goal

SLA service level agreement

SOO statement of objectives

SOW statement of work

SP specific practice

SSD Service System Development (process area)

SST Service System Transition (process area)

STSM Strategic Service Management (process area)

SW-CMM Capability Maturity Model for Software or Software Capability Maturity Model

WBS work breakdown structure

APPENDIX C

CMMI FOR SERVICES PROJECT PARTICIPANTS

Many talented people were part of the product team that developed CMMI-SVC. Listed below are those who participated in one or more of the following teams during the development of CMMI-SVC. The organizations listed by members' names are those they represented at the time of their team membership.

There were five primary groups involved in the development of this model:

- CMMI-SVC, V1.2 Model Team
- CMMI-SVC, V1.2 Training Team
- CMMI-SVC, V1.2 Quality Team
- CMMI for Services Advisory Group
- CMMI Steering Group

CMMI-SVC, V1.2 Model Team

The Version 1.2 CMMI-SVC Model Team collected input from reviewers and users to create CMMI-SVC, Version 1.2.

Drew Allison, Systems and Software Consortium

Rhonda Brown, Software Engineering Institute

Brandon Buteau, Northrop Grumman

Eileen Clark, SRA International, Inc.; Tidewaters Consulting, LLC

Eileen Forrester, Software Engineering Institute[1]

Craig Hollenbach, Northrop Grumman[2]

Mike Konrad, Software Engineering Institute

Frank Niessink, DNV

---

1. SEI Team Lead
2. Industry Team Lead

M. Lynn Penn, Lockheed Martin

Roy Porter, Northrop Grumman

Rich Raphael, MITRE Corporation

Pamela Schoppert, SAIC

Sandy Shrum, Software Engineering Institute

Jerry Simpson, SAIC

Jeff Zeidler, Boeing

Additional team members and contributors:

Roger Bate, Software Engineering Institute

Margaret Glover, Software Engineering Institute

Joanne O'Leary, Software Engineering Institute

Mary Lynn Russo, Software Engineering Institute

Steve Stern, Lockheed Martin

Barbara Tyson, Software Engineering Institute

CMMI-SVC, V1.2 Training Team

The Version 1.2 CMMI-SVC Training Team included a core team of developers and many reviewers. The development team used baselines created by the CMMI-SVC, V1.2 Model Team and the existing *Introduction to CMMI* course to develop training for CMMI-SVC, V1.2.

Eileen Clark, Tidewaters Consulting, LLC

Mary Beth Chrissis, Software Engineering Institute

Bob McFeeley, Software Engineering Institute

Sandy Shrum, Software Engineering Institute

Agapi Svolou, Software Engineering Institute

Barbara Tyson, Software Engineering Institute[3]

CMMI-SVC, V1.2 Quality Team

The Version 1.2 CMMI-SVC Quality Team used a process developed over the years for CMMI model quality assurance. The team tailored the quality assurance (QA) process to CMMI-SVC, V1.2 to prepare it and the training material developed by the CMMI-SVC, V1.2 Training Team for release.

Rhonda Brown, Software Engineering Institute[4]

---

3. Team Lead

4. Team Co-Lead

Mary Lou Russo, Software Engineering Institute

Mary Lynn Russo, Software Engineering Institute

Sandy Shrum, Software Engineering Institute[5]

CMMI for Services Advisory Group

The CMMI for Services Advisory Group was responsible for providing direction to the development work of the CMMI-SVC, Version 1.2 Model Team.

Christian Carmody, University of Pittsburgh Medical Center

Sandra Cepeda, RDECOM AMRDEC Software Engineering Directorate/Cepeda Systems and Software Analysis, Inc.

Annie Combelles, DNV IT Global Services

Jeffrey L. Dutton, Jacobs Technology Inc.

Eileen Forrester, Software Engineering Institute

Craig Hollenbach, Northrop Grumman[6]

Brad Nelson, Office of the Deputy Undersecretary of Defense for Industrial Policy

Lawrence Osiecki, U.S. Army Armament Software Engineering Center

Mike Phillips, Software Engineering Institute

Tim Salerno, Lockheed Martin IS&GS—Civil

Nidhi Srivastava, Tata Consultancy Services

Beth Sumpter, National Security Agency

Dave Swidorsky, Merrill Lynch Global Technology Services

CMMI Steering Group

The CMMI Steering Group has guided and approved the plans of the version 1.2 CMMI Product Team, provided consultation on significant CMMI project issues, ensured involvement from a variety of interested communities, and approved the final release of the model.

Steering Group Members

Kristen Baldwin, OUSD (AT&L) SSE/SSA

Clyde Chittister, Software Engineering Institute

Jim Gill, Boeing Integrated Defense Systems

John Kelly, NASA HQ

---

5. Team Co-Lead

6. Chair

Kathy Lundeen, Defense Contract Management Agency

Larry McCarthy, Motorola, Inc.

Mike Nicol, U.S. Air Force ASC/EN

Lawrence Osiecki, U.S. Army

Bill Peterson, Software Engineering Institute

Bob Rassa, Raytheon Space & Airborne Systems[7]

Kevin Stamey, AFMC/EN

Joan Weszka, Lockheed Martin

Hal Wilson, Northrop Grumman

Brenda Zettervall, U.S. Navy, ASN/RDA CHENG

Ex-Officio Steering Group Members

Lloyd Anderson, Department of Homeland Security

Roger Bate, chief architect, Software Engineering Institute

Mike Phillips, CMMI program manager, Software Engineering Institute

Beth Sumpter, National Security Agency

Steering Group Support: Acquisition

Brian Gallagher, Software Engineering Institute

Steering Group Support: CCB

Mike Konrad, Software Engineering Institute

---

7. Chair

APPENDIX D

GLOSSARY

The glossary defines the basic terms used in CMMI models. Glossary entries are typically multiple-word terms consisting of a noun and one or more restrictive modifiers. (There are some exceptions to this rule that account for one-word terms in the glossary.)

To formulate definitions appropriate for CMMI, we consulted multiple sources. We first consulted the *Merriam-Webster OnLine* dictionary (www.m-w.com). We also consulted other standards as needed, including the following:

- ISO/IEC 12207 [ISO 1995]
- ISO 9000 [ISO 2000]
- ISO/IEC 15288 [ISO 2002a]
- ISO/IEC 15939 [ISO 2002b]
- ISO 20000-1 [ISO 2005]
- ISO/IEC 15504 [ISO 2006]
- IEEE [IEEE 1991]
- CobiT v. 4.0 [IT Governance 2005]
- CMM for Software (SW-CMM) v1.1
- EIA 632 [EIA 2003]
- SA-CMM [SEI 2002]
- People CMM (P-CMM) [Curtis 2001]
- ITIL v3 (Service Improvement, Service Design, Service Operation, Service Strategy, and Service Transition)

We developed the glossary recognizing the importance of using terminology that all model users can understand. We also recognized that words and terms can have different meanings in different contexts and environments. The glossary in CMMI models is designed to document the meanings of words and terms that should have the widest use and understanding by users of CMMI products.

acceptance criteria The criteria that a deliverable must satisfy to be accepted by a user, customer, or other authorized entity. (See also "deliverable.")

acceptance testing Formal testing conducted to enable a user, customer, or other authorized entity to determine whether to accept a deliverable. (See also "unit testing.")

achievement profile In the continuous representation, a list of process areas and their corresponding capability levels that represent the organization's progress for each process area while advancing through the capability levels. (See also "capability level profile," "target profile," and "target staging.")

acquirer The stakeholder that acquires or procures a product or service from a supplier. (See also "stakeholder.")

acquisition The process of obtaining products or services through supplier agreements. (See also "supplier agreement.")

acquisition strategy The specific approach to acquiring products and services that is based on considerations of supply sources, acquisition methods, requirements specification types, contract or agreement types, and related acquisition risks.

adequate Interpretation of goals and practices in light of the organization's business objectives.

When using any CMMI model, practices should be interpreted in a way that works for the organization. This term is used in goals and practices in which certain activities may not be equally relevant in all situations. (See also "appropriate" and "as needed.")

allocated requirement Requirement that levies all or part of the performance and functionality of a higher level requirement on a lower level architectural element or design component.

alternative practice A practice that is a substitute for one or more generic or specific practices contained in CMMI models that achieves an equivalent effect toward satisfying the generic or specific goal associated with it.

Alternative practices are not necessarily one-for-one replacements for generic or specific practices.

amplifications Informative model components that contain information relevant to a particular discipline.

For example, to find amplifications for software engineering, look in the model for items labeled "For Software Engineering." The same is true for amplifications for other disciplines.

appraisal In the CMMI Product Suite, an examination of one or more processes by a trained team of professionals using an appraisal reference model as the basis for determining, at a minimum, strengths and weaknesses. (See also "assessment.")

appraisal findings The results of an appraisal that identify the most important issues, problems, or opportunities for process improvement within the appraisal scope. Appraisal findings are inferences drawn from corroborated objective evidence.

appraisal participants Members of the organizational unit who participate in providing information during an appraisal.

appraisal rating As used in CMMI appraisal materials, the value assigned by an appraisal team to (a) a CMMI goal or process area, (b) the capability level of a process area, or (c) the maturity level of an organizational unit.

A rating is determined by enacting the defined rating process for the appraisal method being employed.

appraisal reference model As used in CMMI appraisal materials, the CMMI model to which an appraisal team correlates implemented process activities.

appraisal scope The definition of the boundaries of an appraisal encompassing the organizational limits and CMMI model limits within which the processes to be investigated operate.

appraisal team leader A person who leads the activities of an appraisal and has satisfied qualification criteria for experience, knowledge, and skills defined by the appraisal method.

appropriate Interpretation of goals and practices in light of the organization's business objectives.

When using any CMMI model, practices should be interpreted in a way that works for the organization. This term is used in goals and practices in which certain activities may not be equally relevant in all situations. (See also "adequate" and "as needed.")

as needed Interpretation of goals and practices in light of the organization's business objectives.

When using any CMMI model, practices should be interpreted in a way that works for the organization. This term is used in goals and practices in which certain activities may not be equally relevant in all situations. (See also "adequate" and "appropriate.")

assessment In the CMMI Product Suite, an appraisal that an organization does internally for the purposes of process improvement.

The word "assessment" is also used in the CMMI Product Suite in an everyday English sense (e.g., risk assessment). (See also "appraisal.")

assignable cause of process variation (See "special cause of process variation.")

In CMMI, the term "special cause of process variation" is used in place of "assignable cause of process variation" to ensure consistency. The two terms are defined identically.

audit In CMMI process improvement work, an objective examination of a work product or set of work products against specific criteria (e.g., requirements).

base measure A distinct property or characteristic of an entity and the method for quantifying it. (See also "derived measure.")

baseline A set of specifications or work products that has been formally reviewed and agreed on, which thereafter serves as the basis for further development, and which can be changed only through change control procedures. (See also "configuration baseline.")

bidirectional traceability An association among two or more logical entities that is discernable in either direction (i.e., to and from an entity). (See also "requirements traceability" and "traceability.")

business objectives (See "organization's business objectives.")

capability level Achievement of process improvement within an individual process area. A capability level is defined by appropriate specific and generic practices for a process area. (See also "generic goal," "generic practice," "maturity level," and "process area.")

capability level profile In the continuous representation, a list of process areas and their corresponding capability levels. (See also "achievement profile," "target profile," and "target staging.")

A capability level profile may be an "achievement profile" when it represents the organization's progress for each process area while advancing through the capability levels. Or, it may be a "target profile" when it represents an objective for process improvement.

capability maturity model A model that contains the essential elements of effective processes for one or more disciplines and describes an evolutionary improvement path from ad hoc, immature processes to disciplined, mature processes with improved quality and effectiveness.

capable process A process that can satisfy its specified product quality, service quality, and process-performance objectives. (See also "stable process," "standard process," and "statistically managed process.")

causal analysis The analysis of defects to determine their cause.

change management Judicious use of means to effect a change, or a proposed change, to a product or service. (See also "configuration management.")

CMMI Framework The basic structure that organizes CMMI components, including elements of current CMMI models as well as rules and methods for generating models, appraisal methods (including associated artifacts), and training materials. The framework enables new disciplines to be added to CMMI so that they will integrate with the existing ones. (See also "CMMI model" and "CMMI Product Suite.")

CMMI model A model generated from the CMMI Framework. (See also "CMMI Framework" and "CMMI Product Suite.")

CMMI model component Any of the main architectural elements that compose a CMMI model. Some of the main elements of a CMMI model include specific practices, generic practices, specific goals, generic goals, process areas, capability levels, and maturity levels.

CMMI Product Suite The complete set of products developed around the CMMI concept. These products include the framework itself, models, appraisal methods, appraisal materials, and training materials. (See also "CMMI Framework" and "CMMI model.")

commercial off-the-shelf Items that can be purchased from a commercial supplier.

common cause of process variation The variation of a process that exists because of normal and expected interactions among components of a process. (See also "special cause of process variation.")

concept of operations (See "operational concept.")

configuration audit An audit conducted to verify that a configuration item or a collection of configuration items that make up a baseline conforms to a specified standard or requirement. (See also "audit," "configuration item," "functional configuration audit," and "physical configuration audit.")

configuration baseline The configuration information formally designated at a specific time during a product's or product component's life. Configuration baselines plus approved changes from those baselines constitute the current configuration information. (See also "product lifecycle.")

configuration control An element of configuration management consisting of the evaluation, coordination, approval or disapproval, and implementation of changes to configuration items after formal establishment of their configuration identification. (See also "configuration identification," "configuration item," and "configuration management.")

configuration control board A group of people responsible for evaluating and approving or disapproving proposed changes to configuration items and for ensuring implementation of approved changes. (See also "configuration item.")

Configuration control boards are also known as "change control boards."

configuration identification An element of configuration management consisting of selecting the configuration items for a product, assigning unique identifiers to them, and recording their functional and physical characteristics in technical documentation. (See also "configuration item," "configuration management," and "product.")

configuration item An aggregation of work products that is designated for configuration management and treated as a single entity in the configuration management process. (See also "configuration management.")

configuration management A discipline applying technical and administrative direction and surveillance to (1) identify and document the functional and physical characteristics of a configuration item, (2) control changes to those characteristics, (3) record and report change processing and implementation status, and (4) verify compliance with specified requirements. (See also "configuration audit," "configuration control," "configuration identification," and "configuration status accounting.")

configuration status accounting An element of configuration management consisting of the recording and reporting of information needed to manage a configuration effectively. This information includes a list of the approved configuration, the status of proposed changes to the configuration, and the implementation status of approved changes. (See also "configuration identification" and "configuration management.")

continuous representation A capability maturity model structure wherein capability levels provide a recommended order for approaching process improvement within each specified process area. (See also "capability level," "process area," and "staged representation.")

contractual requirements The result of the analysis and refinement of customer requirements into a set of requirements suitable to be included in one or more solicitation packages, formal contracts, or supplier agreements between the acquirer and other appropriate organizations. (See also "acquirer," "customer requirement," "solicitation package," and "supplier agreement.")

Contractual requirements include both technical and nontechnical requirements necessary for the acquisition of a product or service.

corrective action Acts or deeds used to remedy a situation, remove an error, or adjust a condition.

customer The party (individual, project, or organization) responsible for accepting the product or for authorizing payment.

The customer is external to the project (except possibly when integrated teams are used) but not necessarily external to the project's organization. The customer may be a higher level project. Customers are a subset of stakeholders. (See also "stakeholder.")

In most cases where this term is used, the preceding definition is intended; however, in some contexts, the term "customer" is intended to include other relevant stakeholders. (See also "customer requirement.")

End users may be distinguished from customers if the parties that directly receive the value of services (i.e., end users) are not the same as the parties that arrange for, pay for, or negotiate service agreements. In contexts where customers and end users are essentially the same parties, the term "customer" may encompass both types. (See also "end user.")

customer requirement The result of eliciting, consolidating, and resolving conflicts among the needs, expectations, constraints, and interfaces of the product's relevant stakeholders in a way that is acceptable to the customer. (See also "customer.")

data Recorded information, regardless of the form or method of recording, including technical data, computer software documents, financial information, management information, representation of facts, numbers, or data of any nature that can be communicated, stored, and processed.

data management The disciplined processes and systems that plan for, acquire, and provide stewardship for business and technical data, consistent with data requirements, throughout the data lifecycle.

defect density Number of defects per unit of product size (e.g., problem reports per thousand lines of code).

defined process A managed process that is tailored from the organization's set of standard processes according to the organization's tailoring guidelines; has a maintained process description; and contributes work products, measures, and other process improvement information to organizational process assets. (See also "managed process" and "measure.")

deliverable An item to be provided to an acquirer or other designated recipient as specified in an agreement. This item can be a document, hardware item, software item, service, or any type of work product. (See also "acquirer.")

delivery environment The complete set of circumstances and conditions under which services are delivered in accordance with service agreements. (See also "service" and "service agreement.")

The delivery environment encompasses everything that has or may have a significant effect on service delivery, including but not limited to service system operation, natural phenomena, and the behavior of all parties, whether or not they intend to have such an effect. For example, consider the effect of weather or traffic patterns on a transportation service. (See also "service system.")

The delivery environment is uniquely distinguished from other environments (e.g., simulation environments, testing environments). The delivery environment is the one in which services are actually delivered and count as satisfying a service agreement.

derived measure Measure that is defined as a function of two or more values of base measures. (See also "base measure.")

derived requirements Requirements that are not explicitly stated in customer requirements but are inferred (1) from contextual requirements (e.g., applicable standards, laws, policies, common practices, management decisions) or (2) from requirements needed to specify a product or service component.

Derived requirements can also arise during analysis and design of components of the product or service. (See also "product requirements.")

design review A formal, documented, comprehensive, and systematic examination of a design to determine if the design meets the applicable requirements, to identify problems, and to propose solutions.

development In the CMMI Product Suite, not only development activities but also maintenance activities. Development projects that benefit from CMMI best practices can focus on development, maintenance, or both.

development plan A plan for guiding, implementing, and controlling the design and development of one or more products or services. (See also "product lifecycle" and "project plan.")

discipline In the CMMI Product Suite, the bodies of knowledge available when selecting a CMMI model (e.g., systems engineering).

The CMMI Product Team envisions that other bodies of knowledge will be integrated into the CMMI Framework in the future.

document A collection of data, regardless of the medium on which it is recorded, that generally has permanence and can be read by humans or machines.

Documents include both paper and electronic documents.

end user A party (individual, project, or organization) that ultimately receives the benefit of a delivered service. (See also "customer.")

End users may or may not also be customers (who can establish and accept agreements or authorize payments).

In contexts where a single service agreement covers multiple service deliveries, any party that initiates a service request may be considered an end user. (See also "service agreement" and "service request.")

enterprise The full composition of a company. A company may consist of many organizations in many locations with different customers. (See also "organization.")

entry criteria States of being that must be present before an effort can begin successfully.

equivalent staging A target staging, created using the continuous representation that is defined so that the results of using the target staging can be compared to maturity levels of the staged representation. (See also "capability level profile," "maturity level," "target profile," and "target staging.")

Such staging permits benchmarking of progress among organizations, enterprises, and projects, regardless of the CMMI representation used. The organization may implement components of CMMI models beyond those reported as part of equivalent staging. Equivalent staging is only a measure to relate how the organization compares to other organizations in terms of maturity levels.

establish and maintain This phrase means more than a combination of its component terms; it includes documentation and use. For example, "Establish and maintain an organizational policy for planning and performing the organizational process focus process" means that not only must a policy be formulated, but it also must be documented and it must be used throughout the organization.

evidence (See "objective evidence.")

executive (See "senior manager.")

exit criteria States of being that must be present before an effort can end successfully.

expected CMMI components CMMI components that explain what may be done to satisfy a required CMMI component.

Model users can implement the expected components explicitly or implement equivalent alternative practices to these components. Specific and generic practices are expected model components.

findings (See "appraisal findings.")

formal evaluation process A structured approach to evaluating alternative solutions against established criteria to determine a recommended solution to address an issue.

framework (See "CMMI Framework.")

functional analysis Examination of a defined function to identify all the subfunctions necessary to accomplish that function; identification of functional relationships and interfaces (internal and external) and capturing these relationships and interfaces in a functional architecture; and flow down of upper-level performance requirements and assignment of these requirements to lower level subfunctions. (See also "functional architecture.")

functional architecture The hierarchical arrangement of functions, their internal and external (external to the aggregation itself) functional interfaces and external physical interfaces, their respective functional and performance requirements, and their design constraints.

functional configuration audit An audit conducted to verify that the development of a configuration item has been completed satisfactorily, that the item has achieved the performance and functional characteristics specified in the functional or allocated configuration identification, and that its operational and support documents are complete and satisfactory. (See also "configuration audit," "configuration management," and "physical configuration audit.")

generic goal A required model component that describes characteristics that must be present to institutionalize processes that implement a process area. (See also "institutionalization.")

generic practice An expected model component that is considered important in achieving the associated generic goal.

    The generic practices associated with a generic goal describe the activities that are expected to result in achievement of the generic goal and contribute to the institutionalization of the processes associated with a process area.

generic practice elaboration An informative model component that appears after a generic practice to provide guidance on how the generic practice should be applied to the process area. (This model component is not present in all CMMI models.)

goal A required CMMI component that can be either a generic goal or a specific goal.

The word "goal" in a CMMI model always refers to a model component (e.g., generic goal, specific goal). (See also "generic goal," "objective," and "specific goal.")

hardware engineering The application of a systematic, disciplined, and quantifiable approach to transforming a set of requirements that represent the collection of stakeholder needs, expectations, and constraints, using documented techniques and technology to design, implement, and maintain a tangible product. (See also "software engineering" and "systems engineering.")

In CMMI, hardware engineering represents all technical fields (e.g., electrical, mechanical) that transform requirements and ideas into tangible and producible products.

higher level management The person or persons who provide the policy and overall guidance for the process but do not provide the direct day-to-day monitoring and controlling of the process. Such persons belong to a level of management in the organization above the immediate level responsible for the process and can be (but are not necessarily) senior managers. (See also "senior manager.")

incomplete process A process that is not performed or is performed only partially (also known as capability level 0). One or more of the specific goals of the process area are not satisfied.

informative CMMI components CMMI components that help model users understand the required and expected components of a model.

These components can contain examples, detailed explanations, or other helpful information. Subpractices, notes, references, goal titles, practice titles, sources, typical work products, amplifications, and generic practice elaborations are informative model components.

institutionalization The ingrained way of doing business that an organization follows routinely as part of its corporate culture.

integrated team A group of people with complementary skills and expertise who are committed to delivering specified work products in timely collaboration.

Integrated team members provide skills and advocacy appropriate to all phases of the work products' life and are collectively responsible for delivering work products as specified. An integrated team should include empowered representatives from organizations, disciplines, and functions that have a stake in the success of the work products.

interface control In configuration management, the process of (1) identifying all functional and physical characteristics relevant to the interfacing of two or more configuration items provided by one or more organizations and (2) ensuring that proposed changes to these characteristics are evaluated and approved prior to implementation. (See also "configuration item" and "configuration management.")

lifecycle model A partitioning of the life of a product, service, or project into phases.

managed process A performed process that is planned and executed in accordance with policy; employs skilled people having adequate resources to produce controlled outputs; involves relevant stakeholders; is monitored, controlled, and reviewed; and is evaluated for adherence to its process description. (See also "performed process.")

manager In the CMMI Product Suite, a person who provides technical and administrative direction and control to those performing tasks or activities within the manager's area of responsibility.

The traditional functions of a manager include planning, organizing, directing, and controlling work within an area of responsibility.

maturity level Degree of process improvement across a predefined set of process areas in which all goals in the set are attained. (See also "capability level" and "process area.")

measure (noun) Variable to which a value is assigned as a result of measurement. (See also "base measure," "derived measure," and "measurement.")

measurement A set of operations to determine the value of a measure. (See also "measure.")

memorandum of agreement Binding document of understanding or agreement between two or more parties.

A memorandum of agreement is also known as a "memorandum of understanding."

natural bounds The inherent process reflected by measures of process performance; sometimes referred to as "voice of the process."

Techniques such as control charts, confidence intervals, and prediction intervals are used to determine whether the variation is due to common causes (i.e., the process is predictable or stable) or is due to some special cause that can and should be identified and removed. (See also "measure" and "process performance.")

nondevelopmental item An item that was developed prior to its current use in an acquisition or development process.

Such an item may require minor modifications to meet the requirements of its current intended use.

nontechnical requirements Requirements affecting product and service acquisition or development that are not properties of the product or service.

Examples include numbers of products or services to be delivered, data rights for delivered COTS nondevelopmental items, delivery dates, and milestones with exit criteria. Other nontechnical requirements include work constraints associated with training, site provisions, and deployment schedules.

objective When used as a noun in the CMMI Product Suite, the term "objective" replaces the word "goal" as used in its common everyday sense, since the word "goal" is reserved for use when referring to CMMI model components called "specific goals" and "generic goals." (See also "goal.")

objective evidence As used in CMMI appraisal materials, documents or interview results used as indicators of the implementation or institutionalization of model practices. Sources of objective evidence can include instruments, presentations, documents, and interviews. (See also "institutionalization.")

objectively evaluate To review activities and work products against criteria that minimize subjectivity and bias by the reviewer. An example of an objective evaluation is an audit against requirements, standards, or procedures by an independent quality assurance function. (See also "audit.")

observation As used in CMMI appraisal materials, a written record that represents the appraisal team members' understanding of information either seen or heard during appraisal data collection activities.

The written record may take the form of a statement or may take alternative forms as long as the content is preserved.

operational concept A general description of the way in which an entity is used or operates. (Also known as "concept of operations.")

operational scenario A description of an imagined sequence of events that includes the interaction of the product or service with its environment and users, as well as interaction among its product or service components.

Operational scenarios are used to evaluate the requirements and design of the system and to verify and validate the system.

optimizing process A quantitatively managed process that is improved based on an understanding of the common causes of variation inherent in the process. The focus of an optimizing process is on continually improving the range of process performance through both incremental and innovative improvements. (See also "common cause of process variation," "defined process," and "quantitatively managed process.")

organization An administrative structure in which people collectively manage one or more projects as a whole and whose projects share a senior manager and operate under the same policies.

However, the word "organization" as used throughout CMMI models can also apply to one person who performs a function in a small organization that might be performed by a group of people in a large organization. (See also "enterprise" and "organizational unit.")

organizational maturity The extent to which an organization has explicitly and consistently deployed processes that are documented, managed, measured, controlled, and continually improved.

Organizational maturity may be measured via appraisals.

organizational policy A guiding principle typically established by senior management that is adopted by an organization to influence and determine decisions.

organizational process assets Artifacts that relate to describing, implementing, and improving processes (e.g., policies, measurements, process descriptions, process implementation support tools).

The term "process assets" is used to indicate that these artifacts are developed or acquired to meet the business objectives of the organization and that they represent investments by the organization that are expected to provide current and future business value. (See also "process asset library.")

organizational unit The part of an organization that is the subject of an appraisal. An organizational unit deploys one or more processes that have a coherent process context and operates within a coherent set of business objectives.

An organizational unit is typically part of a larger organization, although in a small organization, the organizational unit may be the whole organization.

organization's business objectives Senior-management-developed strategies designed to ensure an organization's continued existence and enhance its profitability, market share, and other factors influencing the organization's success. (See also "quality and process-performance objectives" and "quantitative objective.")

Such objectives may include reducing the number of change requests during a system's integration phase, reducing development cycle time, increasing the number of errors found in a product's first or second phase of development, and reducing the number of customer-reported defects when applied to systems engineering activities.

organization's measurement repository A repository used to collect and make measurement data available on processes and work products, particularly as they relate to the organization's set of standard processes. This repository contains or references actual measurement data and related information needed to understand and analyze measurement data.

organization's process asset library A library of information used to store and make process assets available that are useful to those who are defining, implementing, and managing processes in the organization.

This library contains process assets that include process-related documentation, such as policies, defined processes, checklists, lessons-learned documents, templates, standards, procedures, plans, and training materials.

organization's set of standard processes A collection of definitions of the processes that guide activities in an organization.

These process descriptions cover the fundamental process elements (and their relationships to each other, such as ordering and interfaces) that must be incorporated into the defined processes that are implemented in projects across the organization.

A standard process enables consistent development and maintenance activities across the organization and is essential for long-term stability and improvement. (See also "defined process" and "process element.")

outsourcing (See "acquisition.")

peer review The review of work products performed by peers during the development of work products to identify defects for removal. (See also "work product.")

The term "peer review" is used in the CMMI Product Suite instead of the term "work product inspection."

performed process A process that accomplishes the needed work to produce work products. The specific goals of the process area are satisfied.

physical configuration audit An audit conducted to verify that a configuration item, as built, conforms to the technical documentation that defines and describes it. (See also "configuration audit," "configuration management," and "functional configuration audit.")

planned process A process that is documented by both a description and a plan. The description and plan should be coordinated, and the plan should include standards, requirements, objectives, resources, and assignments.

policy (See "organizational policy.")

process In the CMMI Product Suite, activities that can be recognized as implementations of practices in a CMMI model. These activities can be mapped to one or more practices in CMMI process areas to allow a model to be useful for process improvement and process appraisal. (See also "process area," "process element," and "subprocess.")

There is a special use of the phrase "the process" in the statements and descriptions of the generic goals and generic practices. "The process," as used in Part Two, is the process or processes that implement the process area.

process action plan A plan, usually resulting from appraisals, that documents how specific improvements targeting the weaknesses uncovered by an appraisal will be implemented.

process action team A team that has the responsibility to develop and implement process improvement activities for an organization as documented in a process action plan.

process and technology improvements Incremental and innovative improvements to processes and to process, product, or service technologies.

process architecture The ordering, interfaces, interdependencies, and other relationships among the process elements in a standard process. Process architecture also describes the interfaces, interdependencies, and other relationships between process elements and external processes (e.g., contract management).

process area A cluster of related practices in an area that, when implemented collectively, satisfies a set of goals considered important for making improvement in that area. All CMMI process areas are common to both continuous and staged representations.

process asset Anything the organization considers useful in attaining the goals of a process area. (See also "organizational process assets.")

process asset library A collection of process asset holdings that can be used by an organization or project. (See also "organization's process asset library.")

process attribute A measurable characteristic of process capability applicable to any process.

process capability The range of expected results that can be achieved by following a process.

process context The set of factors, documented in the appraisal input, that influences the judgment and comparability of appraisal ratings.

These factors include but are not limited to (a) the size of the organizational unit to be appraised; (b) the demographics of the organizational unit; (c) the application domain of the products or services; (d) the size, criticality, and complexity of the products or services; and (e) the quality characteristics of the products or services.

process definition The act of defining and describing a process. The result of process definition is a process description. (See also "process description.")

process description A documented expression of a set of activities performed to achieve a given purpose.

A process description provides an operational definition of the major components of a process. The description specifies, in a complete, precise, and verifiable manner, the requirements, design, behavior, or other characteristics of a process. It also may include procedures for determining whether these provisions have been satisfied. Process descriptions can be found at the activity, project, or organizational level.

process element The fundamental unit of a process.

A process can be defined in terms of subprocesses or process elements. A subprocess can be further decomposed into subprocesses or process elements; a process element cannot. (See also "process" and "subprocess.")

Each process element covers a closely related set of activities (e.g., estimating element, peer review element). Process elements can be portrayed using templates to be completed, abstractions to be refined, or descriptions to be modified or used. A process element can be an activity or task.

process group A collection of specialists who facilitate the definition, maintenance, and improvement of processes used by the organization.

process improvement A program of activities designed to improve the performance and maturity of the organization's processes, and the results of such a program.

process improvement objectives A set of target characteristics established to guide the effort to improve an existing process in a specific, measurable way either in terms of resultant product or service characteristics (e.g., quality, performance, conformance to standards) or in the way in which the process is executed (e.g., elimination of redundant process steps, combination of process steps, improvement of cycle time). (See also "organization's business objectives" and "quantitative objective.")

process improvement plan A plan for achieving organizational process improvement objectives based on a thorough understanding of current strengths and weaknesses of the organization's processes and process assets.

process measurement A set of operations used to determine values of measures of a process and its resulting products or services for the purpose of characterizing and understanding the process. (See also "measurement.")

process owner The person (or team) responsible for defining and maintaining a process.

At the organizational level, the process owner is the person (or team) responsible for the description of a standard process; at the project level, the process owner is the person (or team) responsible for the description of the defined process. A process may therefore have multiple owners at different levels of responsibility. (See also "defined process" and "standard process.")

process performance A measure of actual results achieved by following a process. It is characterized by both process measures (e.g., effort, cycle time, defect removal efficiency) and product or service measures (e.g., reliability, defect density, response time). (See also "measure.")

process-performance baseline A documented characterization of actual results achieved by following a process, which is used as a benchmark for comparing actual process performance against expected process performance. (See also "process performance.")

process-performance model A description of relationships among attributes of a process and its work products that is developed from historical process-performance data and calibrated using collected process and product or service measures from the project and that is used to predict results to be achieved by following a process. (See also "measure.")

process tailoring Making, altering, or adapting a process description for a particular end.

For example, a project tailors its defined process from the organization's set of standard processes to meet objectives, constraints, and the environment of the project. (See also "defined process," "organization's set of standard processes," and "process description.")

product In the CMMI Product Suite, a work product that is intended for delivery to a customer or end user.

The form of a product can vary in different contexts. (See also "customer," "product component," "service" and "work product.")

product component In the CMMI Product Suite, a work product that is a lower level component of the product. Product components are integrated to produce the product. There may be multiple levels of product components. (See also "product" and "work product.")

Throughout the process areas, where the terms "product" and "product component" are used, their intended meanings also encompass services, service systems, and their components.

product component requirements A complete specification of a product or service component, including fit, form, function, performance, and any other requirement.

product lifecycle The period of time, consisting of phases, that begins when a product or service is conceived and ends when the product or service is no longer available for use.

Since an organization may be producing multiple products or services for multiple customers, one description of a product lifecycle may not be adequate. Therefore, the organization may define a set of approved product lifecycle models. These models are typically found in published literature and are likely to be tailored for use in an organization.

A product lifecycle could consist of the following phases: (1) concept and vision, (2) feasibility, (3) design/development, (4) production, and (5) phase out.

product line A group of products sharing a common, managed set of features that satisfy specific needs of a selected market or mission. (See also "service line.")

product-related lifecycle processes Processes associated with a product or service throughout one or more phases of its life (e.g., from conception through disposal), such as manufacturing and support processes.

product requirements A refinement of customer requirements into the developers' language, making implicit requirements into explicit derived requirements. (See also "derived requirements" and "product component requirements.")

The developer uses product requirements to guide the design and building of the product or service.

product suite (See "CMMI Product Suite.")

profile (See "achievement profile" and "target profile.")

program (1) A project. (2) A collection of related projects and the infrastructure that supports them, including objectives, methods, activities, plans, and success measures. (See also "project.")

project In the CMMI Product Suite, a managed set of interrelated resources that delivers one or more products or services to a customer or end user.

A project has a definite beginning (i.e., project startup) and typically operates according to a plan. Such a plan is frequently documented and specifies what is to be delivered or implemented, the resources and funds to be used, the work to be done, and a schedule for doing the work. A project can be composed of projects. (See also "project startup.")

The term "project" refers to a group of people and resources committed to planning, monitoring, and executing defined processes in a shared endeavor to achieve a set of objectives.

project manager In the CMMI Product Suite, the person responsible for planning, directing, controlling, structuring, and motivating the project. The project manager is responsible for satisfying the customer.

project plan A plan that provides the basis for performing and controlling the project's activities, which address the commitments to the project's customer.

Project planning includes estimating the attributes of work products and tasks, determining the resources needed, negotiating commitments, producing a schedule, and identifying and analyzing project risks. Iterating through these activities may be necessary to establish the project plan.

project progress and performance What a project achieves with respect to implementing project plans, including effort, cost, schedule, and technical performance. (See also "technical performance.")

project startup When a set of interrelated resources are directed to develop or deliver one or more products or services for a customer or end user. (See also "project.")

project's defined process The integrated and defined process that is tailored from the organization's set of standard processes. (See also "defined process.")

prototype A preliminary type, form, or instance of a product, service, product component, or service component that serves as a model for later stages or for the final, complete version of the product or service.

This model of the product or service (e.g., physical, electronic, digital, analytical) can be used for the following (and other) purposes:

- Assessing the feasibility of a new or unfamiliar technology
- Assessing or mitigating technical risk
- Validating requirements
- Demonstrating critical features
- Qualifying a product or service
- Qualifying a process
- Characterizing performance or features of the product or service
- Elucidating physical principles

quality The ability of a set of inherent characteristics of a product, service, product component, service component, or process to fulfill requirements of customers.

quality and process-performance objectives Objectives and requirements for product quality, service quality, and process performance.

Process-performance objectives include quality; however, to emphasize the importance of quality in the CMMI Product Suite, the phrase "quality and process-performance objectives" is used rather than just "process-performance objectives."

quality assurance A planned and systematic means for assuring management that the defined standards, practices, procedures, and methods of the process are applied.

quantitative objective Desired target value expressed as quantitative measures. (See also "measure," "process improvement objectives," and "quality and process-performance objectives.")

quantitatively managed process A defined process that is controlled using statistical and other quantitative techniques.

Product quality, service quality, and process-performance attributes are measurable and controlled throughout the project. (See also "defined process," "optimizing process," and "statistically managed process.")

rating (See "appraisal rating.")

reference An informative model component that points to additional or more detailed information in related process areas.

reference model A model that is used as a benchmark for measuring an attribute.

relevant stakeholder A stakeholder that is identified for involvement in specified activities and is included in a plan. (See also "stakeholder.")

representation The organization, use, and presentation of a CMM's components.

Overall, two types of approaches to presenting best practices are evident: the staged representation and the continuous representation.

required CMMI components CMMI components that are essential to achieving process improvement in a given process area.

These components are used in appraisals to determine process capability. Specific goals and generic goals are required model components.

requirement (1) A condition or capability needed by an end user to solve a problem or achieve an objective. (2) A condition or capability that must be met or possessed by a product, service, product component, or service component to satisfy a supplier agreement, standard, specification, or other formally imposed documents. (3) A documented representation of a condition or capability as in (1) or (2). (See also "supplier agreement.")

requirements analysis The determination of product- or service-specific performance and functional characteristics based on analyses of customer needs, expectations, and constraints; operational concept; projected utilization environments for people, products, services, and processes; and measures of effectiveness. (See also "operational concept.")

requirements elicitation Using systematic techniques, such as prototypes and structured surveys, to proactively identify and document customer and end-user needs.

requirements management The management of all requirements received by or generated by the project, including both technical and nontechnical requirements as well as those requirements levied on the project by the organization. (See also "nontechnical requirement.")

requirements traceability A discernable association between requirements and related requirements, implementations, and verifications. (See also "bidirectional traceability" and "traceability.")

return on investment The ratio of revenue from output (product or service) to production costs, which determines whether an organization benefits from performing an action to produce something.

risk analysis The evaluation, classification, and prioritization of risks.

risk identification An organized, thorough approach to seek out probable or realistic risks in achieving objectives.

risk management An organized, analytic process to identify what might cause harm or loss (identify risks); to assess and quantify the identified risks; and to develop and, if needed, implement an appropriate approach to prevent or handle causes of risk that could result in significant harm or loss.

risk management strategy An organized, technical approach to identify what might cause harm or loss (identify risks); to assess and quantify the identified risks; and to develop and, if needed, implement an appropriate approach to prevent or handle causes of risk that could result in significant harm or loss.

Typically, risk management is performed for a project, an organization, or other organizational units that are developing or delivering products or services.

root cause A source of a defect such that if it is removed, the defect is decreased or removed.

senior manager In the CMMI Product Suite, a management role at a high enough level in an organization that the primary focus of the person filling the role is the long-term vitality of the organization rather than short-term project concerns and pressures. A senior manager has authority to direct the allocation or reallocation of resources in support of organizational process improvement effectiveness. (See also "higher level management.")

A senior manager can be any manager who satisfies this description, including the head of the organization. Synonyms for senior manager include "executive" and "top-level manager." However, to ensure consistency and usability, these synonyms are not used in CMMI models.

service In the CMMI Product Suite, a product that is intangible and nonstorable. (See also "customer," "product," and "work product.")

Services are delivered through the use of service systems that have been designed to satisfy service requirements. (See also "service system.")

Many service providers deliver combinations of services and goods. A single service system can deliver both types of products. For example, a training organization may deliver training materials along with its training services.

Services may be delivered through combinations of manual and automated processes.

service agreement A binding, written record of a promised exchange of value between a service provider and a customer. (See also "customer.")

Service agreements may be fully negotiable, partially negotiable, or non-negotiable, and they may be drafted by the service provider, the customer, or both, depending on the situation.

A "promised exchange of value" means a joint recognition and acceptance of what each party will provide to the other to satisfy

658 PART THREE THE APPENDICES AND GLOSSARY

the agreement. Typically, the customer provides payment in return for delivered services, but other arrangements are possible.

A "written" record need not be contained in a single document or other artifact. Alternatively, it may be extremely brief for some types of services (e.g., a receipt that identifies a service, its price, and its recipient).

service catalog A list or repository of standardized service definitions.

Service catalogs may include varying degrees of detail about available service levels, quality, prices, negotiable/tailorable items, and terms and conditions.

A service catalog need not be contained in a single document or other artifact and may be a combination of items that provide equivalent information (such as Web pages linked to a database). Alternatively, for some services an effective catalog may be a simple printed menu of available services and their prices.

Service catalog information may be partitioned into distinct subsets to support different types of stakeholders (e.g., customers, end users, provider personnel, suppliers).

service incident An indication of an actual or potential interference with a service.

Service incidents may occur in any service domain because customer and end-user complaints are types of incidents, and even the simplest of services may generate complaints.

The word "incident" may used in place of "service incident" for brevity when the context makes the meaning clear.

service level A defined magnitude, degree, or quality of service delivery performance. (See also "service" and "service level measure.")

service level agreement A service agreement that specifies delivered services; service measures; levels of acceptable and unacceptable services; and expected responsibilities, liabilities, and actions of both the provider and customer in anticipated situations. (See also "measure," "service," and "service agreement.")

A service level agreement is a kind of service agreement that documents the details indicated in the definition.

The use of the term "service agreement" always includes "service level agreement" as a subcategory, and the former may be used in place of the latter for brevity. However, "service level agreement" is the preferred term when it is desired to emphasize situations in which there *are* distinct levels of acceptable services, or when other details of a service level agreement are likely to be important to the discussion.

service level measure A method for measuring actual service delivery performance against a service level. (See also "measure" and "service level.")

service line A consolidated and standardized set of services and service levels that satisfy specific needs of a selected market or mission area. (See also "service level.")

service request A communication from a customer or end user that one or more specific instances of service delivery are desired. These requests are made within the context of a service agreement. (See also "service agreement.")

In cases where services are to be delivered continuously or periodically, some service requests may be explicitly identified in the service agreement itself.

In other cases, service requests that fall within the scope of a previously established service agreement are generated over time by customers or end users as their needs develop.

service requirements The complete set of requirements that affect service delivery and service system development. (See also "service system.")

Service requirements include both technical and nontechnical requirements. Technical requirements are properties of the service to be delivered and the service system needed to enable delivery. Nontechnical requirements may include additional conditions, provisions, commitments, and terms identified by contracts, agreements, and regulations, as well as needed capabilities and conditions derived from business objectives.

service system An integrated and interdependent combination of component resources that satisfies service requirements. (See also "service requirements" and "service system component.")

A service system encompasses *everything* required for service delivery, including work products, processes, facilities, tools, consumables, and human resources.

Note that a service system includes the people necessary to perform the service system's processes. In contexts where end users must perform some processes for service delivery to be accomplished, those end users are also part of the service system (at least for the duration of those interactions).

A complex service system may be divisible into multiple distinct delivery and support systems or subsystems. While these divisions and distinctions may be significant to the service provider organization, they may not be as meaningful to other stakeholders.

service system component A resource required for a service system to successfully deliver services.

Some components may remain owned by a customer, end user, or third party before service delivery begins and after service delivery ends. (See also "customer" and "end user.")

Some components may be transient resources that are part of the service system for a limited time (e.g., items that are under repair in a maintenance shop).

Components may include processes and people.

The word "component" may be used in place of "service system component" for brevity when the context makes this meaning clear.

The word "infrastructure" may be used to refer collectively to service system components that are tangible and essentially permanent. Depending on the context and type of service, infrastructure may include human resources.

service system consumable A service system component that ceases to be available or becomes permanently changed by its use during the delivery of a service.

Fuel, office supplies, and disposable containers are examples of commonly used consumables. Particular types of services may have their own specialized consumables (e.g., a health care service may require medications or blood supplies).

People are not consumables, but their labor time is a consumable.

shared vision A common understanding of guiding principles, including mission, objectives, expected behavior, values, and final outcomes, that are developed and used by a project.

software engineering (1) The application of a systematic, disciplined, quantifiable approach to the development, operation, and maintenance of software. (2) The study of approaches as in (1). (See also "hardware engineering," and "systems engineering.")

solicitation The process of preparing a package to be used in selecting a supplier. (See also "solicitation package.")

solicitation package A collection of formal documents that includes a description of the desired form of response from a potential supplier, the relevant statement of work for the supplier, and required provisions in the supplier agreement.

special cause of process variation A cause of a defect that is specific to some transient circumstance and is not an inherent part of a process. (See also "common cause of process variation.")

specific goal A required model component that describes the unique characteristics that must be present to satisfy the process area. (See also "capability level," "generic goal," "organization's business objectives," and "process area.")

specific practice An expected model component that is considered important in achieving the associated specific goal. The specific practices describe the activities expected to result in achievement of the specific goals of a process area. (See also "process area" and "specific goal.")

stable process The state in which all special causes of process variation have been removed and prevented from recurring so that only common causes of process variation of the process remain. (See also "capable process," "common cause of process variation," "special cause of process variation," "standard process," and "statistically managed process.")

staged representation A model structure wherein attaining the goals of a set of process areas establishes a maturity level; each level builds a foundation for subsequent levels. (See also "maturity level" and "process area.")

stakeholder In the CMMI Product Suite, a group or individual that is affected by or is in some way accountable for the outcome of an undertaking. Stakeholders may include project members, suppliers, customers, end users, and others. (See also "customer" and "relevant stakeholder.")

standard (noun) Formal requirements developed and used to prescribe consistent approaches to development (e.g., ISO/IEC standards, IEEE standards, organizational standards).

standard process An operational definition of the basic process that guides the establishment of a common process in an organization.

A standard process describes the fundamental process elements that are expected to be incorporated into any defined process. It also describes relationships (e.g., ordering, interfaces) among these process elements. (See also "defined process.")

statement of work A description of work to be performed.

statistical predictability The performance of a quantitative process that is controlled using statistical and other quantitative techniques.

statistical process control Statistically based analysis of a process and measures of process performance, which identify common and special causes of variation in process performance and maintain process performance within limits. (See also "common cause of process variation," "special cause of process variation," and "statistically managed process.")

statistical techniques An analytic technique that employs statistical methods (e.g., statistical process control, confidence intervals, prediction intervals).

statistically managed process A process that is managed by a statistically based technique in which processes are analyzed, special causes of process variation are identified, and performance is contained within well-defined limits. (See also "capable process," "special cause of process variation," "stable process," "standard process," and "statistical process control.")

subpractice An informative model component that provides guidance for interpreting and implementing specific or generic practices. Subpractices may be worded as if prescriptive, but they are actually meant only to provide ideas that may be useful for process improvement.

subprocess A process that is part of a larger process. A subprocess can be decomposed into subprocesses or process elements. (See also "process," "process description," and "process element.")

supplier (1) An entity delivering products or performing services being acquired. (2) An individual, partnership, company, corporation, association, or other service having an agreement with an acquirer for the design, development, manufacture, maintenance, modification, or supply of items under the terms of an agreement. (See also "acquirer.")

supplier agreement A documented agreement between the acquirer and supplier (e.g., contract, license, memorandum of agreement).

sustainment The processes used to ensure that a product or service remains operational.

systems engineering The interdisciplinary approach governing the total technical and managerial effort required to transform a set of customer needs, expectations, and constraints into a solution and to support that solution throughout its life. (See also "hardware engineering" and "software engineering.")

This approach includes the definition of technical perform-ance measures, the integration of engineering specialties toward the establishment of an architecture, and the definition of sup-porting lifecycle processes that balance cost, performance, and schedule objectives.

system of systems A set or arrangement of systems that results when independent and useful systems are integrated into a large system that delivers unique capabilities.

tailoring The act of making, altering, or adapting something for a particular end.

For example, a project establishes its defined process by tai-loring from the organization's set of standard processes to meet the objectives, constraints, and environment of the project. Like-wise, a service provider tailors standard services for a particular service agreement.

tailoring guidelines Organizational guidelines that enable projects, groups, and organizational functions to appropriately adapt standard processes for their use. The organization's set of stan-dard processes is described at a general level that may not be directly usable to perform a process.

Tailoring guidelines aid those who establish the defined processes for projects. Tailoring guidelines cover (1) selecting a standard process, (2) selecting an approved lifecycle model, and (3) tailoring the selected standard process and lifecycle model to fit project needs. Tailoring guidelines describe what can and can-not be modified and identify process components that are candi-dates for modification.

target profile In the continuous representation, a list of process areas and their corresponding capability levels that represent an objective for process improvement. (See also "achievement pro-file" and "capability level profile.")

target staging In the continuous representation, a sequence of tar-get profiles that describes the path of process improvement to be followed by the organization. (See also "achievement pro-file," "capability level profile," and "target profile.")

technical performance Characteristic of a process, product, or service, generally defined by a functional or technical require-ment (e.g., estimating accuracy, end-user functions, security functions, response time, component accuracy, maximum weight, minimum throughput, allowable range).

technical performance measure Precisely defined technical measure of a requirement, capability, or some combination of requirements and capabilities. (See also "measure.")

technical requirements Properties (i.e., attributes) of products or services to be acquired or developed.

test procedure Detailed instructions for the setup, execution, and evaluation of results for a given test.

traceability A discernable association among two or more logical entities, such as requirements, system elements, verifications, or tasks. (See also "bidirectional traceability" and "requirements traceability.")

trade study An evaluation of alternatives, based on criteria and systematic analysis, to select the best alternative for attaining determined objectives.

training Formal and informal learning options, which may include in-class training, informal mentoring, Web-based training, guided self study, and formalized on-the-job training programs.

The learning options selected for each situation are based on an assessment of the need for training and the performance gap to be addressed.

typical work product An informative model component that provides sample outputs from a specific practice. These examples are called typical work products because there are often other work products that are just as effective but are not listed.

unit testing Testing of individual hardware or software units or groups of related units. (See also "acceptance testing.")

validation Confirmation that the product or service, as provided (or as it will be provided), will fulfill its intended use.

In other words, validation ensures that "you built the right thing." (See also "verification.")

verification Confirmation that work products properly reflect the requirements specified for them.

In other words, verification ensures that "you built it right." (See also "validation.")

version control The establishment and maintenance of baselines and the identification of changes to baselines that make it possible to return to the previous baseline.

work breakdown structure (WBS) An arrangement of work elements and their relationship to each other and to the end product or service.

work product In the CMMI Product Suite, a useful result of a process.

This result can include files, documents, products, parts of a product, services, process descriptions, specifications, and invoices. A key distinction between a work product and a product component is that a work product is not necessarily part of the end product. (See also "product" and "product component.")

In CMMI models, the definition of "work product" includes services; however, the phrase "work products and services" is sometimes used to emphasize the inclusion of services in the discussion.

work product and task attributes Characteristics of products, services, and project tasks used to help in estimating project work. These characteristics include items such as size, complexity, weight, form, fit, and function. They are typically used as one input to deriving other project and resource estimates (e.g., effort, cost, schedule).

Book Contributors

BOOK AUTHORS

Eileen Forrester
Senior Member of the Technical Staff
Software Engineering Institute

Eileen Forrester is a senior member of the technical staff in the Software Engineering Process Management program at the SEI. She is the cochair of the International Process Research Consortium and the SEI lead for CMMI for Services. Eileen is the developer of TransPlant, a transition-planning process, and the editor of the IPRC Process Research Framework. Her current research area is in process-oriented approaches to service delivery, technology change, risk management, and emergent system types. These approaches include GAIT, CMMI for Services, OCTAVE, MDA, and multimodel improvement approaches such as Prime. She has more than thirty years of experience in technology transition, strategic planning, process improvement, communication planning, and managing product, service, and nonprofit organizations.

Brandon L. Buteau
Technical Fellow
Quality Architect
Northrop Grumman

Brandon L. Buteau is a Technical Fellow, technologist, and quality architect at Northrop Grumman. He has been a member of the CMMI for Services model development team from its beginning, and

is both the lead architect for the model and the team's ontologist. His professional career of more than thirty-four years has spanned the analysis and development of advanced systems, technology, and processes. Brandon currently helps to define and develop quality and process architectures as well as supporting tools. He leads, performs, coordinates, and consults on research, strategic analyses, technology assessments, knowledge/information modeling, and business development across a spectrum of technologies needed by customers. He received an AB in applied mathematics (computer science) from Harvard University in 1976.

Sandy Shrum
Senior Writer/Editor
Communications
Software Engineering Institute

Sandy Shrum is a senior writer/editor and communications point of contact for the Software Engineering Process Management program at the Software Engineering Institute. Aside from this book, she has coauthored two other CMMI books: *CMMI-ACQ: Guidelines for Improving the Acquisition of Products and Services* and the first and second editions of *CMMI: Guidelines for Process Integration and Product Improvement*. She has been with the SEI since 1995 and has been a member of the CMMI Development Team since the CMMI project's inception in 1998. Her roles on the project have included model author, small review team member, reviewer, editor, model development process coordinator, and quality assurance process owner. Before joining the SEI, Sandy worked for eight years as a document developer with Legent Corporation, a Virginia-based software company. Her experience as a technical communicator dates back to 1988, when she earned her M.S. in professional writing from Carnegie Mellon University. Her undergraduate degree, a B.S. in business administration, was earned at Gannon University, Erie, PA.

ESSAY AUTHORS

Kevin Behr

Kevin Behr is the founder of the Information Technology Process Institute (ITPI) and the CTO of the CIO Practice at Assemblage Pointe, which helps senior business executives transform IT organizations from chaos to business effectiveness. He has held the post of CTO and CIO at companies ranging from public corporations to technology startups. He is the author of six IT management books, including the popular *The Visible Ops Handbook*, which he coauthored with Gene Kim and George Spafford, and *The Definitive Guide to IT Management for the Adaptive Enterprise*, published by Hewlett-Packard.

Betsey S. Cox-Buteau

Betsey Cox-Buteau is a career educator whose interest is in educational system process continuity and the integration of assessment data into decision-making. Betsey is a school administrator and education consultant who works with struggling schools to improve test scores through data collection, improving processes, and providing high quality professional development.

Sally Cunningham

Sally Cunningham is SEI Counsel, the Deputy Director of Program Development and Transition, and the Business Development Director for the Software Engineering Institute at Carnegie Mellon University. She is responsible for leading SEI's partner and member networks as well as delivery of all SEI courses and certifications worldwide. She is a licensed attorney in the Commonwealth of Pennsylvania, a member of the National Contract Management Association, and a Certified Professional Contracts Manager.

Kieran Doyle

Kieran is a SCAMPI Lead Appraiser based in the United Kingdom and has extensive experience in systems and software engineering, service management, project management, and quality management, covering commercial and defense sectors and encompassing all lifecycle elements from requirements capture through to delivery and operations.

Suzanne Garcia-Miller

SuZ Garcia-Miller is a senior member of the technical staff in the Research, Technology, and System Solutions program at Carnegie Mellon University's Software Engineering Institute. Her research spans organizational issues in systems of systems settings and organizations adopting new architectural practices. Before RTSS, she researched technology transition and process improvement, particularly development and implementation of CMM types of models, and coauthored *CMMI Survival Guide: Just Enough Process Improvement.*

Hillel Glazer

Hillel has been working in process improvement since his first job out of college. He is a CMMI High Maturity Lead Appraiser and CMMI Instructor working with agile teams, as well as an SEI Visiting Scientist. Hillel is the lead author on the SEI's first-ever official publication addressing agile development. His diverse experience base, which includes aerospace/defense and systems engineering, large and small consulting practices, federal agencies, dot-com operations, and financial systems support, is probably what gave him the necessary perspective to pioneer how to bring CMMI and Agile together as far back as his 2001 *CrossTalk* article highlighting the compatibilities of (then) CMM and XP.

Robert K. Green

Robert K. Green is a member of National Government Services' IT Governance Team, which is responsible for the management of corporate IT processes. Robert serves as the coordinator for earned value management on one of the company's major contracts and coordinates the work of National Government Services' Technical Review Board.

Gene Kim

Gene Kim is the CTO and cofounder of Tripwire, Inc. In 2004, he cowrote *The Visible Ops Handbook*, codifying how to successfully transform IT organizations "from good to great." In 2008, he coauthored *Visible Ops Security*, a handbook describing how to link IT security and operational objectives in four practical steps by integrating security controls into IT operational, software development, and project management processes. Gene is a certified IS auditor, and is part of the Institute of Internal Auditors GAIT task force that developed and published the GAIT Principles and Methodology in January of 2007, designed to help management appropriately scope the IT portions of SOX-404. In 2007, *Computerworld* added Gene to the "40 Innovative IT People to Watch, Under the Age of 40" list. Gene was also given the Outstanding Alumnus Award by the Department of Computer Sciences at Purdue University for achievement and leadership in the profession.

Angela Marks

Angela Marks, manager of IT Governance, National Government Services (NGS), is a key member of the NGS SCAMPI appraisal team, which was instrumental in NGS's CMMI-DEV Level III achievement. As the leader of the Engineering Process Group, Angela's team is responsible for IT Process Definition, Organizational Training, and ensuring that NGS Information Technology departments achieve success through continual process improvement.

Barbara Neeb-Bruckner

Barbara Neeb-Bruckner has worked for more than ten years in project lead, senior consultant, and CMMI specialist roles in different industries, including telco, airline, finance and in different countries—Germany, China, Denmark, and Switzerland. As well as having degrees in mathematics and sustainable tourism management, she has also trained in organizational development and corporate social responsibility.

Brad Nelson

Brad Nelson is an engineer with the Department of Defense (DoD) Office of the Deputy Under Secretary of Defense for Industrial Policy (ODUSD (IP)), serving as an Industrial Base Analyst for C4, Information Technology, and Contract Services. Brad has over twenty-six years experience in systems engineering and technical leadership as a manager, project manager, headquarters program manager, and network systems engineer in the government, military, and private sectors. Prior to joining ODUSD (IP) in late 2006, Brad was a civilian employee of the U.S. Army, where he held a variety of IT positions, including Chief Systems Engineer for the Program Executive Officer for Enterprise Information Systems (PEO EIS.) Previously, he has held engineering and management positions with WorldCom, the Department of Energy, and the Environmental Protection Agency. He also served on active duty with the U.S. Navy as a submariner and retired from reserve duty as a captain.

Mike Phillips

Mike Phillips is the Program Manager for CMMI at the Software Engineering Institute (SEI), a position created to lead the Capability Maturity Model Integration (CMMI) project for the SEI. He has coauthored *CMMI-ACQ: Guidelines for Improving the Acquisition of Products and Services*. He was previously responsible for Transition Enabling activities at the SEI. Prior to his retirement as a colonel from the Air Force, he was the program manager of the $36 billion development program for the B-2 stealth bomber in the B-2 System Program Office at Wright-Patterson AFB, OH.

Hal Wilson

Wilson is Director of Engineering within the Northrop Grumman Information Systems Sector's Defense Systems Division (DSD). He has over forty-two years of experience in designing, implementing, and managing large programs. Hal is the vice chairman of the NDIA Systems Engineering Division and is the industry colead of the Government/Industry NDIA Working Group analyzing Systemic Root Causes of Acquisition Problems. Hal is a charter member of the Capability Maturity Model Integration (CMMI) Steering Group and a member of the author teams for CMMI-AM and CMMI-Architecture, and coauthor of *Understanding and Leveraging a Supplier's CMMI Efforts: A Guidebook for Acquirers*.

INDEX

The SEI Partner Network:
Helping hands with a global reach.

Do you need help getting started with CMMI for Services adoption in your organization? Or are you an experienced professional in the field who wants to join a global network of CMMI for Services providers? Regardless of your level of experience with CMMI for Services tools and methods, the SEI Partner Network can provide the assistance and the support you need to make your CMMI for Services adoption a success.

The SEI Partner Network is a world-wide group of licensed organizations with individuals qualified by the SEI to deliver SEI services. SEI Partners can provide you with training courses, CMMI for Services adoption assistance, proven appraisal methods, and teamwork and management processes that aid in implementation of the SEI's tools and methods.

**To find an SEI Partner near you, or to learn more
about this global network of professionals,
please visit the SEI Partner Network website at
*http://www.sei.cmu.edu/partners***

ESSENTIAL GUIDES TO CMMI®

CMMI®: Guidelines for Process Integration and Product Improvement, Second Edition

Mary Beth Chrissis, Mike Konrad, and Sandy Shrum

ISBN-13: 978-0-321-27967-5

The definitive guide to CMMI—now updated for CMMI v1.2! Whether you are new to CMMI or already familiar with some version of it, this book is the essential resource for managers, practitioners, and process improvement team members who to need to understand, evaluate, and/or implement a CMMI model.

CMMI® for Services: Guidelines for Superior Service

Eileen C. Forrester, Brandon L. Buteau, and Sandy Shrum

ISBN-13: 978-0-321-63589-1

The authoritative guide to CMMI for Services, a model designed to help service-provider organizations improve their processes and thereby gain business advantage. This book, which contains the complete model, also includes helpful commentary by the authors and case studies to illustrate how the model is being used.

CMMI®-ACQ: Guidelines for Improving the Acquisition of Products and Services

Brian P. Gallagher, Mike Phillips, Karen J. Richter, and Sandy Shrum

ISBN-13: 978-0-321-58035-1

The official guide to CMMI-ACQ—an extended CMMI framework for improving product and service acquisition processes. In addition to the complete CMMI-ACQ itself, the book includes tips, hints, and case studies to enhance your understanding and to provide valuable, practical advice.

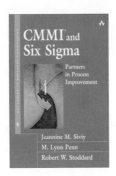

CMMI® and Six Sigma: Partners in Process Improvement

Jeannine M. Siviy, M. Lynn Penn, and Robert W. Stoddard

ISBN-13: 978-0-321-51608-4

Focuses on the synergistic, rather than competitive, implementation of CMMI and Six Sigma—with synergy translating to "faster, better, cheaper" achievement of mission success.

CMMI® Survival Guide: Just Enough Process Improvement

Suzanne Garcia and Richard Turner

ISBN-13: 978-0-321-42277-4

Practical guidance for any organization, large or small, considering or undertaking process improvement, with particular advice for implementing CMMI successfully in resource-strapped environments.

CMMI® Distilled: A Practical Introduction to Integrated Process Improvement, Third Edition

Dennis M. Ahern, Aaron Clouse, and Richard Turner

ISBN-13: 978-0-321-46108-7

Updated for CMMI version 1.2, this third edition again provides a concise and readable introduction to the model, as well as straightforward, no-nonsense information on integrated, continuous process improvement.

For more information on these and other CMMI-related books, as well as on all titles in The SEI Series in Software Engineering, please visit informit.com/seiseries.